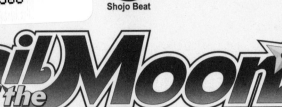

Shojo Beat

Tail of the Moon™

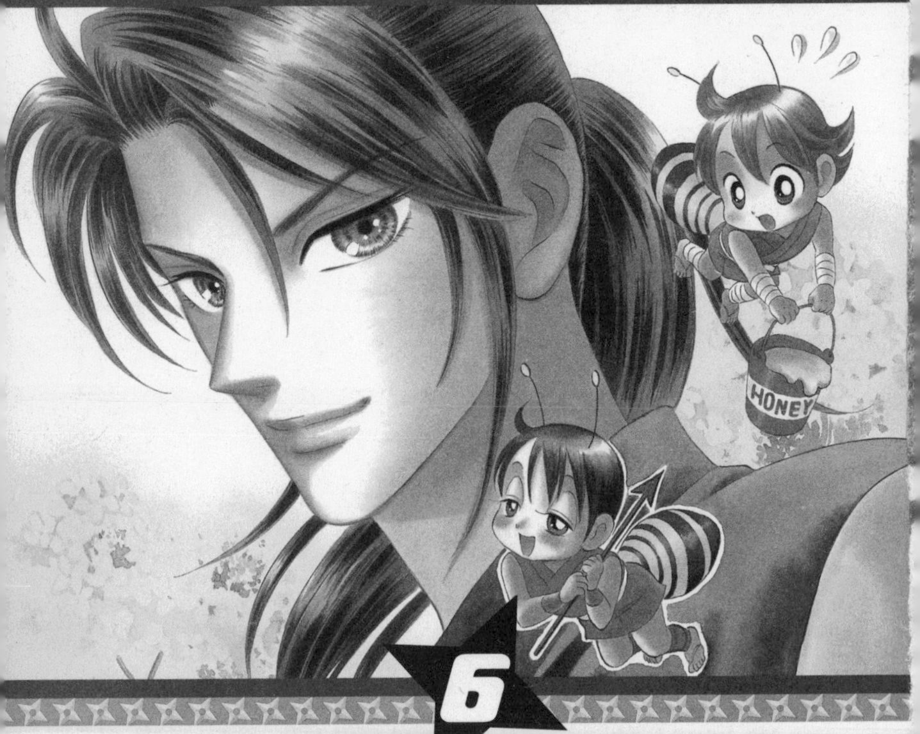
HONEY

6

Story & Art by

Rinko Ueda

Volume 6

CONTENTS

Story Thus Far...

It is the Era of the Warring States. Usagi is a failure as a ninja, but she is a skilled herbalist. She is working hard to qualify as a ninja so she can be the bride of Hattori Hanzo (aka "Shimo no Hanzo").

After fulfilling her assignment in Hamamatsu, Usagi is finally able to return to Iga. But suddenly Hanzo's elder sister Suzune appears before her! Usagi is overjoyed when Hanzo introduces her to Suzune as his bride-elect. Unfortunately, Suzune is totally against the marriage! In the hope that Suzune will accept her, Usagi begins to train under Suzune to learn the know-hows of becoming a good wife. Even with her diet, Usagi works hard and is finally accepted by Suzune!

One day, Usagi heads for Hamamatsu to learn the secrets of how to lose weight. On the way, she is captured by Hikaru and taken to Kouga. At the village, Usagi is ordered to make a poison with Goemon as a hostage...?!

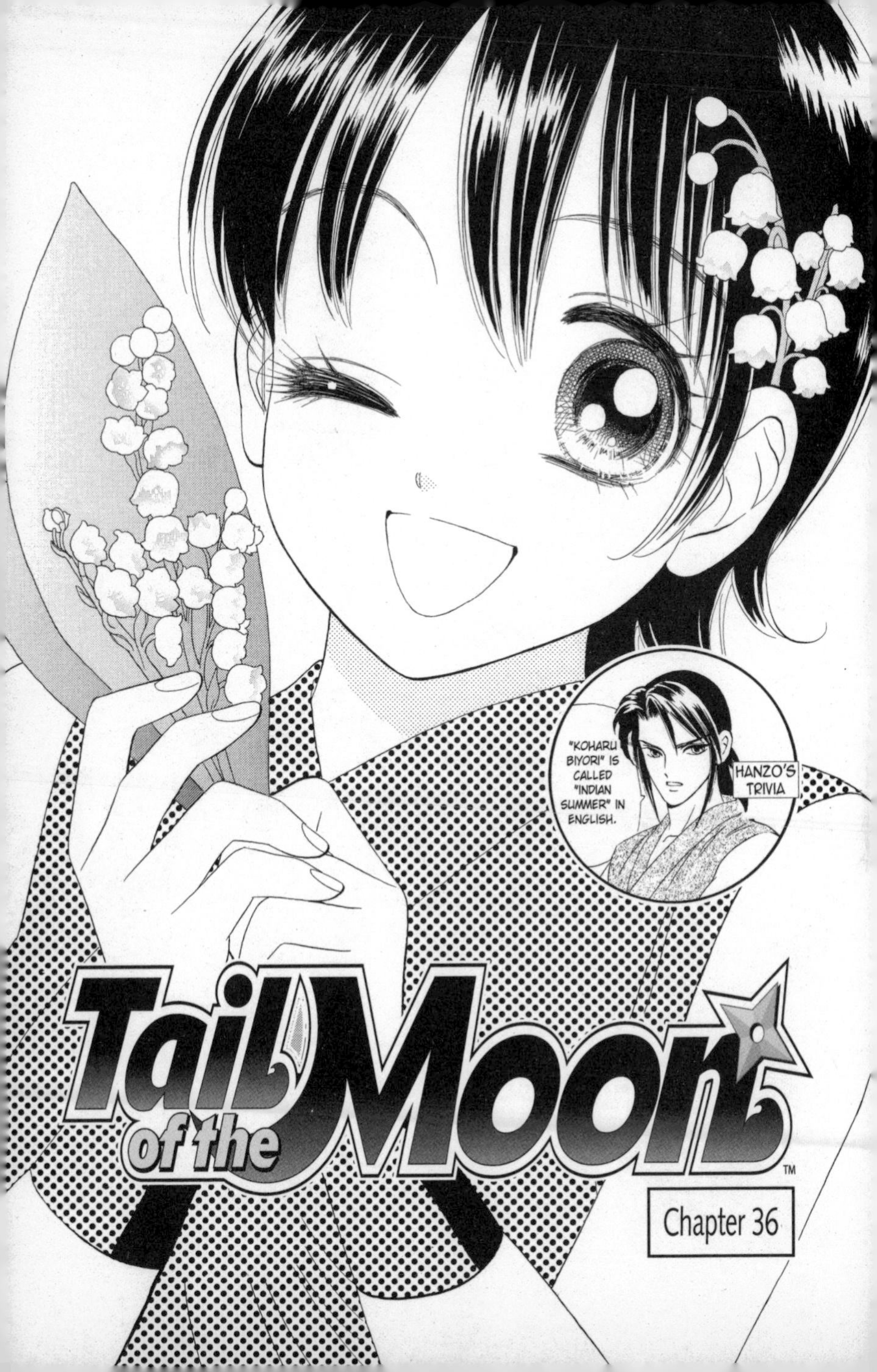
"KOHARU BIYORI" IS CALLED "INDIAN SUMMER" IN ENGLISH.
HANZO'S TRIVIA
Tail of the Moon™
Chapter 36

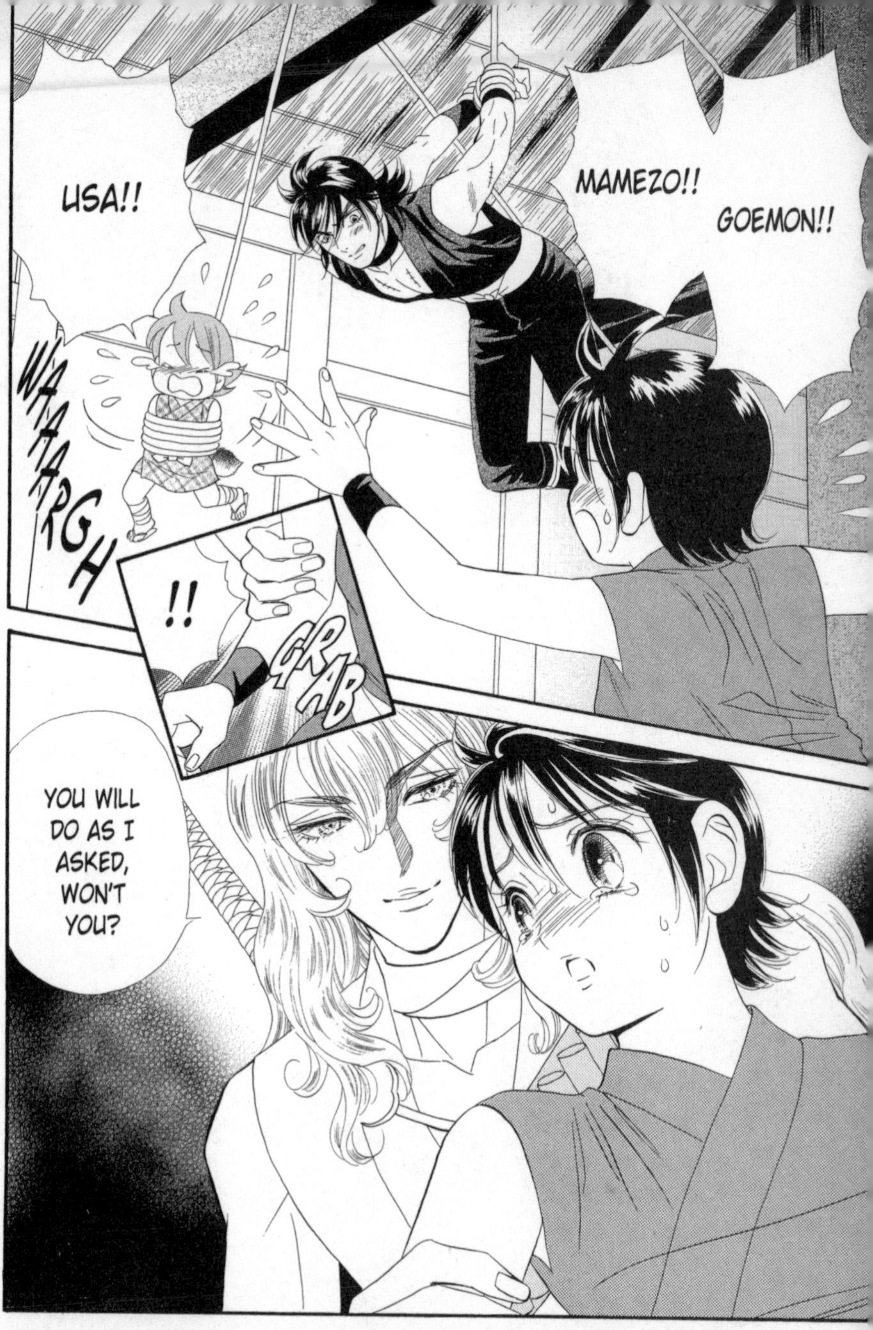
MAMEZO!!
GOEMON!!
USA!!
WAAAARGH
!!
GRAB
YOU WILL DO AS I ASKED, WON'T YOU?

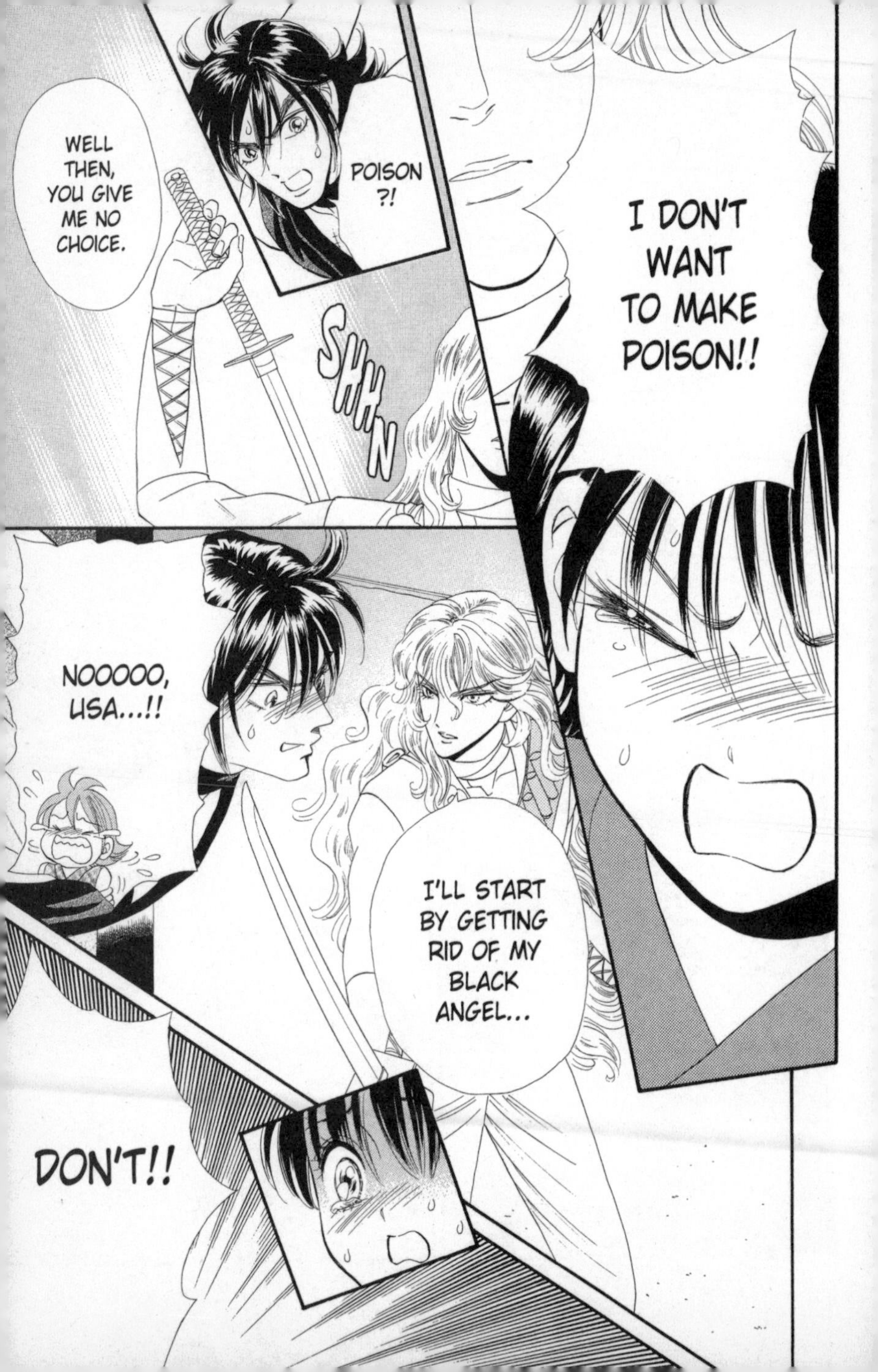
I DON'T WANT TO MAKE POISON!!
POISON ?!
WELL THEN, YOU GIVE ME NO CHOICE.
SHHN
I'LL START BY GETTING RID OF MY BLACK ANGEL...
NOOOOO, USA...!!
DON'T!!

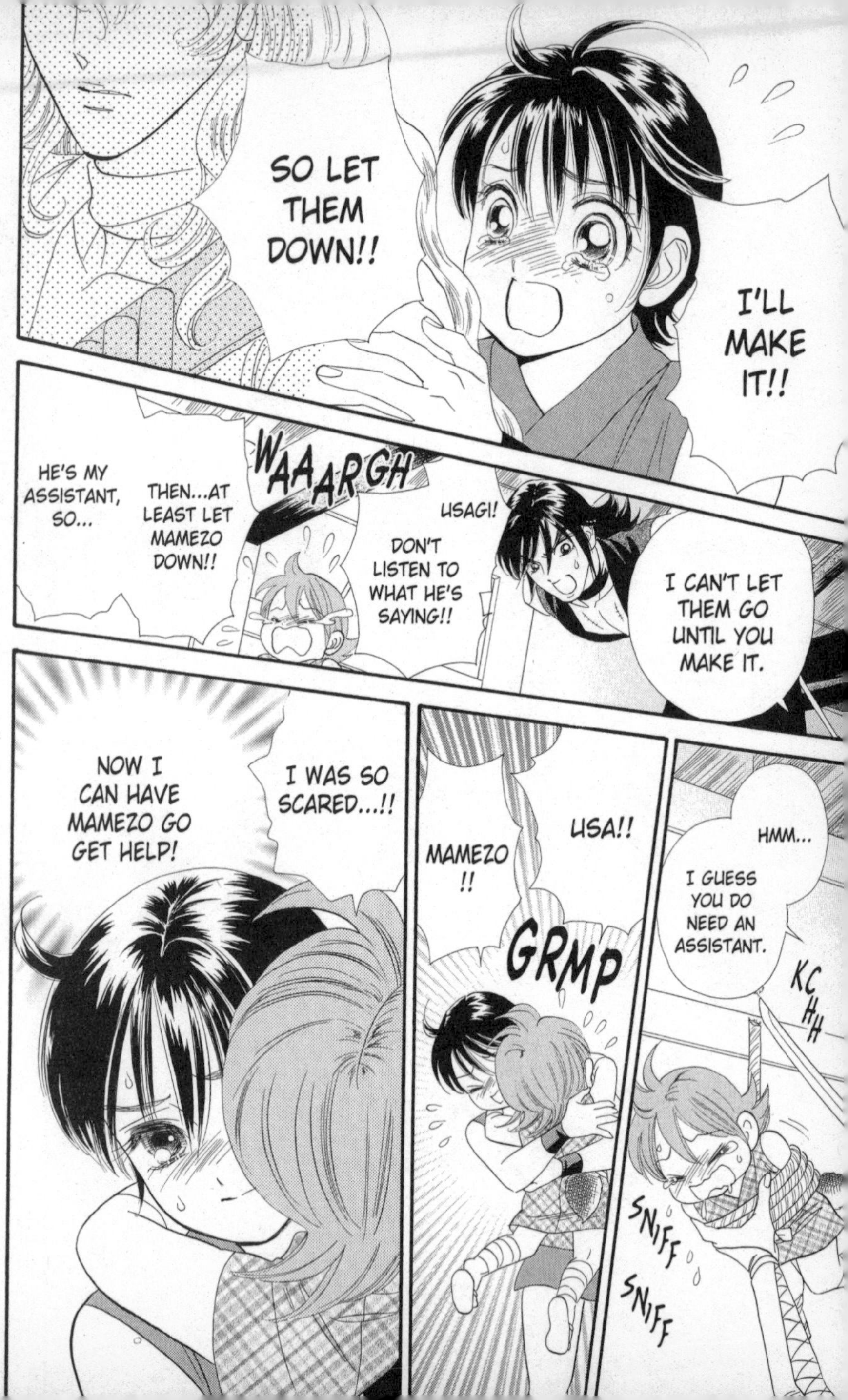
I'LL MAKE IT!!
SO LET THEM DOWN!!
I CAN'T LET THEM GO UNTIL YOU MAKE IT.
USAGI!
DON'T LISTEN TO WHAT HE'S SAYING!!
WAAARGH
THEN...AT LEAST LET MAMEZO DOWN!!
HE'S MY ASSISTANT, SO...
HMM...
I GUESS YOU DO NEED AN ASSISTANT.
KCHH
SNIFF
SNIFF
USA!!
MAMEZO!!
GRMP
I WAS SO SCARED...!!
NOW I CAN HAVE MAMEZO GO GET HELP!

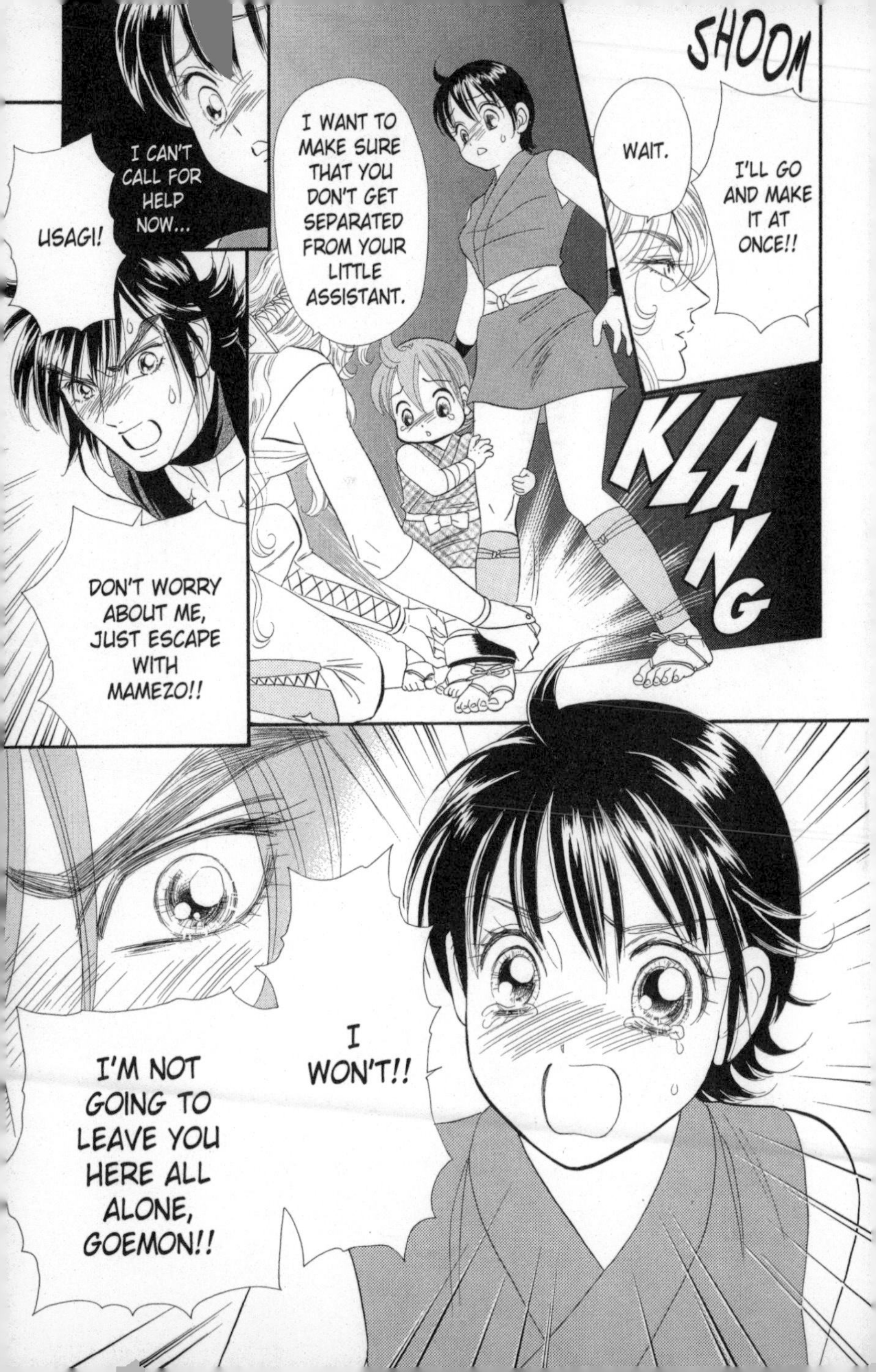
SHOOM
WAIT.
I'LL GO AND MAKE IT AT ONCE!!
KLANG
I WANT TO MAKE SURE THAT YOU DON'T GET SEPARATED FROM YOUR LITTLE ASSISTANT.
I CAN'T CALL FOR HELP NOW...
USAGI!
DON'T WORRY ABOUT ME, JUST ESCAPE WITH MAMEZO!!
I WON'T!!
I'M NOT GOING TO LEAVE YOU HERE ALL ALONE, GOEMON!!

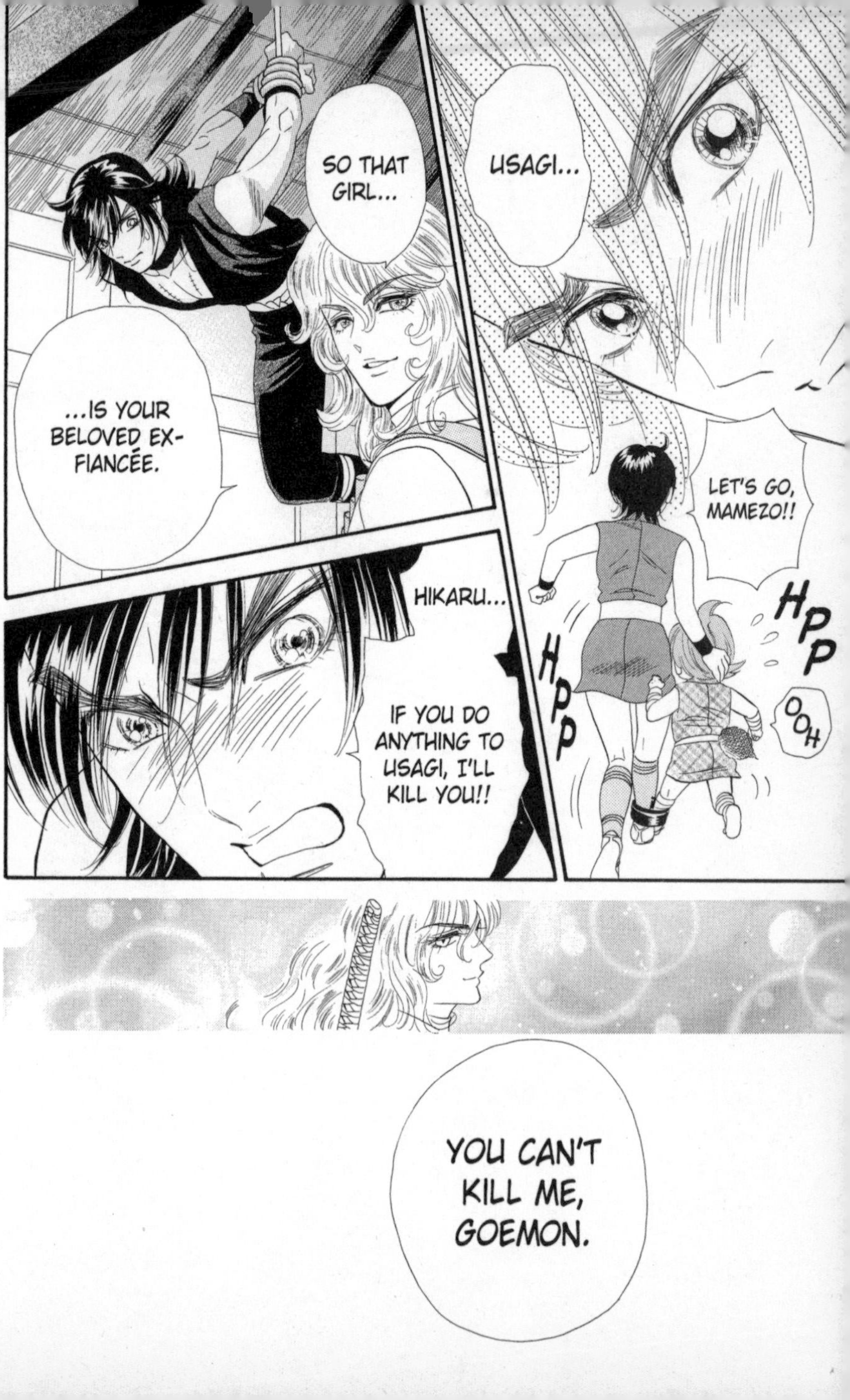
USAGI...
LET'S GO, MAMEZO!!
HPP
OOH
HPP
SO THAT GIRL...
...IS YOUR BELOVED EX-FIANCÉE.
HIKARU...
IF YOU DO ANYTHING TO USAGI, I'LL KILL YOU!!
YOU CAN'T KILL ME, GOEMON.

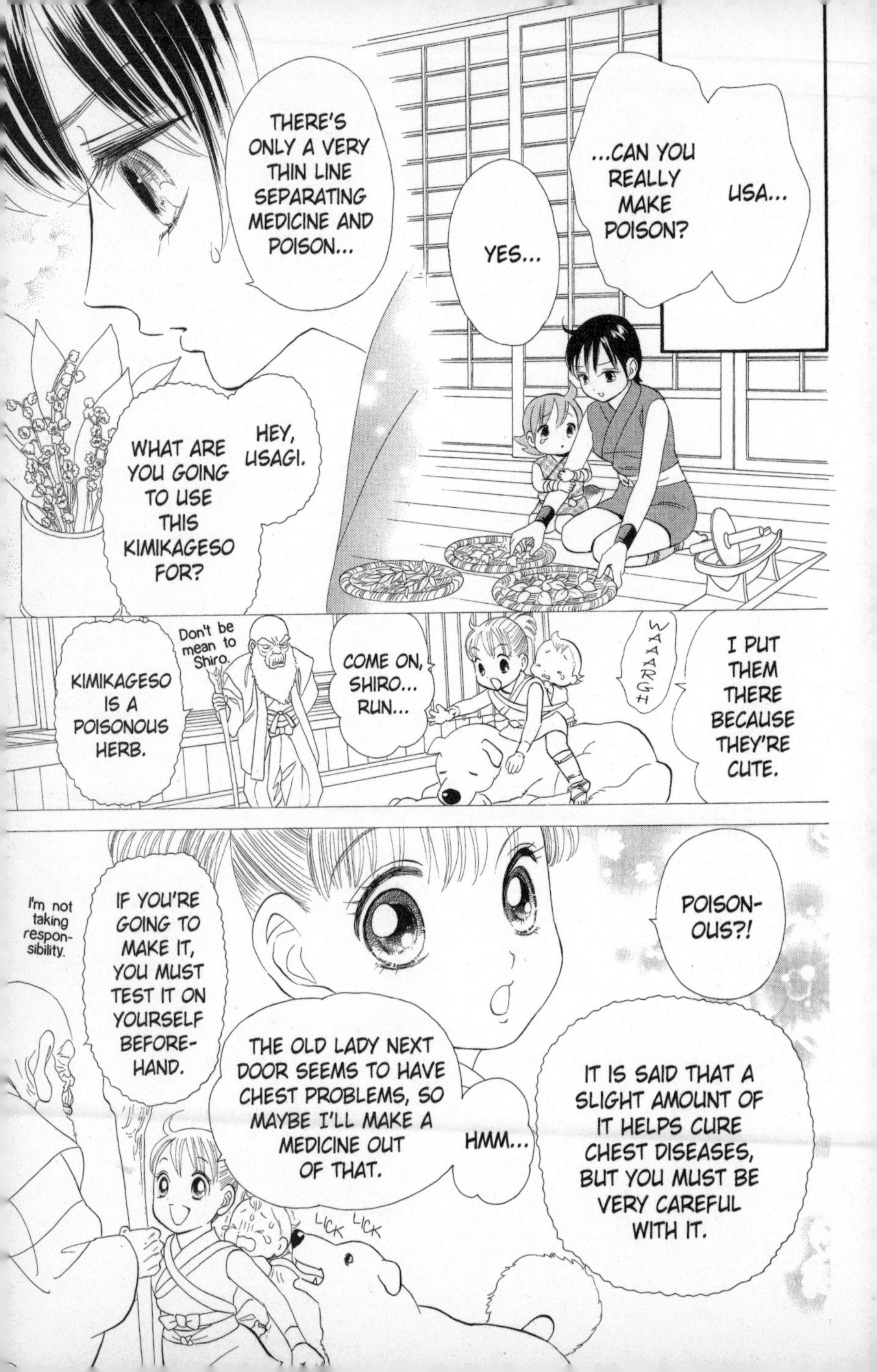
USA...
...CAN YOU REALLY MAKE POISON?
YES...
THERE'S ONLY A VERY THIN LINE SEPARATING MEDICINE AND POISON...
HEY, USAGI.
WHAT ARE YOU GOING TO USE THIS KIMIKAGESO FOR?
I PUT THEM THERE BECAUSE THEY'RE CUTE.
WAAAARGH
COME ON, SHIRO... RUN...
Don't be mean to Shiro.
KIMIKAGESO IS A POISONOUS HERB.
POISON-OUS?!
IT IS SAID THAT A SLIGHT AMOUNT OF IT HELPS CURE CHEST DISEASES, BUT YOU MUST BE VERY CAREFUL WITH IT.
HMM...
THE OLD LADY NEXT DOOR SEEMS TO HAVE CHEST PROBLEMS, SO MAYBE I'LL MAKE A MEDICINE OUT OF THAT.
IF YOU'RE GOING TO MAKE IT, YOU MUST TEST IT ON YOURSELF BEFORE-HAND.
I'm not taking respon-sibility.
LICK LICK

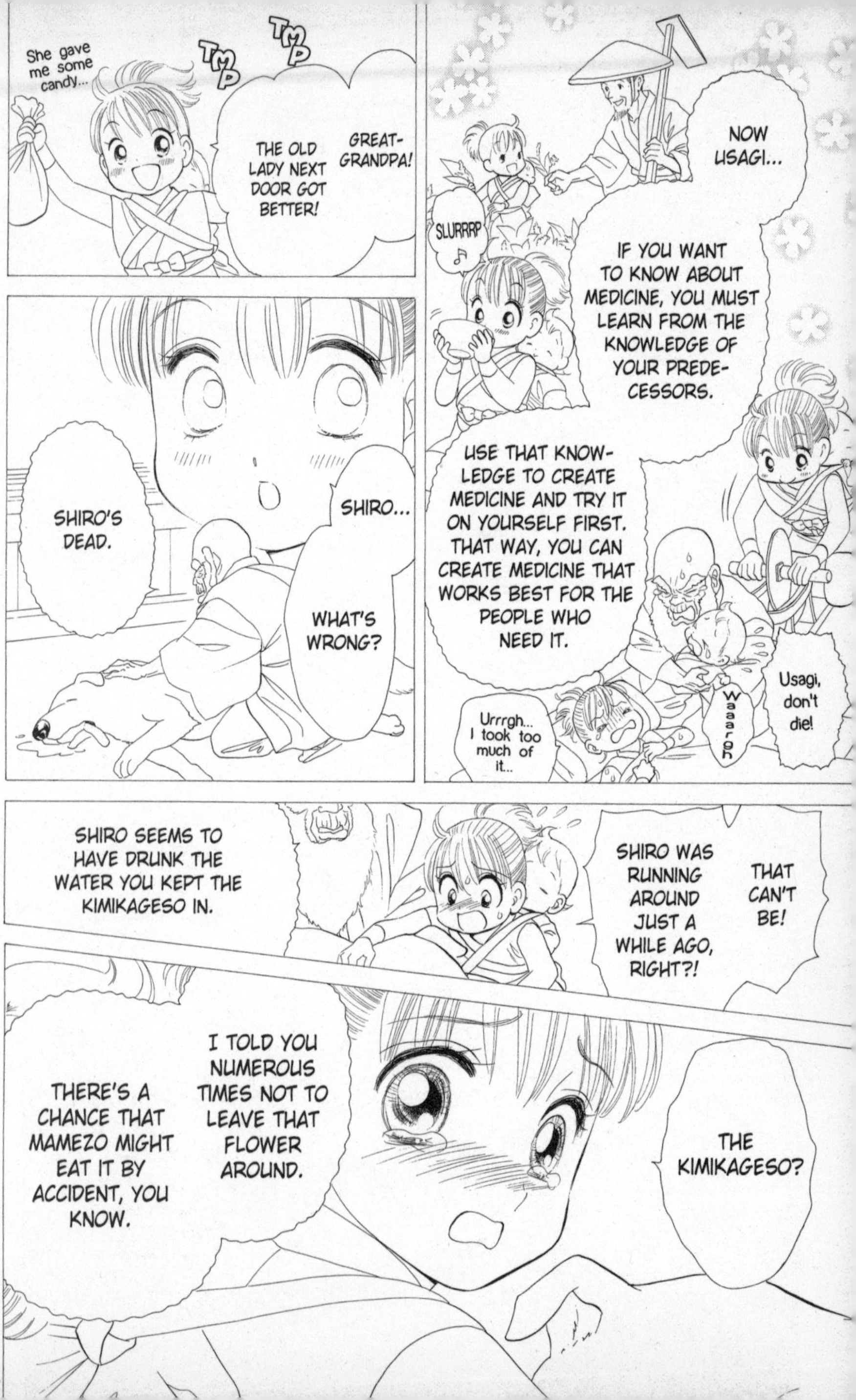
NOW USAGI...
IF YOU WANT TO KNOW ABOUT MEDICINE, YOU MUST LEARN FROM THE KNOWLEDGE OF YOUR PREDE-CESSORS.
SLURRRP ♪
USE THAT KNOW-LEDGE TO CREATE MEDICINE AND TRY IT ON YOURSELF FIRST. THAT WAY, YOU CAN CREATE MEDICINE THAT WORKS BEST FOR THE PEOPLE WHO NEED IT.
Usagi, don't die!
Waaargh
Urrrgh... I took too much of it...
TMP
TMP
GREAT-GRANDPA!
THE OLD LADY NEXT DOOR GOT BETTER!
She gave me some candy...
SHIRO...
WHAT'S WRONG?
SHIRO'S DEAD.
THAT CAN'T BE!
SHIRO WAS RUNNING AROUND JUST A WHILE AGO, RIGHT?!
SHIRO SEEMS TO HAVE DRUNK THE WATER YOU KEPT THE KIMIKAGESO IN.
THE KIMIKAGESO?
I TOLD YOU NUMEROUS TIMES NOT TO LEAVE THAT FLOWER AROUND.
THERE'S A CHANCE THAT MAMEZO MIGHT EAT IT BY ACCIDENT, YOU KNOW.

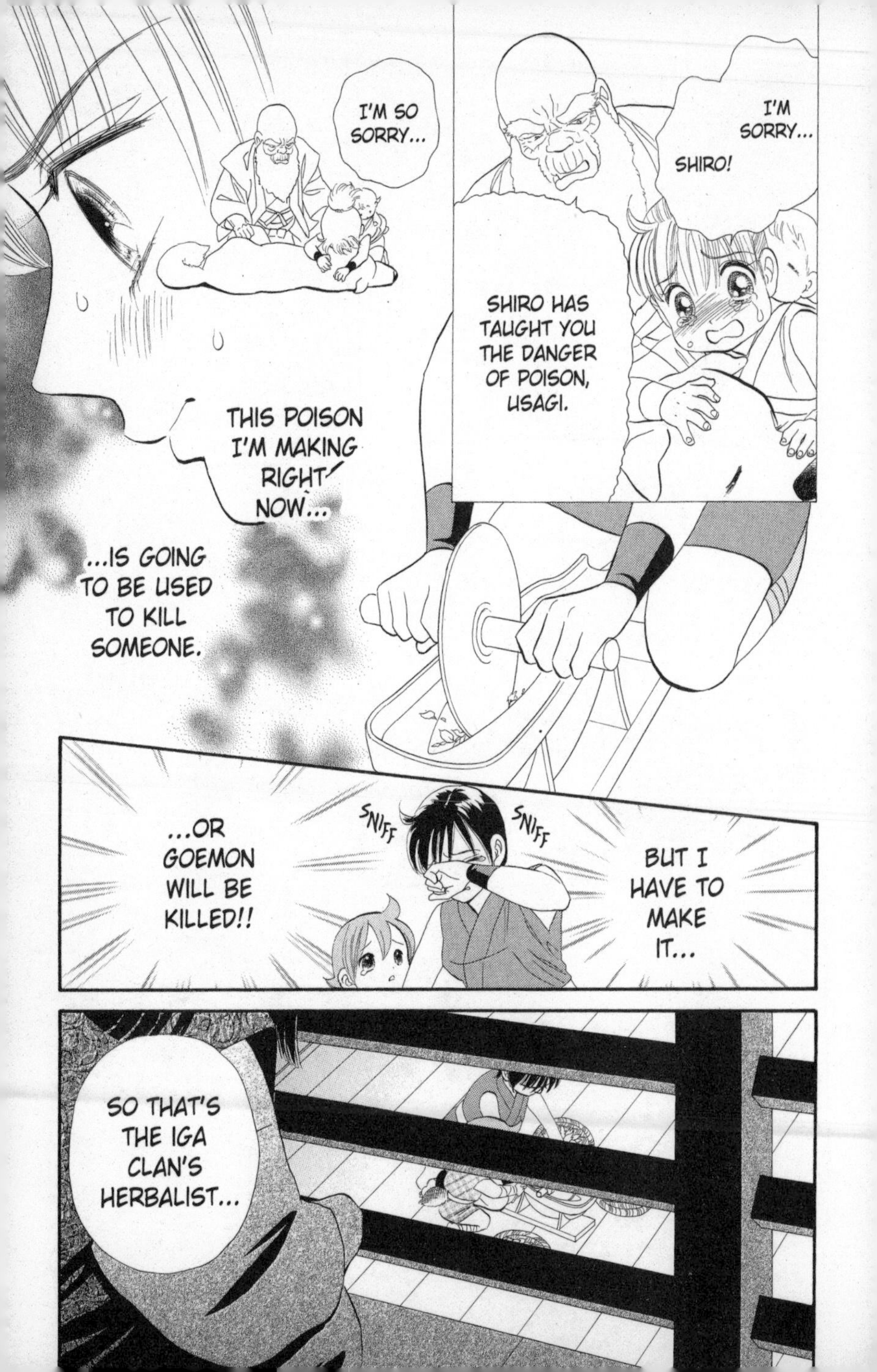
I'M SORRY...
SHIRO!
SHIRO HAS TAUGHT YOU THE DANGER OF POISON, USAGI.
I'M SO SORRY...
THIS POISON I'M MAKING RIGHT NOW...
...IS GOING TO BE USED TO KILL SOMEONE.
BUT I HAVE TO MAKE IT...
SNIFF
SNIFF
...OR GOEMON WILL BE KILLED!!
SO THAT'S THE IGA CLAN'S HERBALIST...

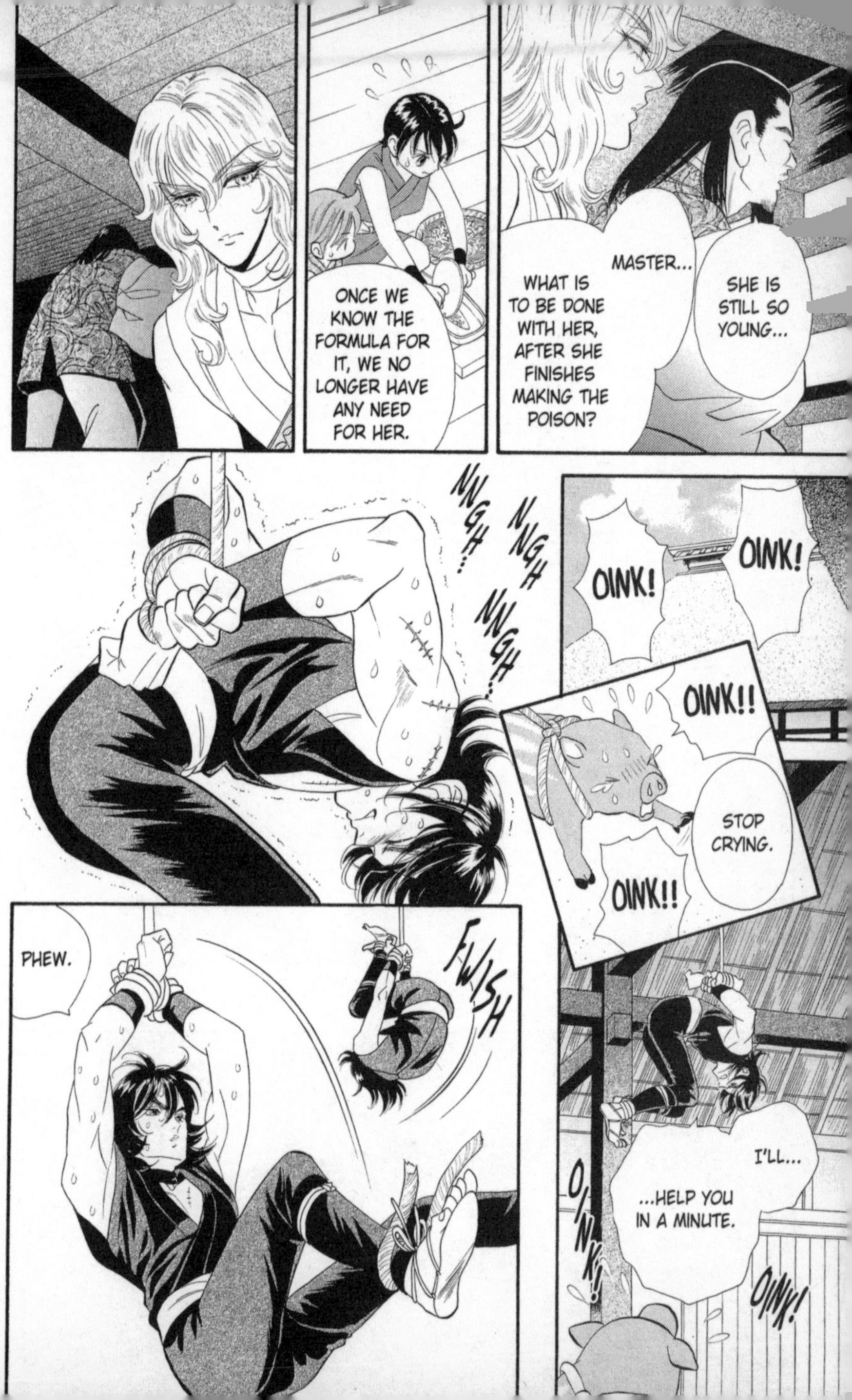
SHE IS STILL SO YOUNG...
MASTER... WHAT IS TO BE DONE WITH HER, AFTER SHE FINISHES MAKING THE POISON?
ONCE WE KNOW THE FORMULA FOR IT, WE NO LONGER HAVE ANY NEED FOR HER.
OINK!
OINK!
OINK!!
STOP CRYING.
OINK!!
NNGH...
NNGH
NNGH...
I'LL...
...HELP YOU IN A MINUTE.
OINK!
OINK!
FWISH
PHEW.

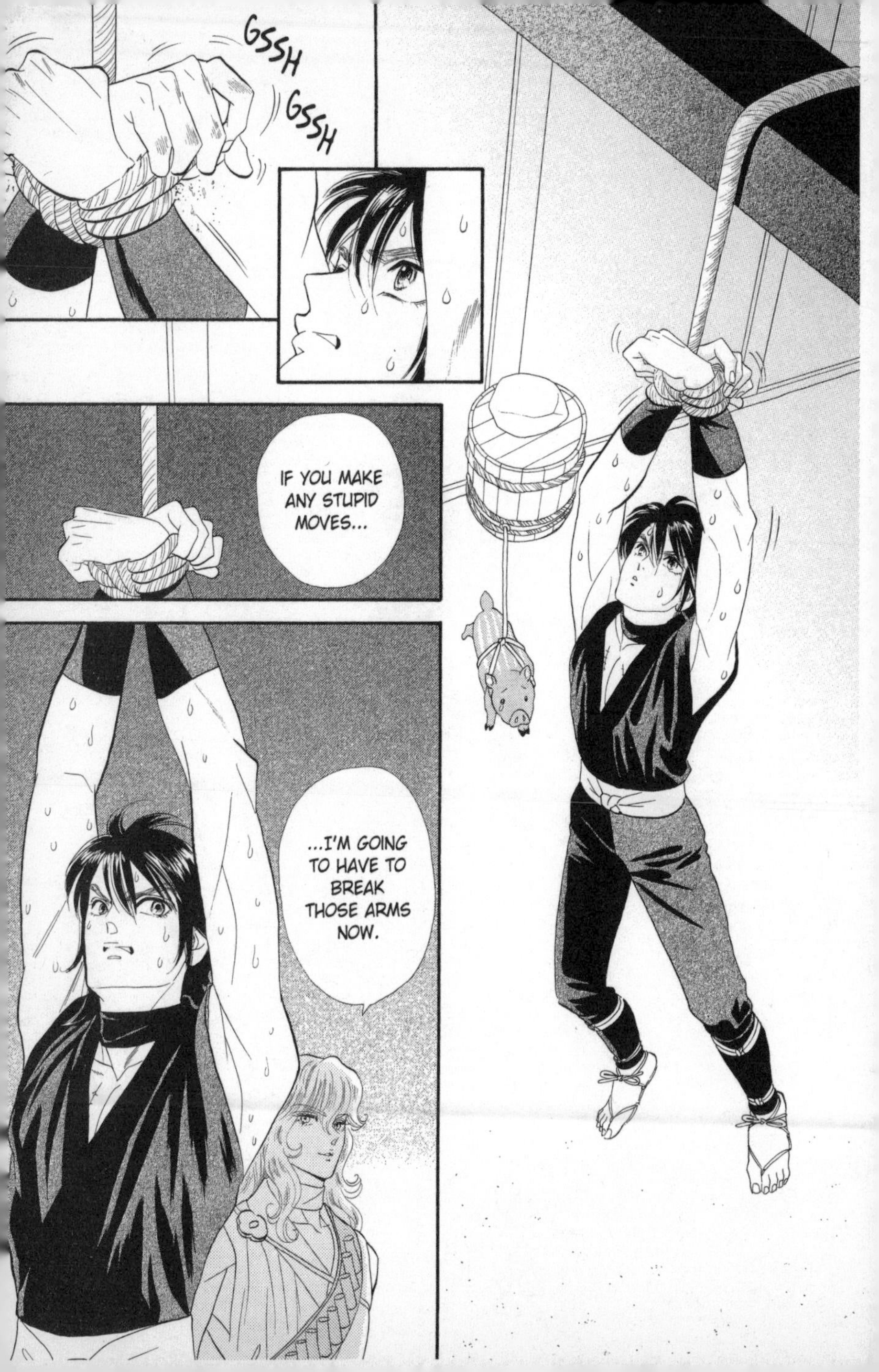
GSSH
GSSH
IF YOU MAKE ANY STUPID MOVES...
...I'M GOING TO HAVE TO BREAK THOSE ARMS NOW.

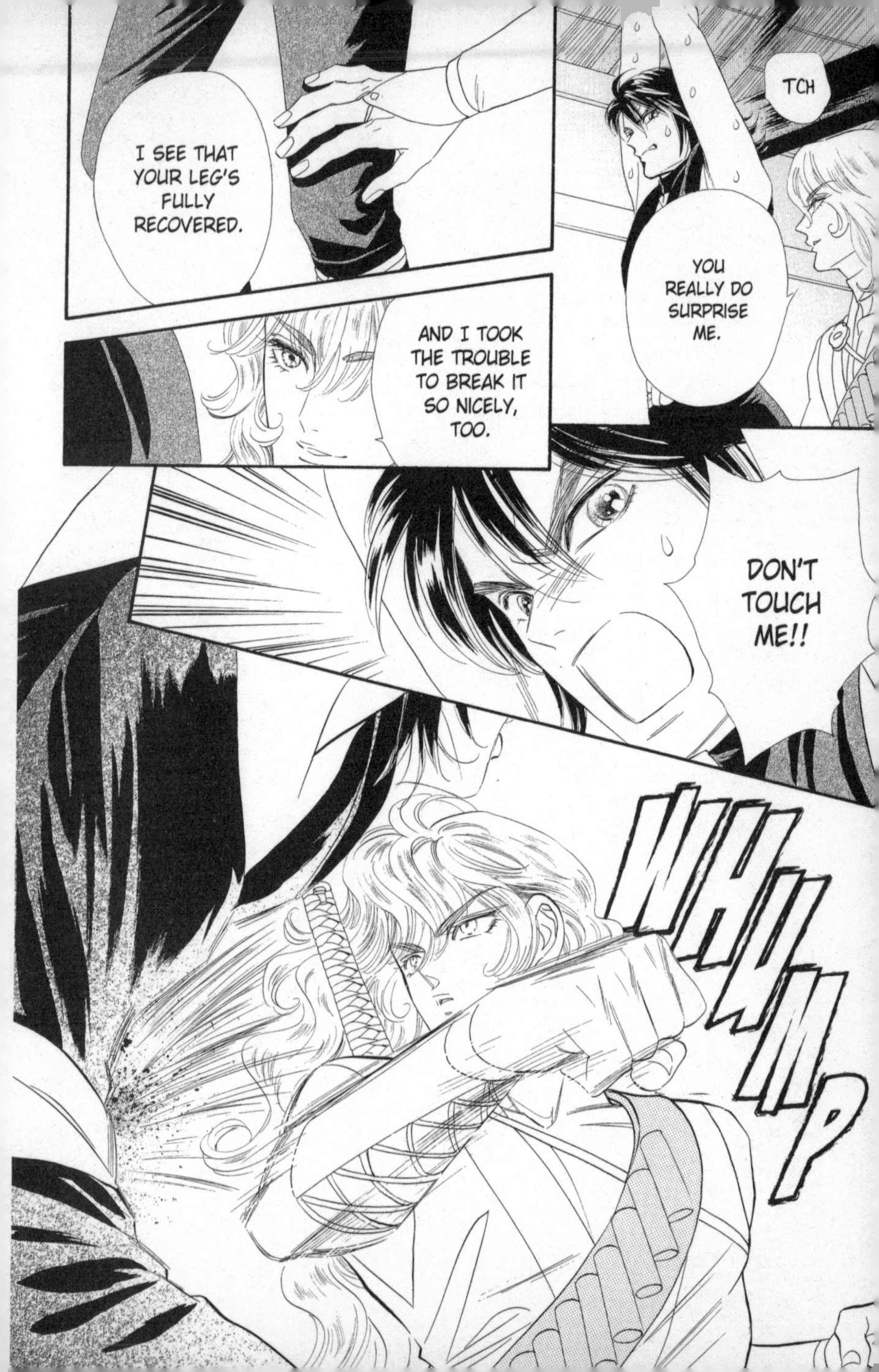
TCH
YOU REALLY DO SURPRISE ME.
I SEE THAT YOUR LEG'S FULLY RECOVERED.
AND I TOOK THE TROUBLE TO BREAK IT SO NICELY, TOO.
DON'T TOUCH ME!!
WHUMP

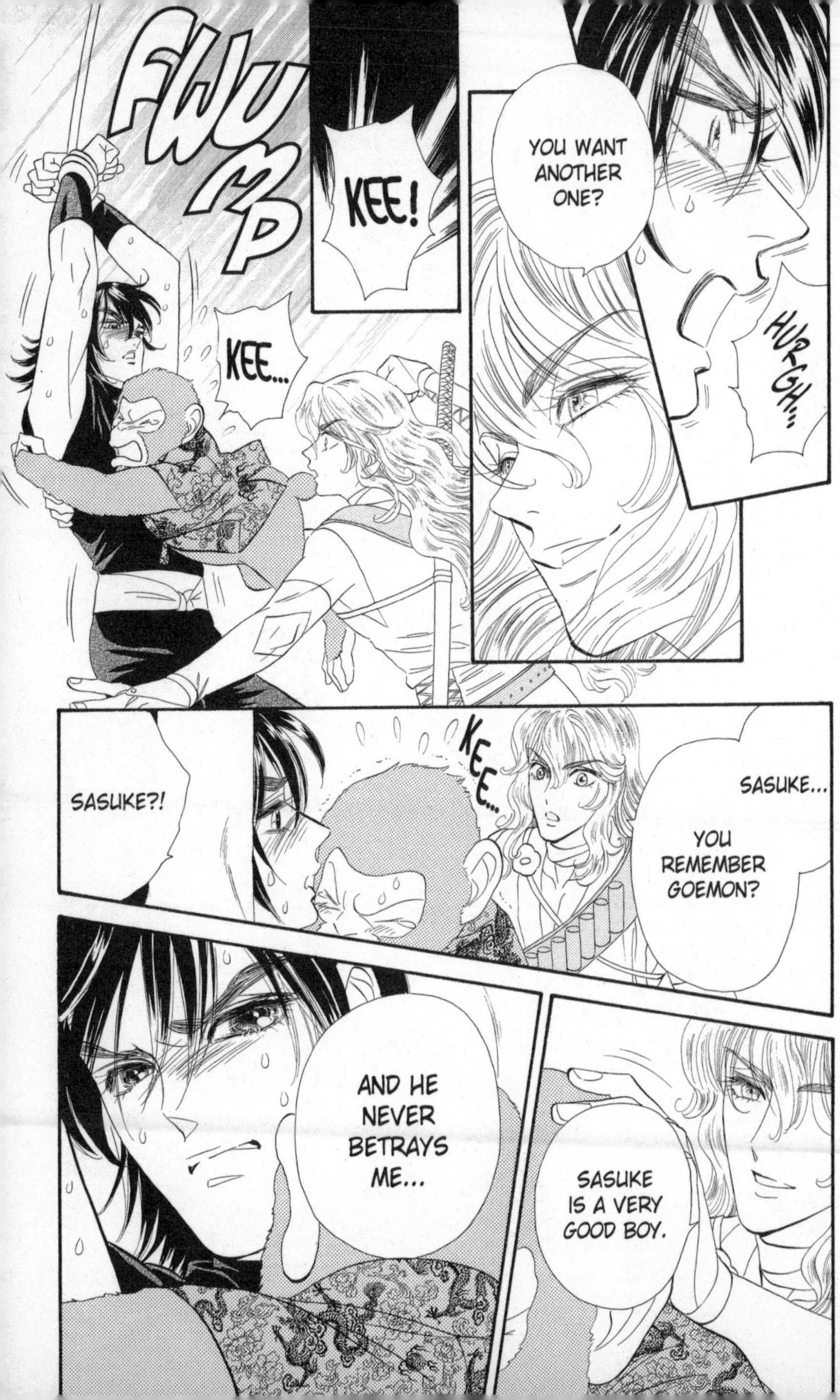
YOU WANT ANOTHER ONE?
HURGH...
KEE!
FWUMP
KEE...
SASUKE...
YOU REMEMBER GOEMON?
KEE...
SASUKE?!
SASUKE IS A VERY GOOD BOY.
AND HE NEVER BETRAYS ME...

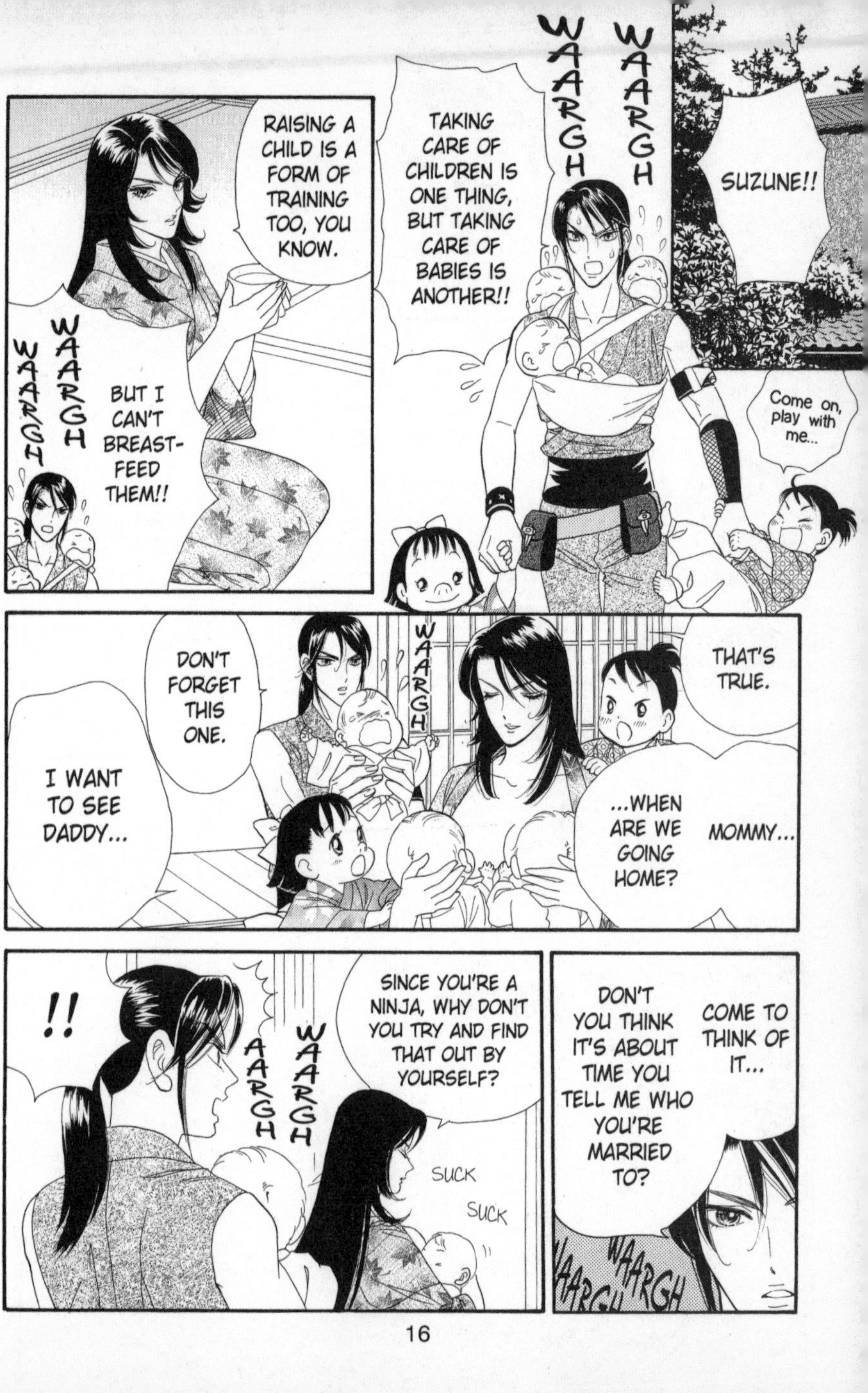
SUZUNE!!
WAARGH
WAARGH
TAKING CARE OF CHILDREN IS ONE THING, BUT TAKING CARE OF BABIES IS ANOTHER!!
Come on, play with me...
RAISING A CHILD IS A FORM OF TRAINING TOO, YOU KNOW.
WAARGH
WAARGH
BUT I CAN'T BREAST-FEED THEM!!
THAT'S TRUE.
MOMMY...
...WHEN ARE WE GOING HOME?
WAARGH
DON'T FORGET THIS ONE.
I WANT TO SEE DADDY...
COME TO THINK OF IT...
DON'T YOU THINK IT'S ABOUT TIME YOU TELL ME WHO YOU'RE MARRIED TO?
WAARGH
WAARGH
SINCE YOU'RE A NINJA, WHY DON'T YOU TRY AND FIND THAT OUT BY YOURSELF?
WAARGH
WAARGH
SUCK
SUCK
!!

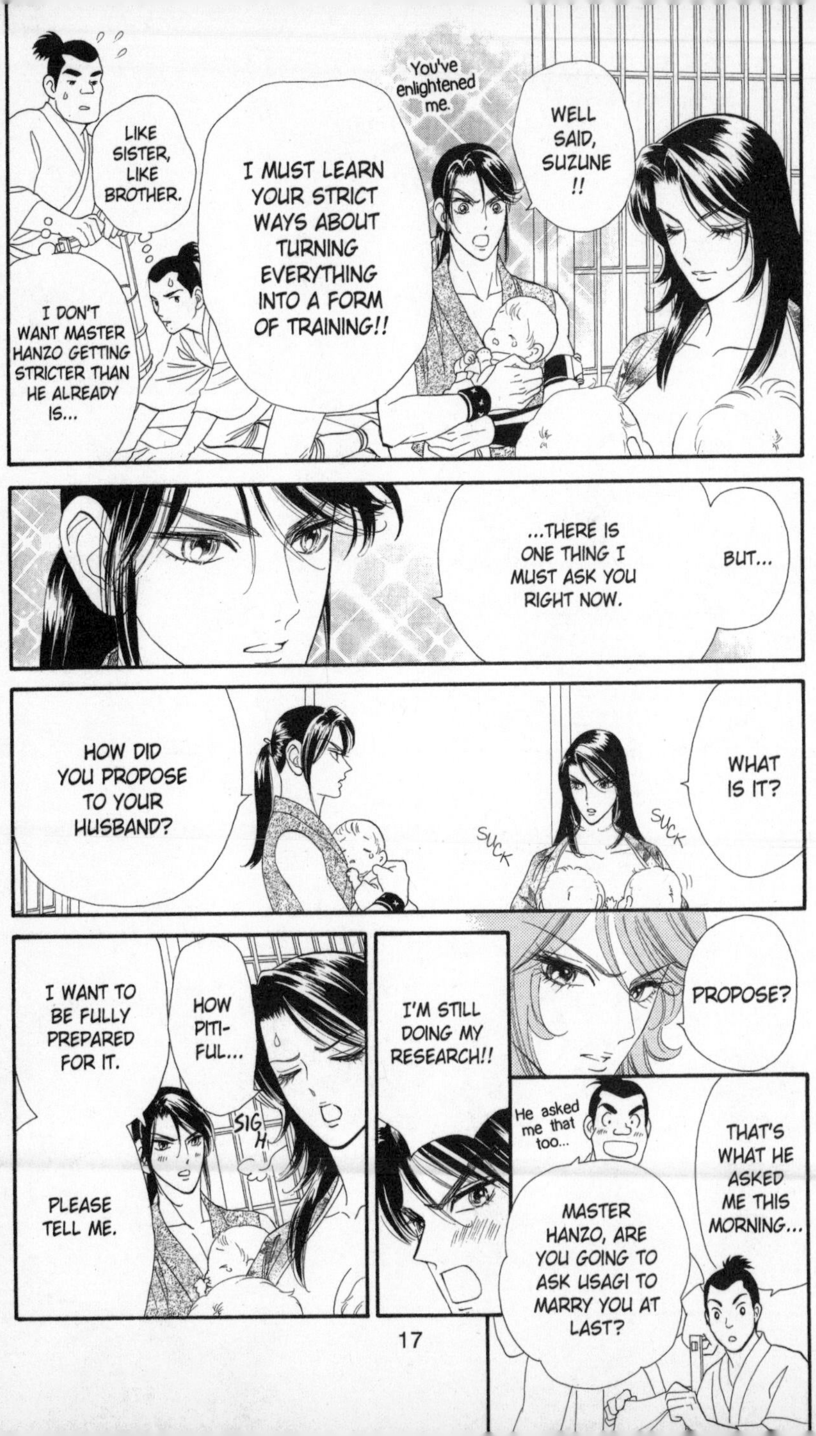
WELL SAID, SUZUNE!!
You've enlightened me.
I MUST LEARN YOUR STRICT WAYS ABOUT TURNING EVERYTHING INTO A FORM OF TRAINING!!
LIKE SISTER, LIKE BROTHER.
I DON'T WANT MASTER HANZO GETTING STRICTER THAN HE ALREADY IS...
BUT...
...THERE IS ONE THING I MUST ASK YOU RIGHT NOW.
WHAT IS IT?
SUCK
SUCK
HOW DID YOU PROPOSE TO YOUR HUSBAND?
PROPOSE?
THAT'S WHAT HE ASKED ME THIS MORNING...
He asked me that too...
MASTER HANZO, ARE YOU GOING TO ASK USAGI TO MARRY YOU AT LAST?
I'M STILL DOING MY RESEARCH!!
HOW PITIFUL...
SIGH
I WANT TO BE FULLY PREPARED FOR IT.
PLEASE TELL ME.

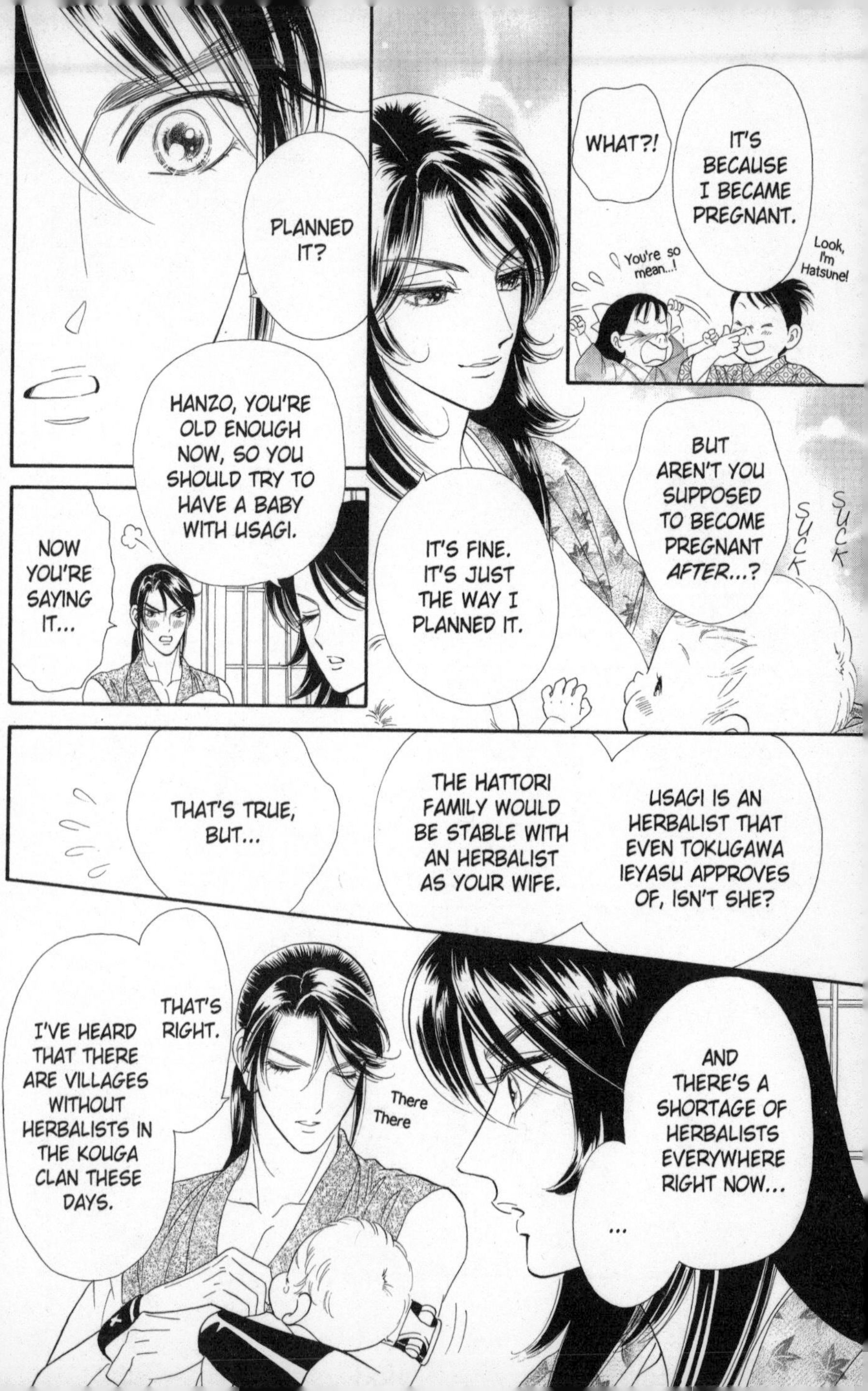
IT'S BECAUSE I BECAME PREGNANT.
WHAT?!
Look, I'm Hatsune!
You're so mean...!
BUT AREN'T YOU SUPPOSED TO BECOME PREGNANT *AFTER*...?
SUCK SUCK
IT'S FINE. IT'S JUST THE WAY I PLANNED IT.
PLANNED IT?
HANZO, YOU'RE OLD ENOUGH NOW, SO YOU SHOULD TRY TO HAVE A BABY WITH USAGI.
NOW YOU'RE SAYING IT...
USAGI IS AN HERBALIST THAT EVEN TOKUGAWA IEYASU APPROVES OF, ISN'T SHE?
THE HATTORI FAMILY WOULD BE STABLE WITH AN HERBALIST AS YOUR WIFE.
THAT'S TRUE, BUT...
AND THERE'S A SHORTAGE OF HERBALISTS EVERYWHERE RIGHT NOW...
...
There There
THAT'S RIGHT.
I'VE HEARD THAT THERE ARE VILLAGES WITHOUT HERBALISTS IN THE KOUGA CLAN THESE DAYS.

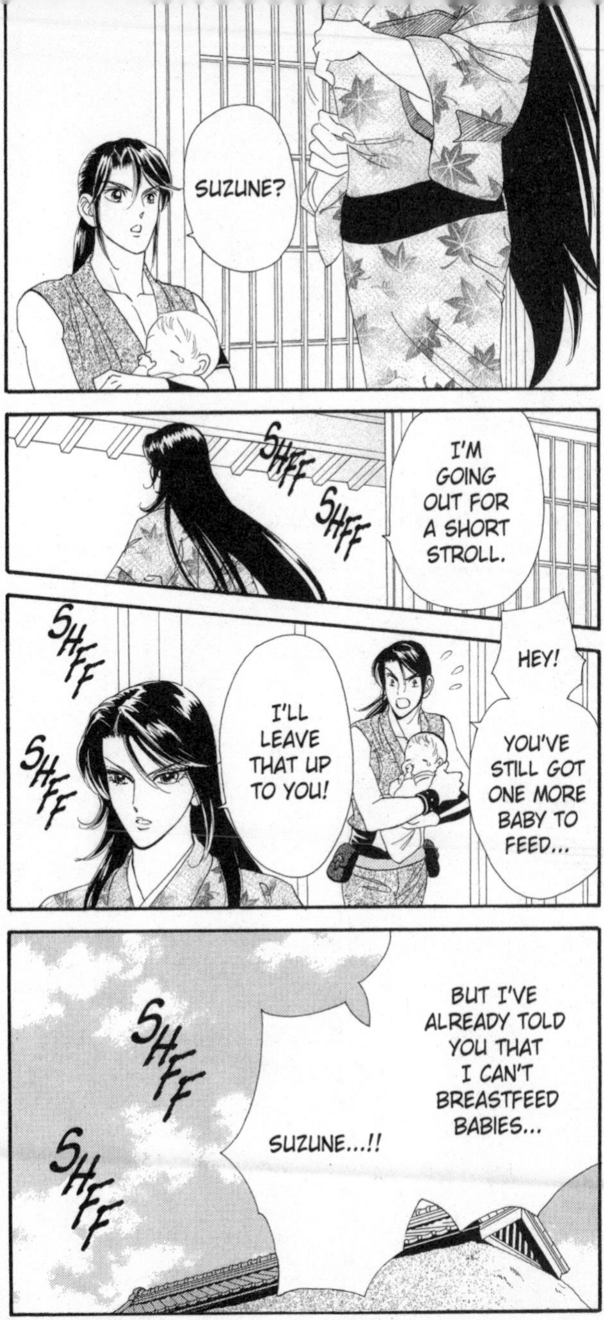
SUZUNE?
I'M GOING OUT FOR A SHORT STROLL.
SHFF
SHFF
HEY!
YOU'VE STILL GOT ONE MORE BABY TO FEED...
I'LL LEAVE THAT UP TO YOU!
SHFF
SHFF
BUT I'VE ALREADY TOLD YOU THAT I CAN'T BREASTFEED BABIES...
SUZUNE...!!
SHFF
SHFF

GREETINGS

Hi there! Ue-Rin here.

Thanks to everyone, volume 6 of "Tail of the Moon" is now out.

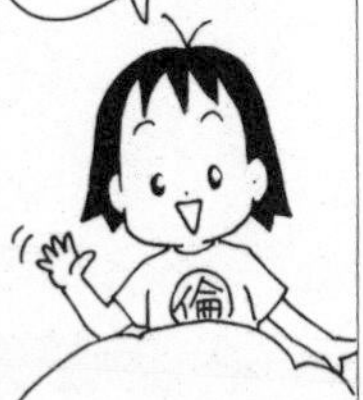

In this volume, I'm going to be writing about "Ue-Rin's Manga School" in my column, just as I said I would last time. ♪

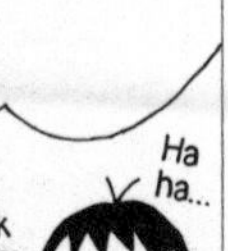
Ha ha...

Miss Ue-Rin's trademark are these papillon glasses.

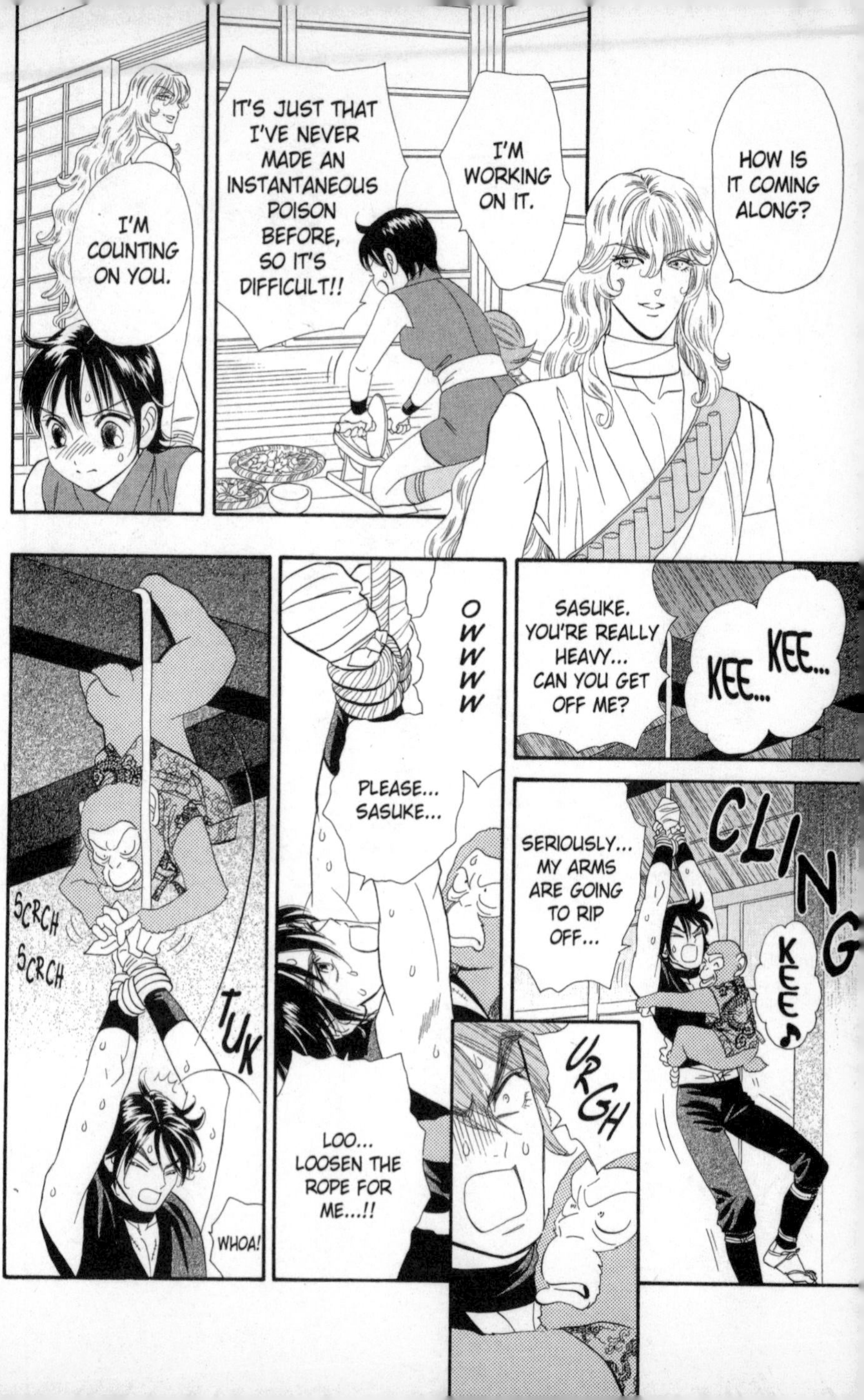
HOW IS IT COMING ALONG?
I'M WORKING ON IT.
IT'S JUST THAT I'VE NEVER MADE AN INSTANTANEOUS POISON BEFORE, SO IT'S DIFFICULT!!
I'M COUNTING ON YOU.
KEE... KEE...
SASUKE. YOU'RE REALLY HEAVY... CAN YOU GET OFF ME?
CLING
KEE♪
SERIOUSLY... MY ARMS ARE GOING TO RIP OFF...
OWWWW
PLEASE... SASUKE...
URGH
LOO... LOOSEN THE ROPE FOR ME...!!
SCRCH SCRCH
TUK
WHOA!

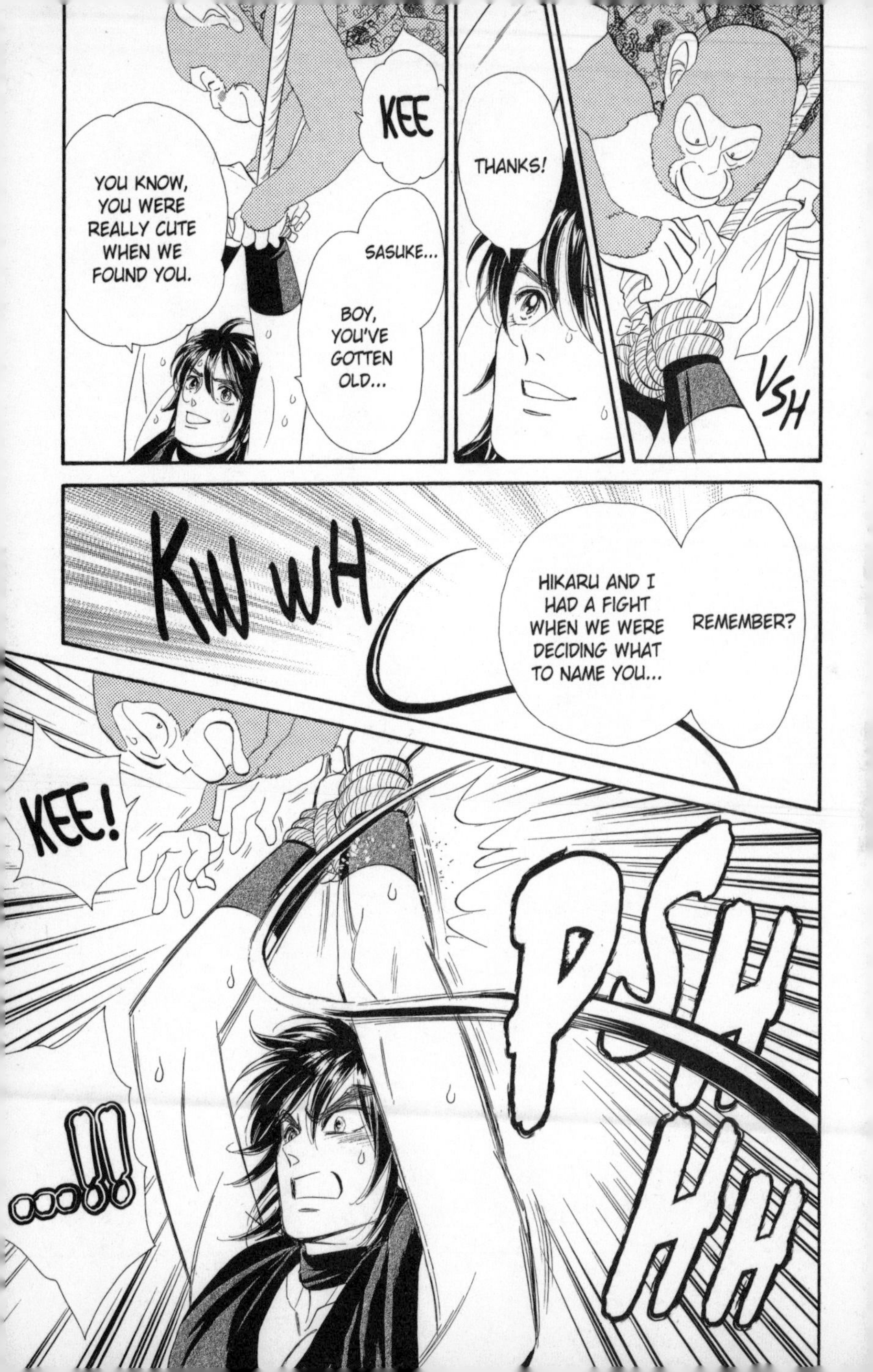
THANKS!
VSH
KEE
SASUKE...
BOY, YOU'VE GOTTEN OLD...
YOU KNOW, YOU WERE REALLY CUTE WHEN WE FOUND YOU.
KWWH
HIKARU AND I HAD A FIGHT WHEN WE WERE DECIDING WHAT TO NAME YOU...
REMEMBER?
KEE!
DSHHH
...!!

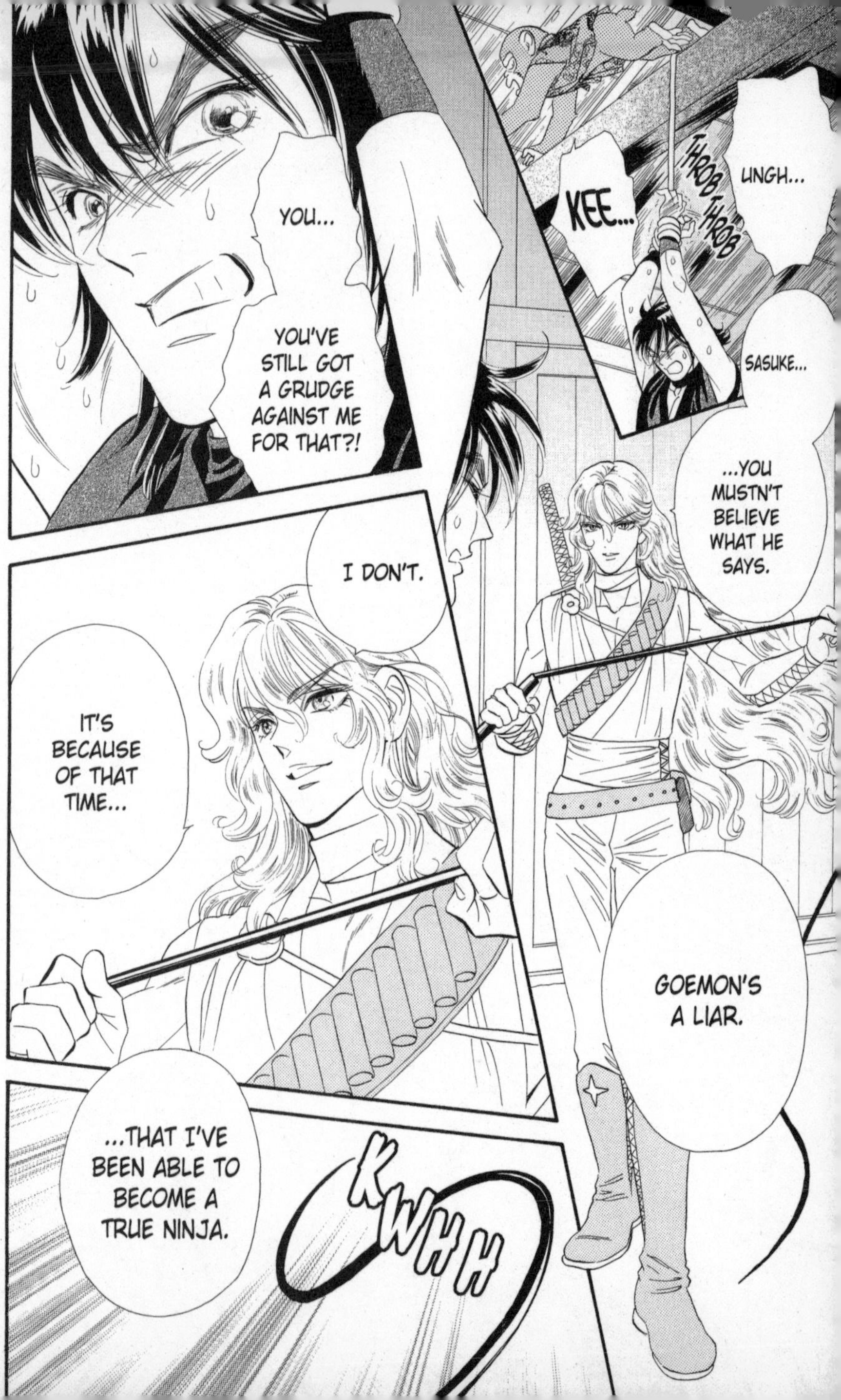
UNGH...
THROB THROB
KEE...
SASUKE...
...YOU MUSTN'T BELIEVE WHAT HE SAYS.
GOEMON'S A LIAR.
YOU...
YOU'VE STILL GOT A GRUDGE AGAINST ME FOR THAT?!
I DON'T.
IT'S BECAUSE OF THAT TIME...
...THAT I'VE BEEN ABLE TO BECOME A TRUE NINJA.
KWHH

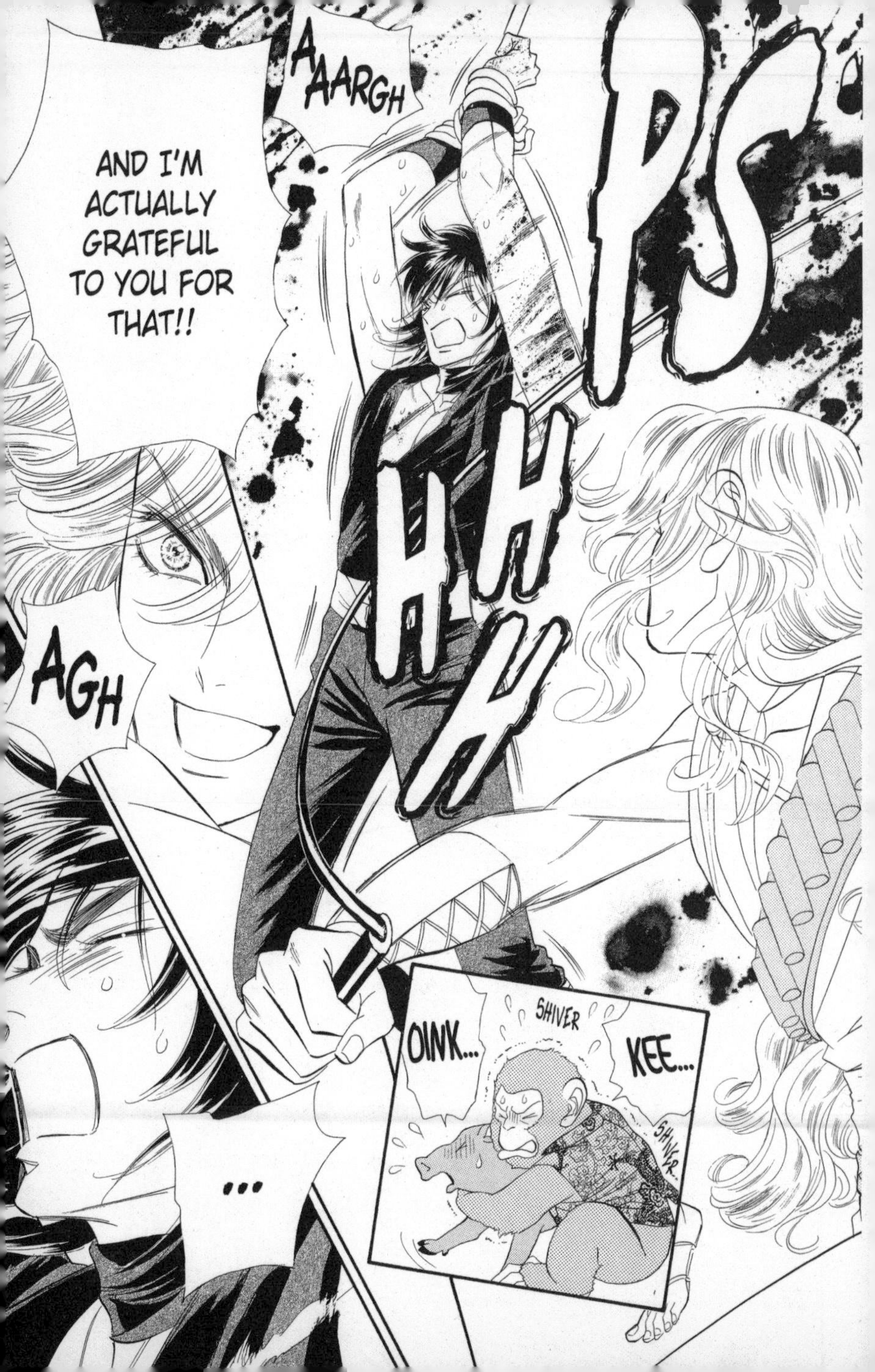
PSHHH
AAARGH
AND I'M ACTUALLY GRATEFUL TO YOU FOR THAT!!
AGH
KEE...
SHIVER
SHIVER
OINK...
...

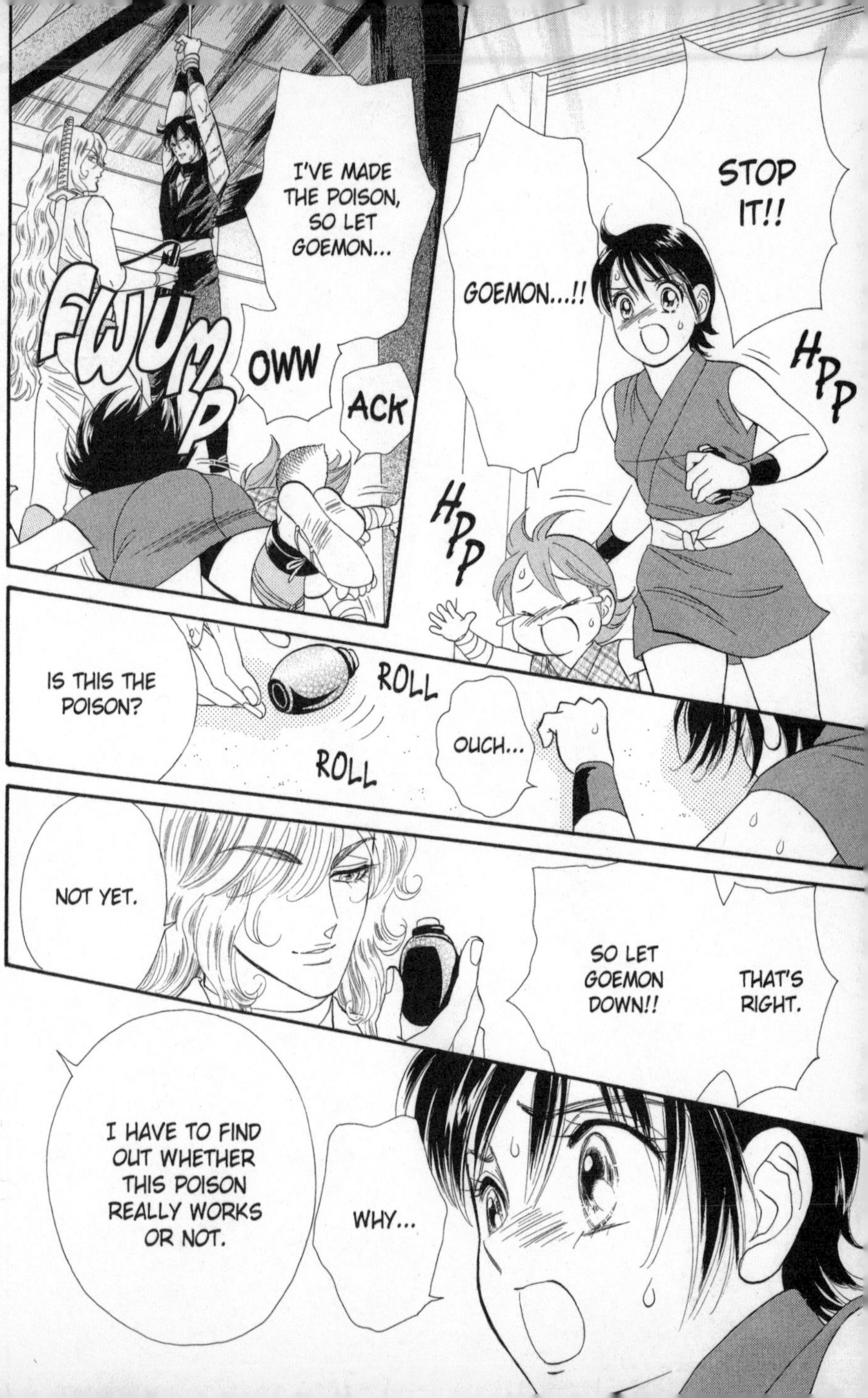
STOP IT!!
GOEMON...!!
HPP
HPP
I'VE MADE THE POISON, SO LET GOEMON...
FWUMP
OWW
ACK
OUCH...
ROLL
IS THIS THE POISON?
ROLL
THAT'S RIGHT.
SO LET GOEMON DOWN!!
NOT YET.
WHY...
I HAVE TO FIND OUT WHETHER THIS POISON REALLY WORKS OR NOT.

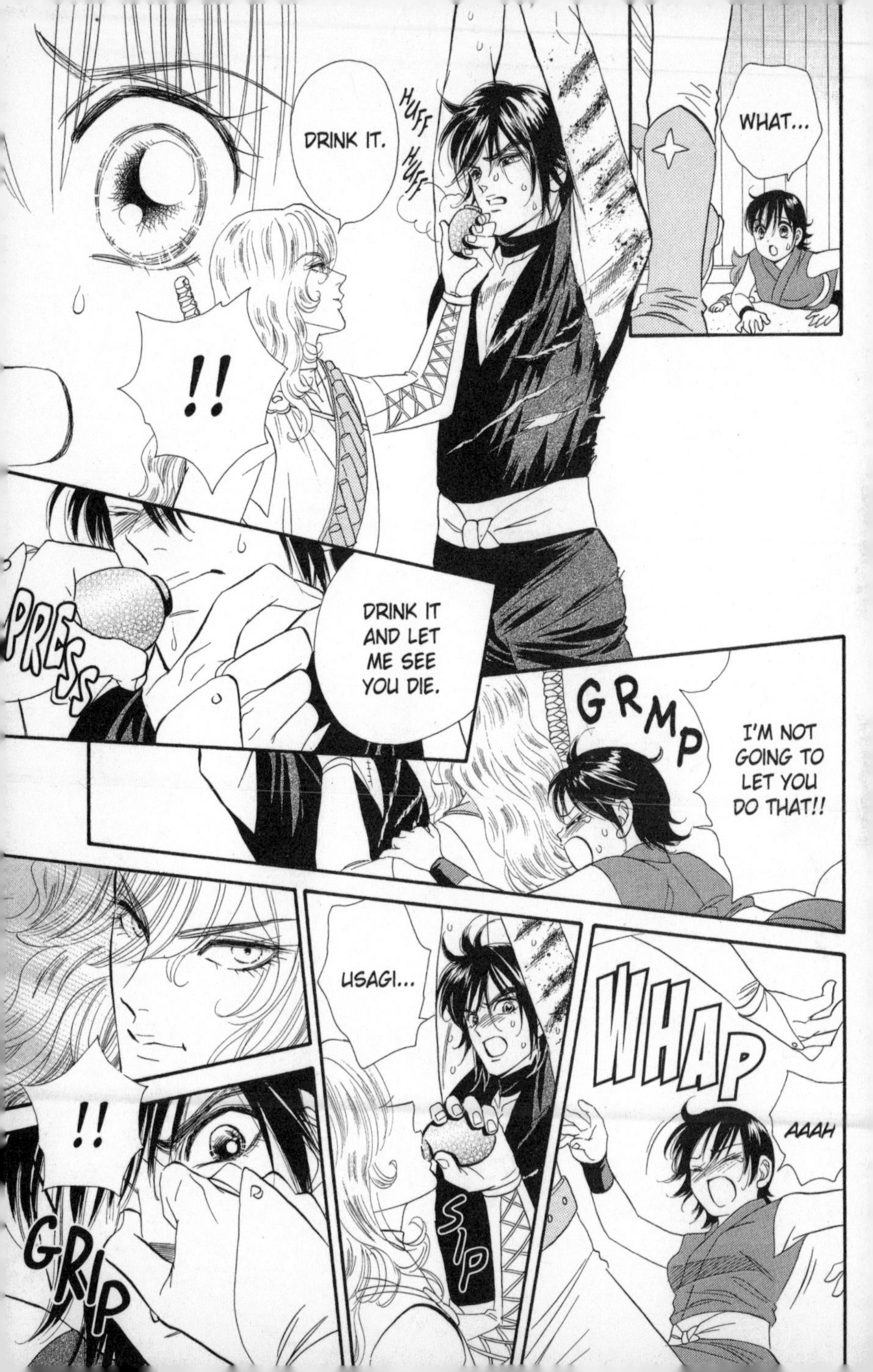
WHAT...
DRINK IT.
HUFF HUFF
!!
DRINK IT AND LET ME SEE YOU DIE.
PRESS
GRMP
I'M NOT GOING TO LET YOU DO THAT!!
WHAP
AAAH
USAGI...
SIP
!!
GRIP

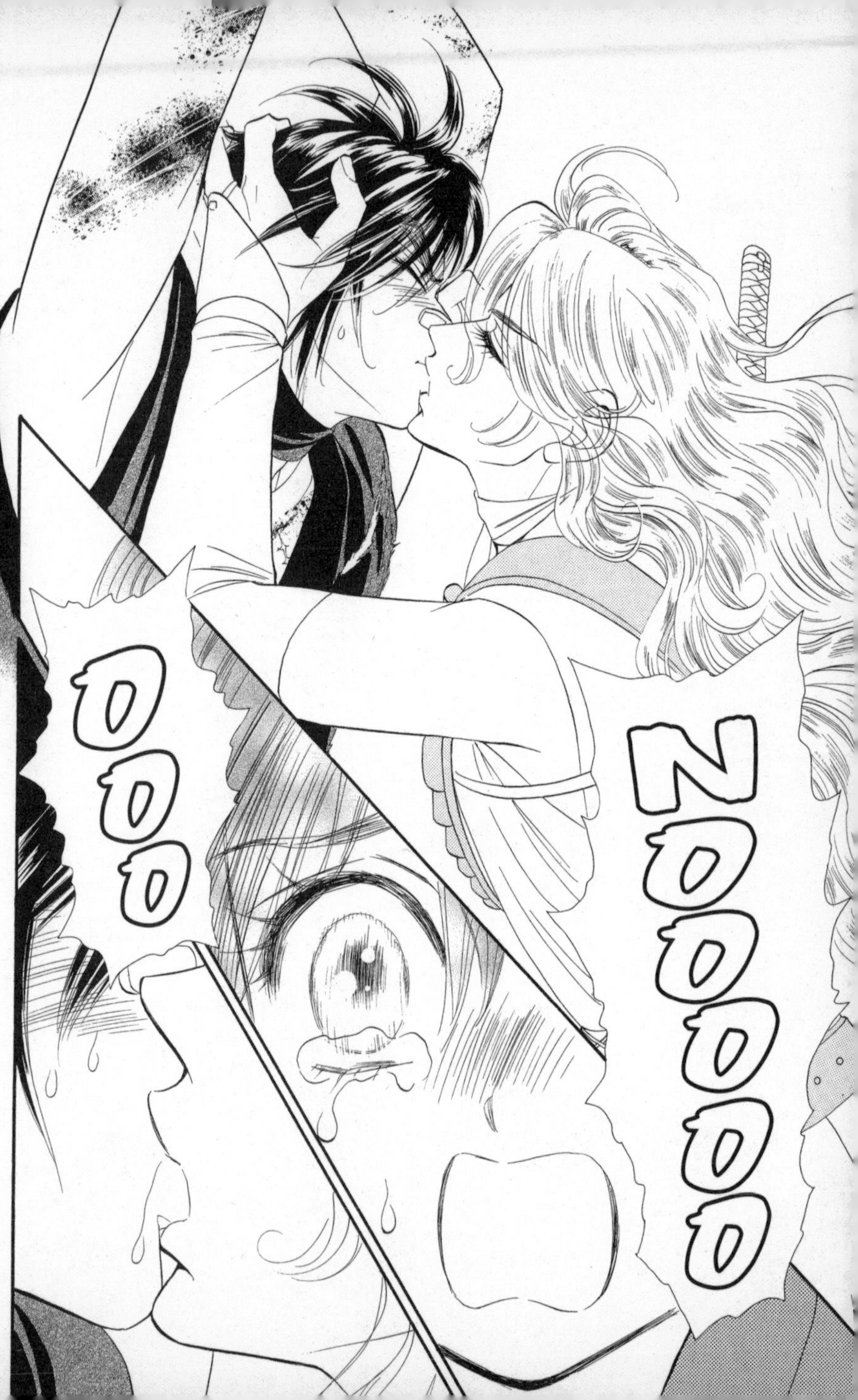
NOOOOOO
OOO

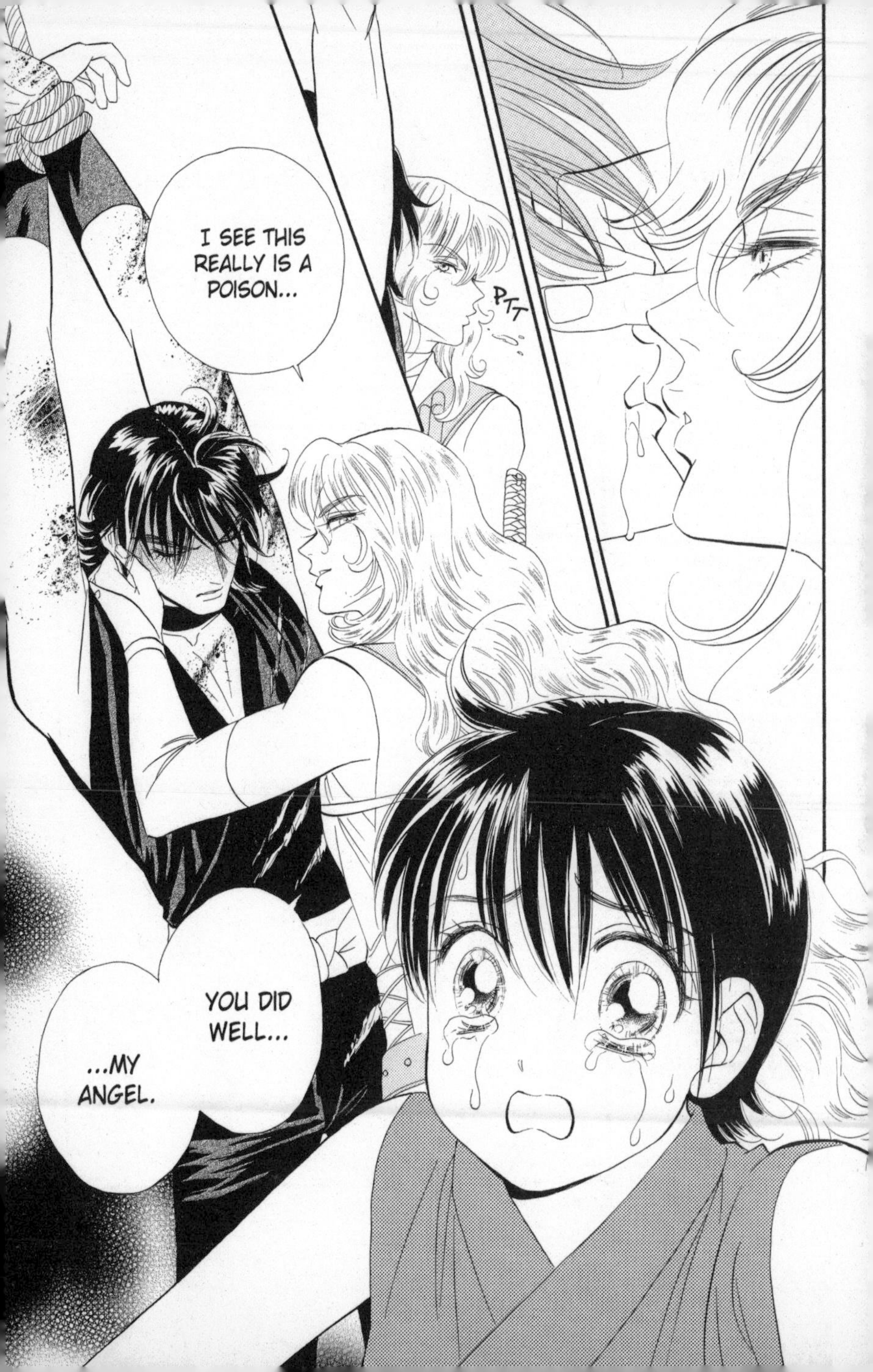
PTT
I SEE THIS REALLY IS A POISON...
YOU DID WELL...
...MY ANGEL.

TAIL OF THE MOON EXTRA: TODAY'S MISSION

"I WANT PRINCE HANZOU TO ESCORT ME!"

-MIKA, MIYAZAKI PREFECTURE

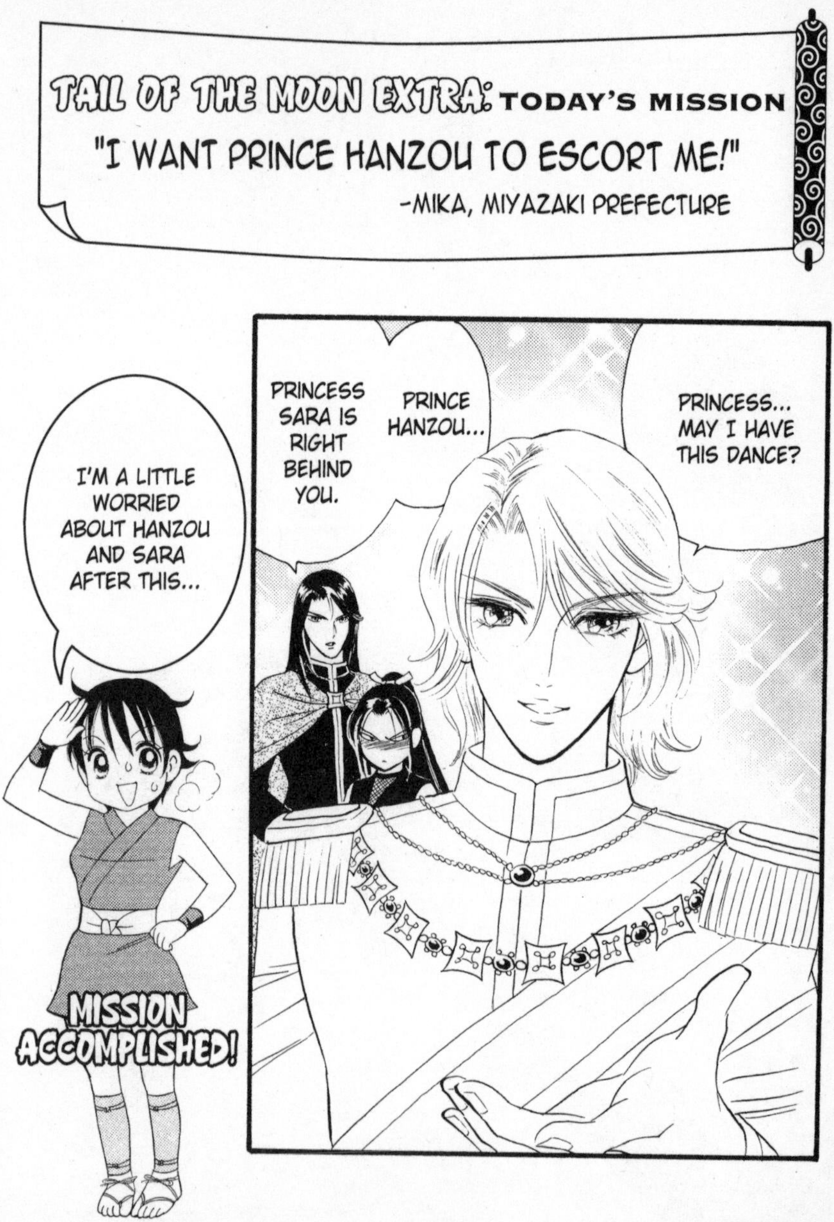
PRINCESS... MAY I HAVE THIS DANCE?
PRINCE HANZOU...
PRINCESS SARA IS RIGHT BEHIND YOU.
I'M A LITTLE WORRIED ABOUT HANZOU AND SARA AFTER THIS...
MISSION ACCOMPLISHED!

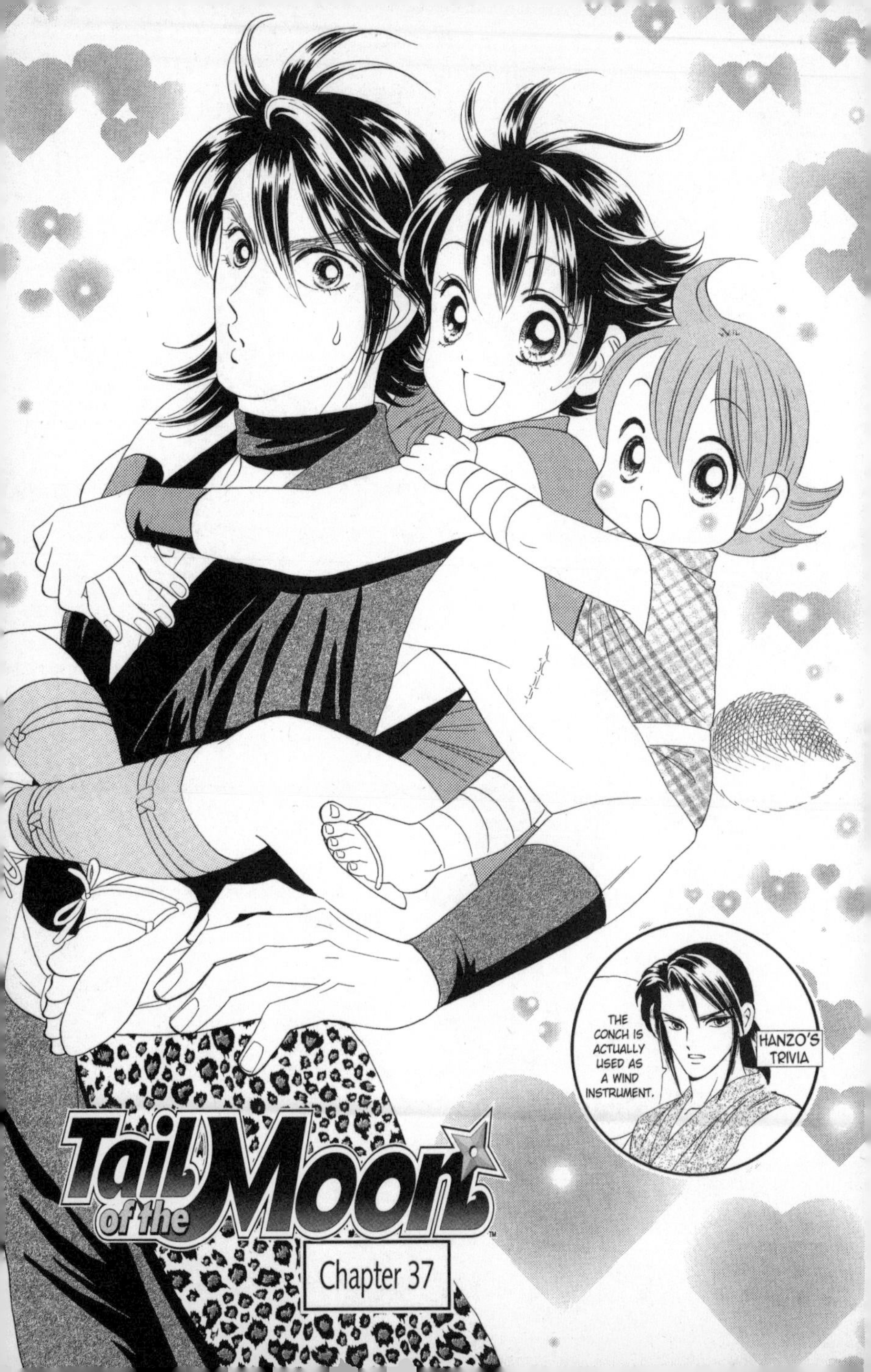
HANZO'S TRIVIA
THE CONCH IS ACTUALLY USED AS A WIND INSTRUMENT.
Tail of the Moon™
Chapter 37

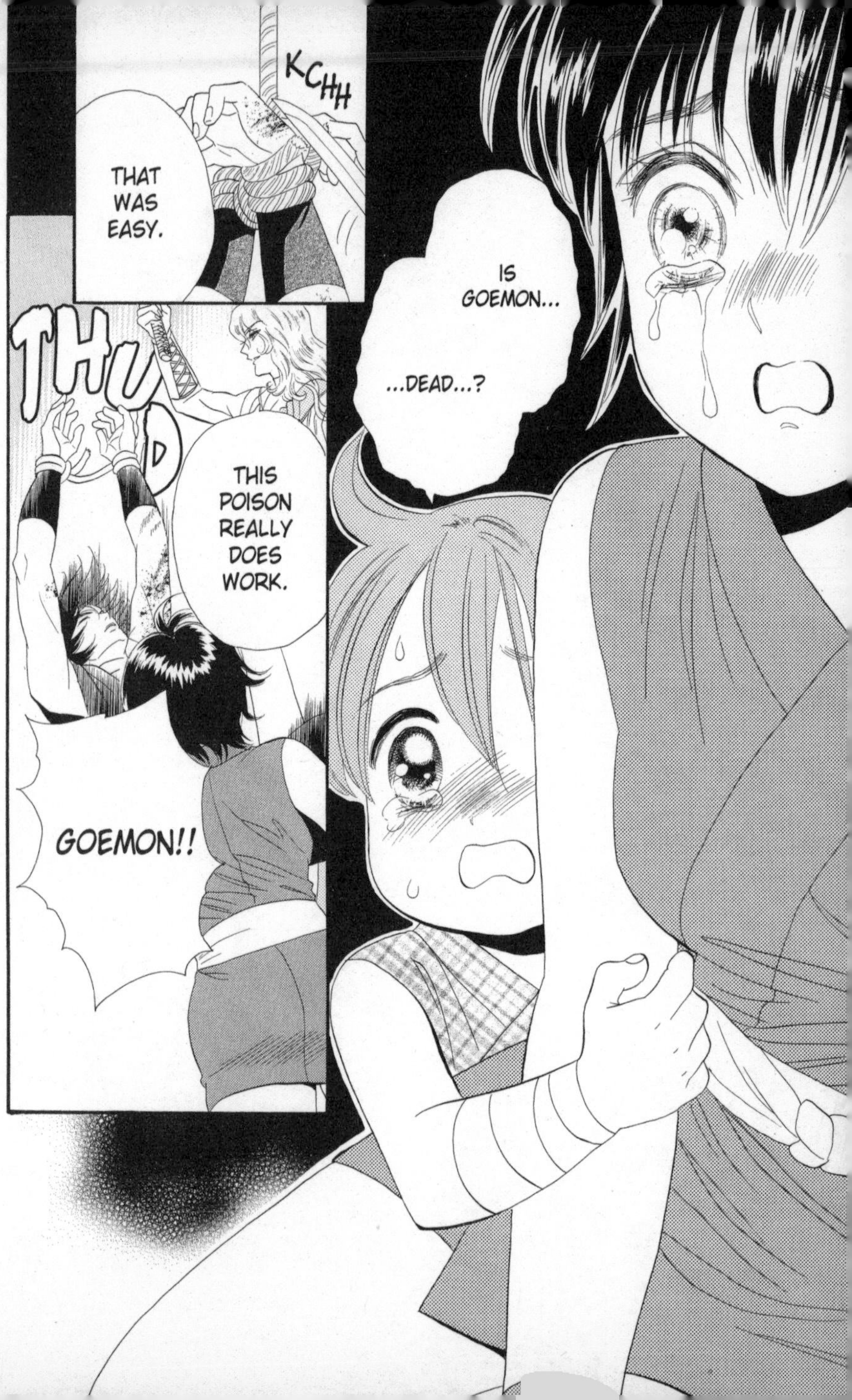
IS GOEMON...
...DEAD...?
KCHH
THAT WAS EASY.
THUD
THIS POISON REALLY DOES WORK.
GOEMON!!

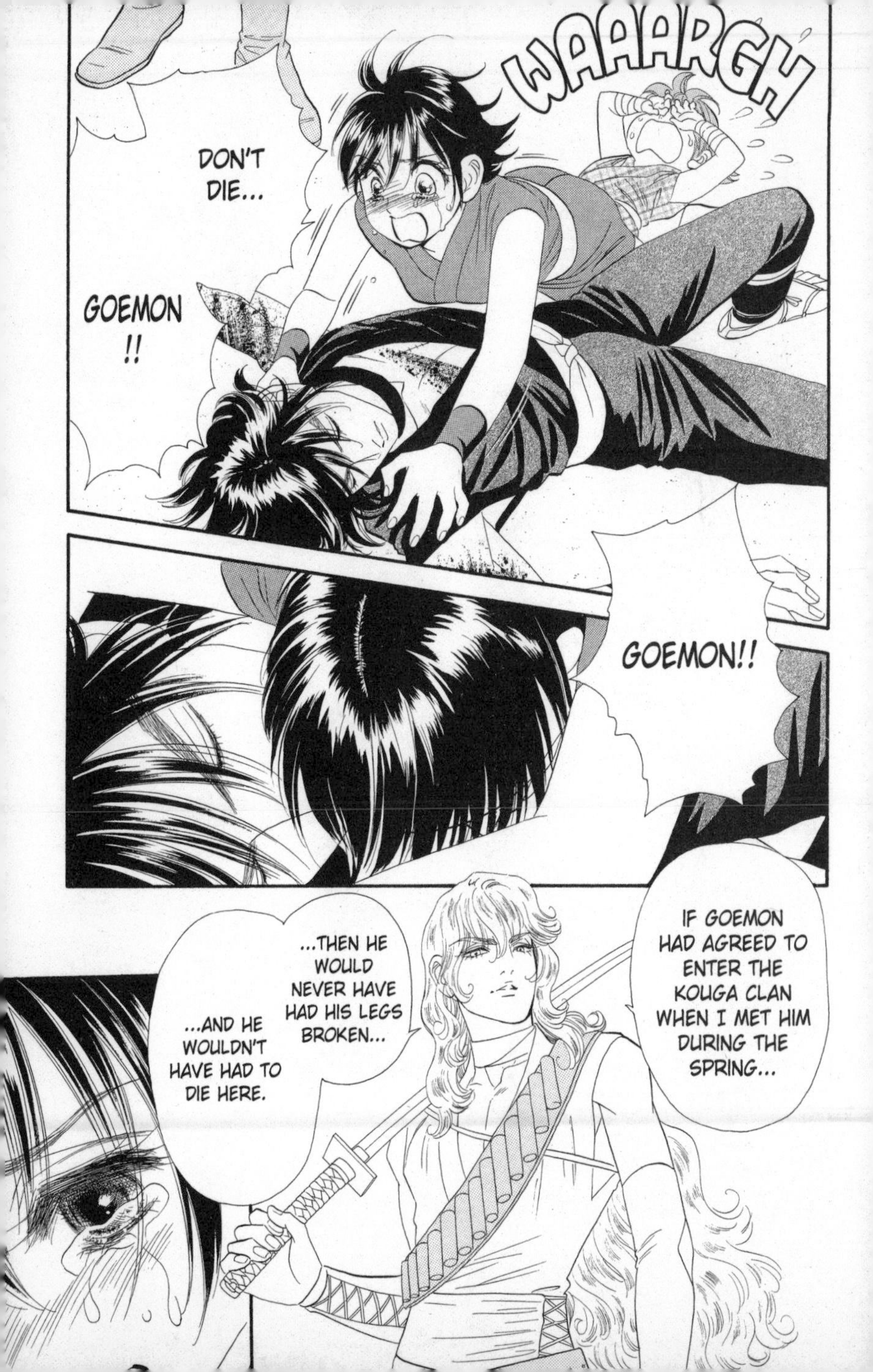
WAAARGH
DON'T DIE...
GOEMON !!
GOEMON!!
IF GOEMON HAD AGREED TO ENTER THE KOUGA CLAN WHEN I MET HIM DURING THE SPRING...
...THEN HE WOULD NEVER HAVE HAD HIS LEGS BROKEN...
...AND HE WOULDN'T HAVE HAD TO DIE HERE.

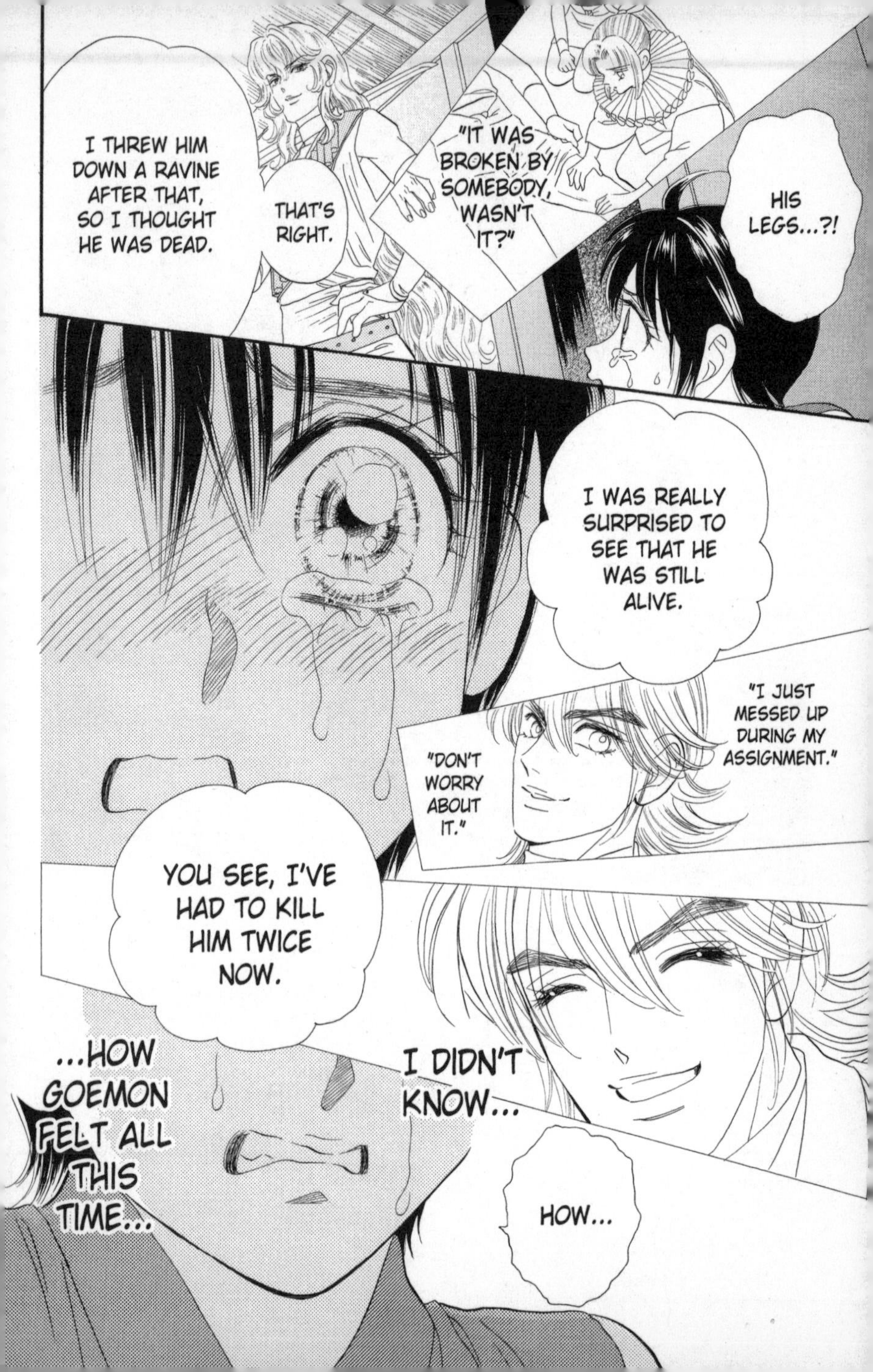
HIS LEGS...?!
"IT WAS BROKEN BY SOMEBODY, WASN'T IT?"
THAT'S RIGHT.
I THREW HIM DOWN A RAVINE AFTER THAT, SO I THOUGHT HE WAS DEAD.
I WAS REALLY SURPRISED TO SEE THAT HE WAS STILL ALIVE.
"I JUST MESSED UP DURING MY ASSIGNMENT."
"DON'T WORRY ABOUT IT."
YOU SEE, I'VE HAD TO KILL HIM TWICE NOW.
HOW...
I DIDN'T KNOW...
...HOW GOEMON FELT ALL THIS TIME...

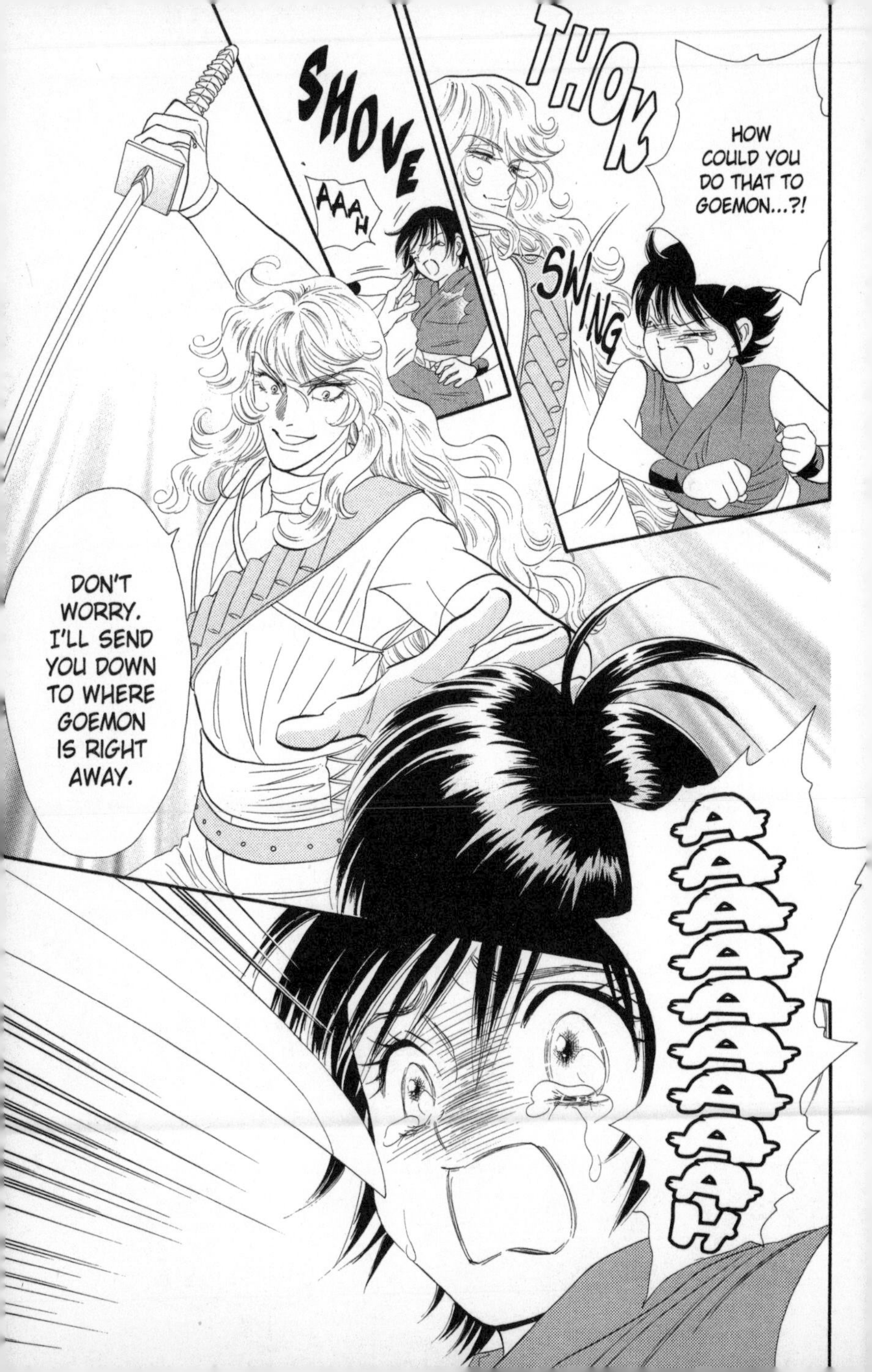
THOK
HOW COULD YOU DO THAT TO GOEMON...?!
SWING
SHOVE
AAAH
DON'T WORRY. I'LL SEND YOU DOWN TO WHERE GOEMON IS RIGHT AWAY.
AAAAAAAAAH

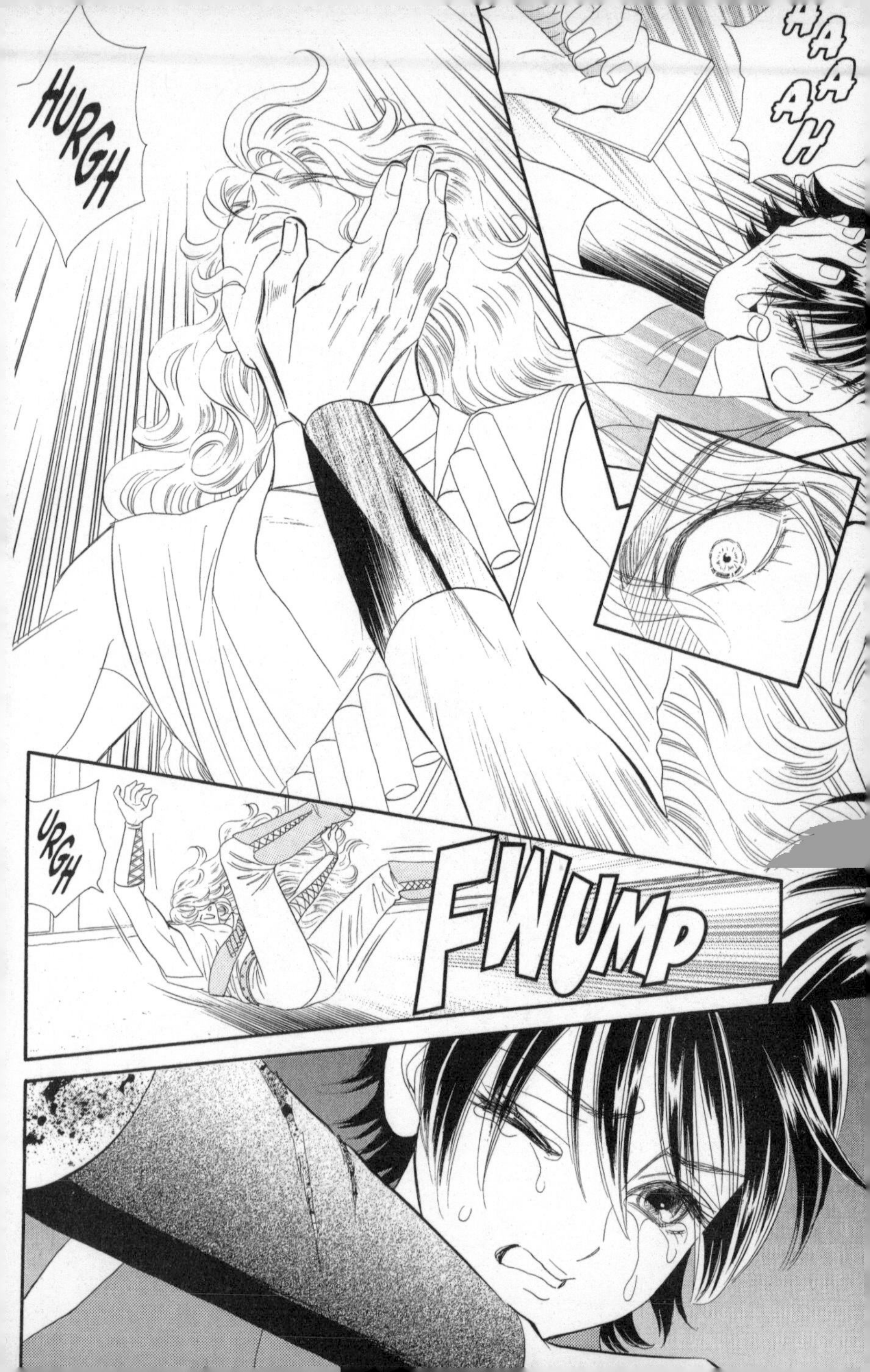
HAAAAH
HURGH
F-WUMP
URGH

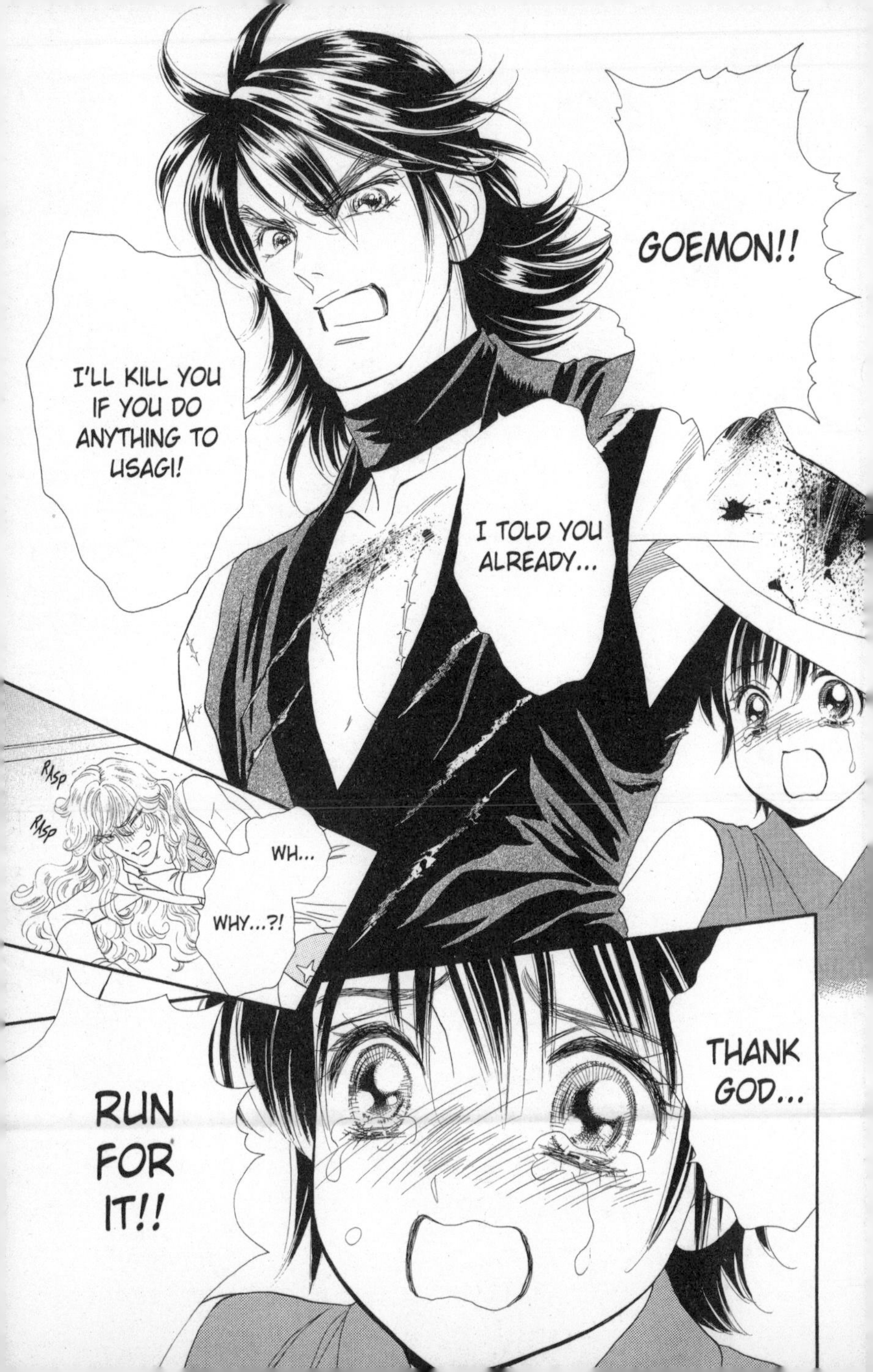
GOEMON!!
I TOLD YOU ALREADY...
I'LL KILL YOU IF YOU DO ANYTHING TO USAGI!
RASP
RASP
WH...
WHY...?!
THANK GOD...
RUN FOR IT!!

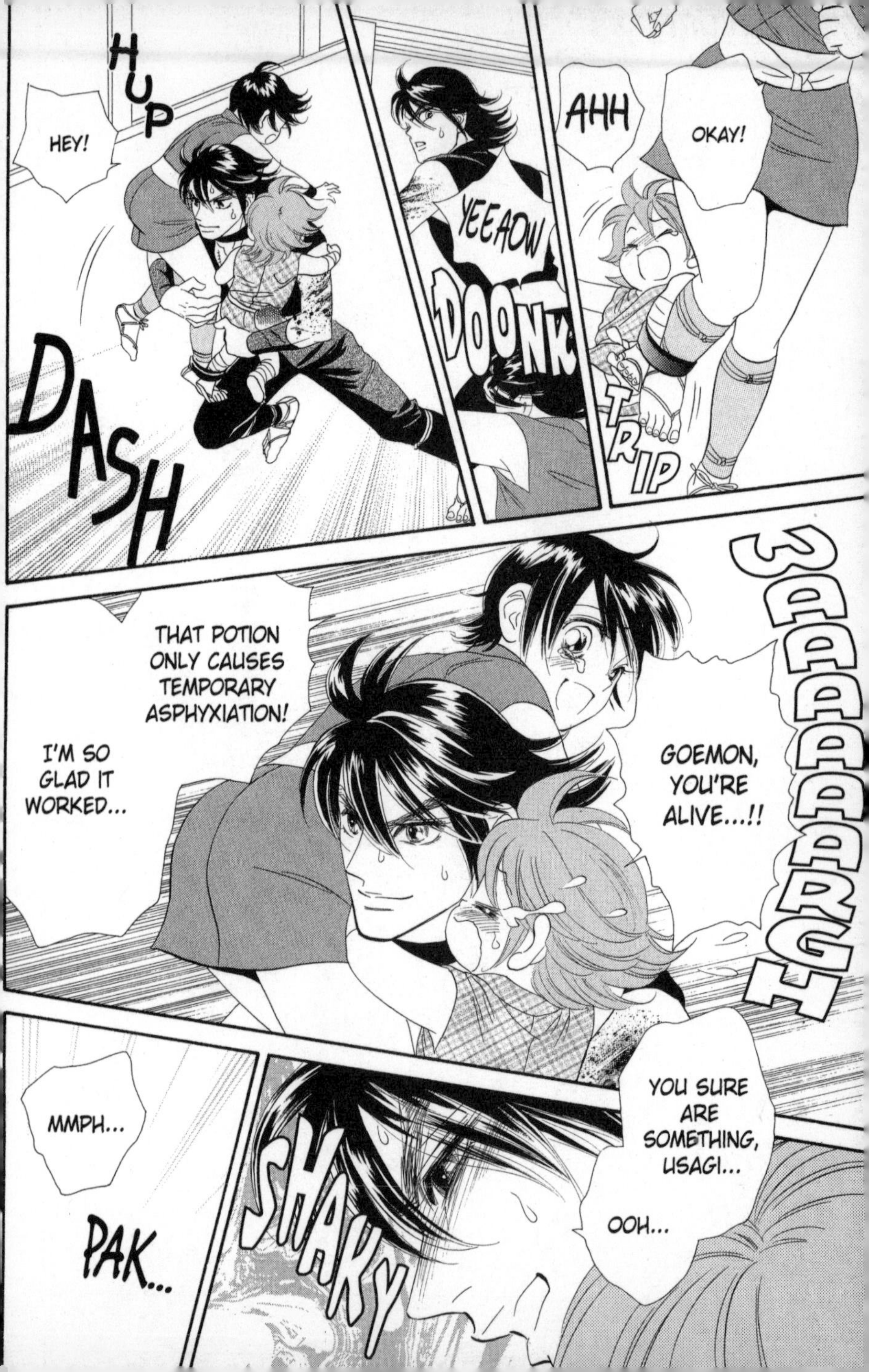
OKAY!
AHH
TRIP
YEEAOW
DOONK
HEY!
HUP
DASH
WAAAAAARGH
GOEMON, YOU'RE ALIVE...!!
THAT POTION ONLY CAUSES TEMPORARY ASPHYXIATION!
I'M SO GLAD IT WORKED...
YOU SURE ARE SOMETHING, USAGI...
OOH...
SHAKY
MMPH...
PAK...

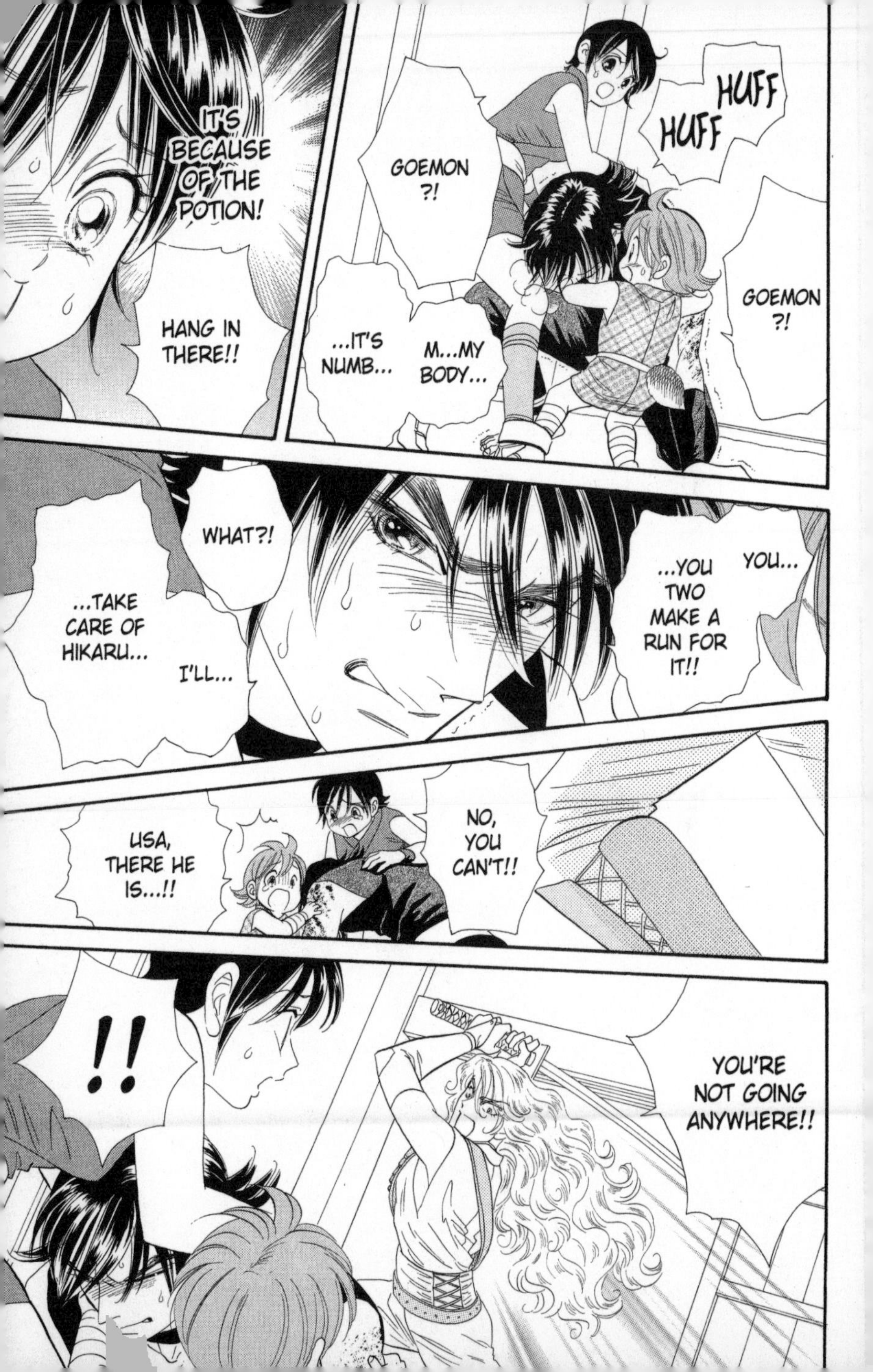
HUFF HUFF
GOEMON ?!
GOEMON ?!
M...MY BODY...
...IT'S NUMB...
IT'S BECAUSE OF THE POTION!
HANG IN THERE!!
YOU...
...YOU TWO MAKE A RUN FOR IT!!
WHAT?!
I'LL...
...TAKE CARE OF HIKARU...
NO, YOU CAN'T!!
USA, THERE HE IS...!!
YOU'RE NOT GOING ANYWHERE!!
!!

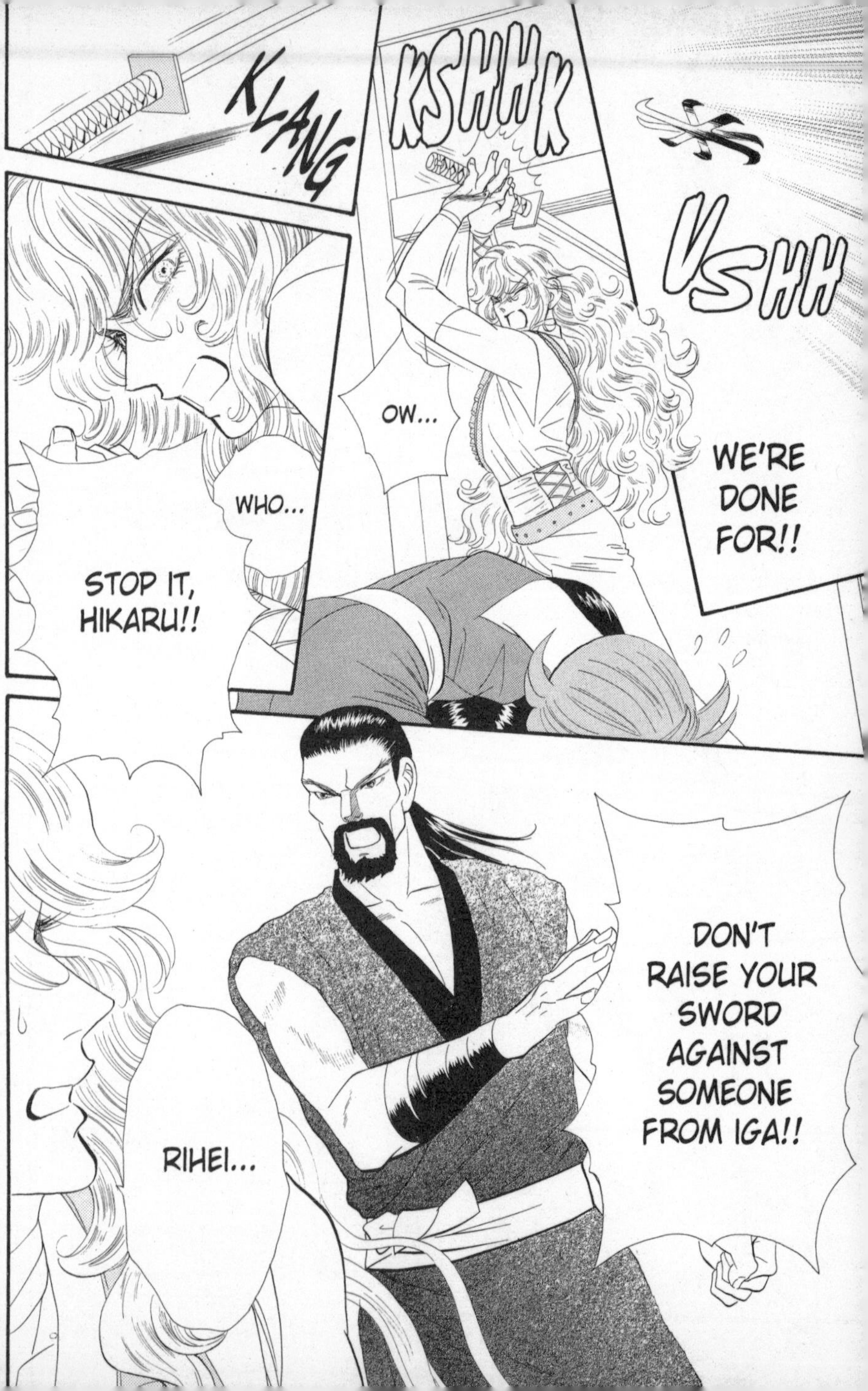

VSHH
WE'RE DONE FOR!!
KSHHK
OW...
KLANG
WHO...
STOP IT, HIKARU!!
DON'T RAISE YOUR SWORD AGAINST SOMEONE FROM IGA!!
RIHEI...

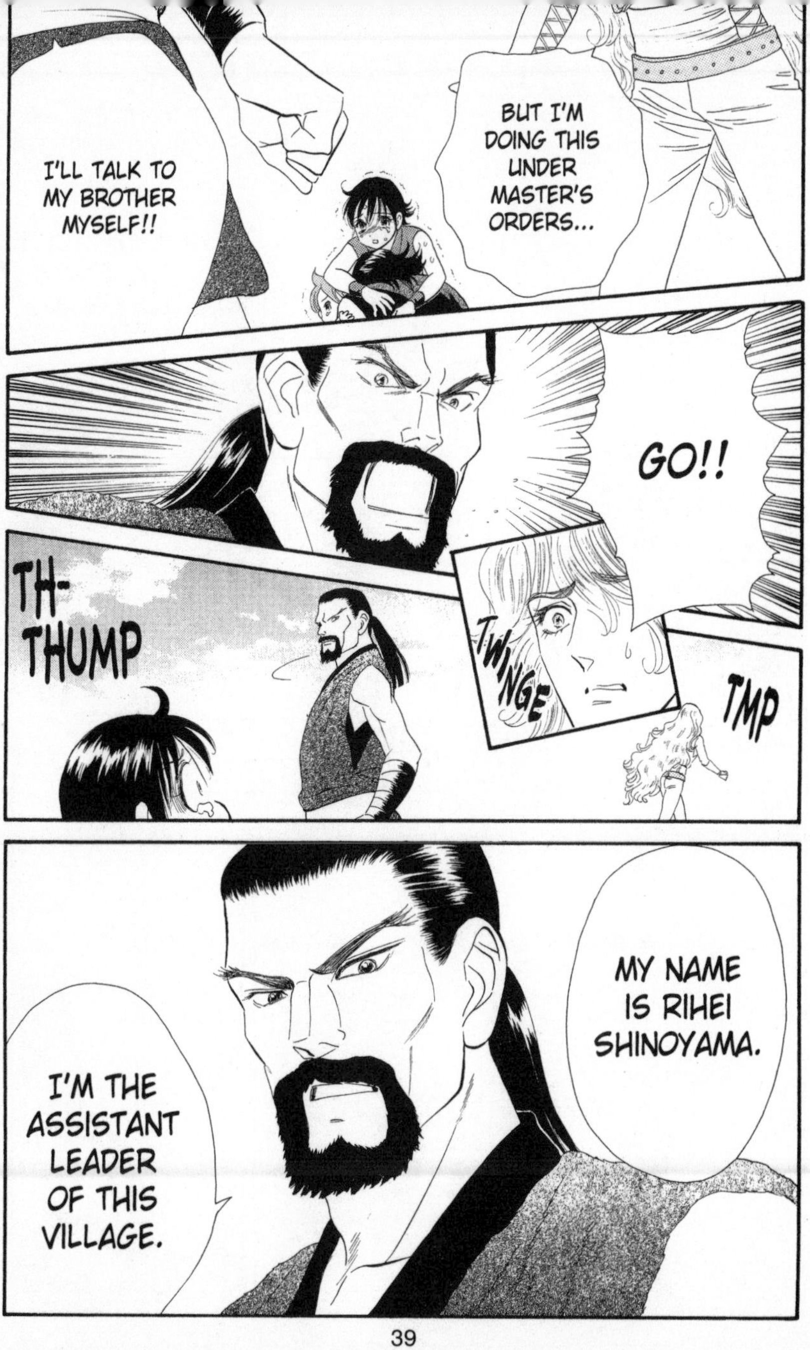
BUT I'M DOING THIS UNDER MASTER'S ORDERS...
I'LL TALK TO MY BROTHER MYSELF!!
GO!!
TWINGE
TMP
TH-THUMP
MY NAME IS RIHEI SHINOYAMA.
I'M THE ASSISTANT LEADER OF THIS VILLAGE.

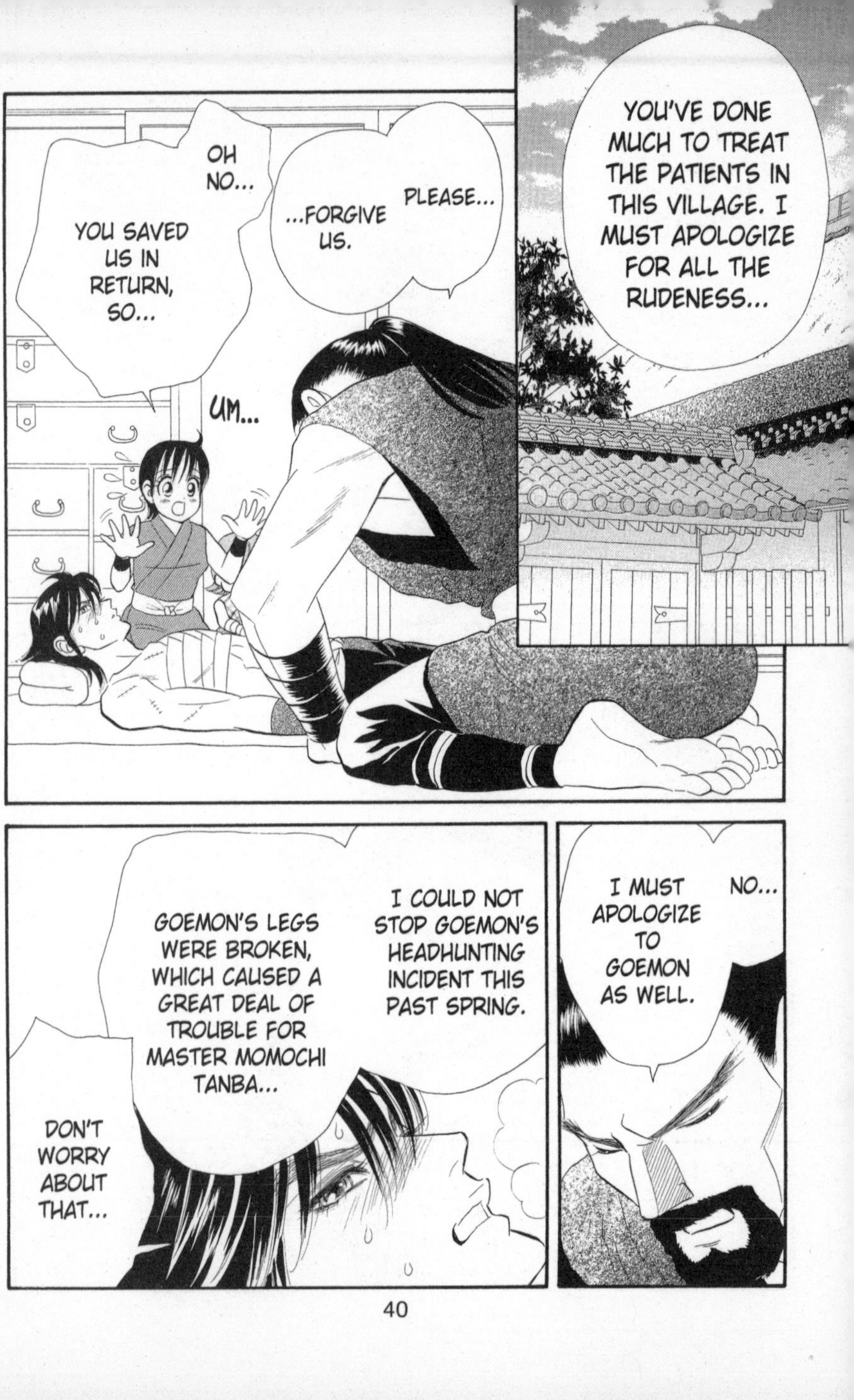
YOU'VE DONE MUCH TO TREAT THE PATIENTS IN THIS VILLAGE. I MUST APOLOGIZE FOR ALL THE RUDENESS...
PLEASE...
...FORGIVE US.
OH NO...
YOU SAVED US IN RETURN, SO...
UM...
NO...
I MUST APOLOGIZE TO GOEMON AS WELL.
I COULD NOT STOP GOEMON'S HEADHUNTING INCIDENT THIS PAST SPRING.
GOEMON'S LEGS WERE BROKEN, WHICH CAUSED A GREAT DEAL OF TROUBLE FOR MASTER MOMOCHI TANBA...
DON'T WORRY ABOUT THAT...

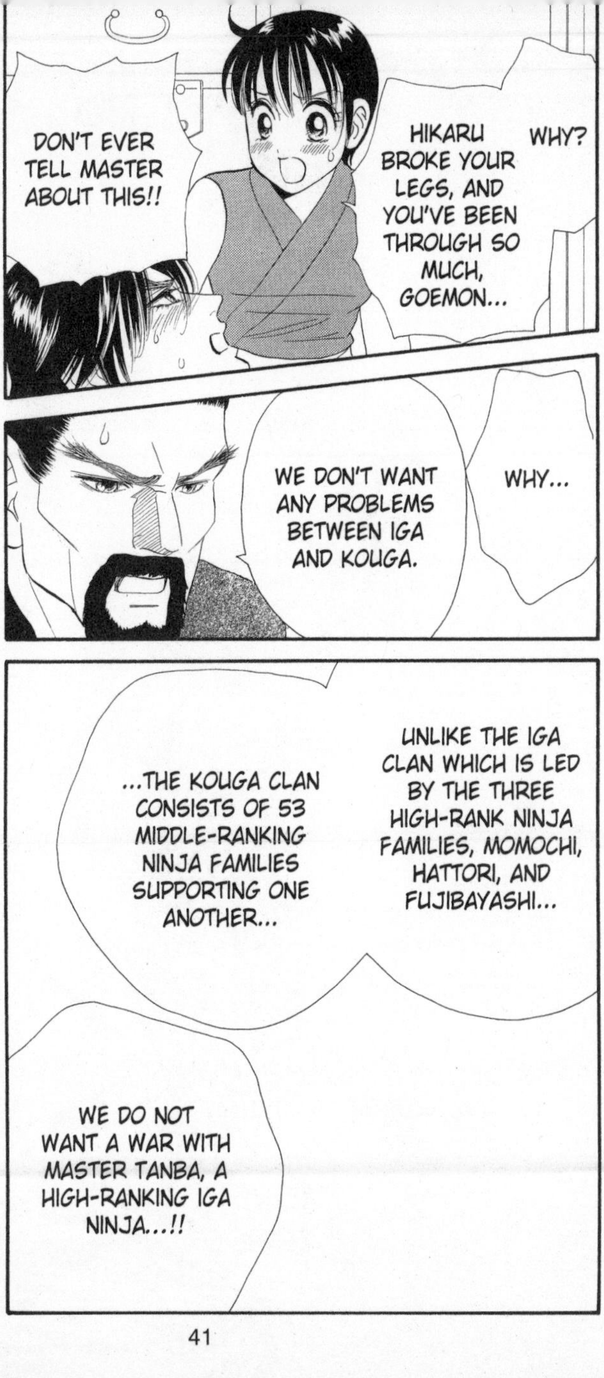
WHY?
HIKARU BROKE YOUR LEGS, AND YOU'VE BEEN THROUGH SO MUCH, GOEMON...
DON'T EVER TELL MASTER ABOUT THIS!!
WHY...
WE DON'T WANT ANY PROBLEMS BETWEEN IGA AND KOUGA.
UNLIKE THE IGA CLAN WHICH IS LED BY THE THREE HIGH-RANK NINJA FAMILIES, MOMOCHI, HATTORI, AND FUJIBAYASHI...
...THE KOUGA CLAN CONSISTS OF 53 MIDDLE-RANKING NINJA FAMILIES SUPPORTING ONE ANOTHER...
WE DO NOT WANT A WAR WITH MASTER TANBA, A HIGH-RANKING IGA NINJA...!!

UE-RIN'S WAY OF THE MANGA ①

Ue-Rin's encounter with Manga was pretty late...No one in my family read manga, so I had never read manga until I entered middle school. I liked to draw even before that, so I spent my early years drawing pictures after watching anime or looking through illustration books...

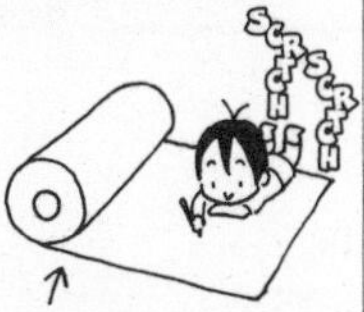
SCRATCH SCRATCH

↑
I kept wasting huge rolls of paper that my parents brought back from the factory. Well, so I heard... (I hardly remember any of it.) In middle school, my classmate brought *Weekly Margaret*, a manga magazine, to school.

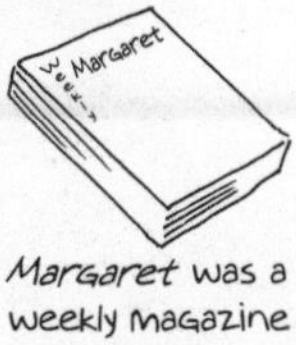
Weekly Margaret

Margaret was a weekly magazine back then.

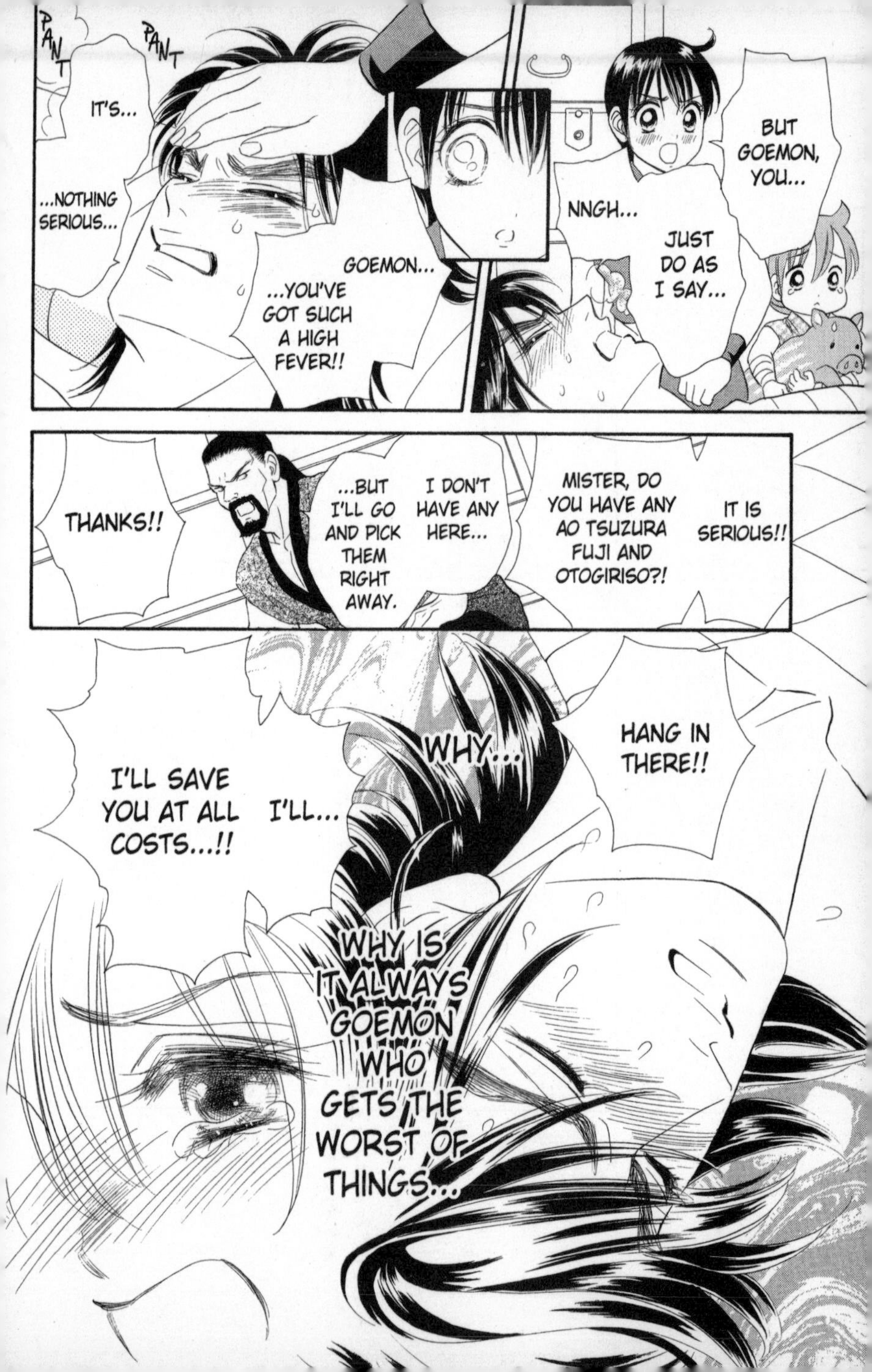
BUT GOEMON, YOU...
NNGH...
JUST DO AS I SAY...
GOEMON...
...YOU'VE GOT SUCH A HIGH FEVER!!
PANT PANT
IT'S...
...NOTHING SERIOUS...
IT IS SERIOUS!!
MISTER, DO YOU HAVE ANY AO TSUZURA FUJI AND OTOGIRISO?!
I DON'T HAVE ANY HERE...
...BUT I'LL GO AND PICK THEM RIGHT AWAY.
THANKS!!
HANG IN THERE!!
WHY...
I'LL...
I'LL SAVE YOU AT ALL COSTS...!!
WHY IS IT ALWAYS GOEMON WHO GETS THE WORST OF THINGS...

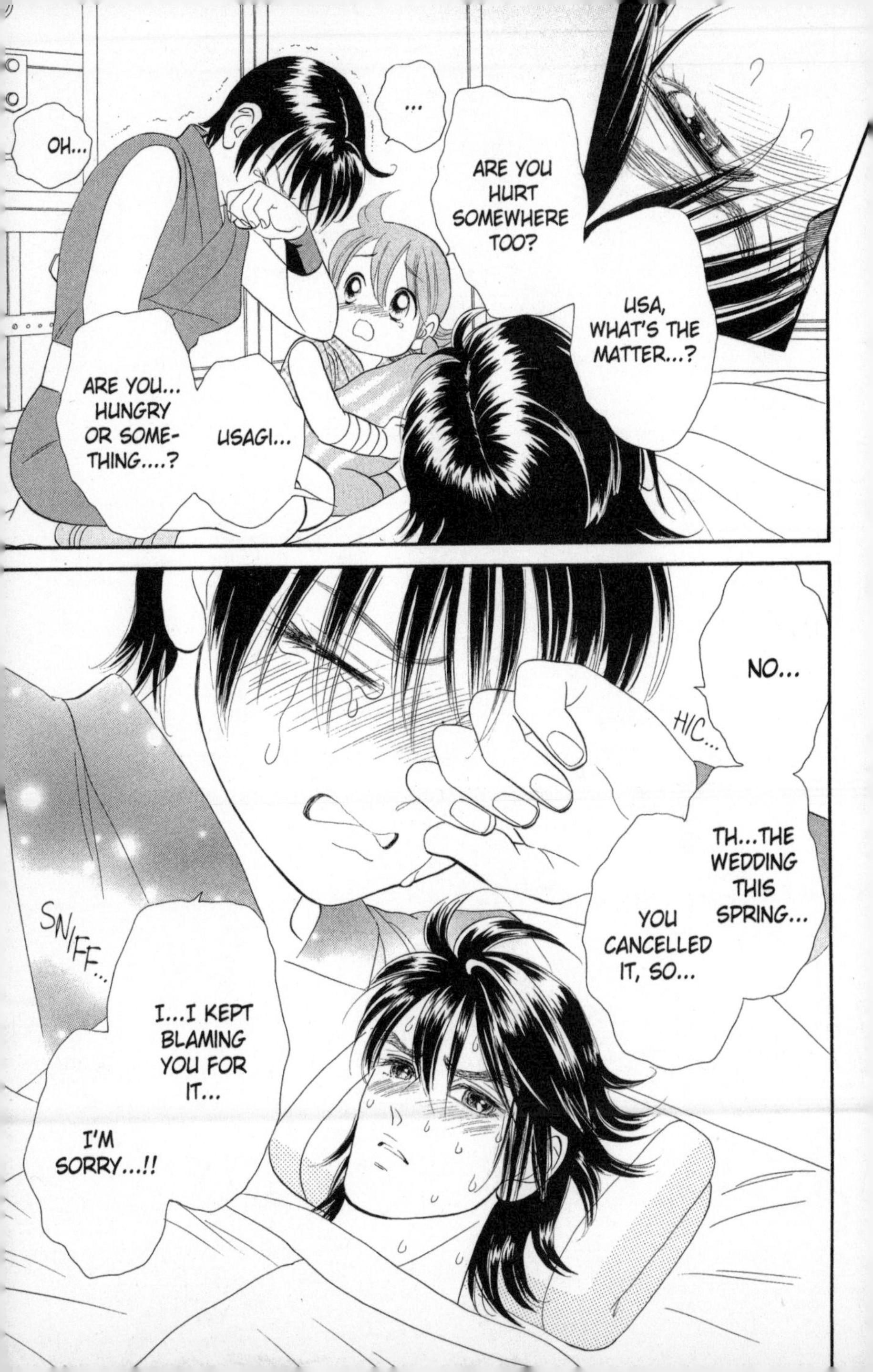
USA, WHAT'S THE MATTER...?
ARE YOU HURT SOMEWHERE TOO?
...
USAGI...
ARE YOU... HUNGRY OR SOME-THING....?
OH...
NO...
HIC...
TH...THE WEDDING THIS SPRING...
YOU CANCELLED IT, SO...
SNIFF...
I...I KEPT BLAMING YOU FOR IT...
I'M SORRY...!!

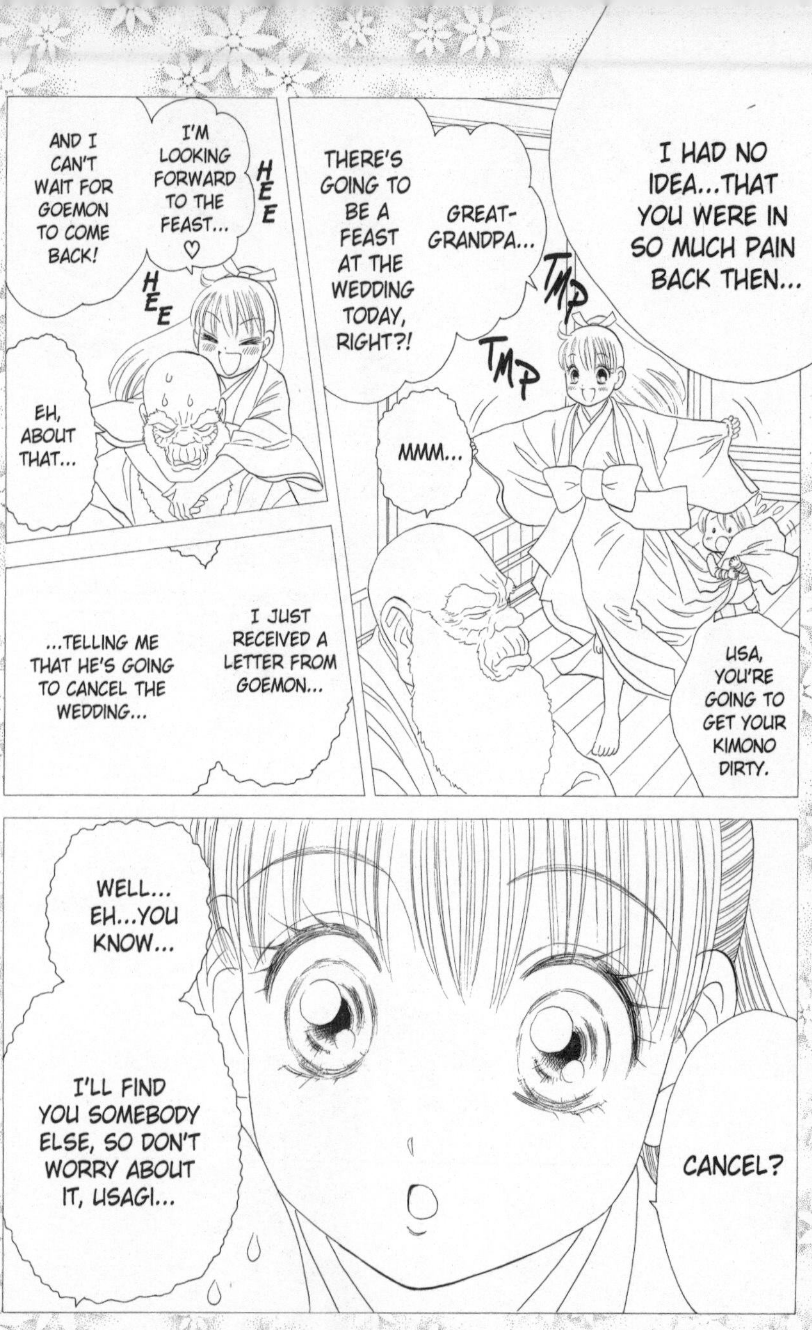
I HAD NO IDEA...THAT YOU WERE IN SO MUCH PAIN BACK THEN...
TMP
TMP
GREAT-GRANDPA...
THERE'S GOING TO BE A FEAST AT THE WEDDING TODAY, RIGHT?!
USA, YOU'RE GOING TO GET YOUR KIMONO DIRTY.
MMM...
I'M LOOKING FORWARD TO THE FEAST... ♡
HEE
HEE
AND I CAN'T WAIT FOR GOEMON TO COME BACK!
EH, ABOUT THAT...
I JUST RECEIVED A LETTER FROM GOEMON...
...TELLING ME THAT HE'S GOING TO CANCEL THE WEDDING...
CANCEL?
WELL... EH...YOU KNOW...
I'LL FIND YOU SOMEBODY ELSE, SO DON'T WORRY ABOUT IT, USAGI...

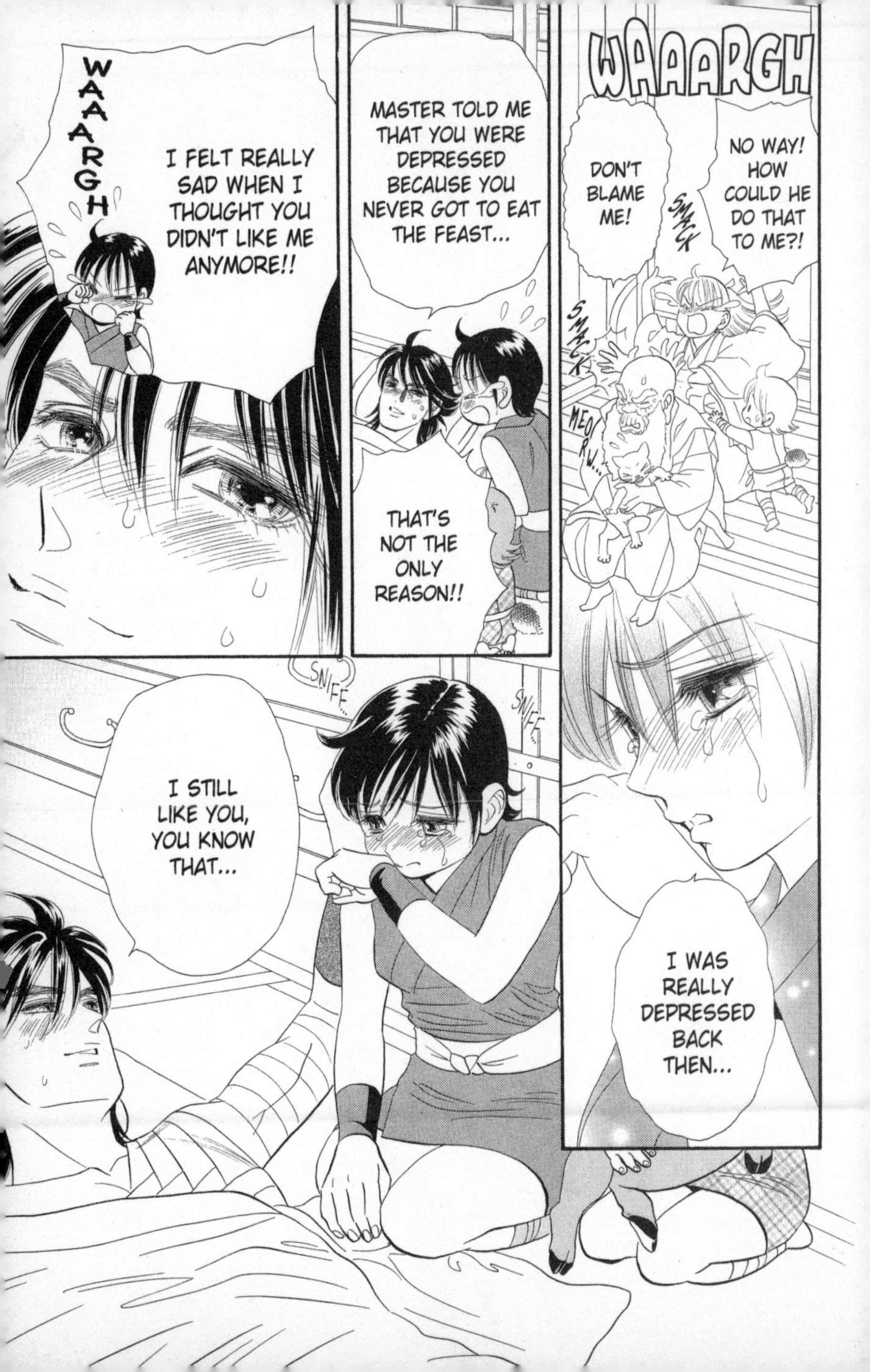
WAAARGH
NO WAY! HOW COULD HE DO THAT TO ME?!
DON'T BLAME ME!
SMACK
SMACK
MEOWRW...
I WAS REALLY DEPRESSED BACK THEN...
MASTER TOLD ME THAT YOU WERE DEPRESSED BECAUSE YOU NEVER GOT TO EAT THE FEAST...
THAT'S NOT THE ONLY REASON!!
WAAARGH
I FELT REALLY SAD WHEN I THOUGHT YOU DIDN'T LIKE ME ANYMORE!!
SNIFF
SNIFF...
I STILL LIKE YOU, YOU KNOW THAT...

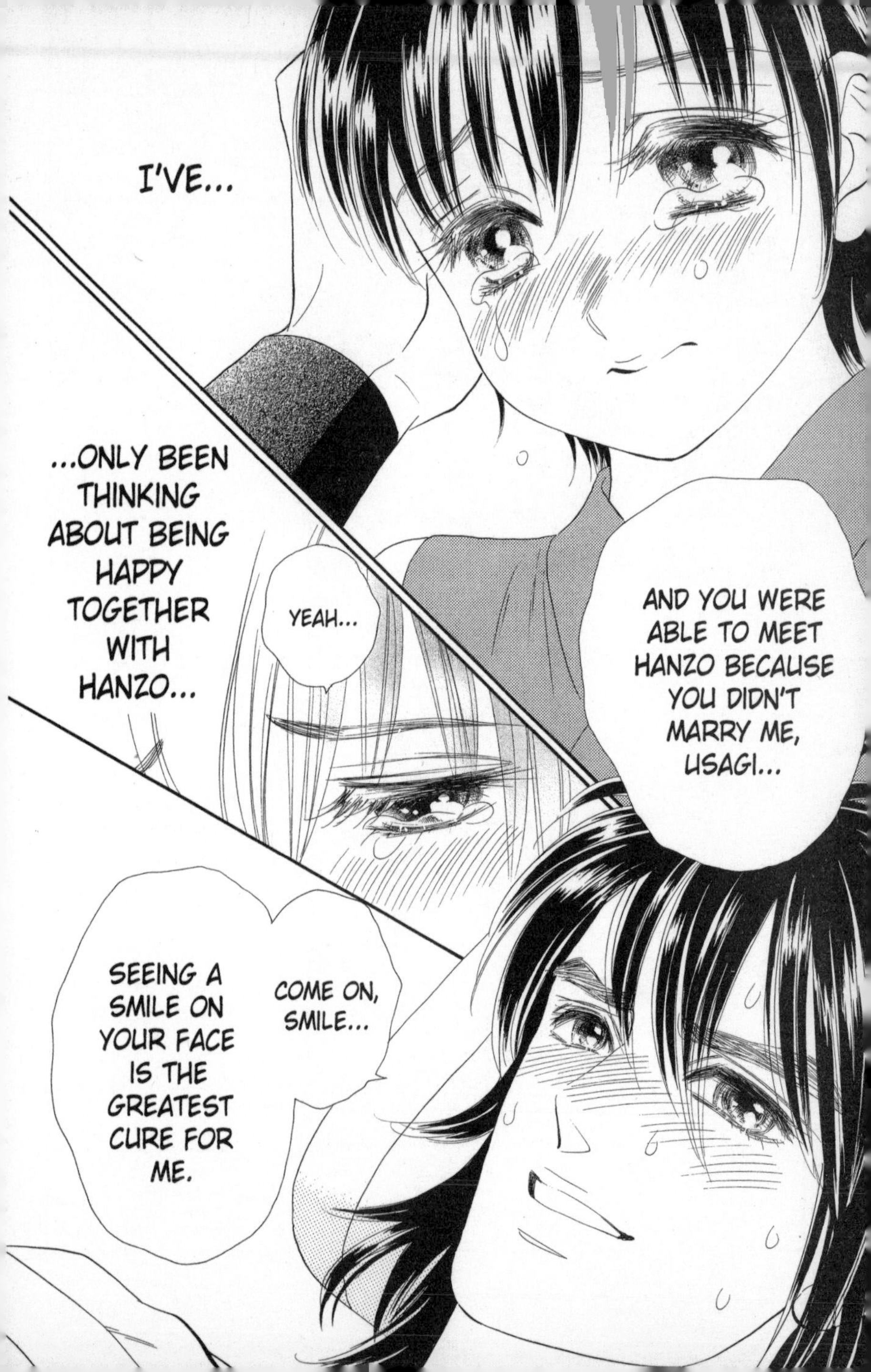
I'VE...
...ONLY BEEN THINKING ABOUT BEING HAPPY TOGETHER WITH HANZO...
AND YOU WERE ABLE TO MEET HANZO BECAUSE YOU DIDN'T MARRY ME, USAGI...
YEAH...
COME ON, SMILE...
SEEING A SMILE ON YOUR FACE IS THE GREATEST CURE FOR ME.

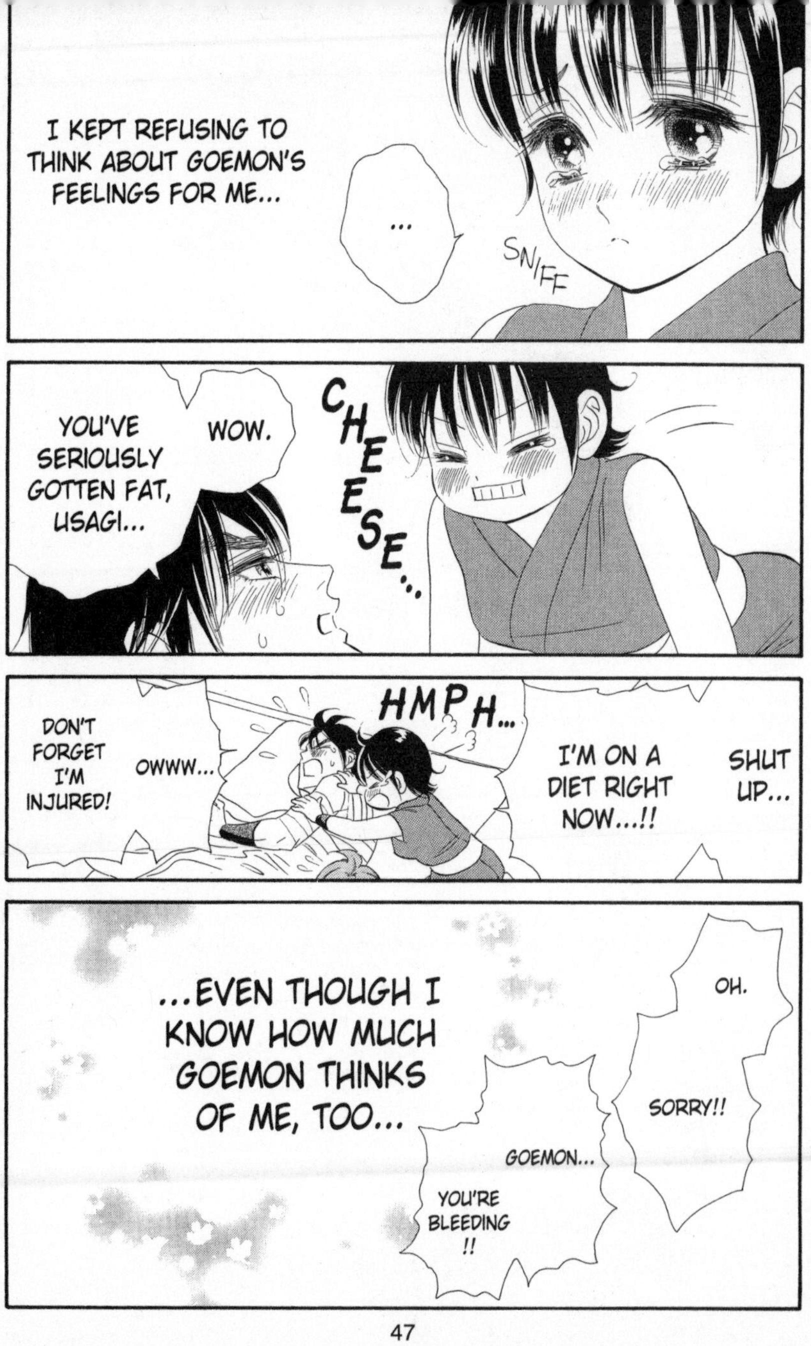
I KEPT REFUSING TO THINK ABOUT GOEMON'S FEELINGS FOR ME...
...
SNIFF
CHEESE...
WOW.
YOU'VE SERIOUSLY GOTTEN FAT, USAGI...
SHUT UP...
I'M ON A DIET RIGHT NOW...!!
HMPH...
OWWW...
DON'T FORGET I'M INJURED!
OH.
SORRY!!
GOEMON...
YOU'RE BLEEDING !!
...EVEN THOUGH I KNOW HOW MUCH GOEMON THINKS OF ME, TOO...

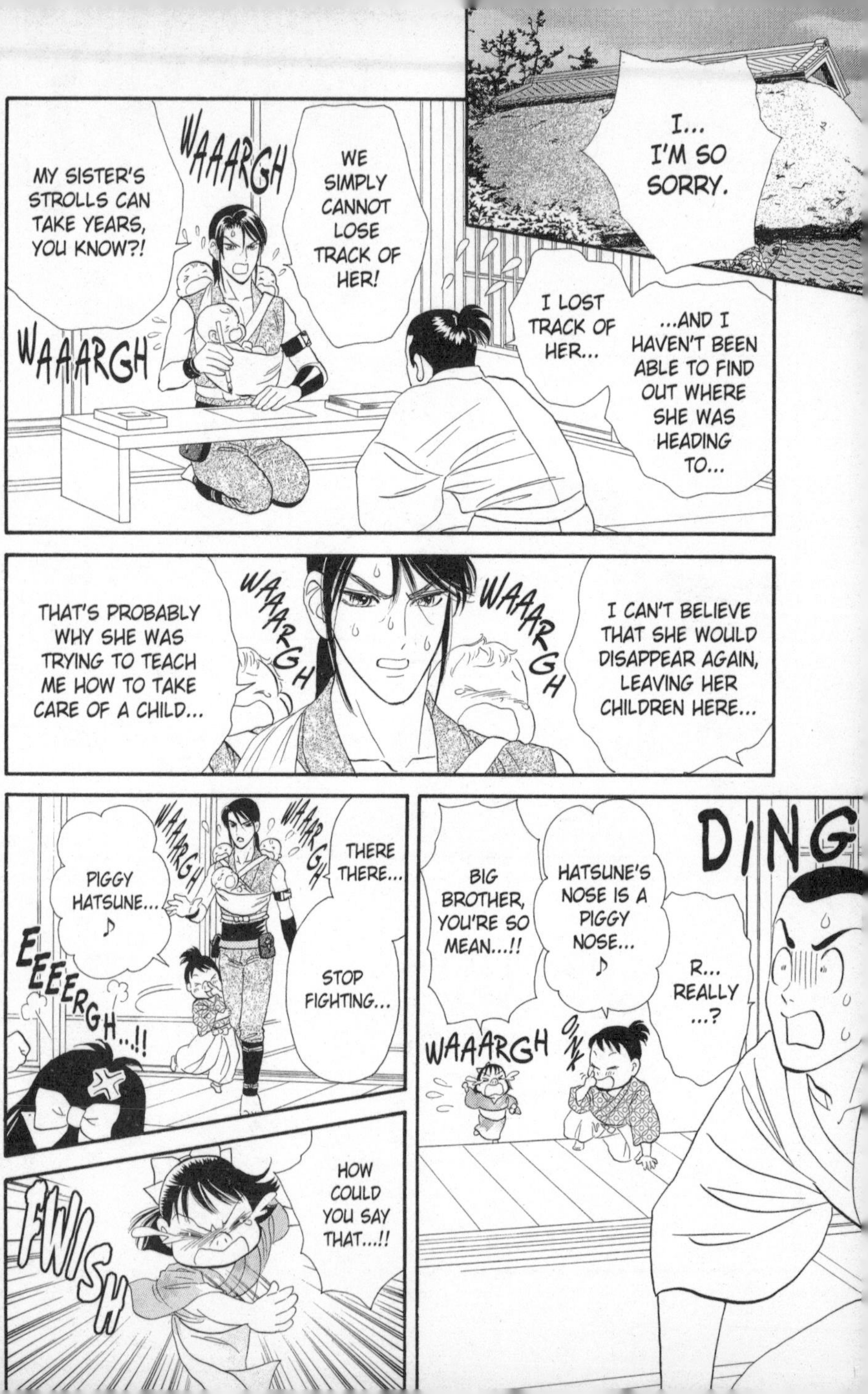
I... I'M SO SORRY.
I LOST TRACK OF HER...
...AND I HAVEN'T BEEN ABLE TO FIND OUT WHERE SHE WAS HEADING TO...
WE SIMPLY CANNOT LOSE TRACK OF HER!
WAAARGH
MY SISTER'S STROLLS CAN TAKE YEARS, YOU KNOW?!
WAAARGH
I CAN'T BELIEVE THAT SHE WOULD DISAPPEAR AGAIN, LEAVING HER CHILDREN HERE...
WAAARGH
WAAARGH
THAT'S PROBABLY WHY SHE WAS TRYING TO TEACH ME HOW TO TAKE CARE OF A CHILD...
DING
R... REALLY ...?
HATSUNE'S NOSE IS A PIGGY NOSE... ♪
BIG BROTHER, YOU'RE SO MEAN...!!
OINK
WAAARGH
THERE THERE...
WAAARGH
STOP FIGHTING...
WAAARGH
PIGGY HATSUNE... ♪
EEEERGH..!!
HOW COULD YOU SAY THAT...!!
FWISH

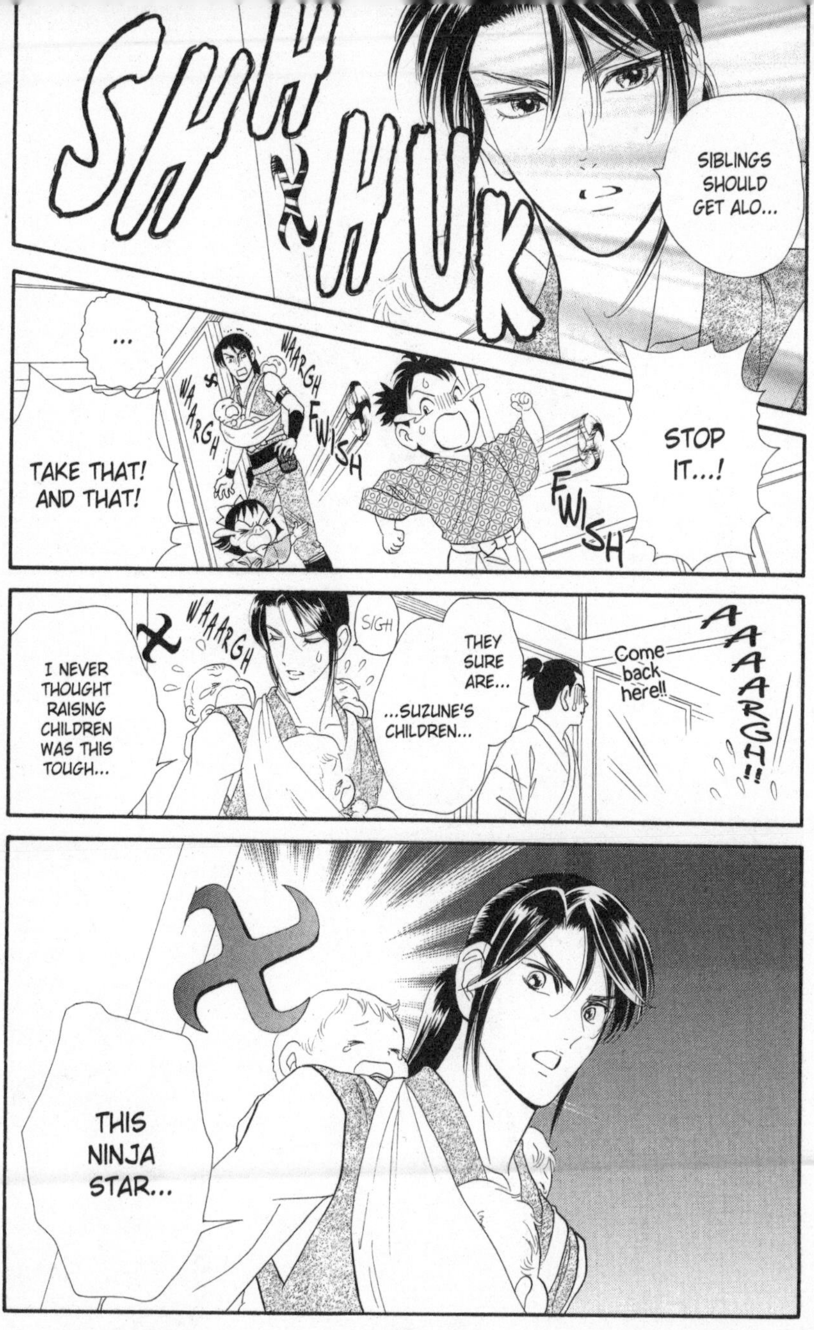
SIBLINGS SHOULD GET ALO...
SHH
HUK
STOP IT...!
FWISH
FWISH
WAARGH
WAARGH
...
TAKE THAT! AND THAT!
AAAAARGH!!
Come back here!!
THEY SURE ARE...
...SUZUNE'S CHILDREN...
SIGH
WAAARGH
I NEVER THOUGHT RAISING CHILDREN WAS THIS TOUGH...
THIS NINJA STAR...

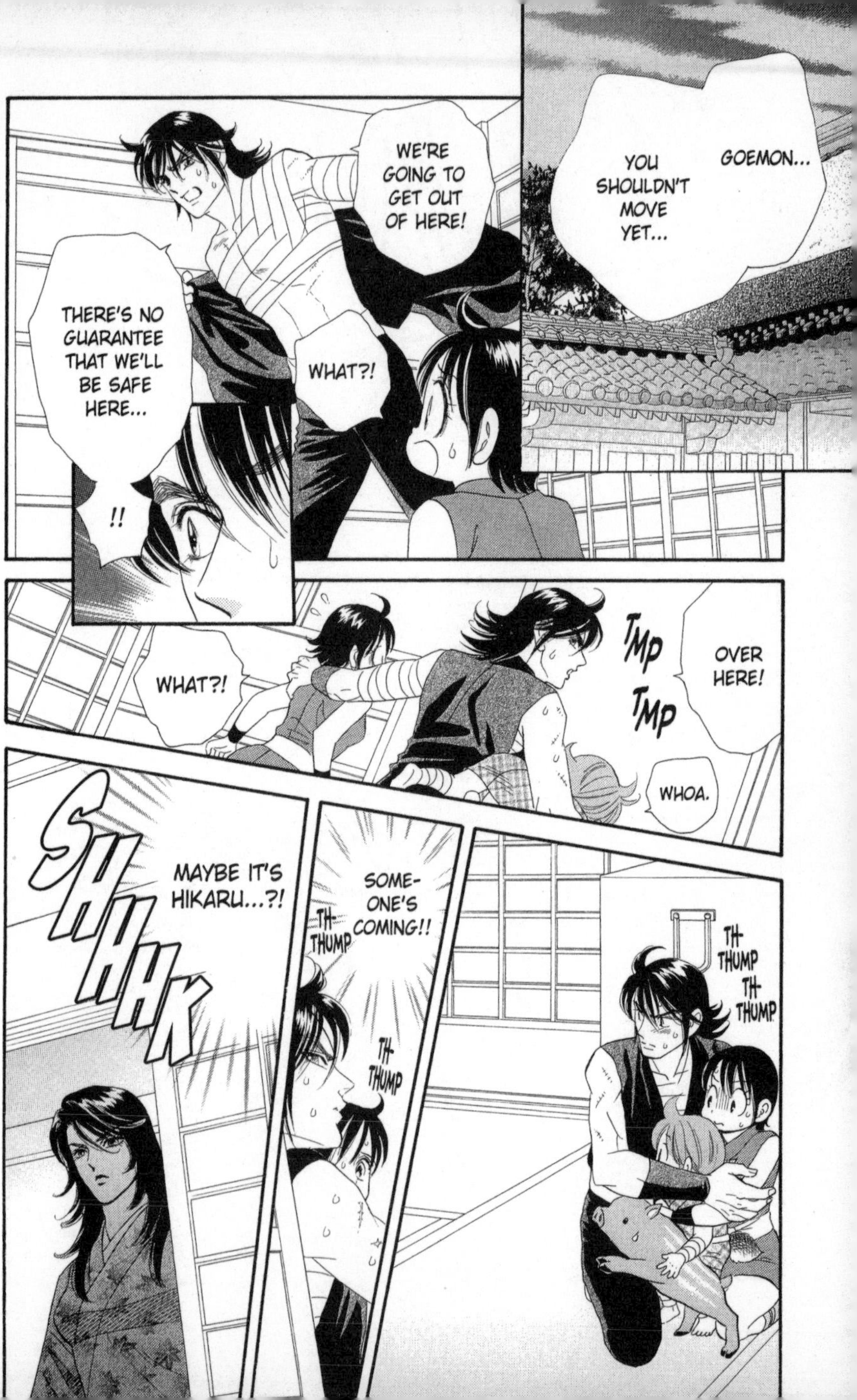
GOEMON...
YOU SHOULDN'T MOVE YET...
WE'RE GOING TO GET OUT OF HERE!
WHAT?!
THERE'S NO GUARANTEE THAT WE'LL BE SAFE HERE...
!!
OVER HERE!
TMP TMP
WHOA.
WHAT?!
TH-THUMP TH-THUMP
SOME-ONE'S COMING!!
TH-THUMP
TH-THUMP
MAYBE IT'S HIKARU...?!
SHHHK

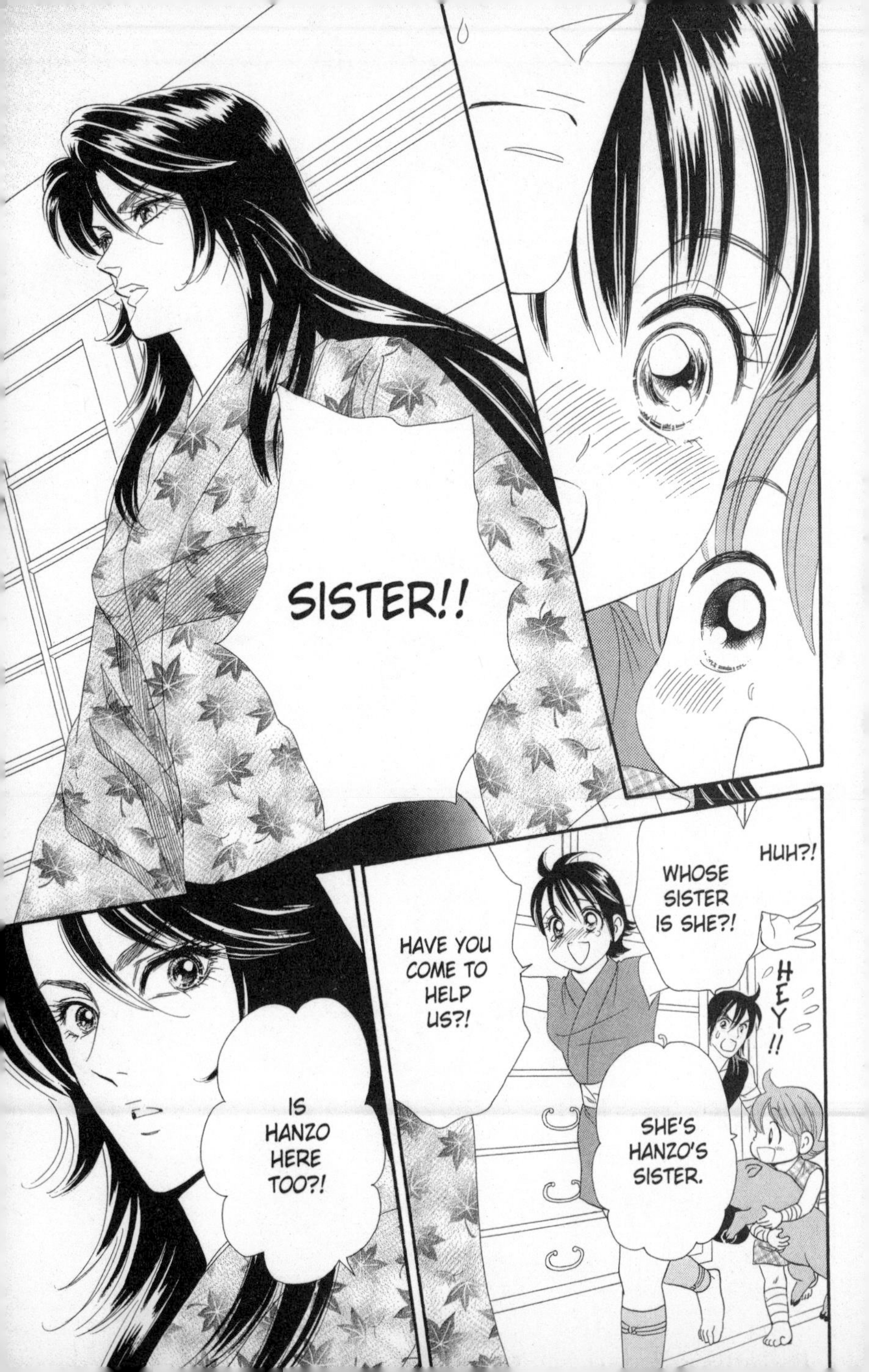
SISTER!!
HUH?!
WHOSE SISTER IS SHE?!
HEY!!
HAVE YOU COME TO HELP US?!
SHE'S HANZO'S SISTER.
IS HANZO HERE TOO?!

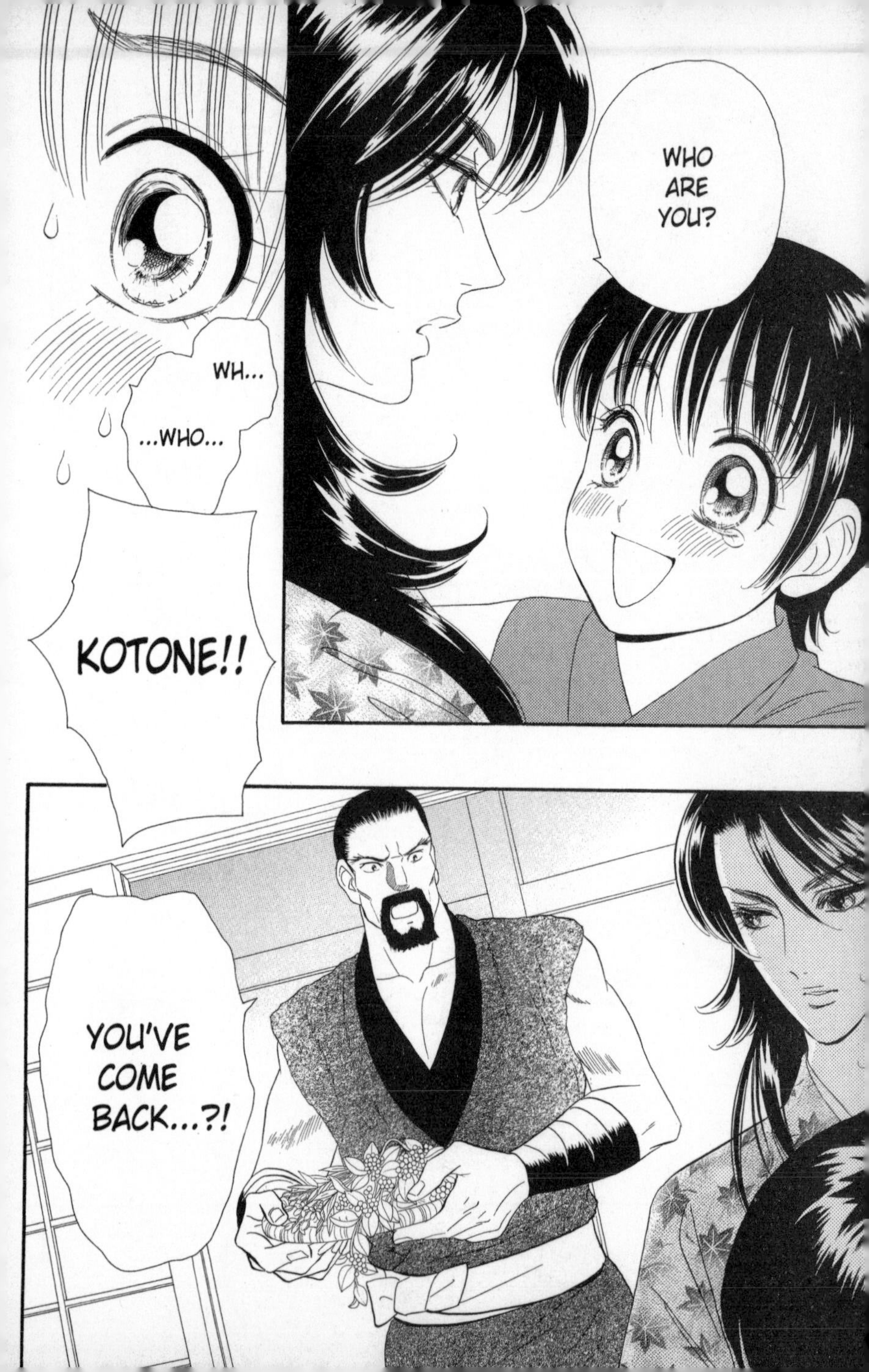
WHO ARE YOU?
WH...
...WHO...
KOTONE!!
YOU'VE COME BACK...?!

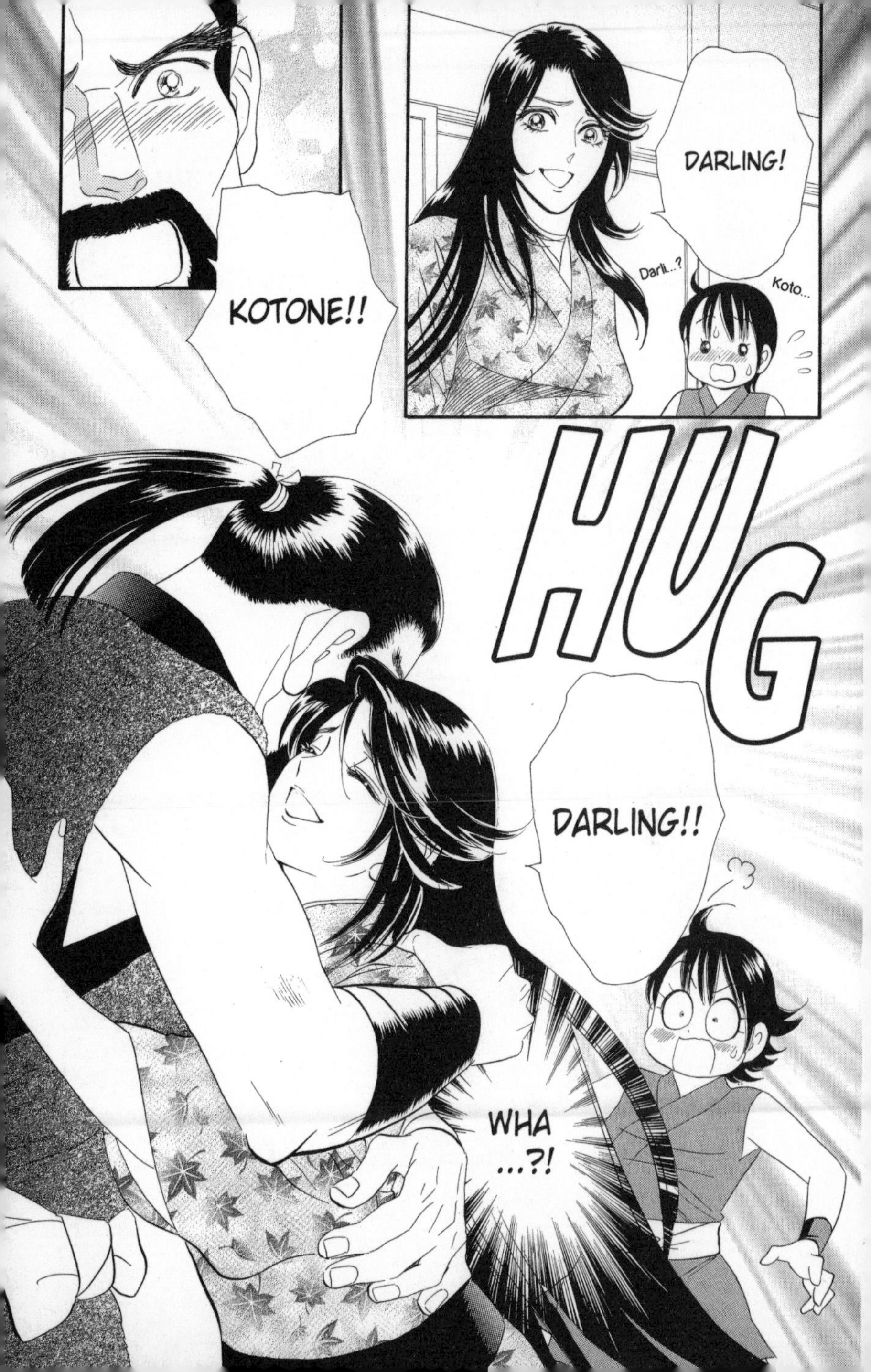
DARLING!
Koto...
Darli...?
KOTONE!!
HUG
DARLING!!
WHA ...?!

TAIL OF THE MOON EXTRA: TODAY'S MISSION

"I WANT TO SEE HANZO SURROUNDED BY ROSES."

-MICHIYO, SAGA PREFECTURE

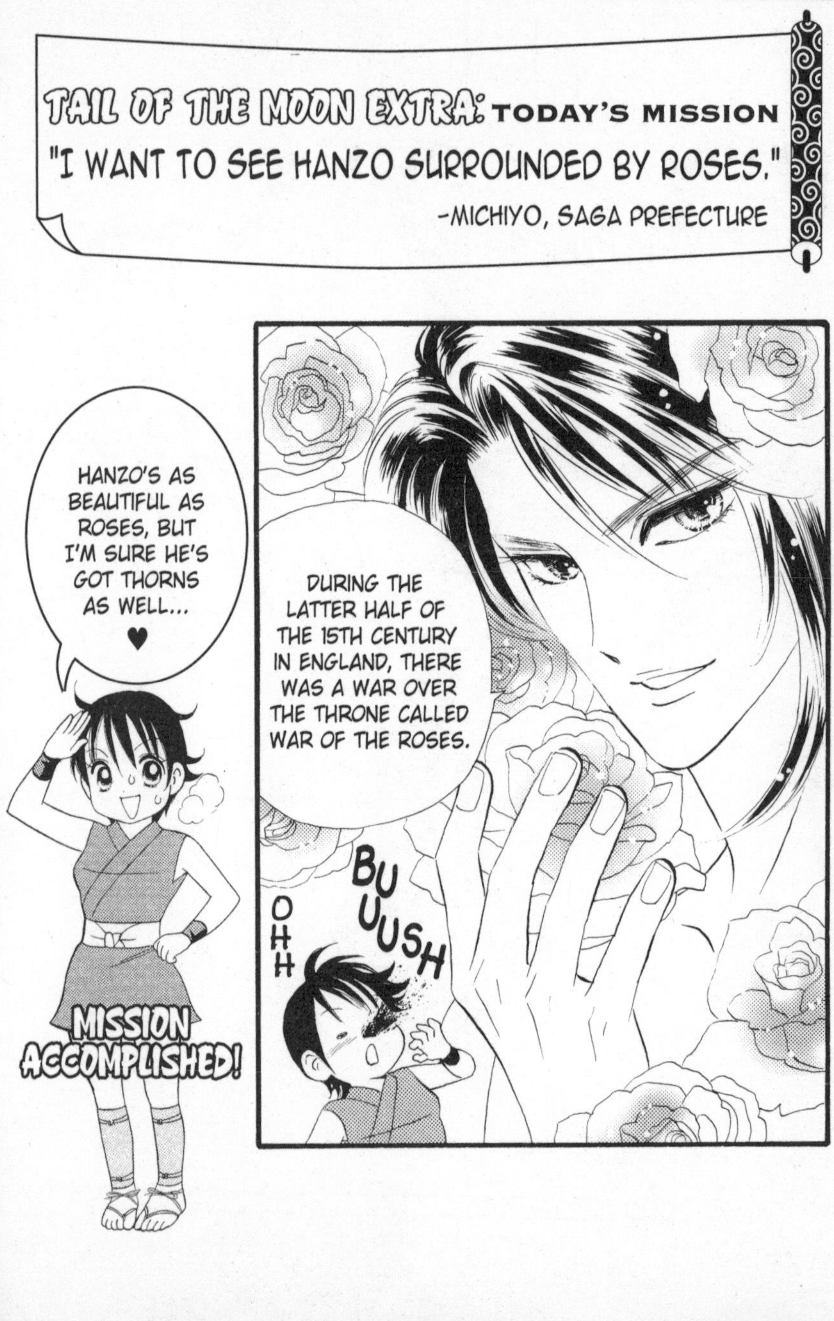
DURING THE LATTER HALF OF THE 15TH CENTURY IN ENGLAND, THERE WAS A WAR OVER THE THRONE CALLED WAR OF THE ROSES.
BUUUSH
OHH
HANZO'S AS BEAUTIFUL AS ROSES, BUT I'M SURE HE'S GOT THORNS AS WELL... ♥
MISSION ACCOMPLISHED!

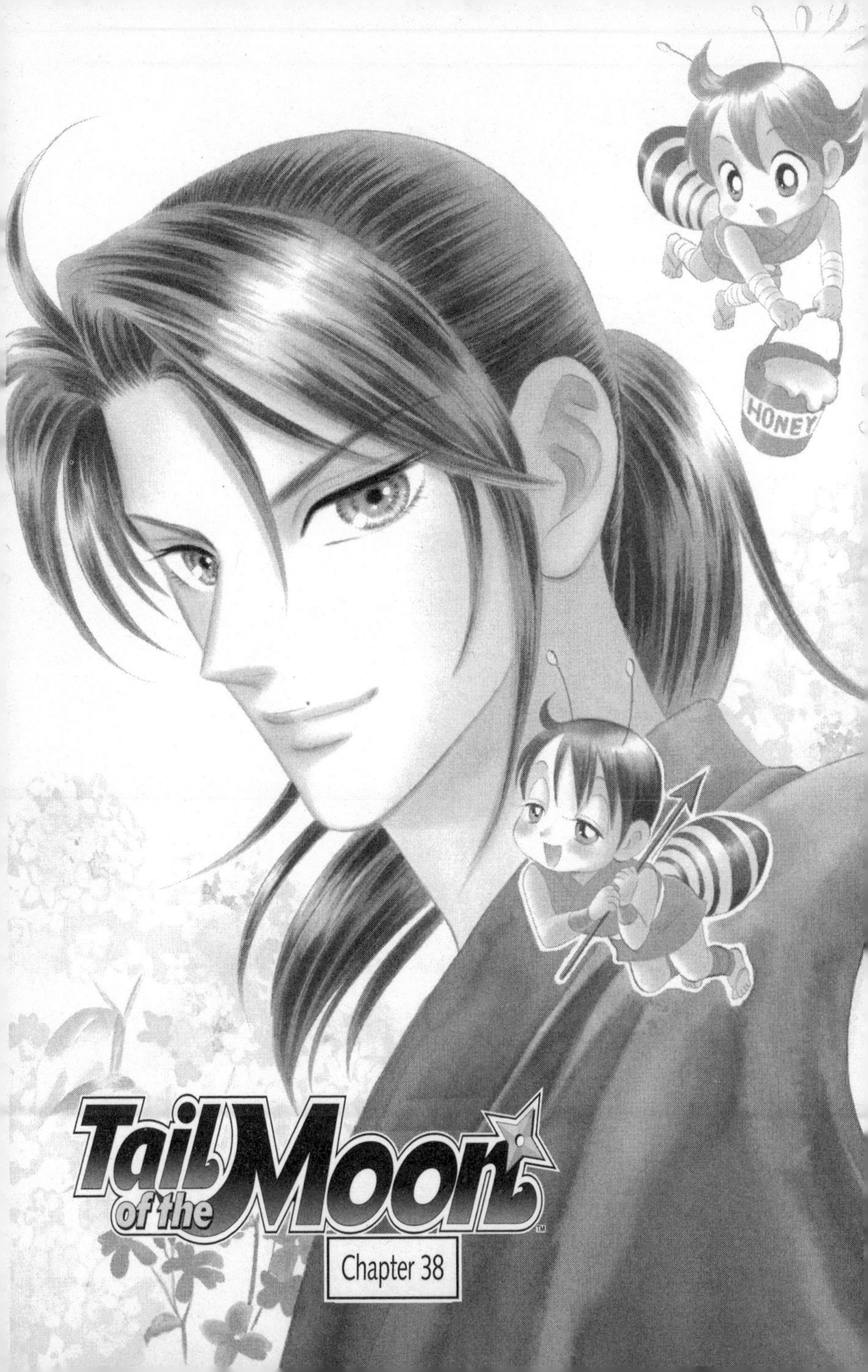
HONEY
Tail of the Moon™
Chapter 38

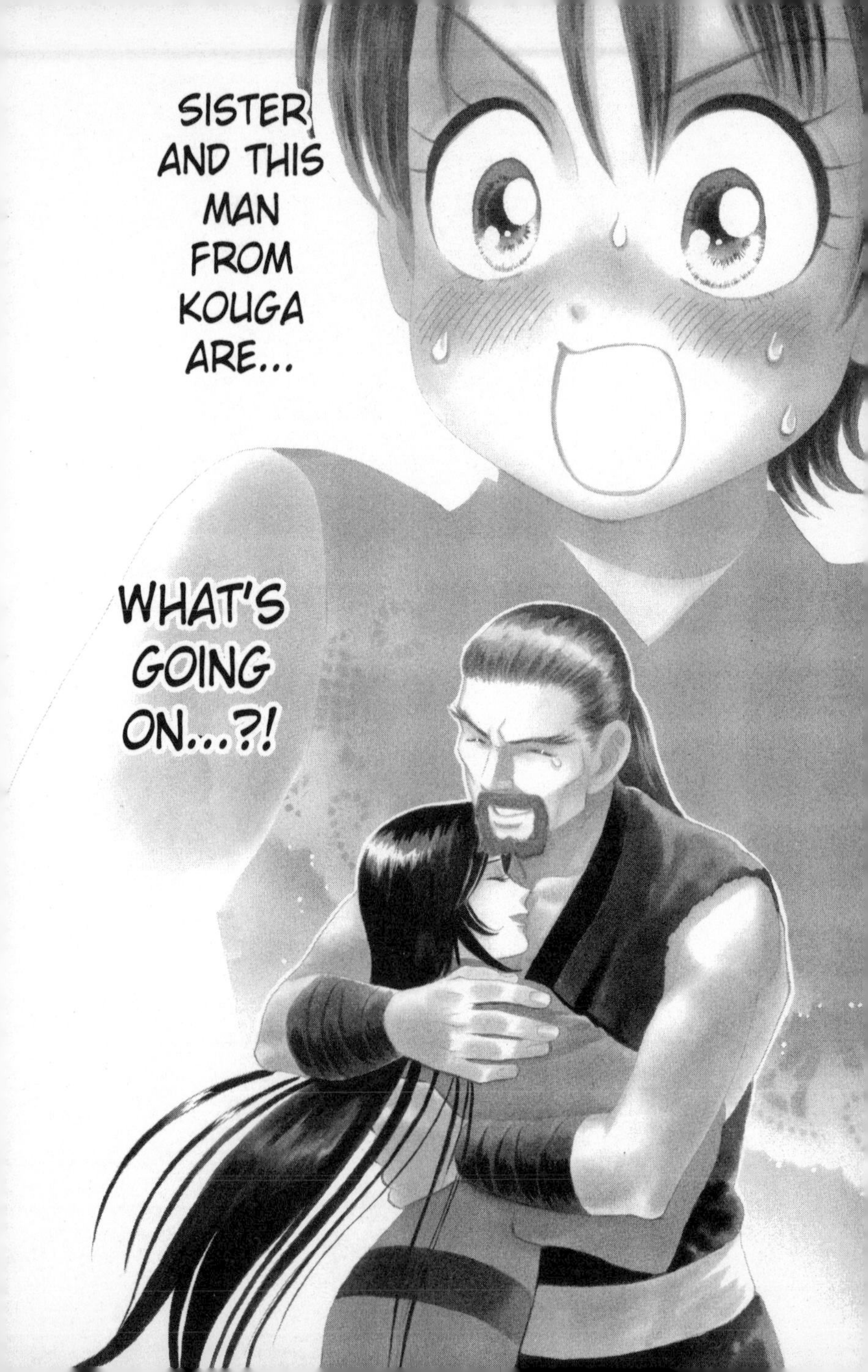
SISTER AND THIS MAN FROM KOUGA ARE...
WHAT'S GOING ON...?!

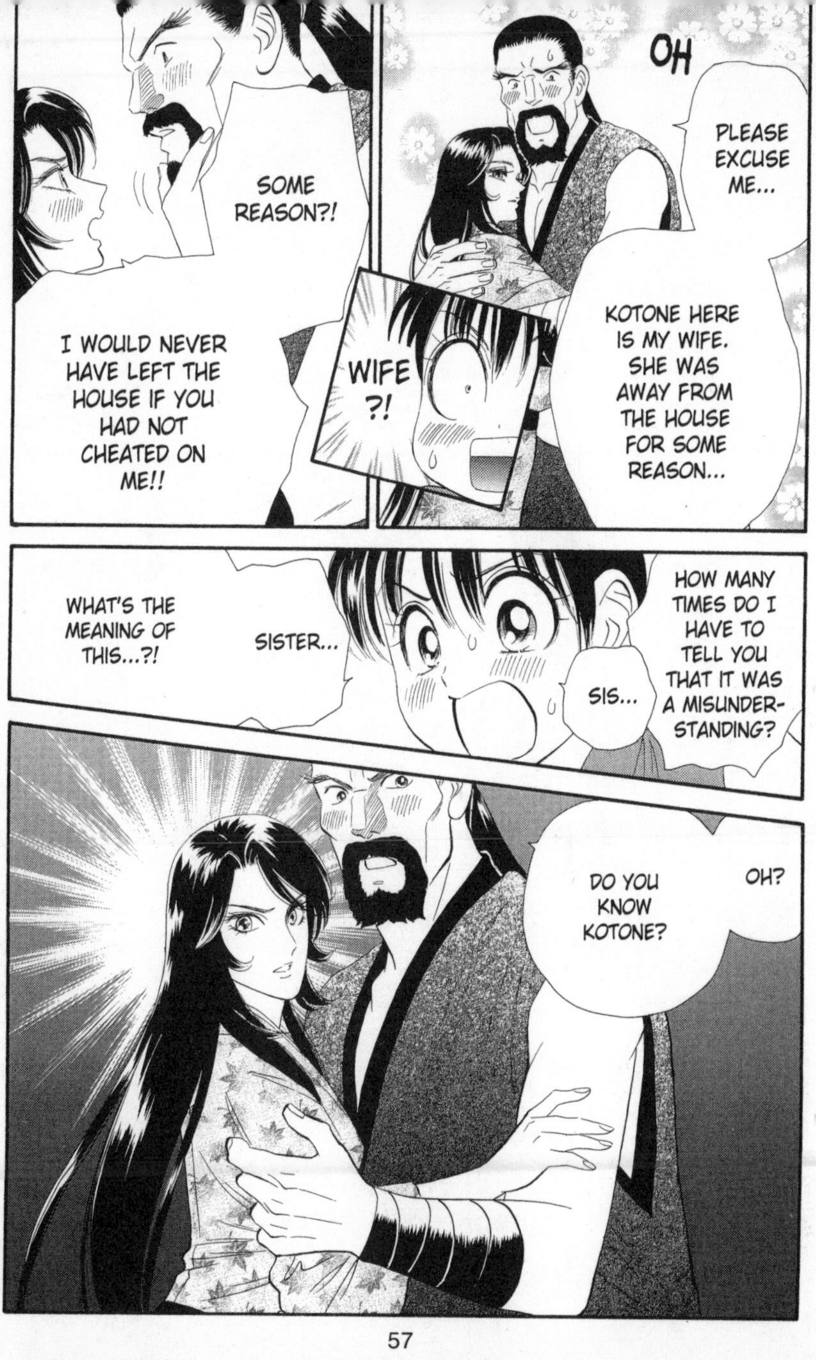
OH
PLEASE EXCUSE ME...
KOTONE HERE IS MY WIFE. SHE WAS AWAY FROM THE HOUSE FOR SOME REASON...
WIFE ?!
SOME REASON?!
I WOULD NEVER HAVE LEFT THE HOUSE IF YOU HAD NOT CHEATED ON ME!!
HOW MANY TIMES DO I HAVE TO TELL YOU THAT IT WAS A MISUNDER-STANDING?
SIS...
SISTER...
WHAT'S THE MEANING OF THIS...?!
OH?
DO YOU KNOW KOTONE?

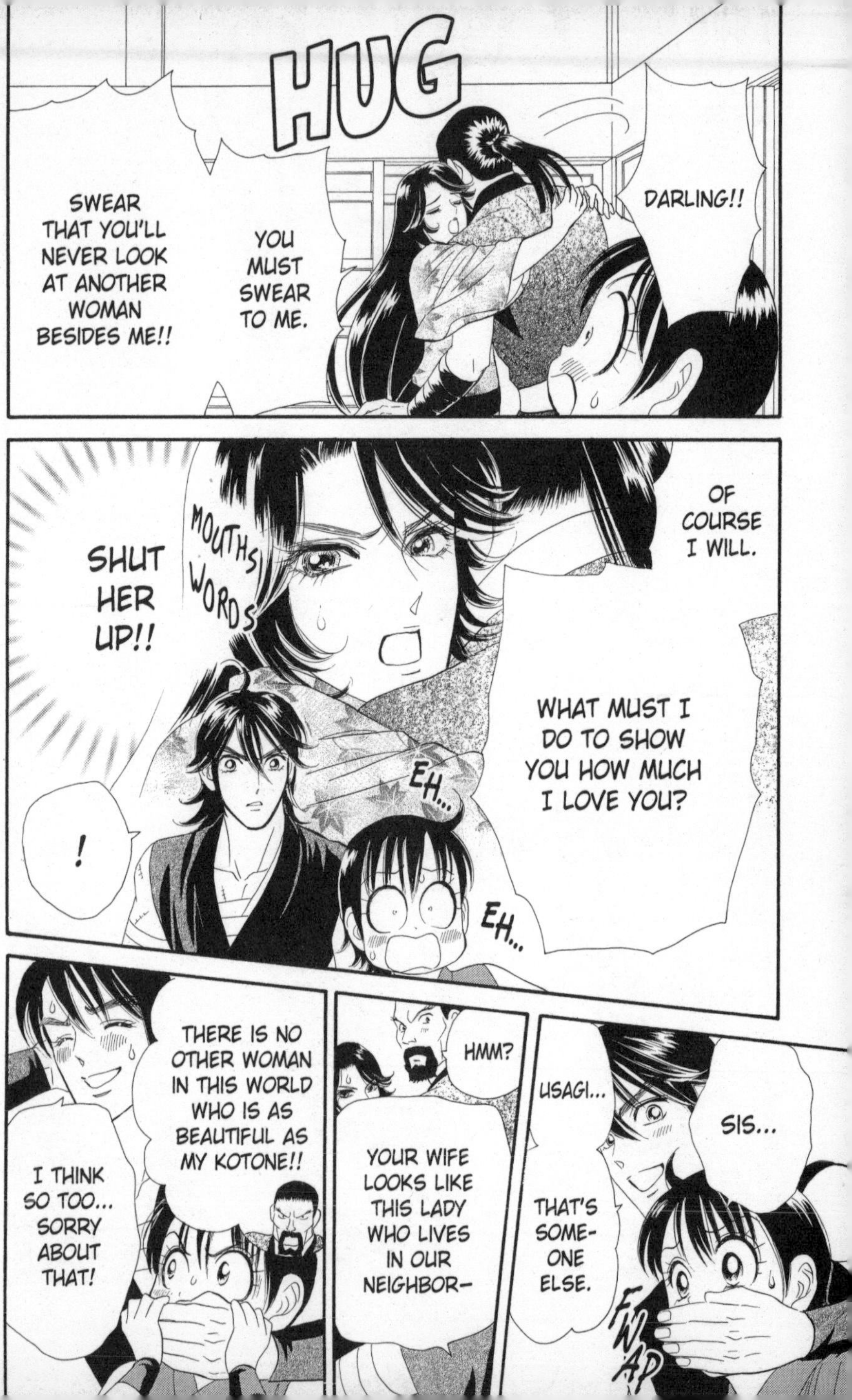
HUG
DARLING!!
YOU MUST SWEAR TO ME.
SWEAR THAT YOU'LL NEVER LOOK AT ANOTHER WOMAN BESIDES ME!!
OF COURSE I WILL.
MOUTHS WORDS
SHUT HER UP!!
WHAT MUST I DO TO SHOW YOU HOW MUCH I LOVE YOU?
EH...
!
EH...
SIS...
USAGI...
THAT'S SOME-ONE ELSE.
FWAP
HMM?
YOUR WIFE LOOKS LIKE THIS LADY WHO LIVES IN OUR NEIGHBOR-
THERE IS NO OTHER WOMAN IN THIS WORLD WHO IS AS BEAUTIFUL AS MY KOTONE!!
I THINK SO TOO... SORRY ABOUT THAT!

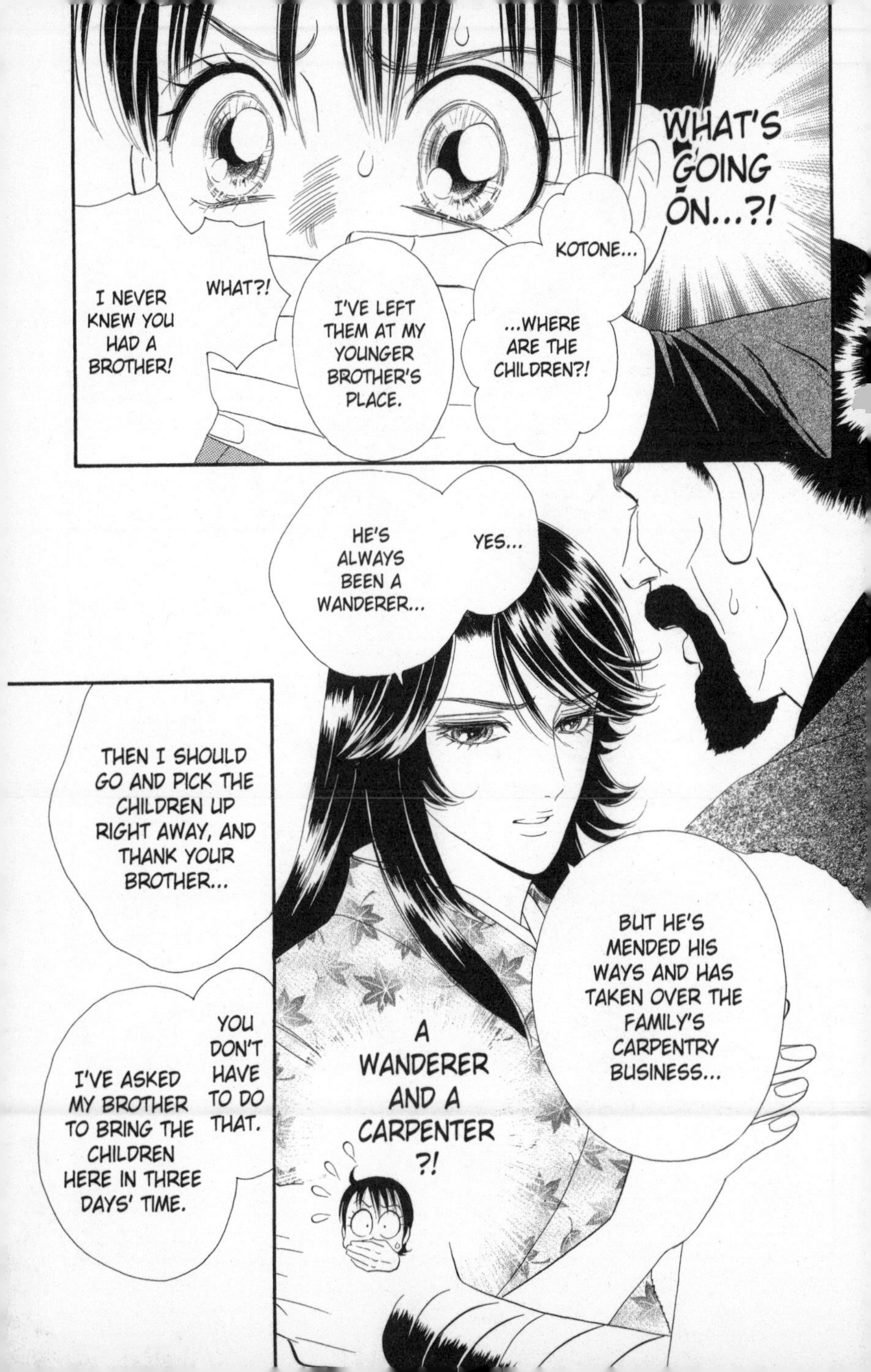
WHAT'S GOING ON...?!
KOTONE...
...WHERE ARE THE CHILDREN?!
I'VE LEFT THEM AT MY YOUNGER BROTHER'S PLACE.
WHAT?!
I NEVER KNEW YOU HAD A BROTHER!
YES...
HE'S ALWAYS BEEN A WANDERER...
BUT HE'S MENDED HIS WAYS AND HAS TAKEN OVER THE FAMILY'S CARPENTRY BUSINESS...
A WANDERER AND A CARPENTER ?!
THEN I SHOULD GO AND PICK THE CHILDREN UP RIGHT AWAY, AND THANK YOUR BROTHER...
YOU DON'T HAVE TO DO THAT.
I'VE ASKED MY BROTHER TO BRING THE CHILDREN HERE IN THREE DAYS' TIME.

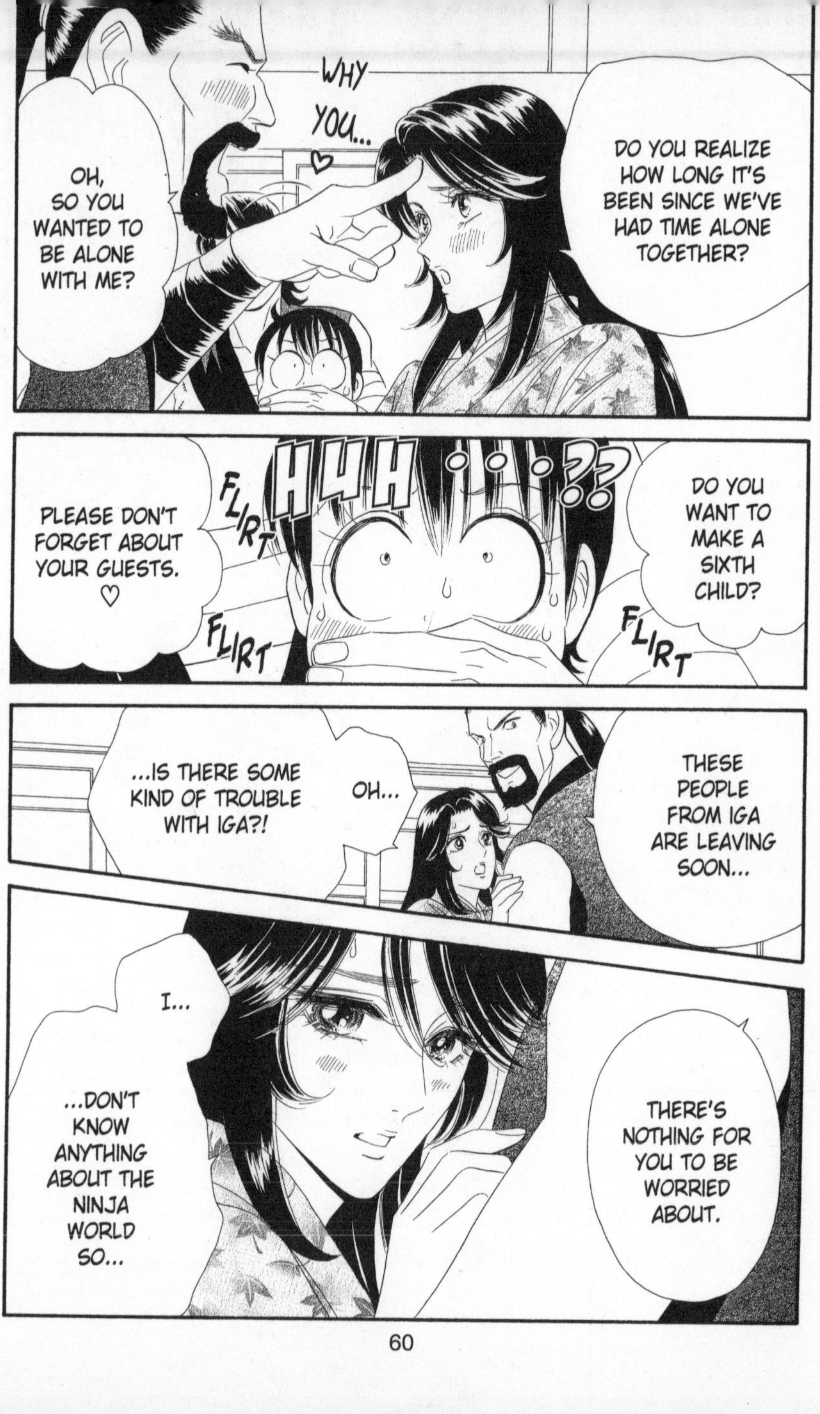
DO YOU REALIZE HOW LONG IT'S BEEN SINCE WE'VE HAD TIME ALONE TOGETHER?
WHY YOU... ♡
OH, SO YOU WANTED TO BE ALONE WITH ME?
DO YOU WANT TO MAKE A SIXTH CHILD?
FLIRT
HUH...??
FLIRT
PLEASE DON'T FORGET ABOUT YOUR GUESTS. ♡
FLIRT
THESE PEOPLE FROM IGA ARE LEAVING SOON...
OH...
...IS THERE SOME KIND OF TROUBLE WITH IGA?!
THERE'S NOTHING FOR YOU TO BE WORRIED ABOUT.
I...
...DON'T KNOW ANYTHING ABOUT THE NINJA WORLD SO...

DON'T WORRY.
YOU'RE WEAK, BUT I'LL PROTECT YOU WILL ALL THAT I'VE GOT.
DARLING... ♡
WEAK ...?!
I'LL GO AND SQUARE THINGS OUT WITH MY BROTHER.
KOTONE, GIVE THESE PEOPLE FROM IGA SOMETHING TO EAT.
OF COURSE.
SHHK
MAYBE SHE REALLY IS A DIFFERENT PERSON?!
PHEW
UH... UM...

UE-RIN'S WAY OF THE MANGA ②

The first thing that came to my mind when I saw a manga magazine for the first time in my life was...

Hey, even I can draw something like this.

TALK ABOUT BE-ING BRASSY.

Sorry to all the creators back then!

My youthful enthusiasm and naiveté was the starting point for my drawing manga.

But when I tried to draw manga, I didn't know how to do it exactly nor did I know what tools I needed...

So during my 1st year in middle school, I just kept copying the manga I liked and drew random original manga in my notebook.

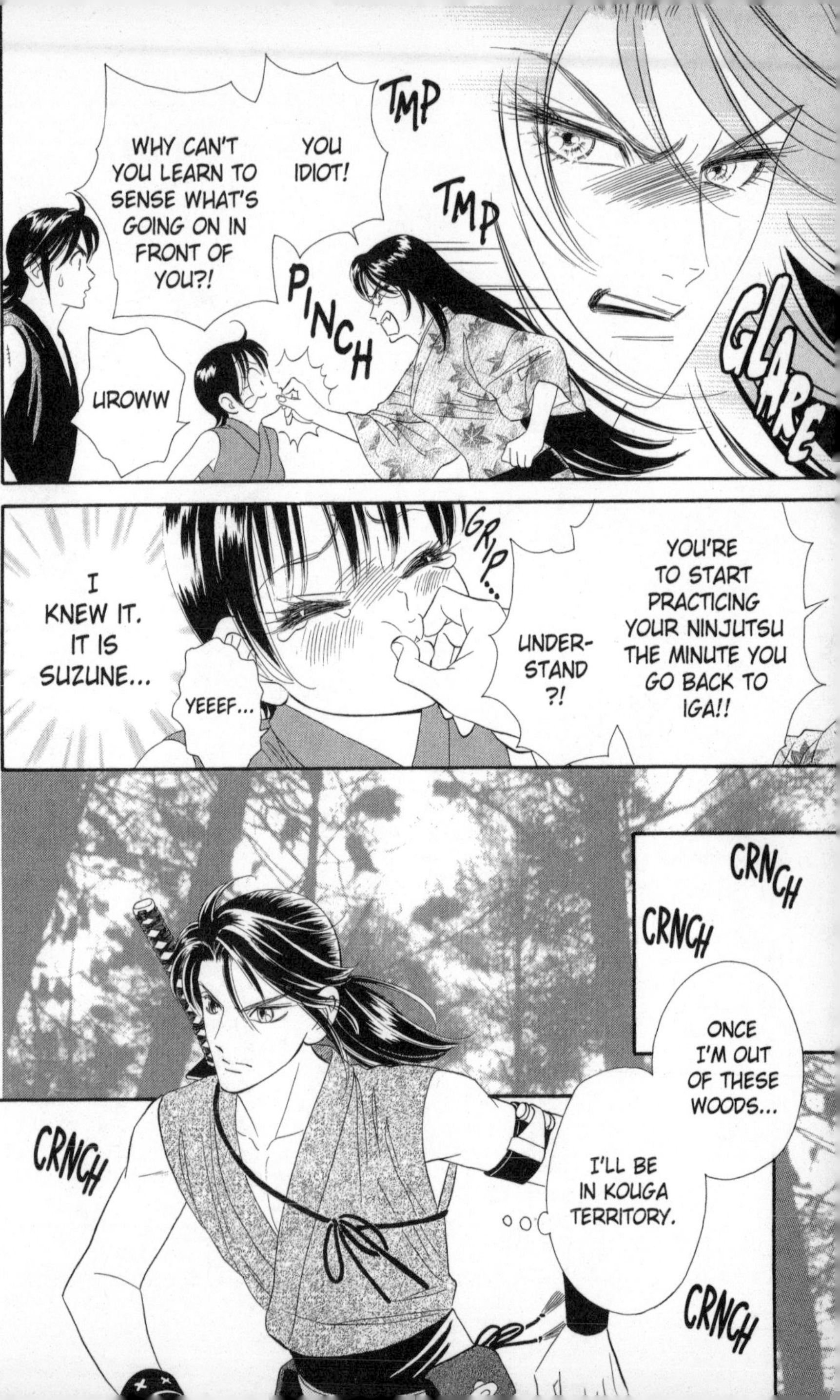
TMP
TMP
GLARE
YOU IDIOT!
WHY CAN'T YOU LEARN TO SENSE WHAT'S GOING ON IN FRONT OF YOU?!
PINCH
UROWW
YOU'RE TO START PRACTICING YOUR NINJUTSU THE MINUTE YOU GO BACK TO IGA!!
UNDER-STAND?!
GRIP...
YEEEF...
I KNEW IT. IT IS SUZUNE...
CRNCH
CRNCH
ONCE I'M OUT OF THESE WOODS...
I'LL BE IN KOUGA TERRITORY.
CRNCH
CRNCH

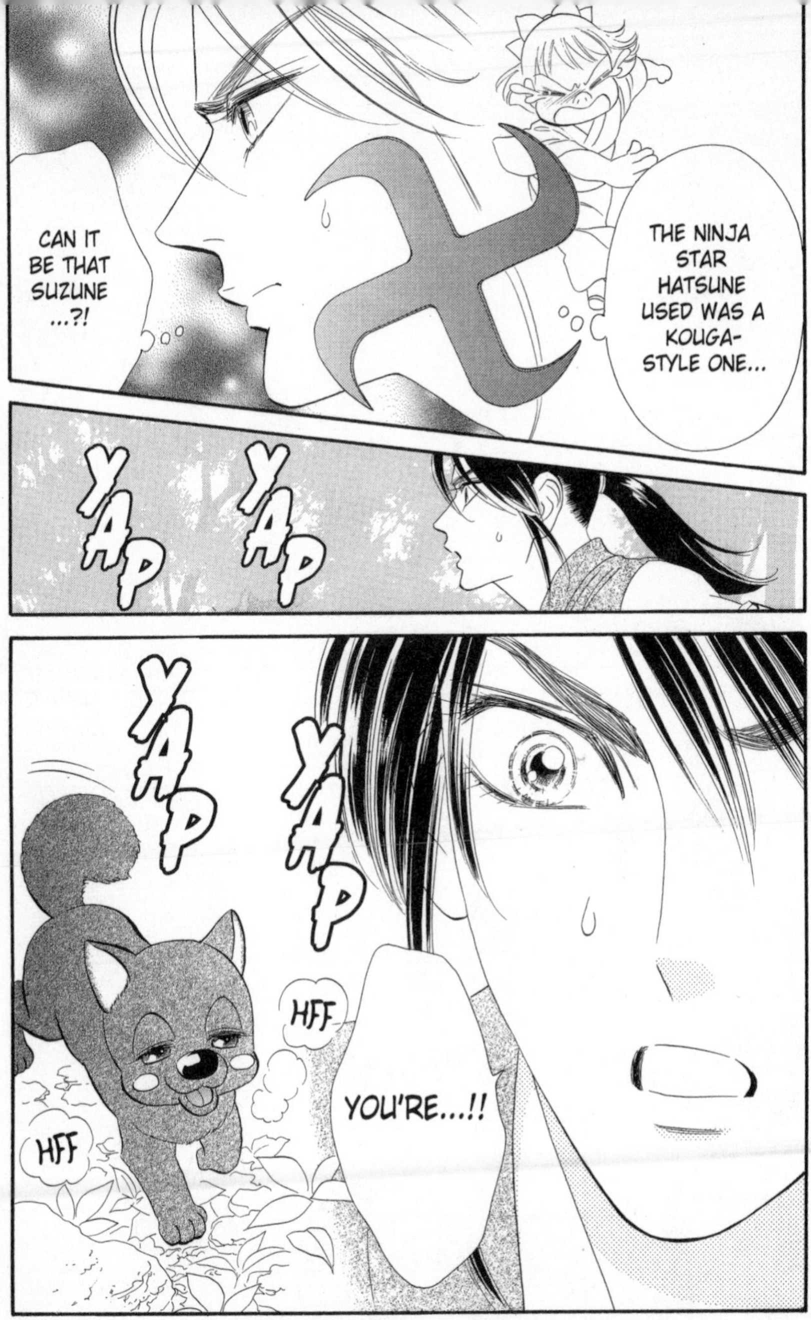
THE NINJA STAR HATSUNE USED WAS A KOUGA-STYLE ONE...
CAN IT BE THAT SUZUNE ...?!
YAP
YAP
YAP
YAP
YOU'RE...!!
HFF
HFF

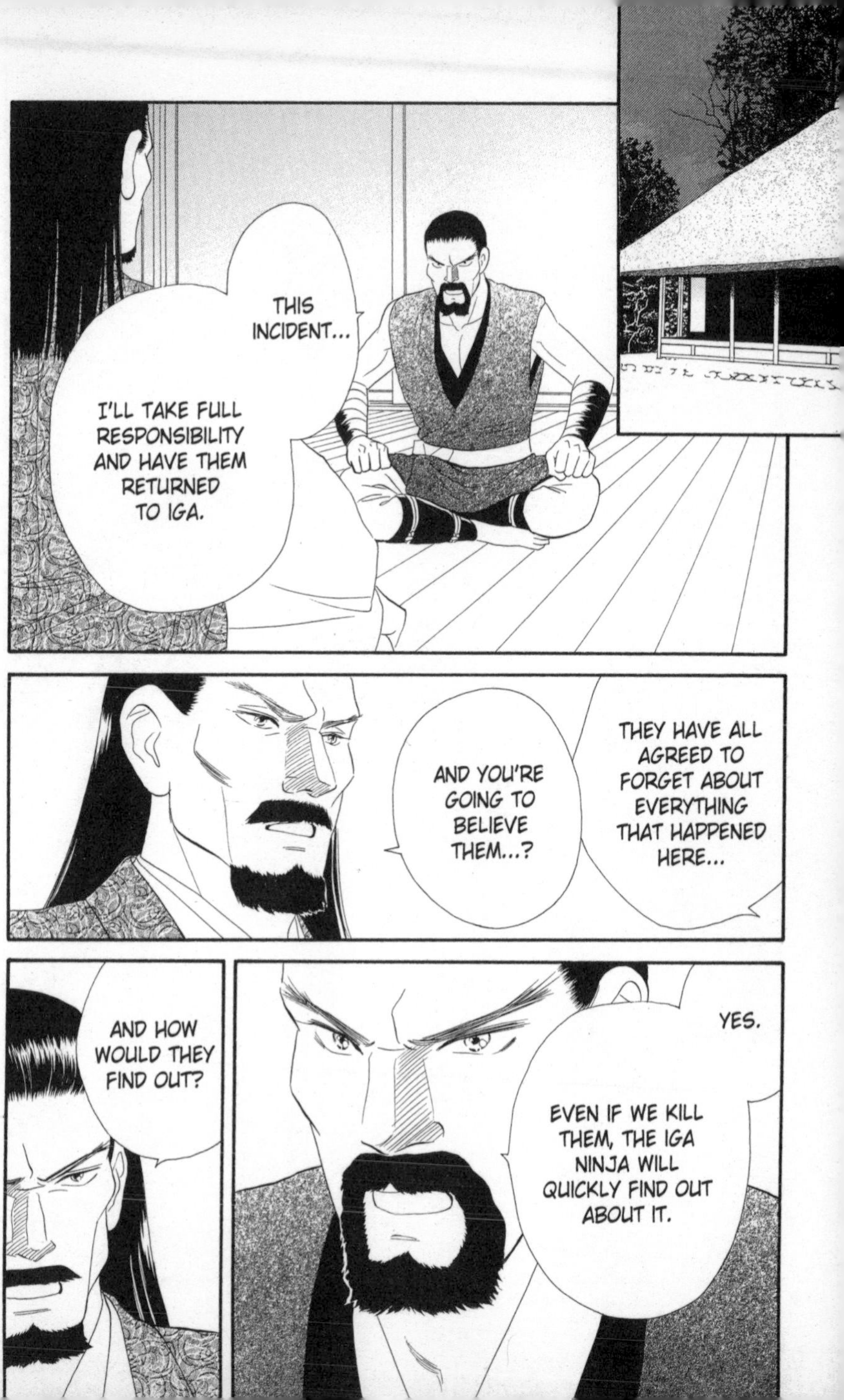
THIS INCIDENT...
I'LL TAKE FULL RESPONSIBILITY AND HAVE THEM RETURNED TO IGA.
THEY HAVE ALL AGREED TO FORGET ABOUT EVERYTHING THAT HAPPENED HERE...
AND YOU'RE GOING TO BELIEVE THEM...?
YES.
EVEN IF WE KILL THEM, THE IGA NINJA WILL QUICKLY FIND OUT ABOUT IT.
AND HOW WOULD THEY FIND OUT?

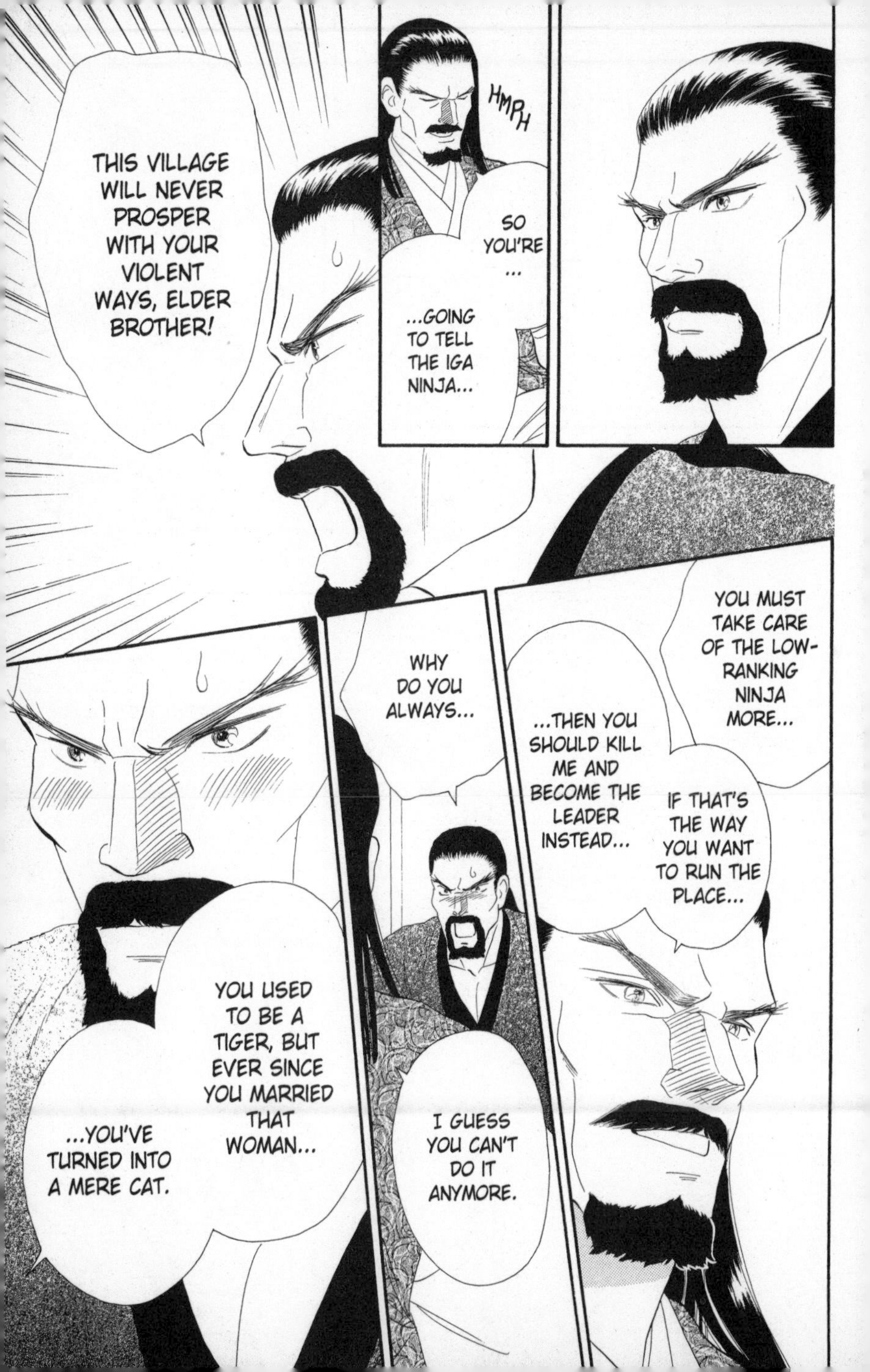
HMPH
SO YOU'RE ...
...GOING TO TELL THE IGA NINJA...
THIS VILLAGE WILL NEVER PROSPER WITH YOUR VIOLENT WAYS, ELDER BROTHER!
YOU MUST TAKE CARE OF THE LOW-RANKING NINJA MORE...
IF THAT'S THE WAY YOU WANT TO RUN THE PLACE...
...THEN YOU SHOULD KILL ME AND BECOME THE LEADER INSTEAD...
WHY DO YOU ALWAYS...
I GUESS YOU CAN'T DO IT ANYMORE.
YOU USED TO BE A TIGER, BUT EVER SINCE YOU MARRIED THAT WOMAN...
...YOU'VE TURNED INTO A MERE CAT.

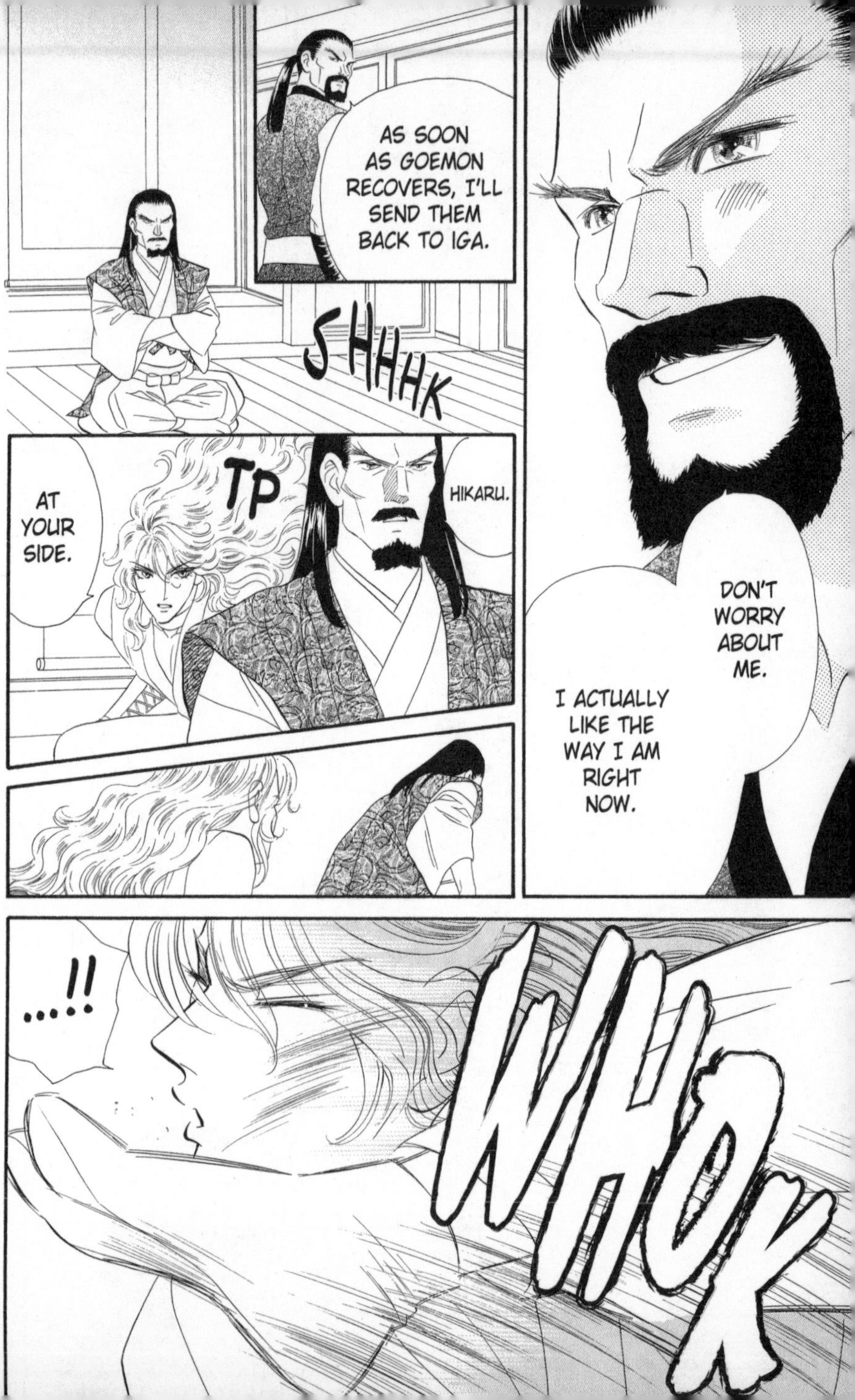
DON'T WORRY ABOUT ME.
I ACTUALLY LIKE THE WAY I AM RIGHT NOW.
AS SOON AS GOEMON RECOVERS, I'LL SEND THEM BACK TO IGA.
SHHHK
HIKARU.
TP
AT YOUR SIDE.
...!!
WHACK

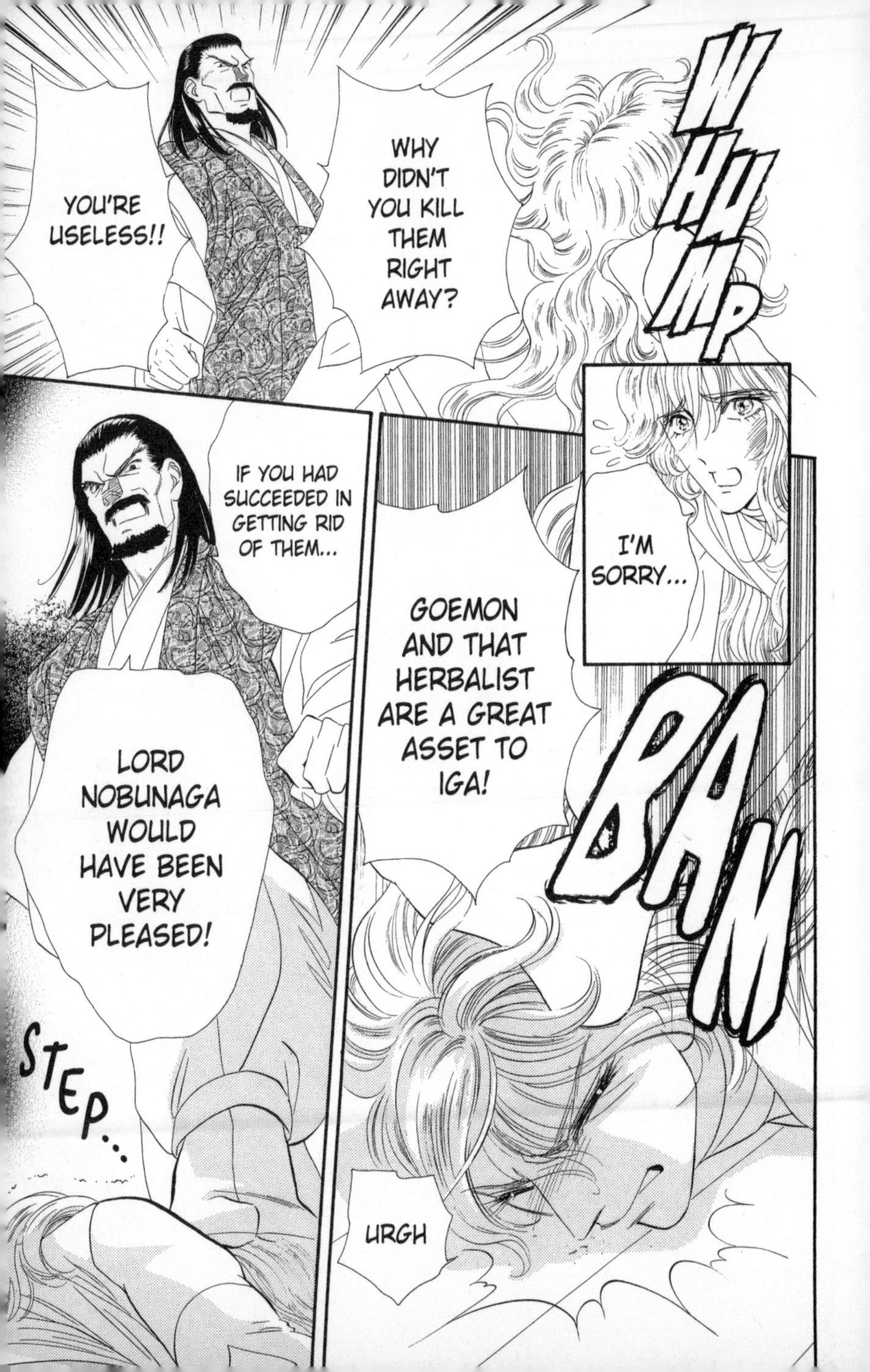
WHHUMP
WHY DIDN'T YOU KILL THEM RIGHT AWAY?
YOU'RE USELESS!!
I'M SORRY...
BAM
GOEMON AND THAT HERBALIST ARE A GREAT ASSET TO IGA!
URGH
IF YOU HAD SUCCEEDED IN GETTING RID OF THEM...
LORD NOBUNAGA WOULD HAVE BEEN VERY PLEASED!
STEP...

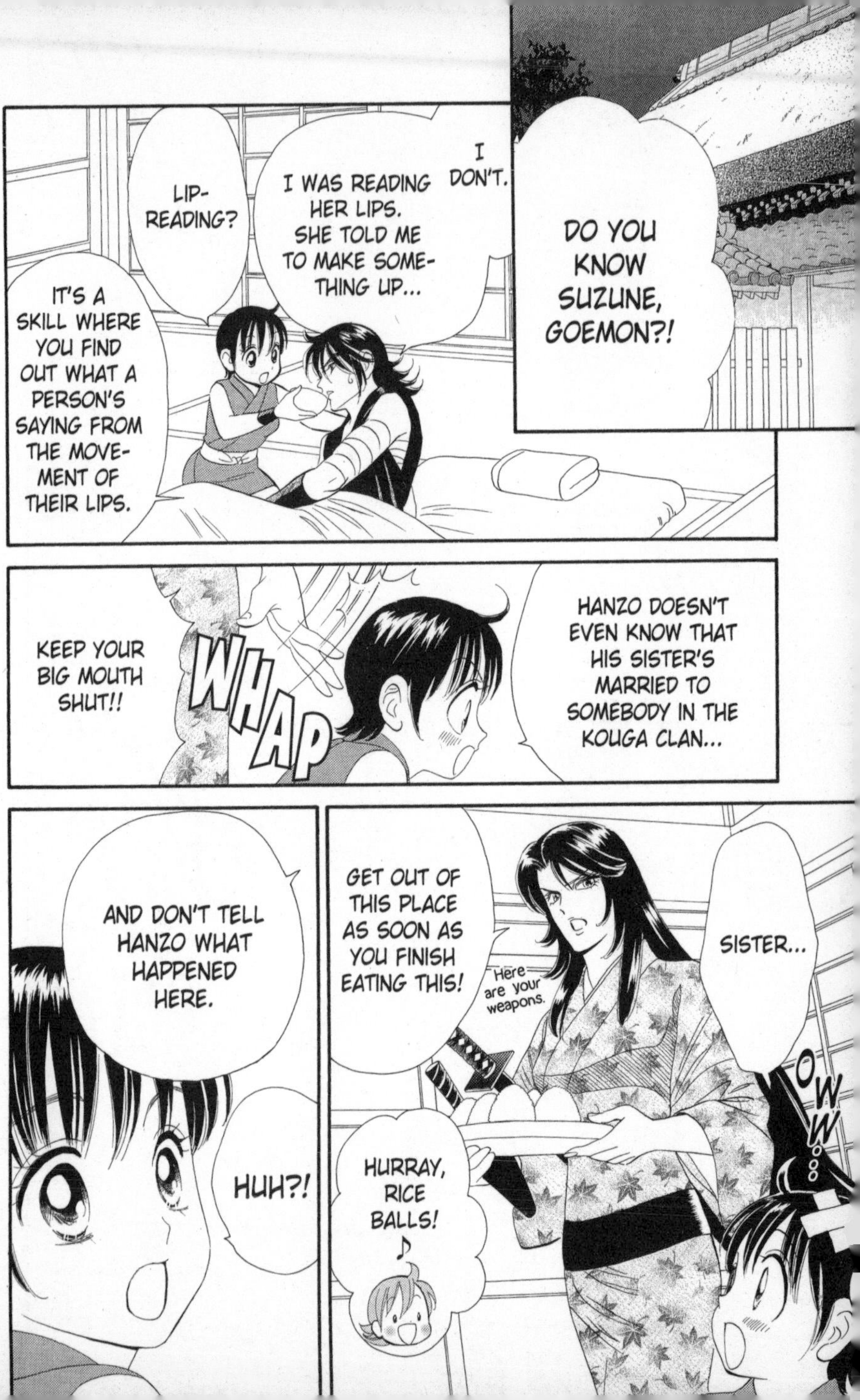
DO YOU KNOW SUZUNE, GOEMON?!
I DON'T.
I WAS READING HER LIPS. SHE TOLD ME TO MAKE SOME-THING UP...
LIP-READING?
IT'S A SKILL WHERE YOU FIND OUT WHAT A PERSON'S SAYING FROM THE MOVE-MENT OF THEIR LIPS.
HANZO DOESN'T EVEN KNOW THAT HIS SISTER'S MARRIED TO SOMEBODY IN THE KOUGA CLAN...
WHAP
KEEP YOUR BIG MOUTH SHUT!!
SISTER...
OWWooo
GET OUT OF THIS PLACE AS SOON AS YOU FINISH EATING THIS!
Here are your weapons.
HURRAY, RICE BALLS! ♪
AND DON'T TELL HANZO WHAT HAPPENED HERE.
HUH?!

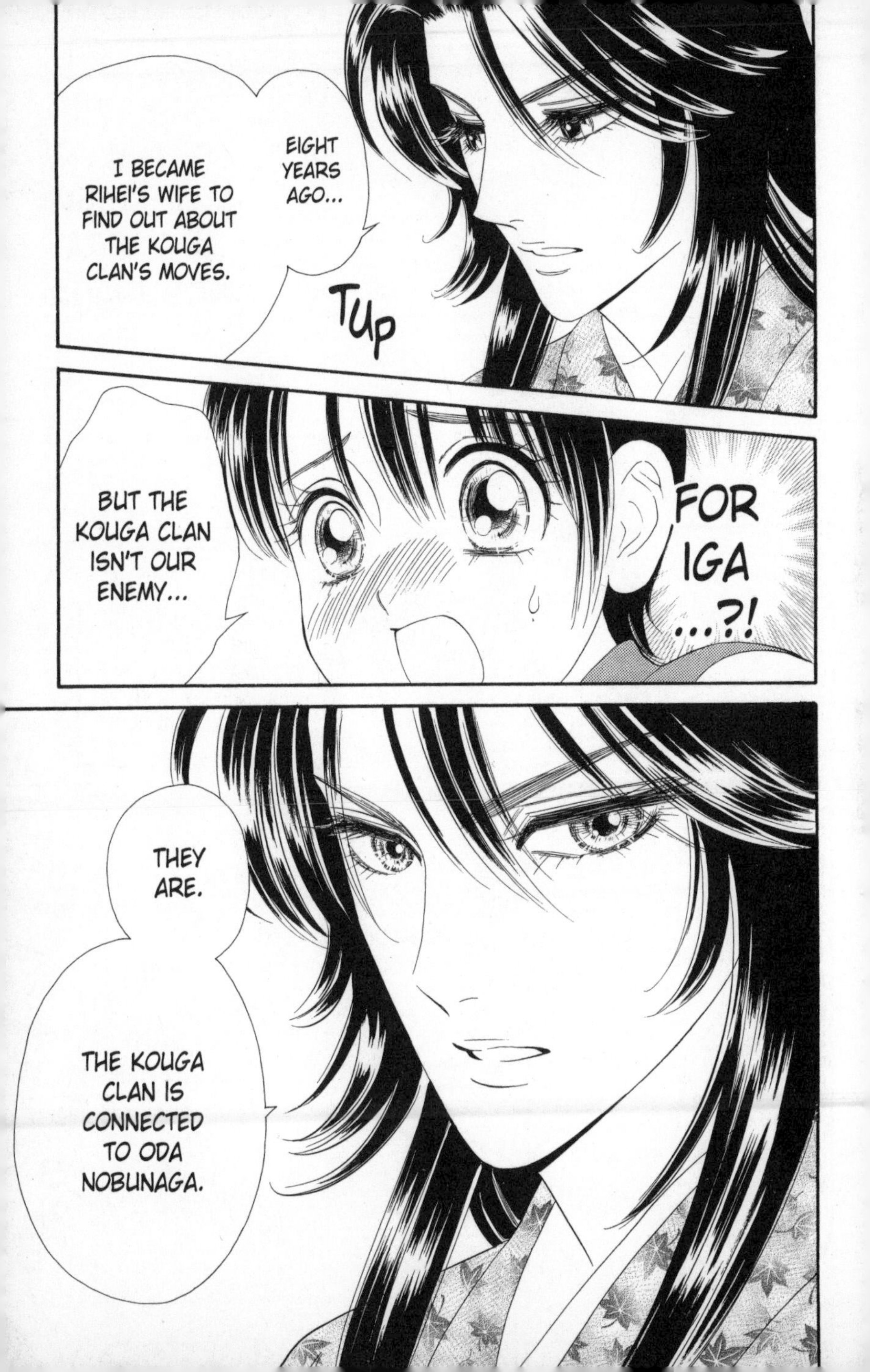
EIGHT YEARS AGO...
I BECAME RIHEI'S WIFE TO FIND OUT ABOUT THE KOUGA CLAN'S MOVES.
TUP
FOR IGA...?!
BUT THE KOUGA CLAN ISN'T OUR ENEMY...
THEY ARE.
THE KOUGA CLAN IS CONNECTED TO ODA NOBUNAGA.

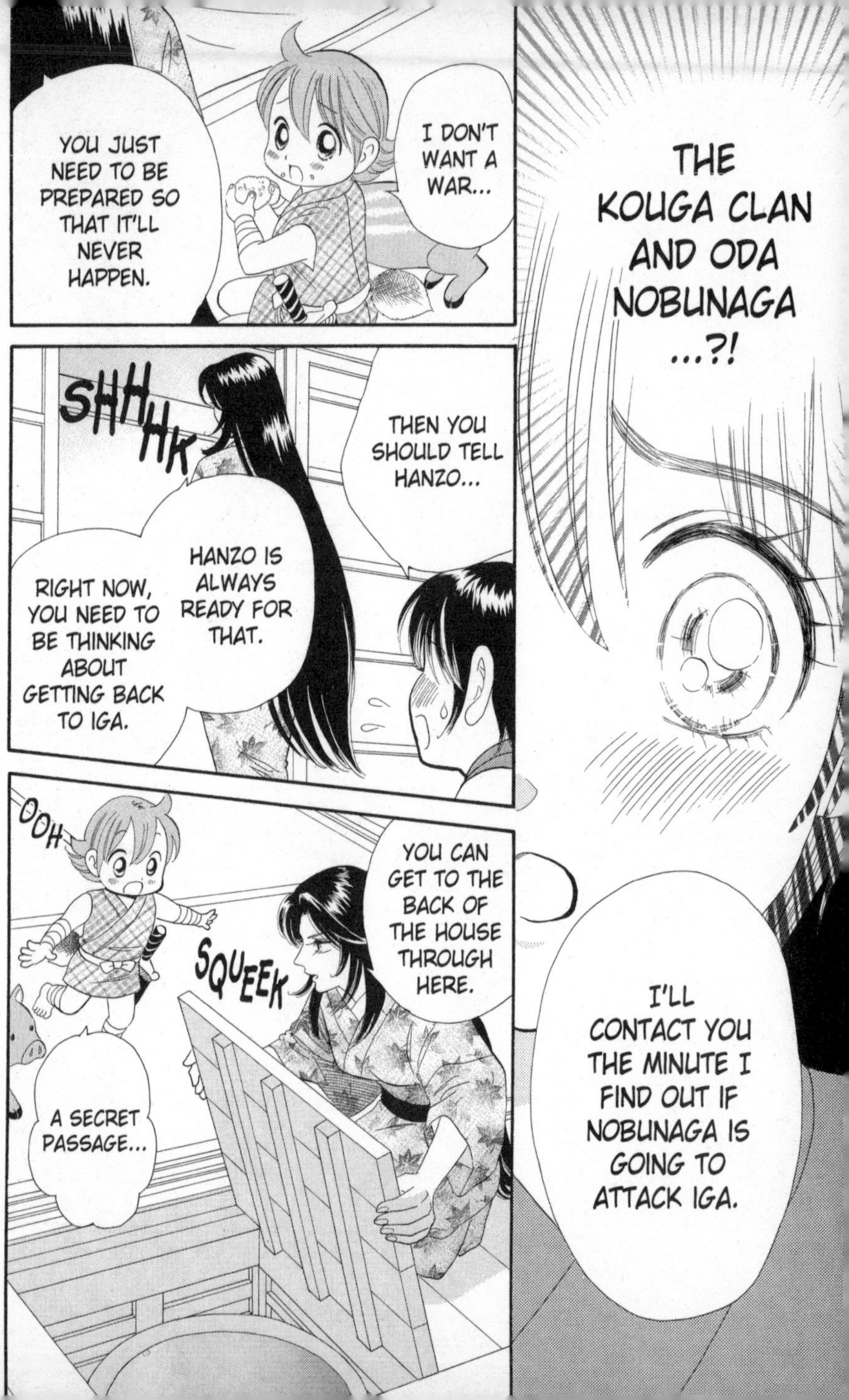
THE KOUGA CLAN AND ODA NOBUNAGA ...?!
I'LL CONTACT YOU THE MINUTE I FIND OUT IF NOBUNAGA IS GOING TO ATTACK IGA.
I DON'T WANT A WAR...
YOU JUST NEED TO BE PREPARED SO THAT IT'LL NEVER HAPPEN.
THEN YOU SHOULD TELL HANZO...
SHHHK
HANZO IS ALWAYS READY FOR THAT.
RIGHT NOW, YOU NEED TO BE THINKING ABOUT GETTING BACK TO IGA.
YOU CAN GET TO THE BACK OF THE HOUSE THROUGH HERE.
SQUEEEK
OOH
A SECRET PASSAGE...

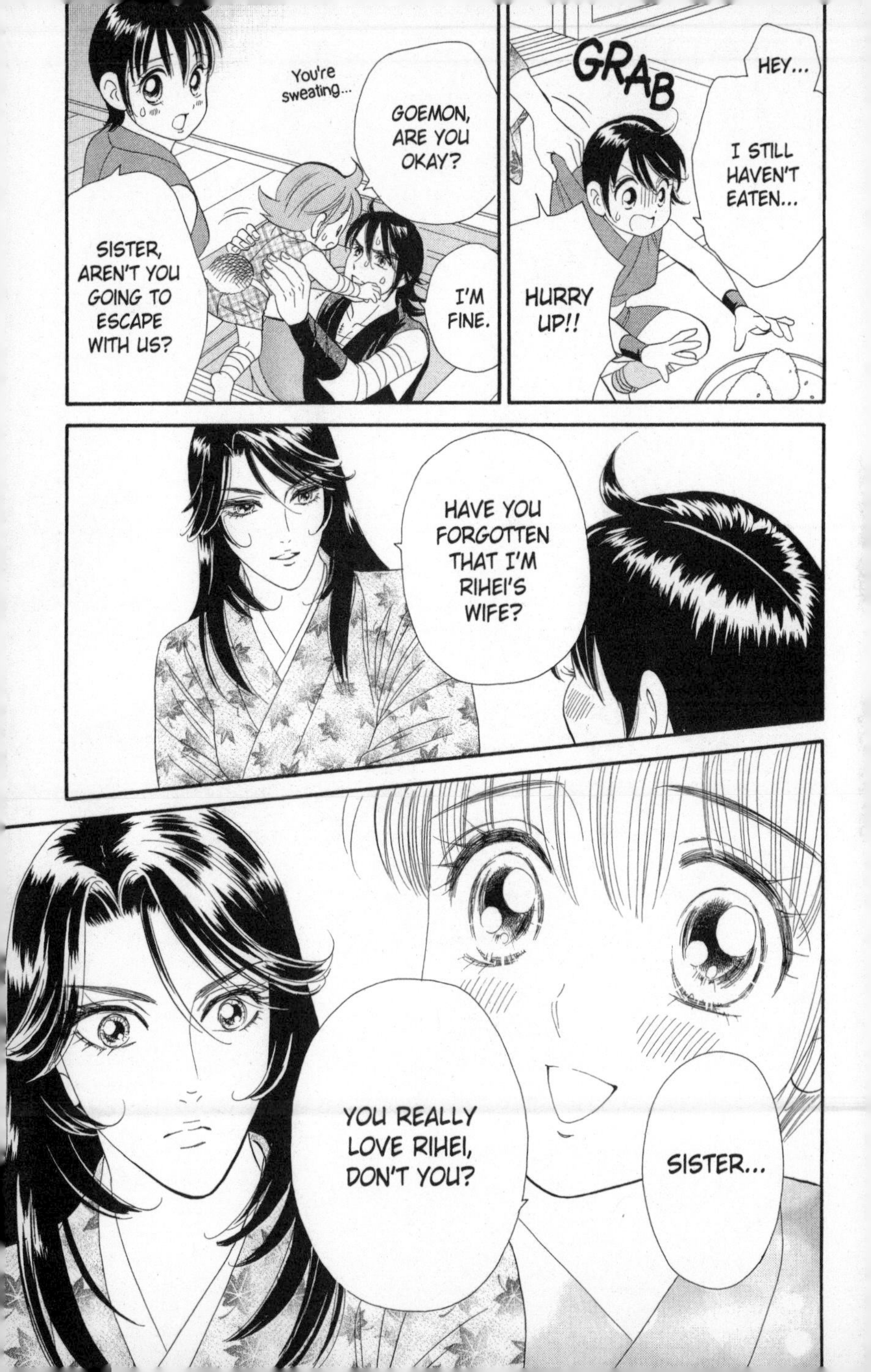
GRAB
HEY...
I STILL HAVEN'T EATEN...
HURRY UP!!
GOEMON, ARE YOU OKAY?
You're sweating...
I'M FINE.
SISTER, AREN'T YOU GOING TO ESCAPE WITH US?
HAVE YOU FORGOTTEN THAT I'M RIHEI'S WIFE?
SISTER...
YOU REALLY LOVE RIHEI, DON'T YOU?

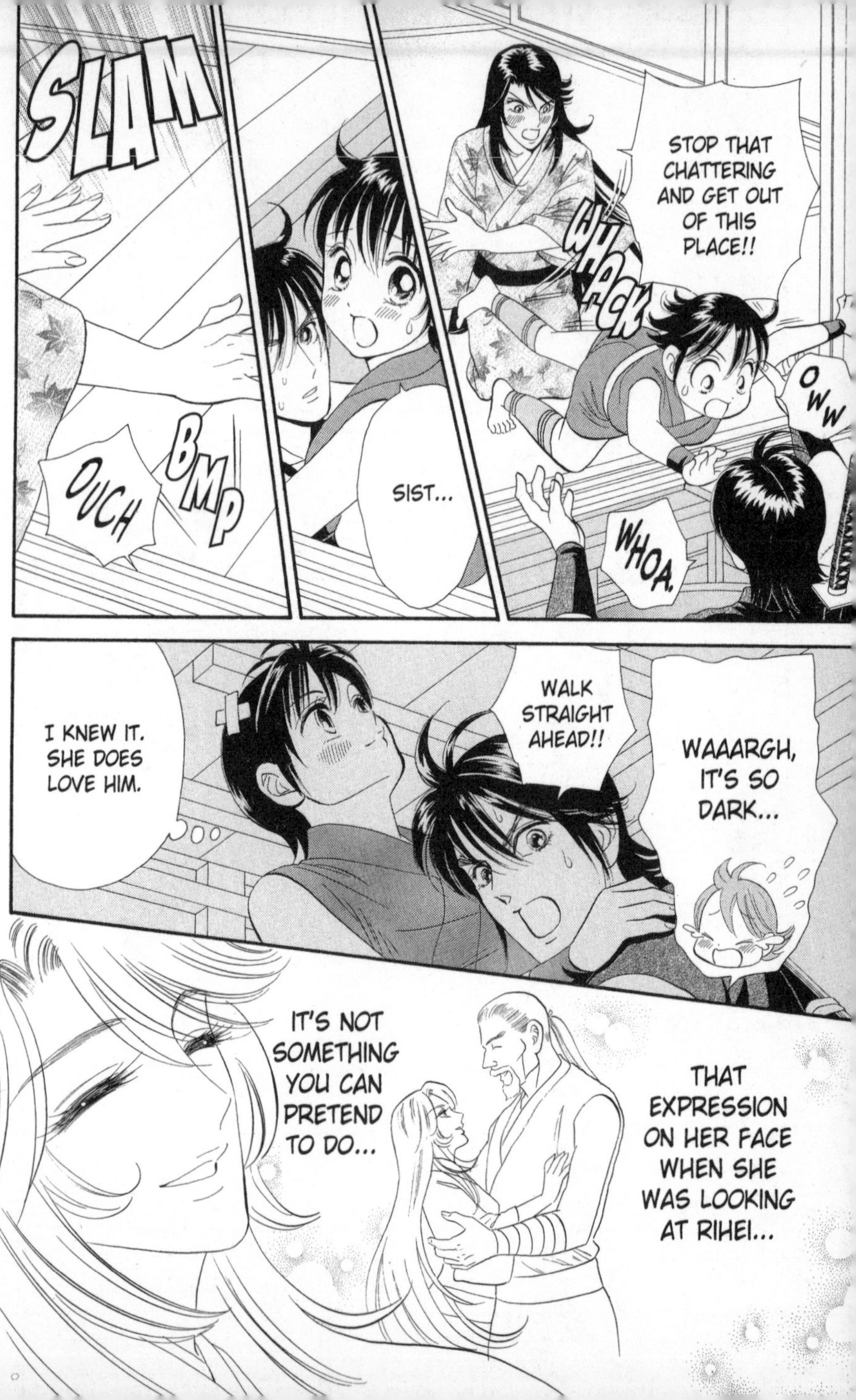
STOP THAT CHATTERING AND GET OUT OF THIS PLACE!!
WHACK
OWW
WHOA.
SIST...
SLAM
BMP
OUCH
WAAARGH, IT'S SO DARK...
WALK STRAIGHT AHEAD!!
I KNEW IT. SHE DOES LOVE HIM.
THAT EXPRESSION ON HER FACE WHEN SHE WAS LOOKING AT RIHEI...
IT'S NOT SOMETHING YOU CAN PRETEND TO DO...

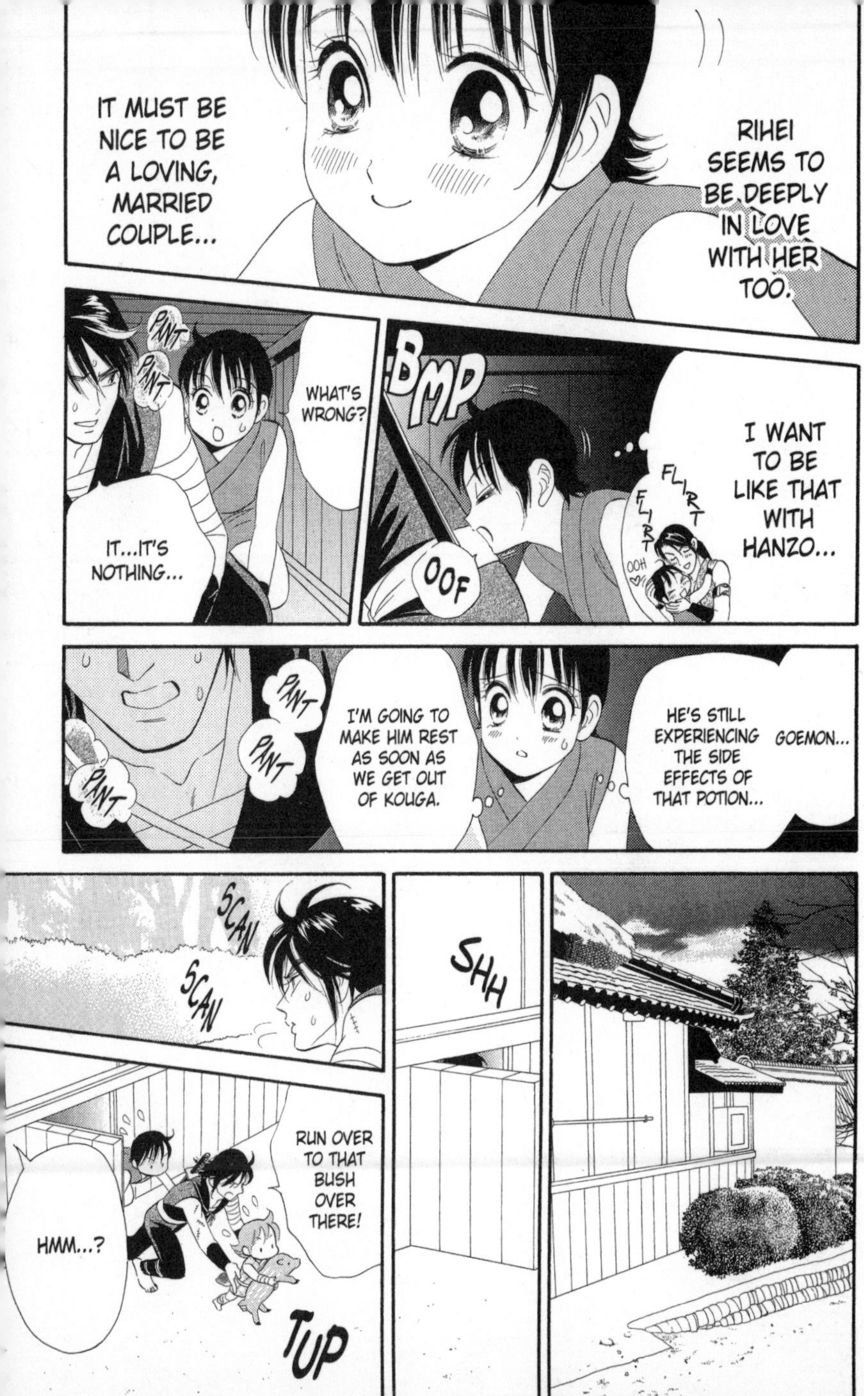
RIHEI SEEMS TO BE DEEPLY IN LOVE WITH HER TOO.
IT MUST BE NICE TO BE A LOVING, MARRIED COUPLE...
I WANT TO BE LIKE THAT WITH HANZO...
FLIRT
FLIRT
OOH
BMP
OOF
PANT
PANT
PANT
WHAT'S WRONG?
IT...IT'S NOTHING...
GOEMON...
HE'S STILL EXPERIENCING THE SIDE EFFECTS OF THAT POTION...
I'M GOING TO MAKE HIM REST AS SOON AS WE GET OUT OF KOUGA.
PANT
PANT
PANT
SHH
SCAN
SCAN
RUN OVER TO THAT BUSH OVER THERE!
HMM...?
TUP

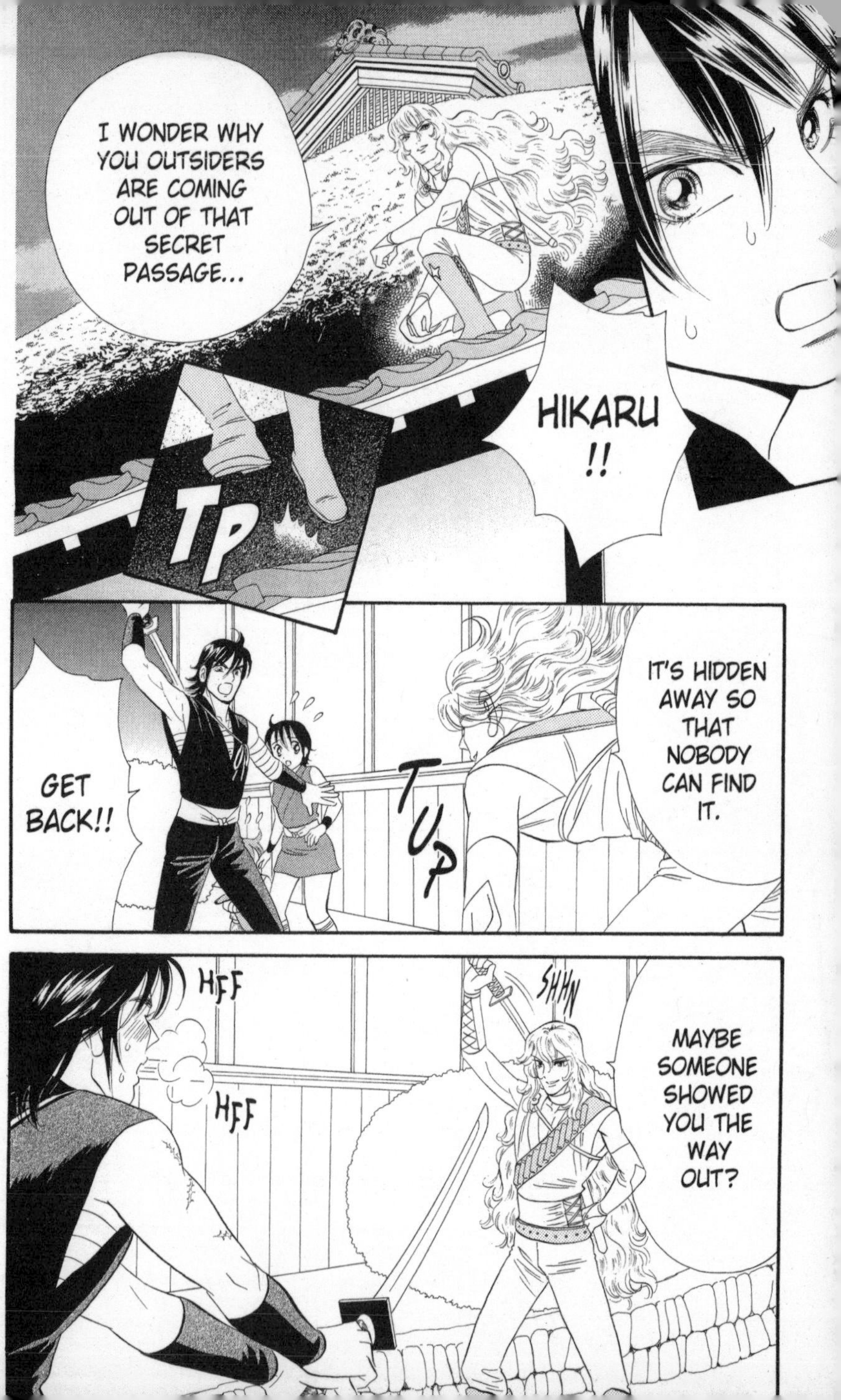
HIKARU !!
I WONDER WHY YOU OUTSIDERS ARE COMING OUT OF THAT SECRET PASSAGE...
TP
IT'S HIDDEN AWAY SO THAT NOBODY CAN FIND IT.
TUP
GET BACK!!
MAYBE SOMEONE SHOWED YOU THE WAY OUT?
SHHN
HFF
HFF

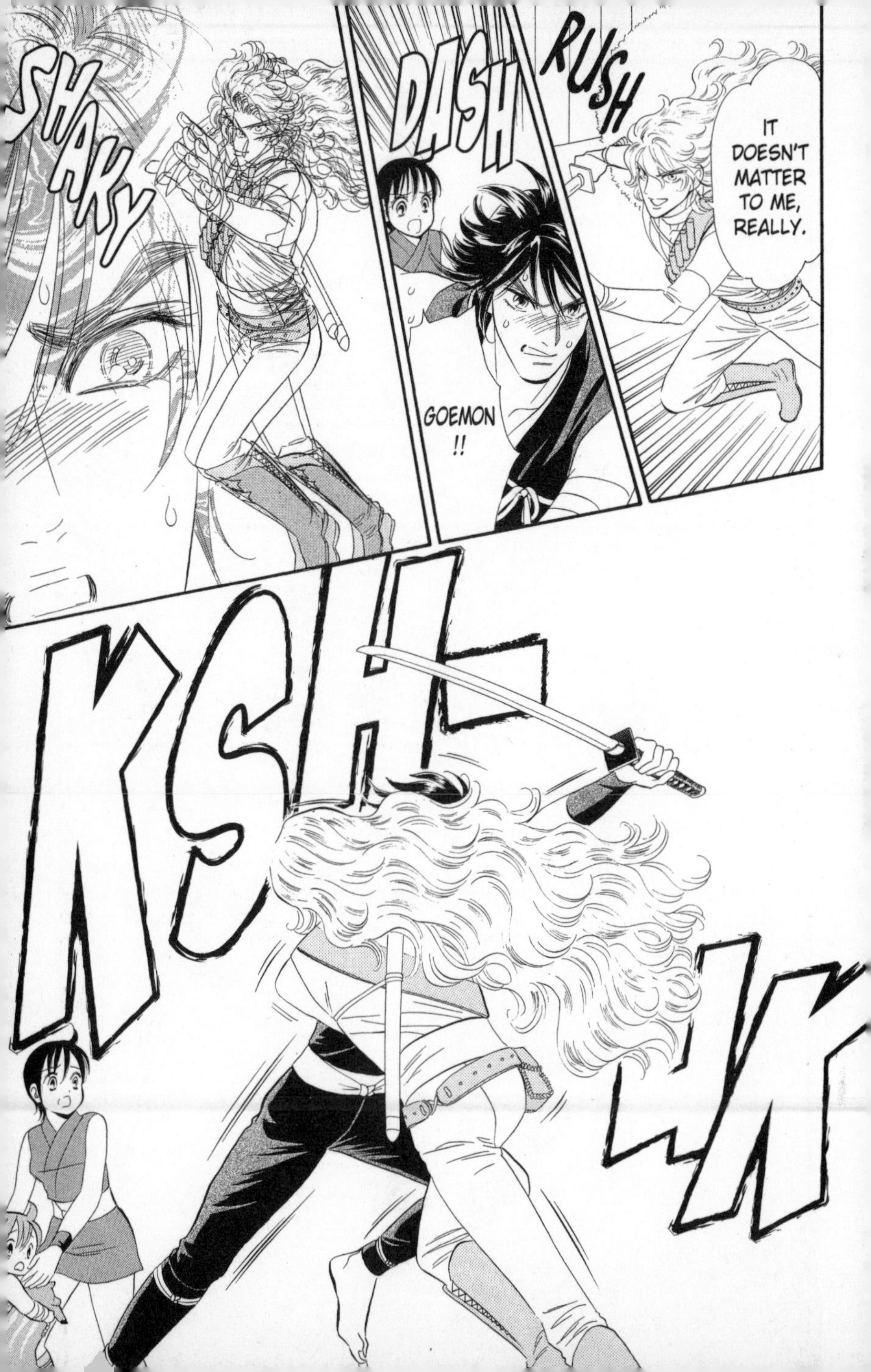
RUSH
IT DOESN'T MATTER TO ME, REALLY.
DASH
GOEMON!!
SHAKY

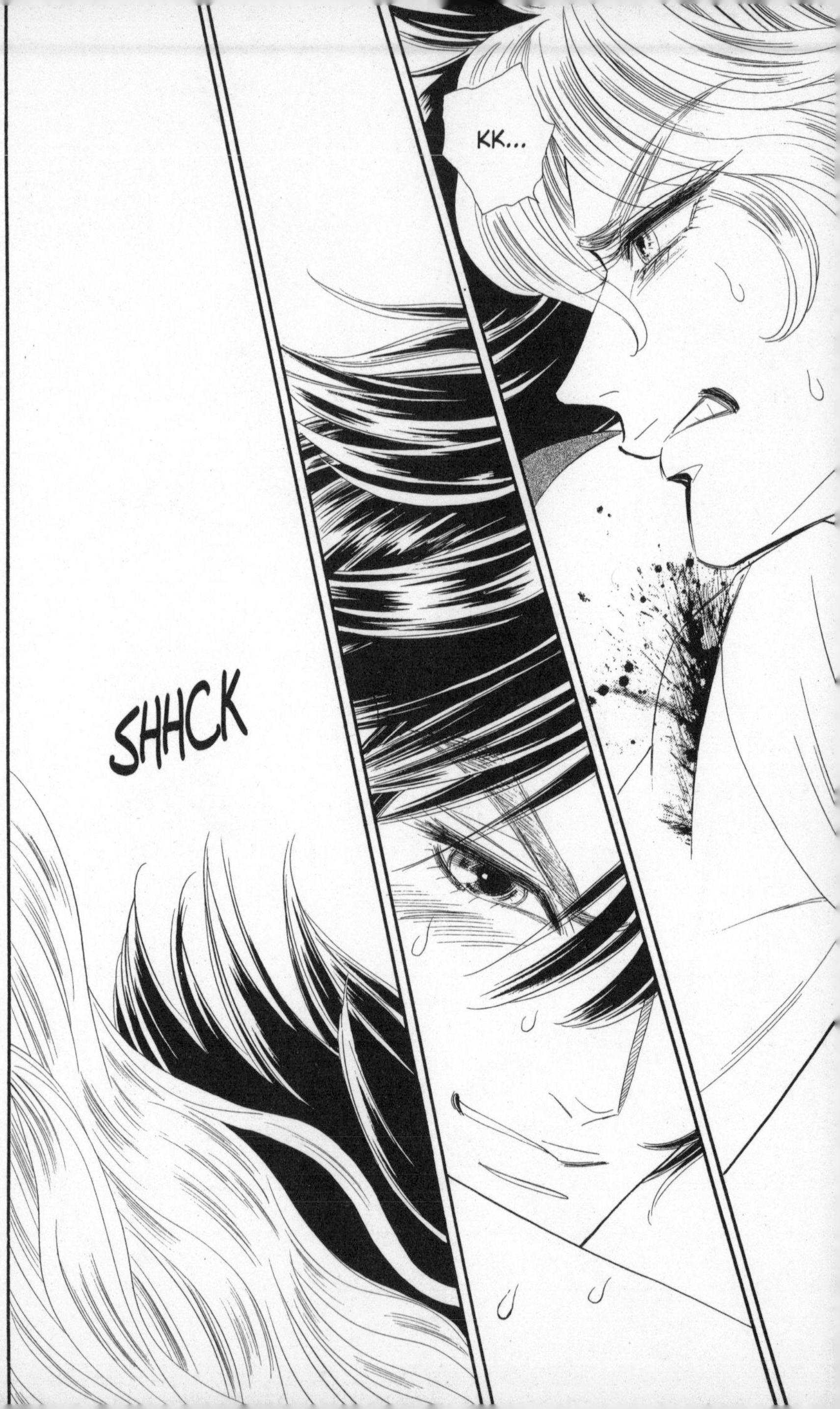
KK...
SHHCK

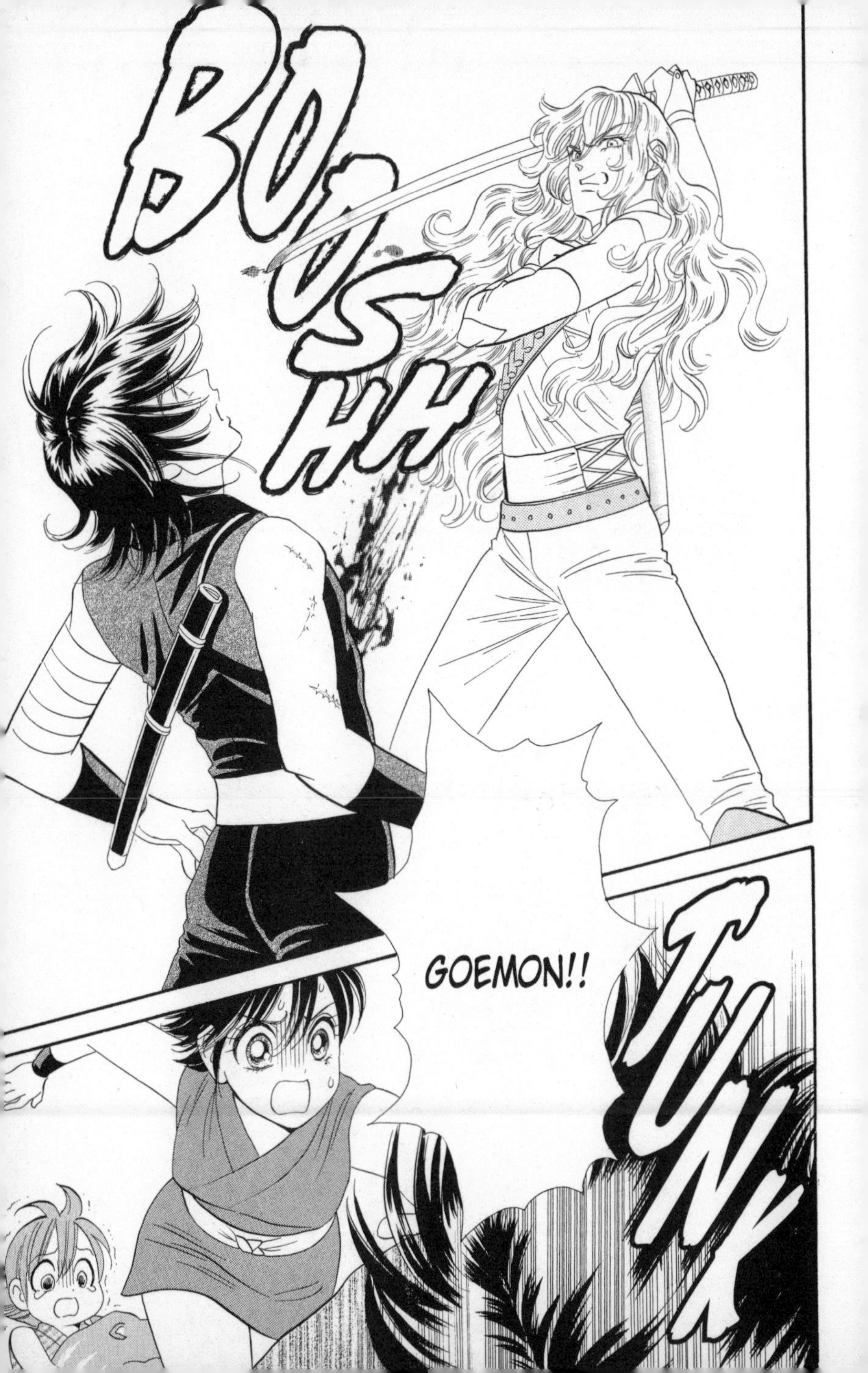
BOOSHH
GOEMON!!
THUNK

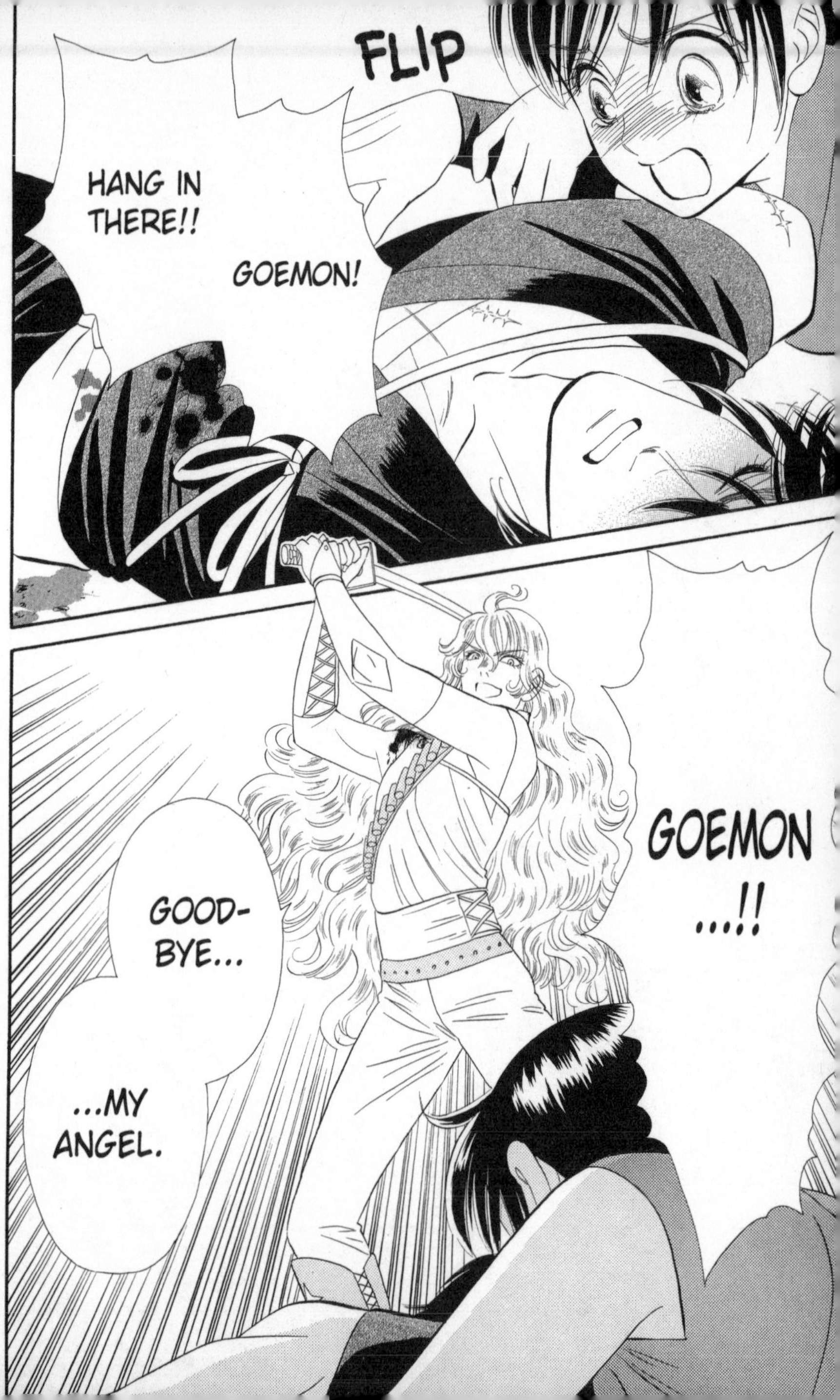
FLIP
HANG IN THERE!! GOEMON!
GOEMON ...!!
GOOD-BYE...
...MY ANGEL.

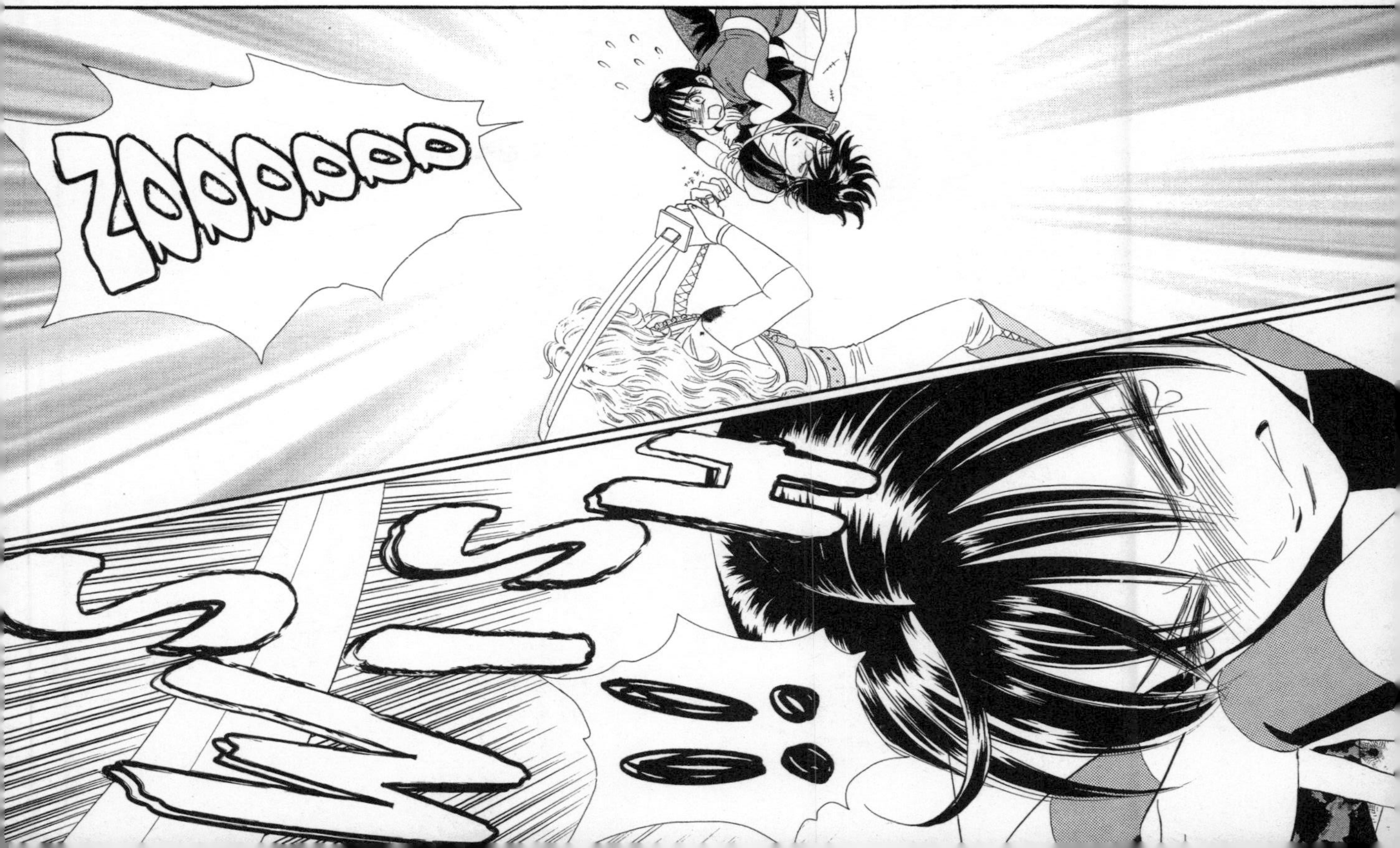
ZOOOOOOO
SWISH!!

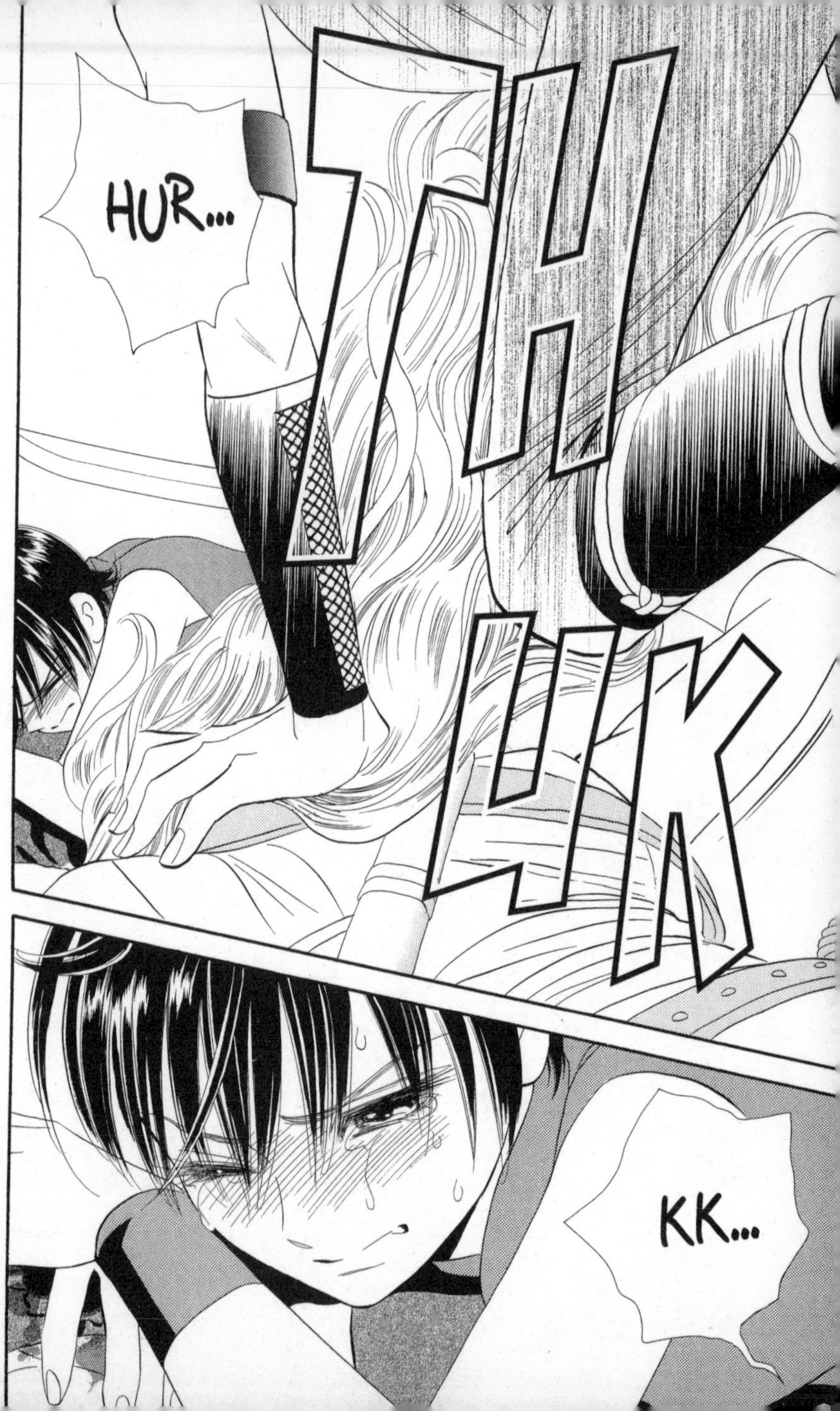
THUNK
HUR...
KK...

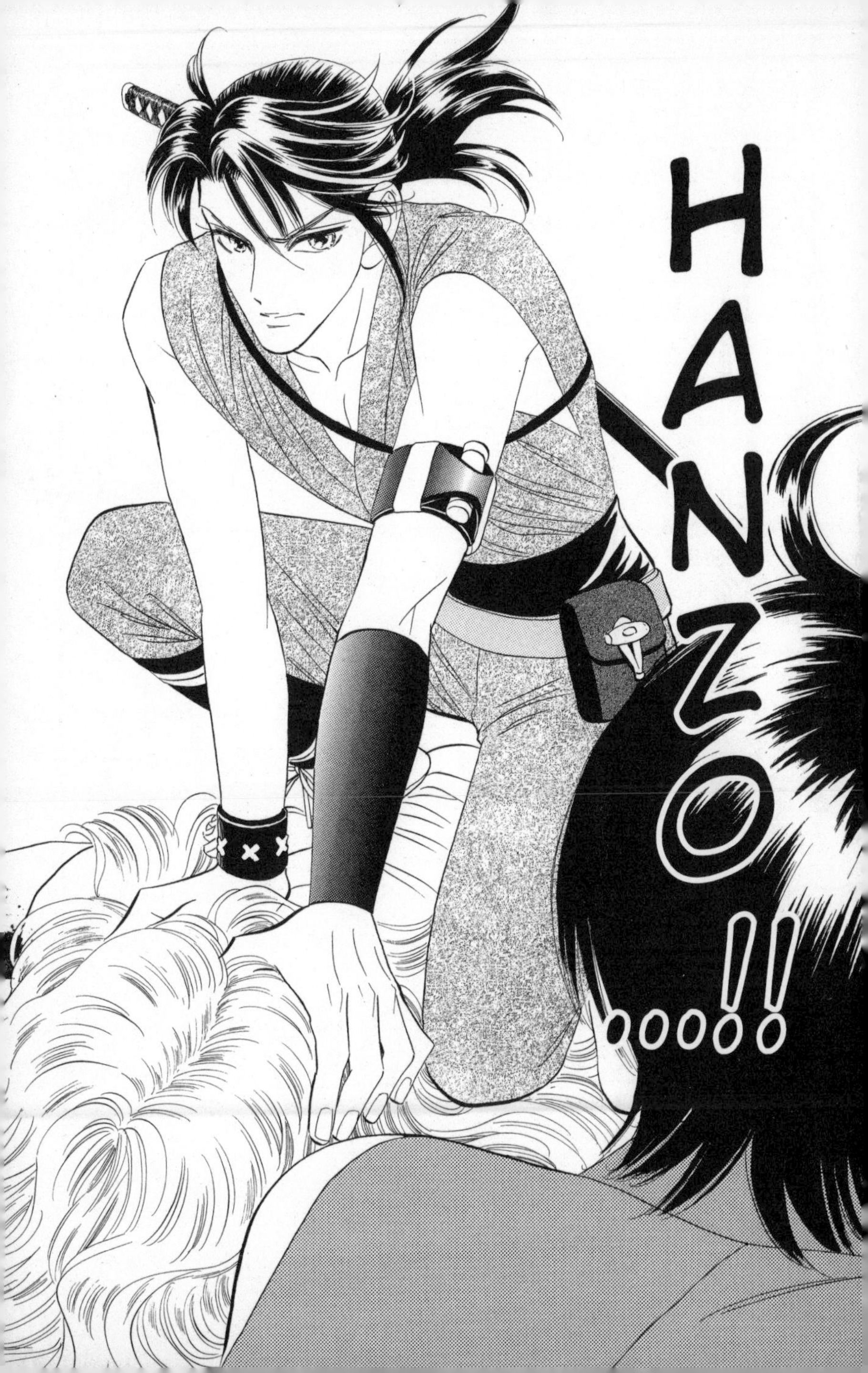
HANZO!!

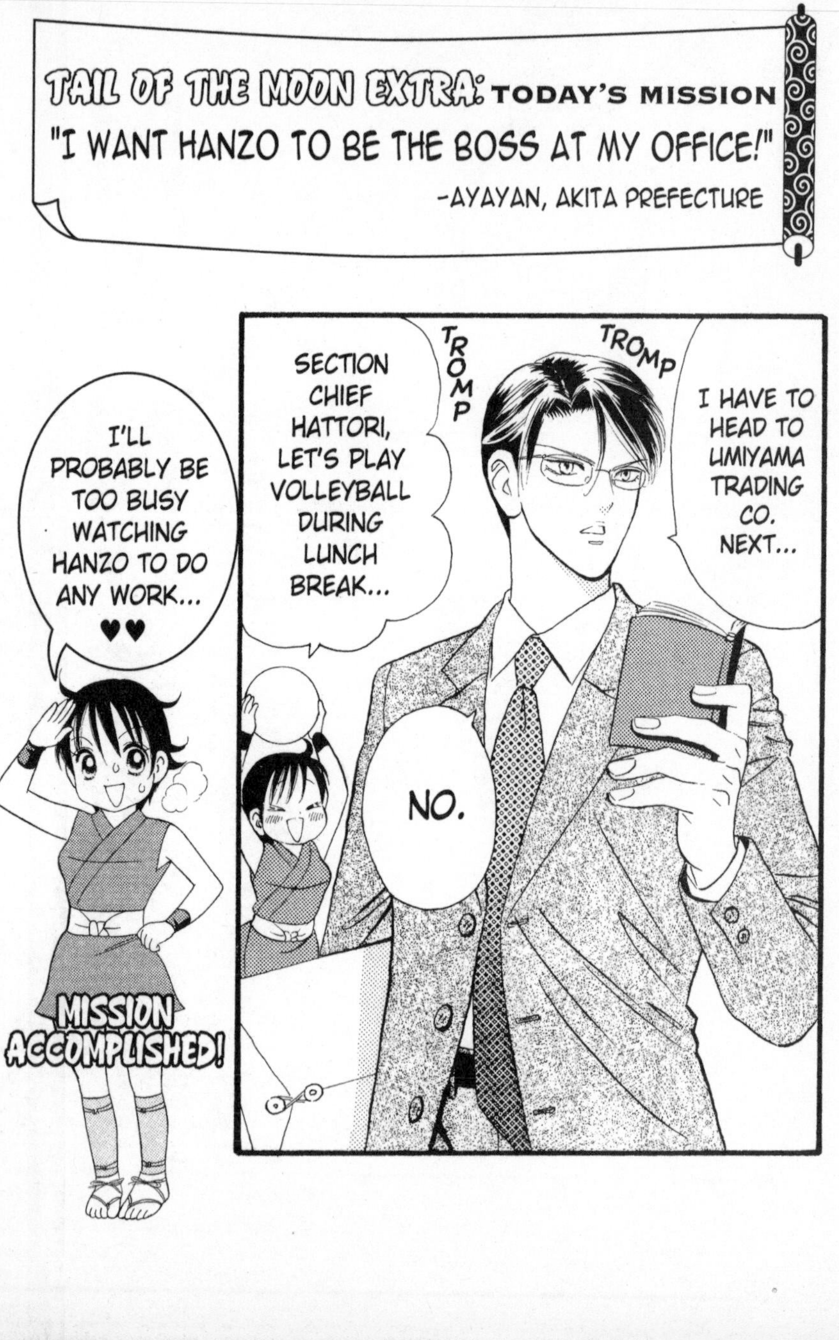
TAIL OF THE MOON EXTRA: TODAY'S MISSION
"I WANT HANZO TO BE THE BOSS AT MY OFFICE!"
-AYAYAN, AKITA PREFECTURE
I HAVE TO HEAD TO UMIYAMA TRADING CO. NEXT...
TROMP
TROMP
SECTION CHIEF HATTORI, LET'S PLAY VOLLEYBALL DURING LUNCH BREAK...
NO.
I'LL PROBABLY BE TOO BUSY WATCHING HANZO TO DO ANY WORK... ♥♥
MISSION ACCOMPLISHED!

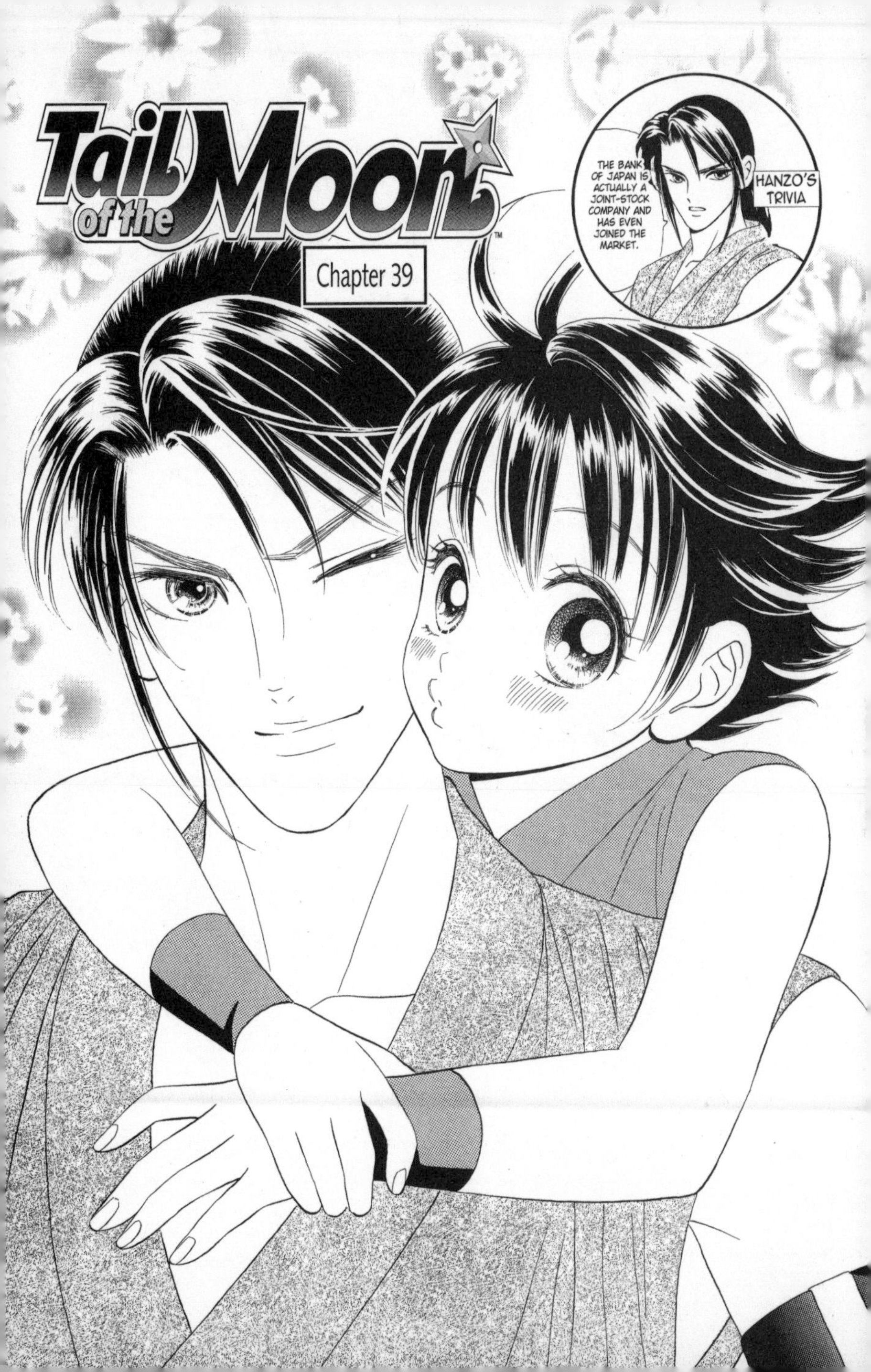
Tail of the Moon™
Chapter 39
HANZO'S TRIVIA
THE BANK OF JAPAN IS ACTUALLY A JOINT-STOCK COMPANY AND HAS EVEN JOINED THE MARKET.

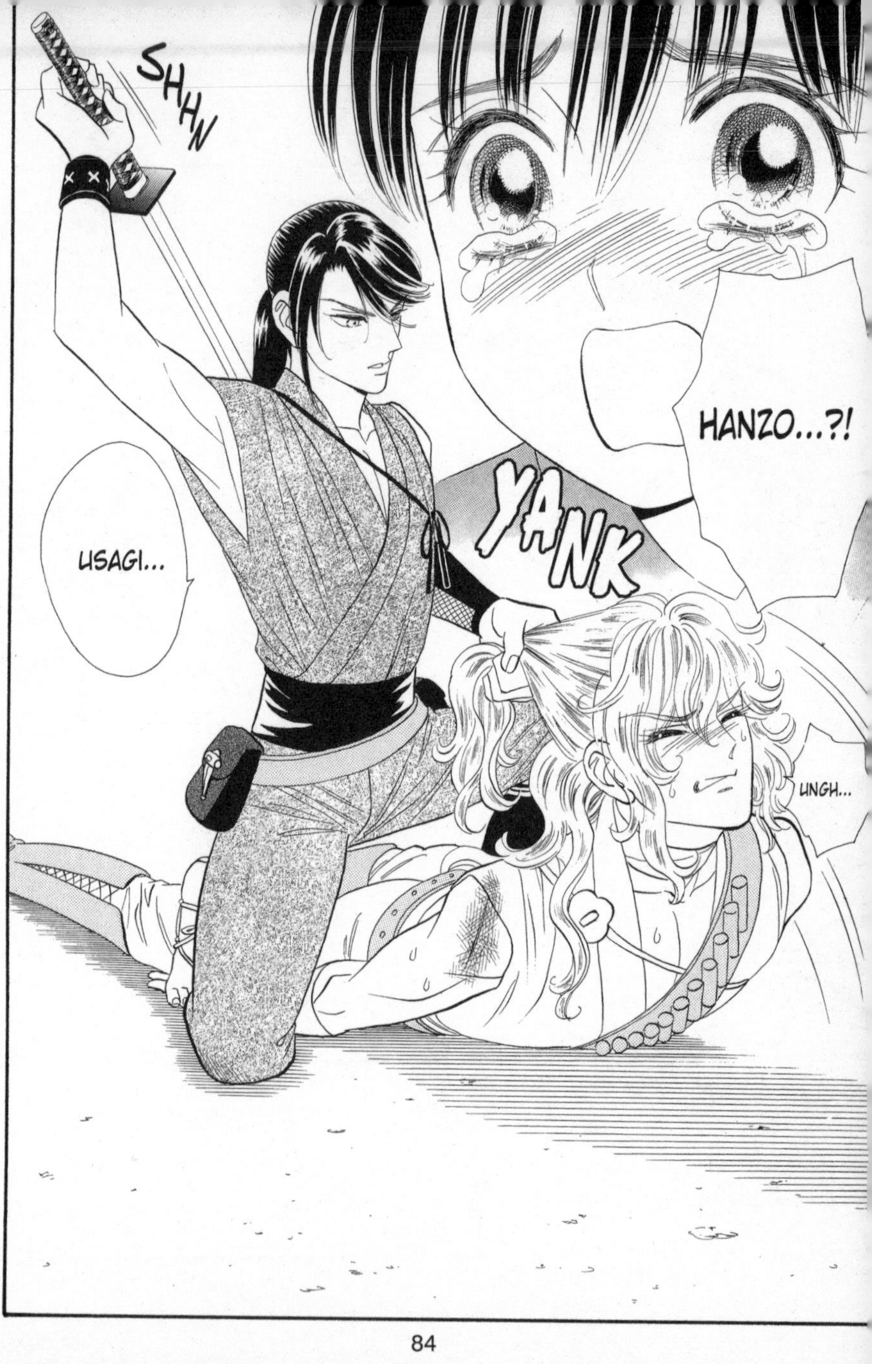
HANZO...?!
YANK
UNGH...
SHHN
USAGI...

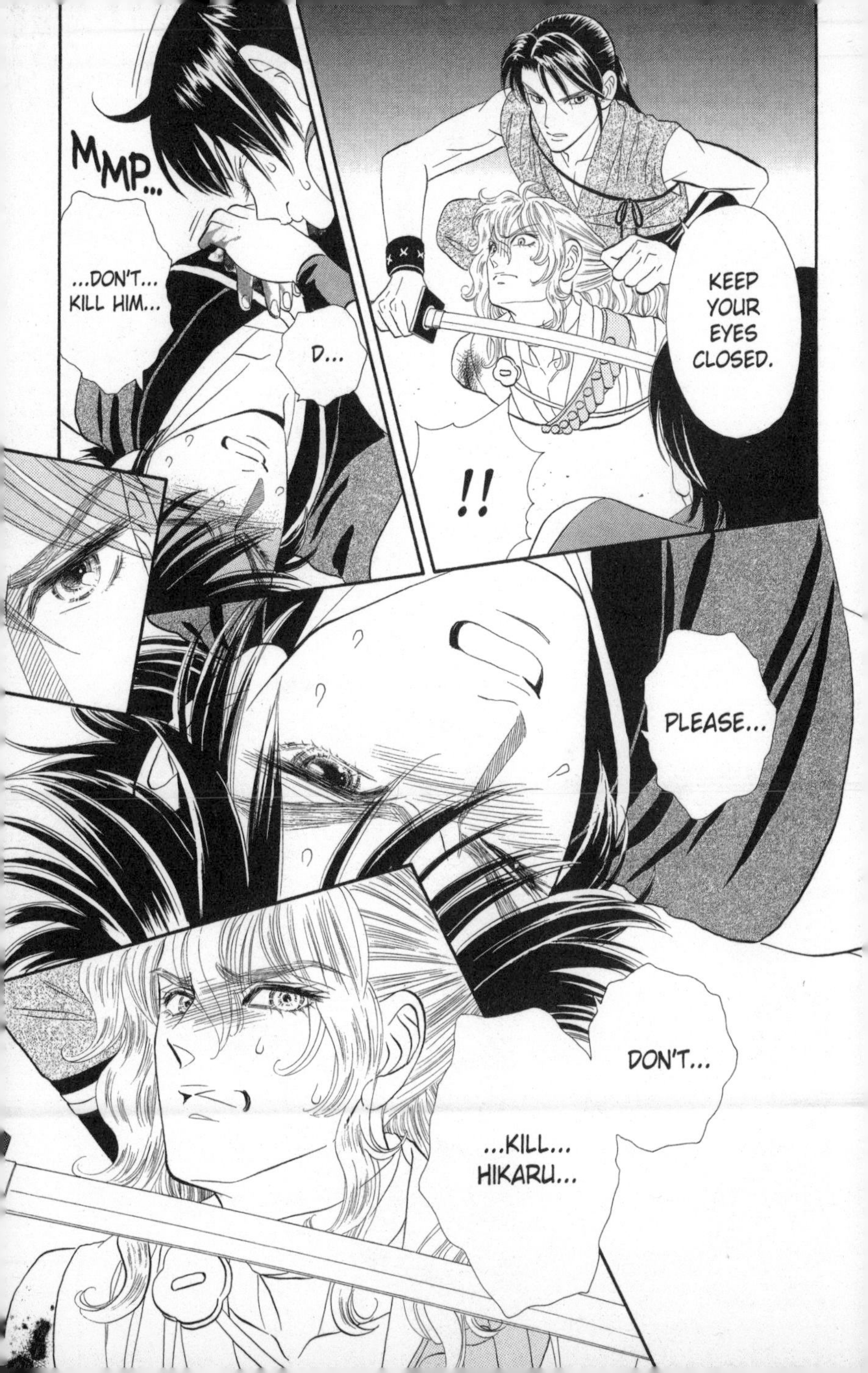
KEEP YOUR EYES CLOSED.
!!
MMP...
...DON'T... KILL HIM...
D...
PLEASE...
DON'T...
...KILL... HIKARU...

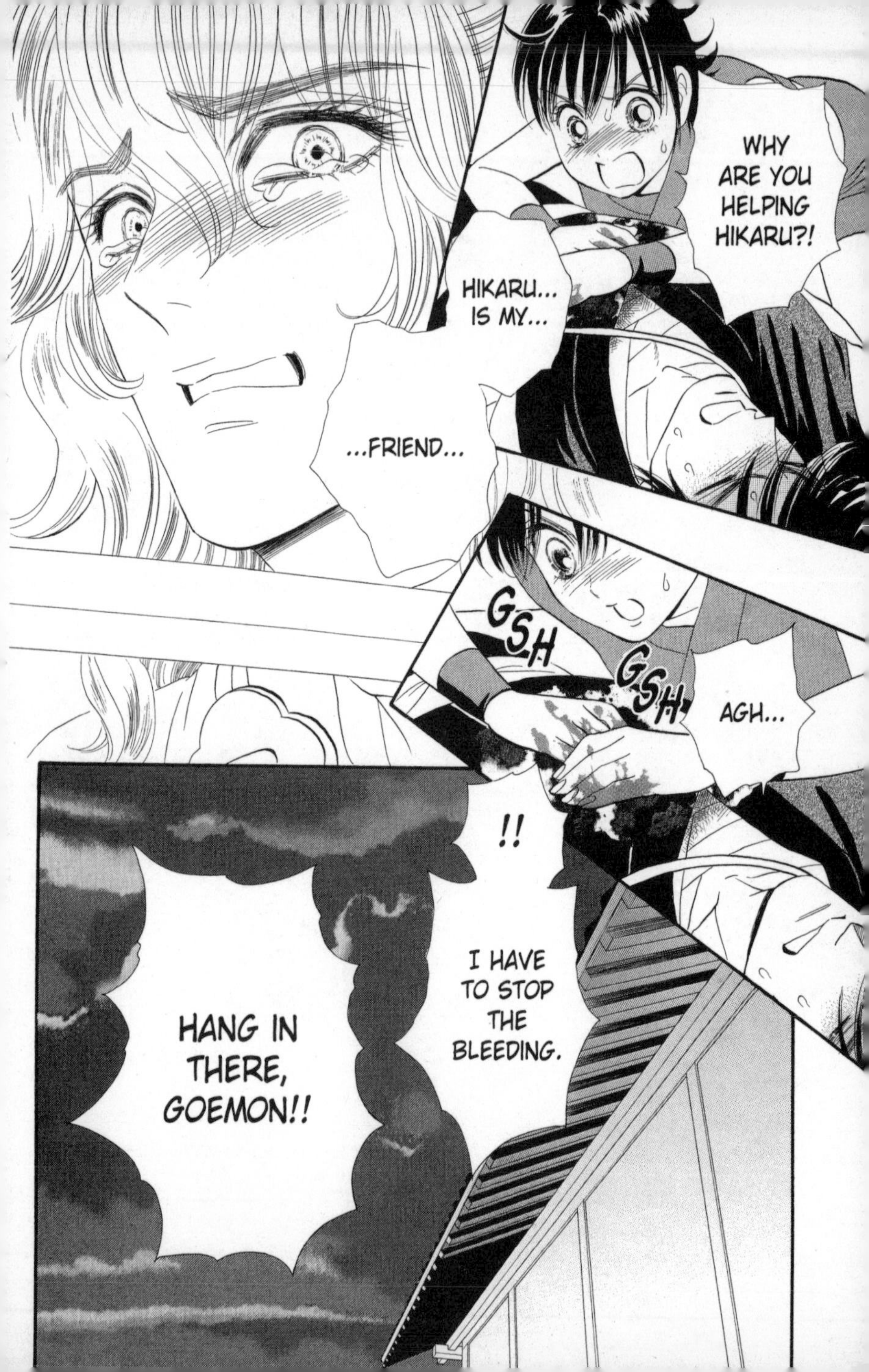
WHY ARE YOU HELPING HIKARU?!
HIKARU... IS MY...
...FRIEND...
GSH
GSH
AGH...
!!
I HAVE TO STOP THE BLEEDING.
HANG IN THERE, GOEMON!!

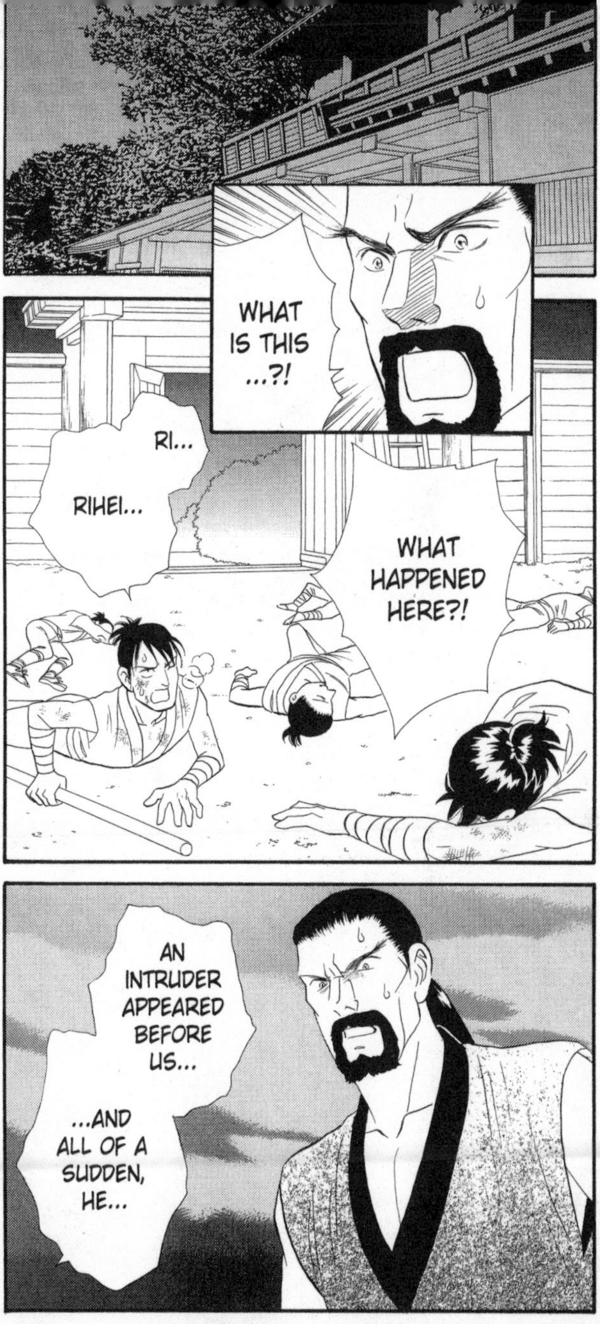
WHAT IS THIS ...?!
WHAT HAPPENED HERE?!
RI...
RIHEI...
AN INTRUDER APPEARED BEFORE US...
...AND ALL OF A SUDDEN, HE...

UE-RIN'S WAY OF THE MANGA ③

Back then, there was quite a lot of people who made their shojo manga debut in high school or middle school. Every time I read about people like that in the "Manga School" section, I...

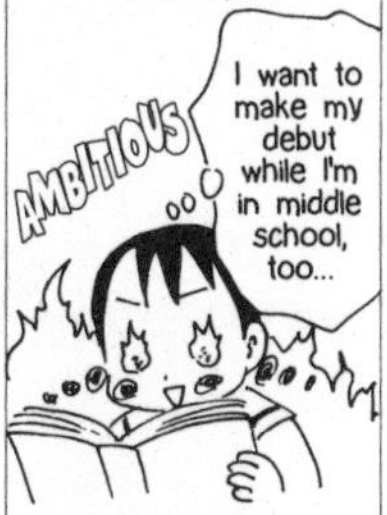
AMBITIOUS
I want to make my debut while I'm in middle school, too...

And once again, with that brassy attitude of mine, I got started.

I bought a How to Draw Manga book by Hikaru Yuzuki, a former *Ribon* manga artist. In that book it said, "When drawing people, you should start with the eyes." So without a shadow of a doubt, I started practicing that way.

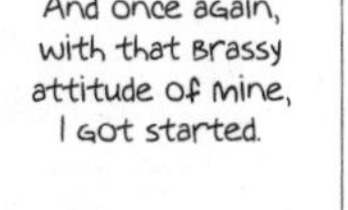

I still draw starting with the eyes.

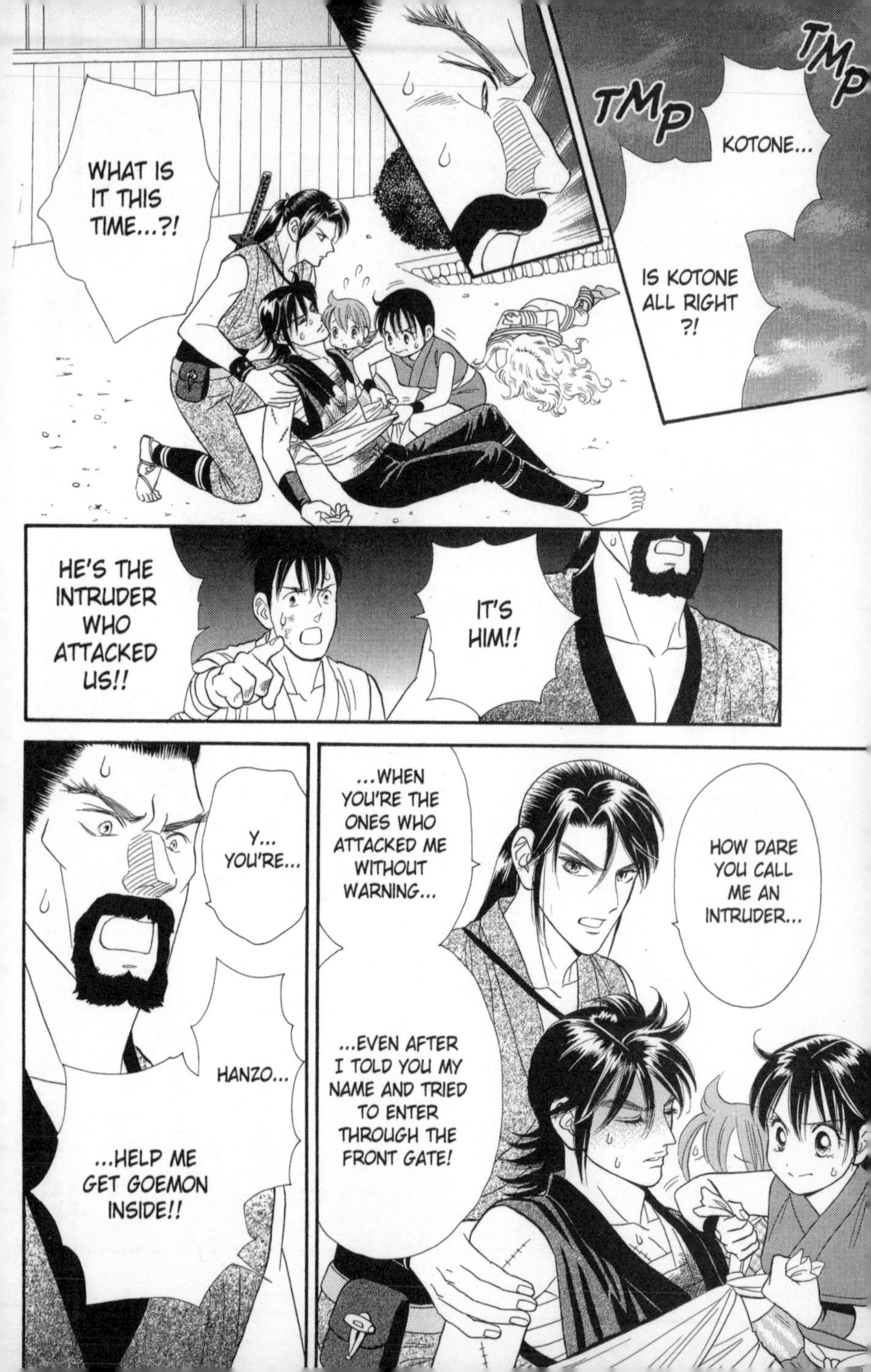
TMP
TMP
KOTONE...
IS KOTONE ALL RIGHT ?!
WHAT IS IT THIS TIME...?!
IT'S HIM!!
HE'S THE INTRUDER WHO ATTACKED US!!
HOW DARE YOU CALL ME AN INTRUDER...
...WHEN YOU'RE THE ONES WHO ATTACKED ME WITHOUT WARNING...
...EVEN AFTER I TOLD YOU MY NAME AND TRIED TO ENTER THROUGH THE FRONT GATE!
Y... YOU'RE...
HANZO...
...HELP ME GET GOEMON INSIDE!!

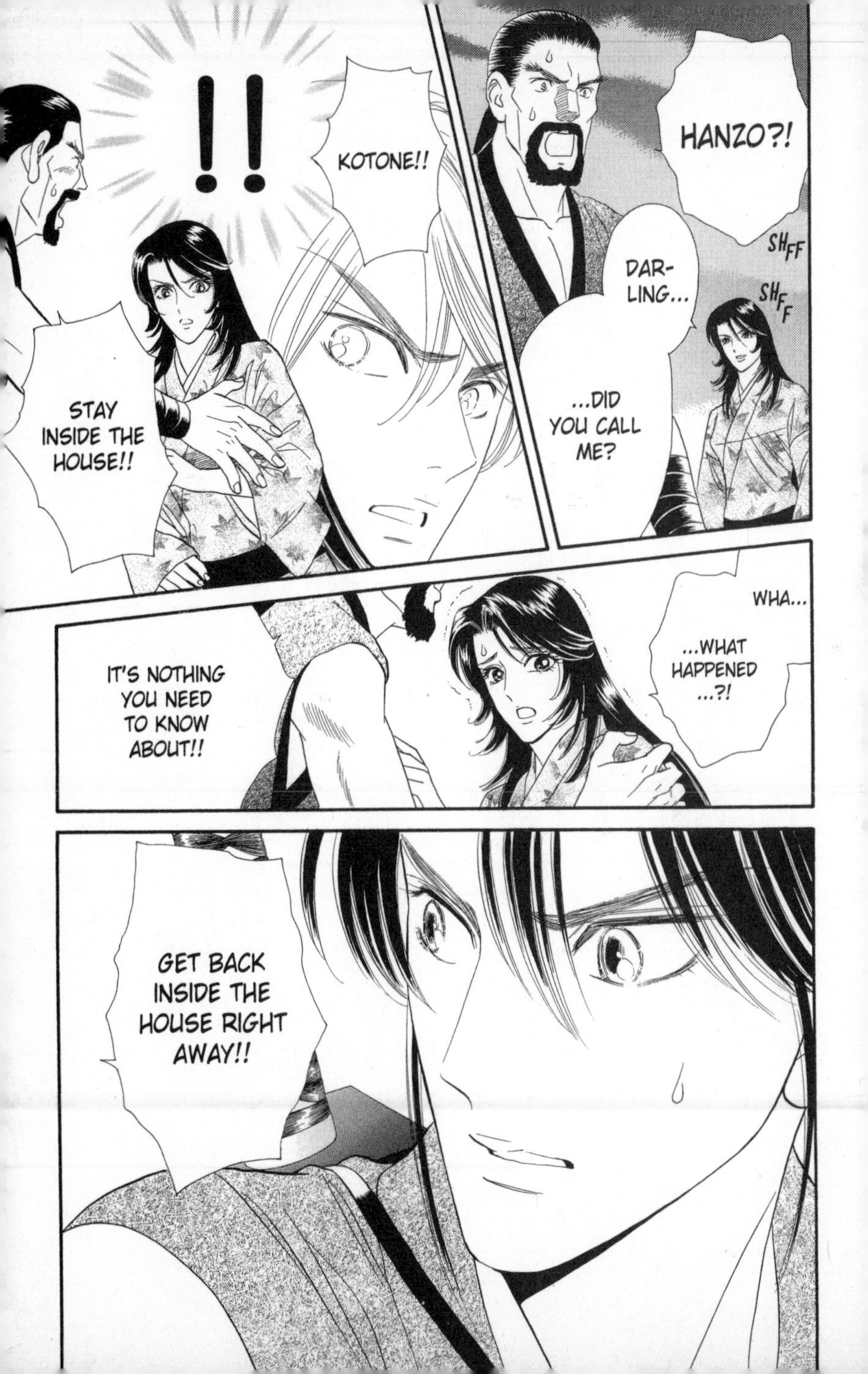
HANZO?!
SHFF
SHFF
DAR-
LING...
...DID YOU CALL ME?
!!
KOTONE!!
STAY INSIDE THE HOUSE!!
WHA...
...WHAT HAPPENED ...?!
IT'S NOTHING YOU NEED TO KNOW ABOUT!!
GET BACK INSIDE THE HOUSE RIGHT AWAY!!

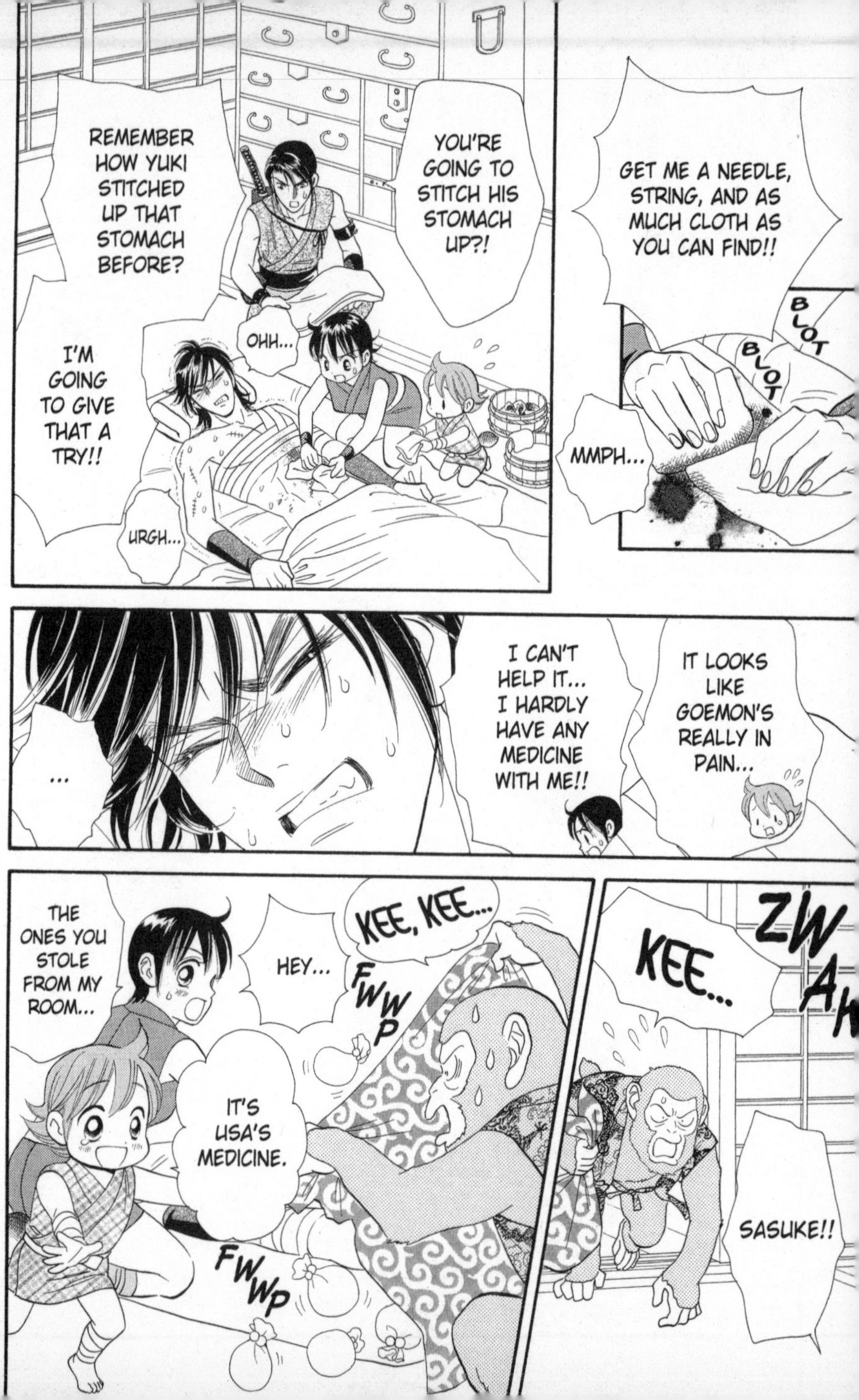
GET ME A NEEDLE, STRING, AND AS MUCH CLOTH AS YOU CAN FIND!!
BLOT
BLOT
MMPH...
YOU'RE GOING TO STITCH HIS STOMACH UP?!
REMEMBER HOW YUKI STITCHED UP THAT STOMACH BEFORE?
OHH...
I'M GOING TO GIVE THAT A TRY!!
URGH...
IT LOOKS LIKE GOEMON'S REALLY IN PAIN...
I CAN'T HELP IT... I HARDLY HAVE ANY MEDICINE WITH ME!!
...
ZWAK
KEE...
SASUKE!!
KEE, KEE...
HEY...
THE ONES YOU STOLE FROM MY ROOM...
FWWP
IT'S USA'S MEDICINE.
FWWP

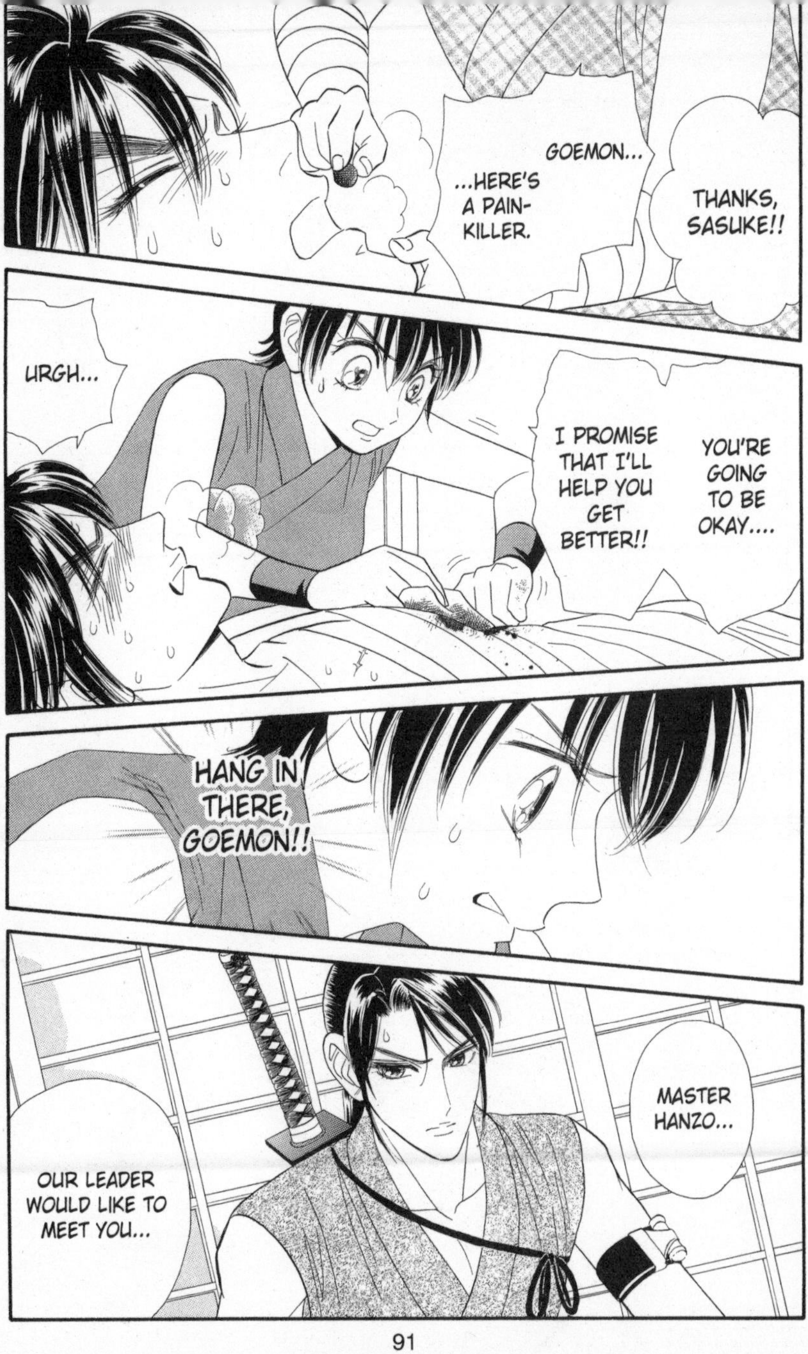
THANKS, SASUKE!!
GOEMON...
...HERE'S A PAIN-KILLER.
YOU'RE GOING TO BE OKAY....
I PROMISE THAT I'LL HELP YOU GET BETTER!!
URGH...
HANG IN THERE, GOEMON!!
MASTER HANZO...
OUR LEADER WOULD LIKE TO MEET YOU...

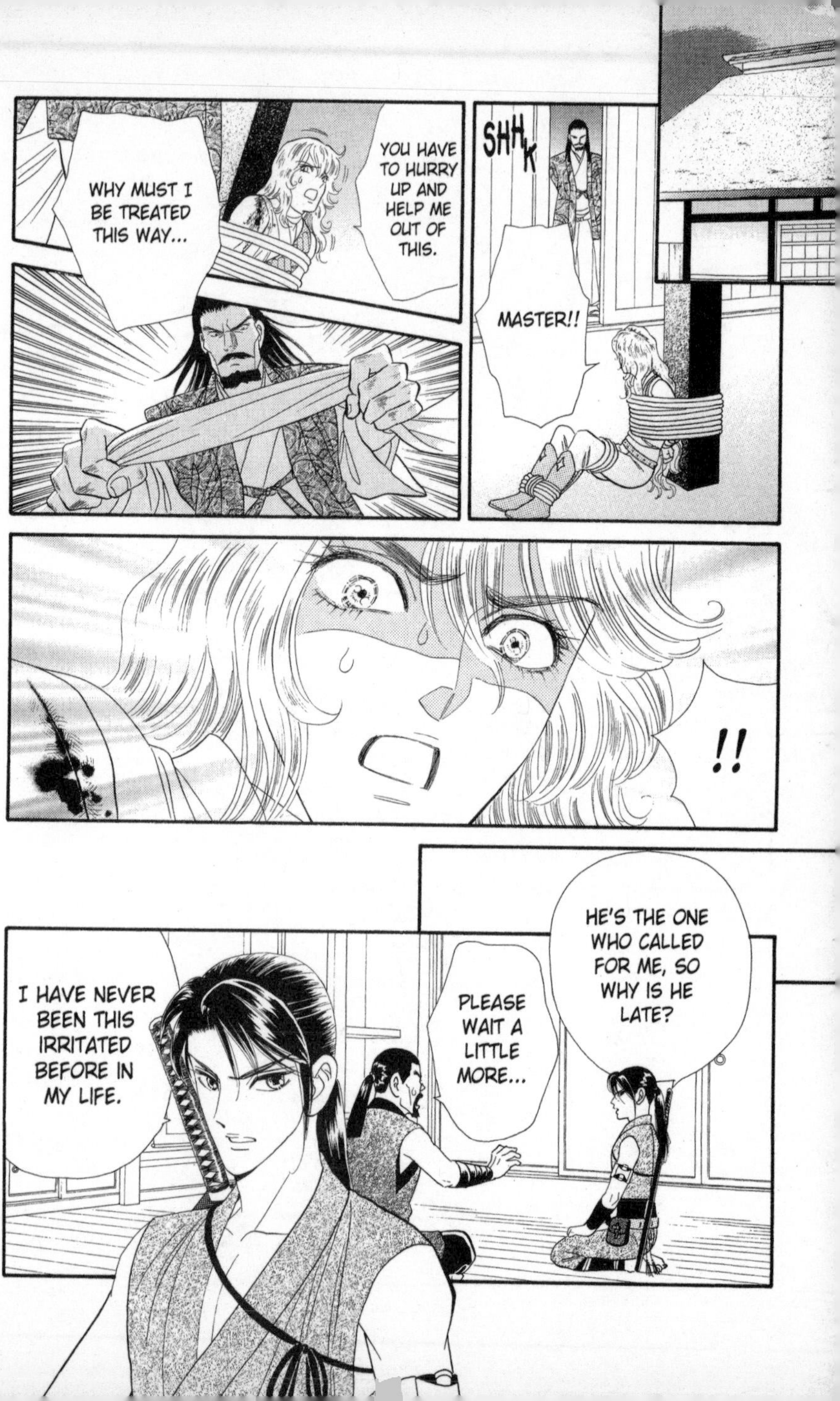
SHHK
MASTER!!
YOU HAVE TO HURRY UP AND HELP ME OUT OF THIS.
WHY MUST I BE TREATED THIS WAY...
!!
HE'S THE ONE WHO CALLED FOR ME, SO WHY IS HE LATE?
PLEASE WAIT A LITTLE MORE...
I HAVE NEVER BEEN THIS IRRITATED BEFORE IN MY LIFE.

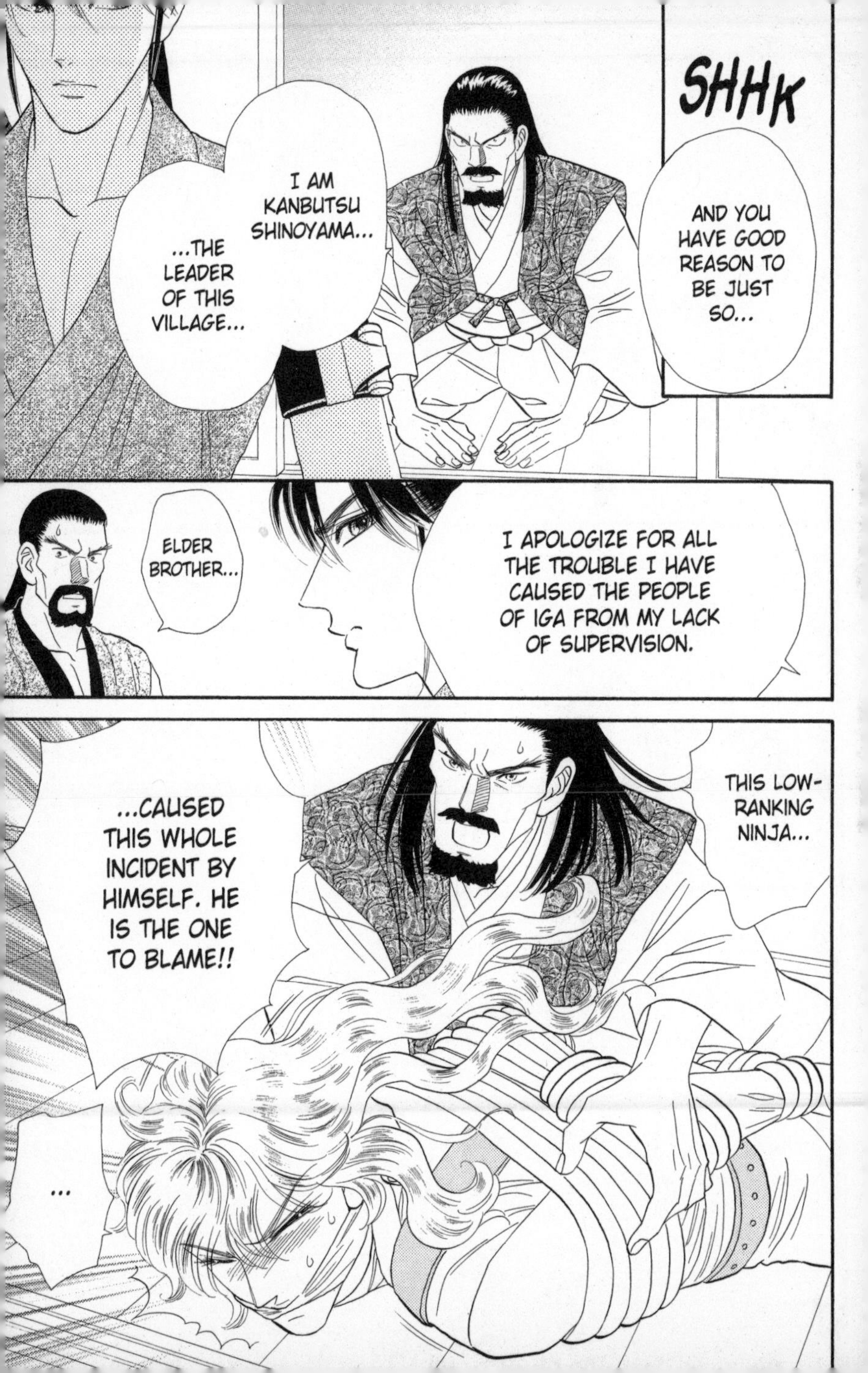
SHHK
AND YOU HAVE GOOD REASON TO BE JUST SO...
I AM KANBUTSU SHINOYAMA...
...THE LEADER OF THIS VILLAGE...
I APOLOGIZE FOR ALL THE TROUBLE I HAVE CAUSED THE PEOPLE OF IGA FROM MY LACK OF SUPERVISION.
ELDER BROTHER...
THIS LOW-RANKING NINJA...
...CAUSED THIS WHOLE INCIDENT BY HIMSELF. HE IS THE ONE TO BLAME!!
...

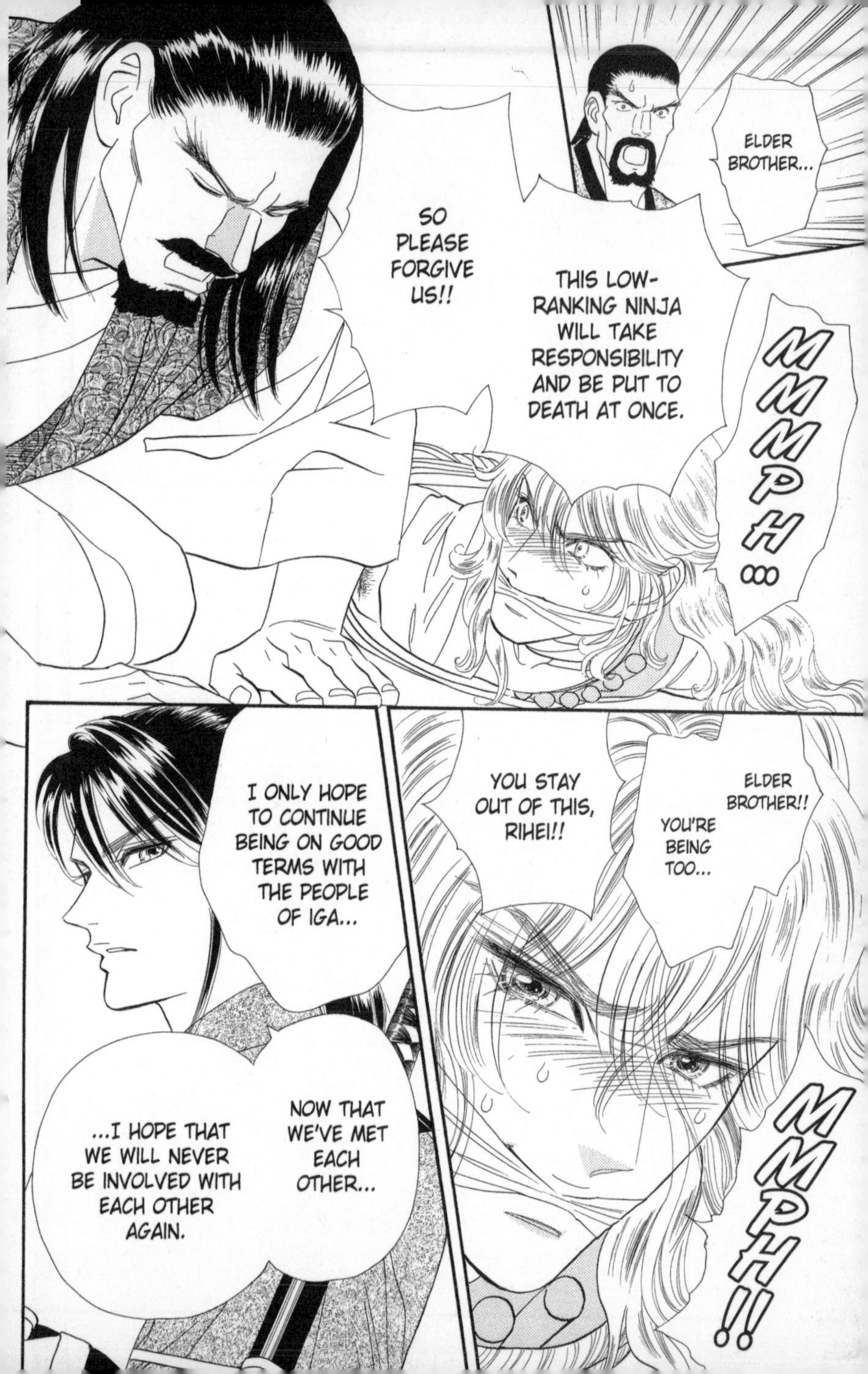
THIS LOW-RANKING NINJA WILL TAKE RESPONSIBILITY AND BE PUT TO DEATH AT ONCE.
SO PLEASE FORGIVE US!!
ELDER BROTHER...
MMMPH...
ELDER BROTHER!!
YOU'RE BEING TOO...
YOU STAY OUT OF THIS, RIHEI!!
MMMPH!!
I ONLY HOPE TO CONTINUE BEING ON GOOD TERMS WITH THE PEOPLE OF IGA...
NOW THAT WE'VE MET EACH OTHER...
...I HOPE THAT WE WILL NEVER BE INVOLVED WITH EACH OTHER AGAIN.

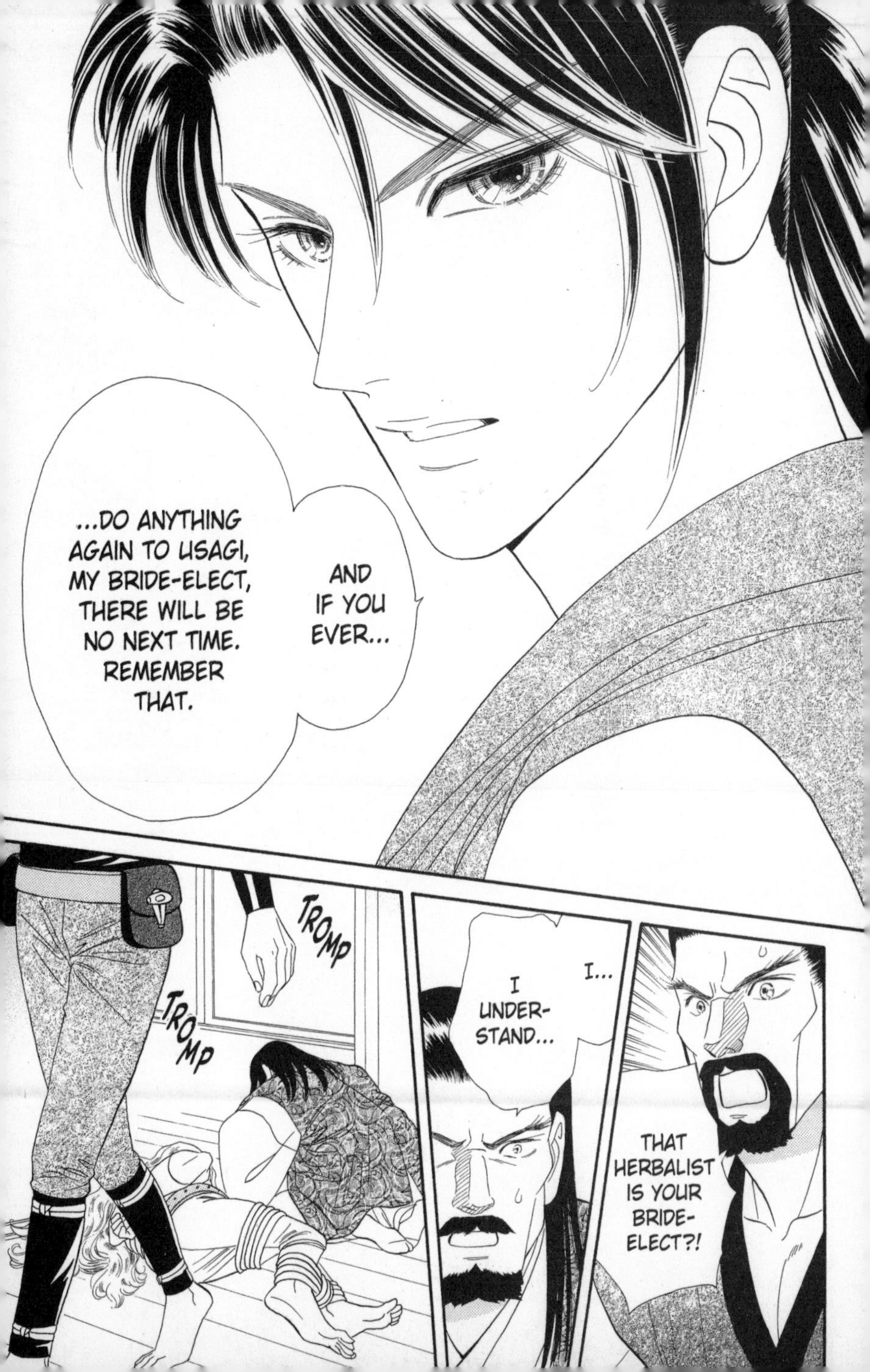
AND IF YOU EVER...
...DO ANYTHING AGAIN TO USAGI, MY BRIDE-ELECT, THERE WILL BE NO NEXT TIME. REMEMBER THAT.
THAT HERBALIST IS YOUR BRIDE-ELECT?!
I...
I UNDER-STAND...
TROMP
TROMP

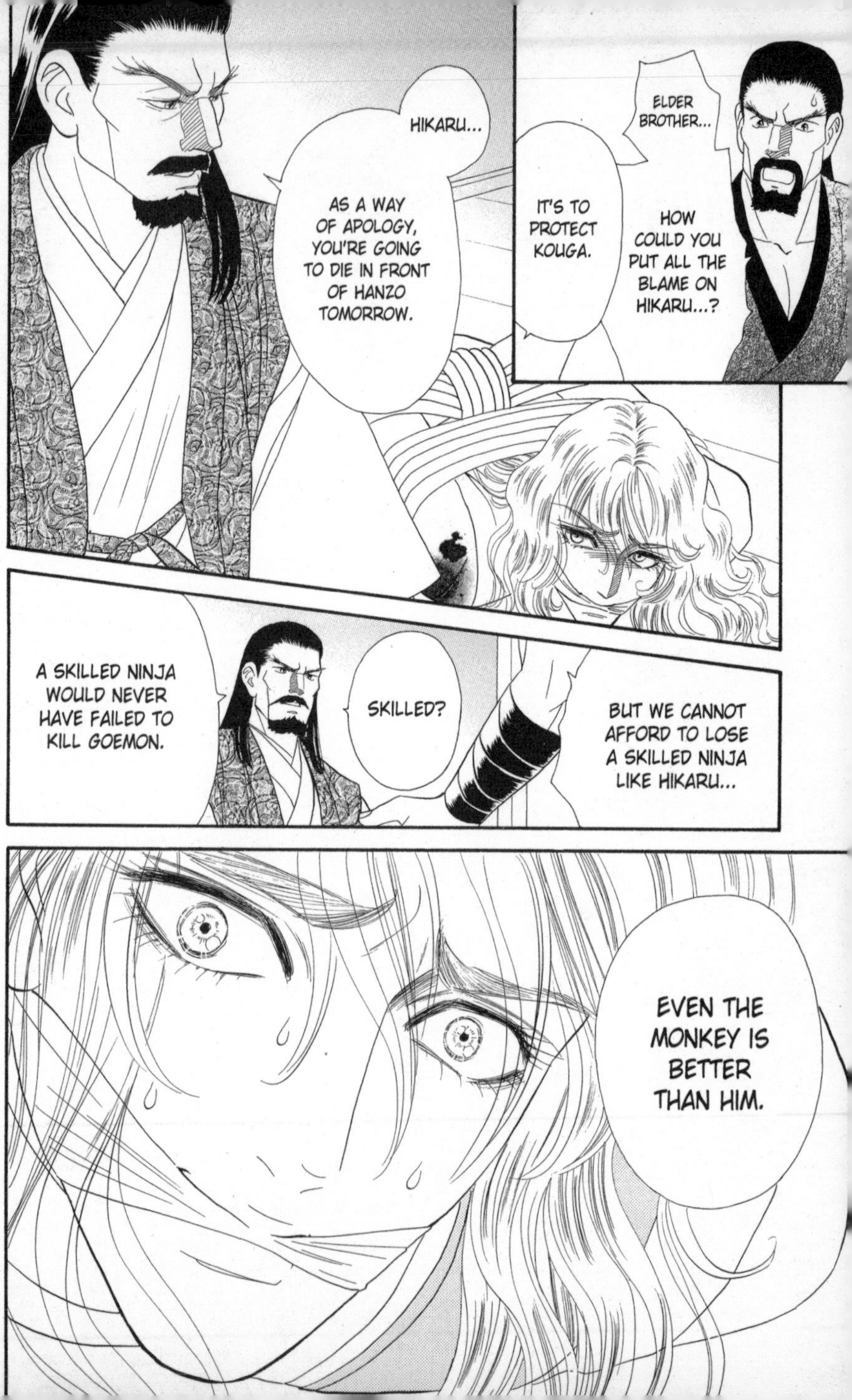
ELDER BROTHER...
HOW COULD YOU PUT ALL THE BLAME ON HIKARU...?
IT'S TO PROTECT KOUGA.
HIKARU...
AS A WAY OF APOLOGY, YOU'RE GOING TO DIE IN FRONT OF HANZO TOMORROW.
BUT WE CANNOT AFFORD TO LOSE A SKILLED NINJA LIKE HIKARU...
SKILLED?
A SKILLED NINJA WOULD NEVER HAVE FAILED TO KILL GOEMON.
EVEN THE MONKEY IS BETTER THAN HIM.

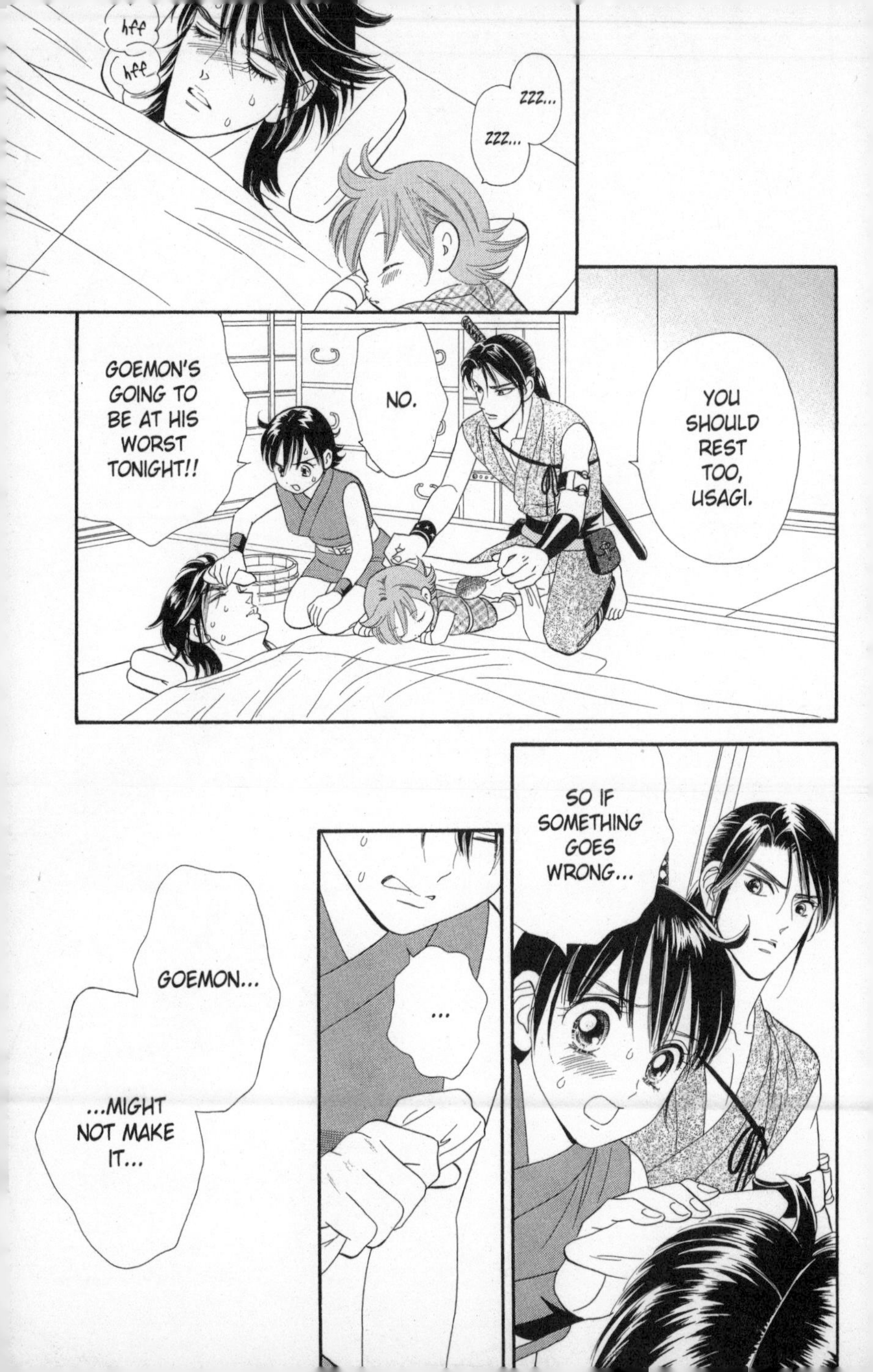
ZZZ...
ZZZ...
hff
hff
YOU SHOULD REST TOO, USAGI.
NO.
GOEMON'S GOING TO BE AT HIS WORST TONIGHT!!
SO IF SOMETHING GOES WRONG...
...
GOEMON...
...MIGHT NOT MAKE IT...

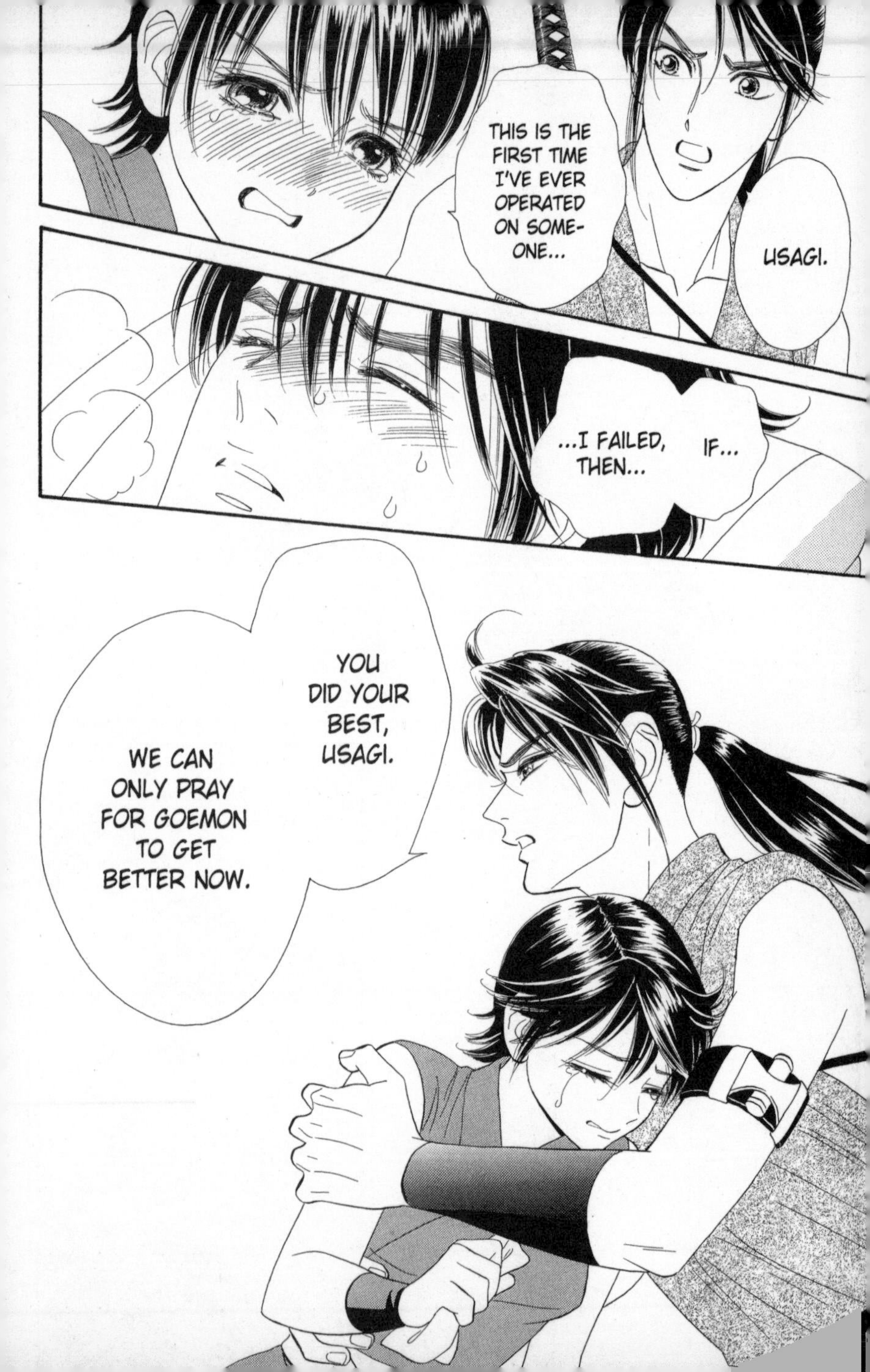
USAGI.
THIS IS THE FIRST TIME I'VE EVER OPERATED ON SOME-ONE...
IF...
...I FAILED, THEN...
YOU DID YOUR BEST, USAGI.
WE CAN ONLY PRAY FOR GOEMON TO GET BETTER NOW.

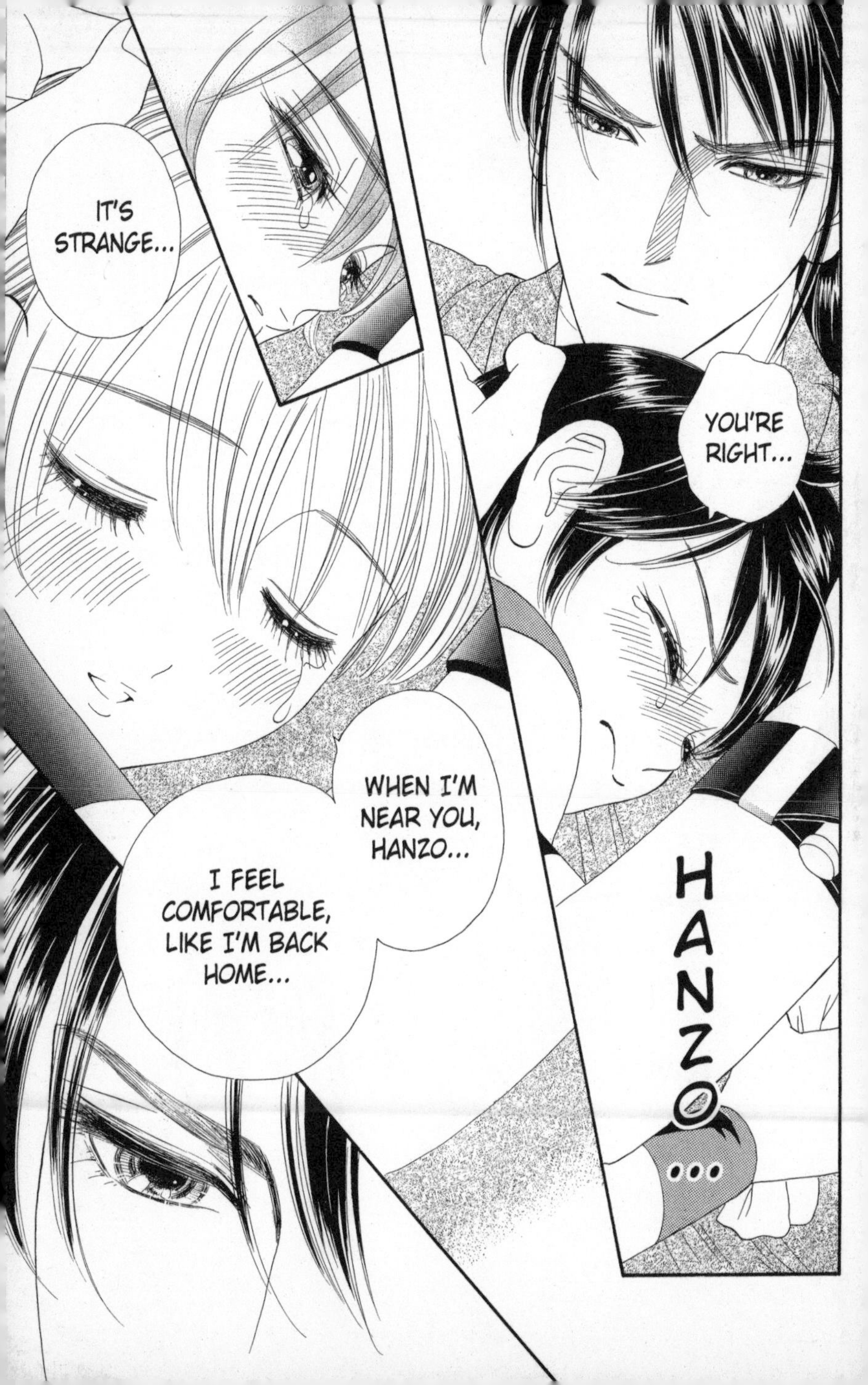
YOU'RE RIGHT...
HANZO...
IT'S STRANGE...
WHEN I'M NEAR YOU, HANZO...
I FEEL COMFORTABLE, LIKE I'M BACK HOME...

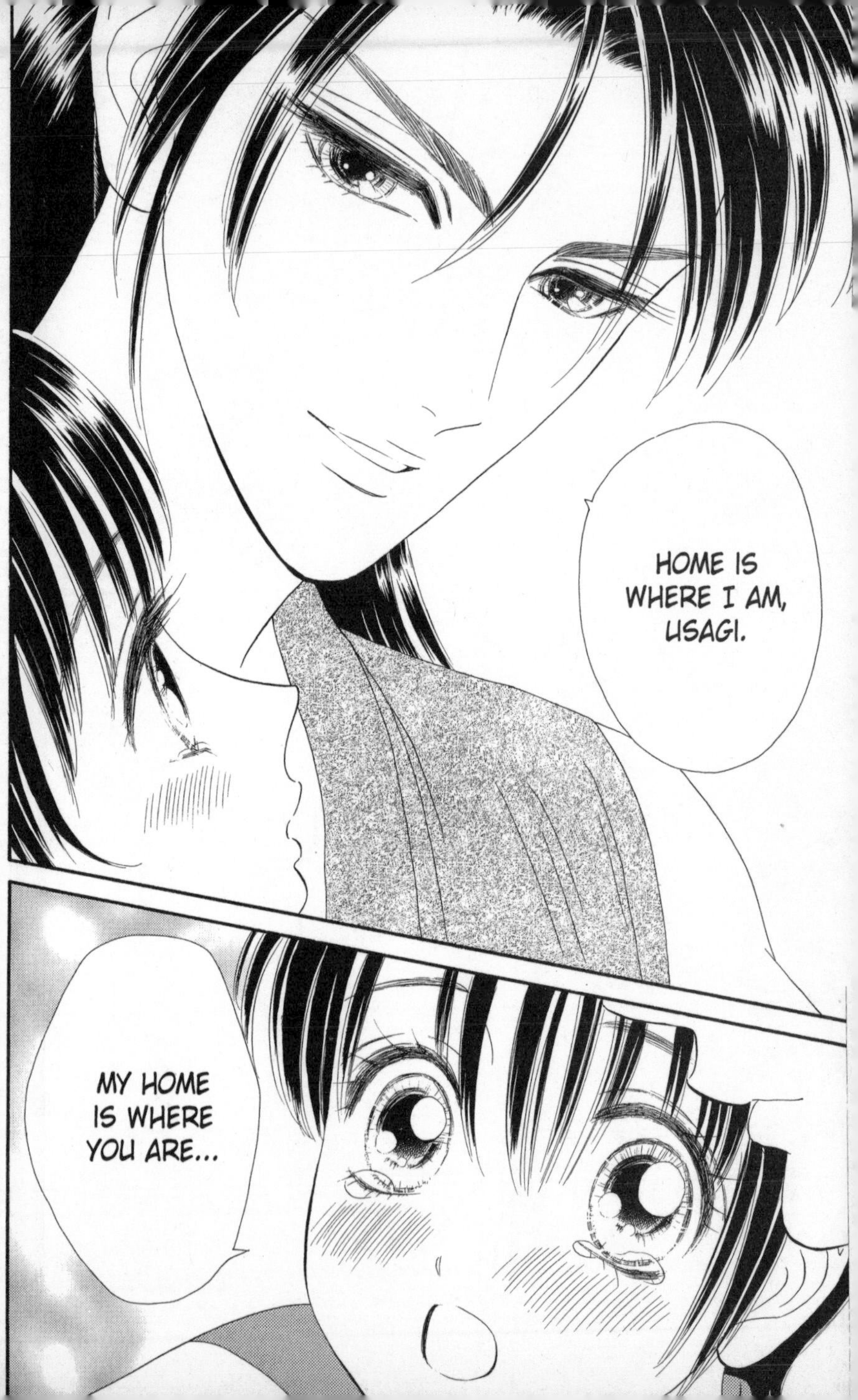
HOME IS WHERE I AM, USAGI.
MY HOME IS WHERE YOU ARE...

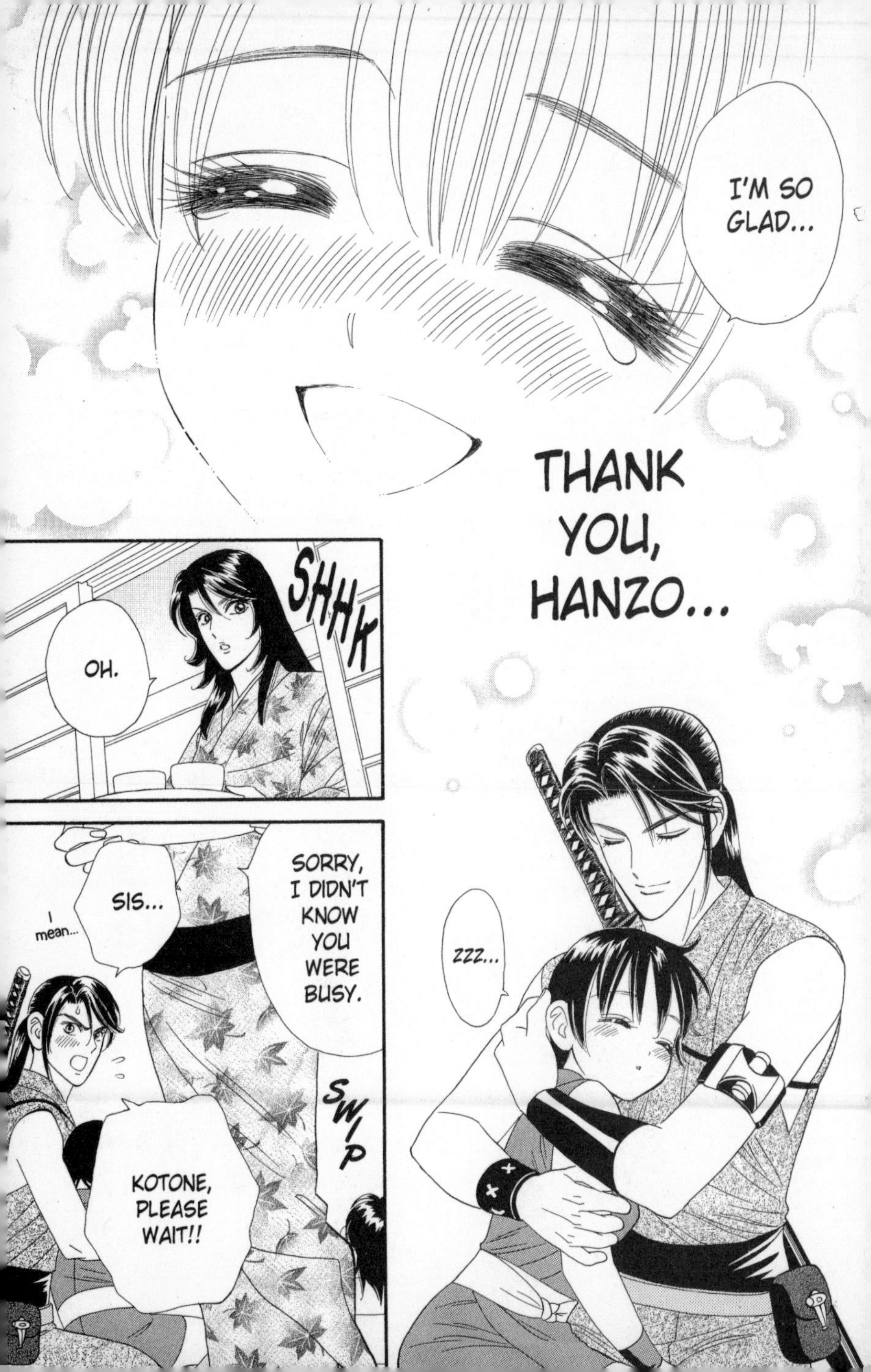
I'M SO GLAD...
THANK YOU, HANZO...
ZZZ...
SHHK
OH.
SORRY, I DIDN'T KNOW YOU WERE BUSY.
SWIP
SIS...
I mean...
KOTONE, PLEASE WAIT!!

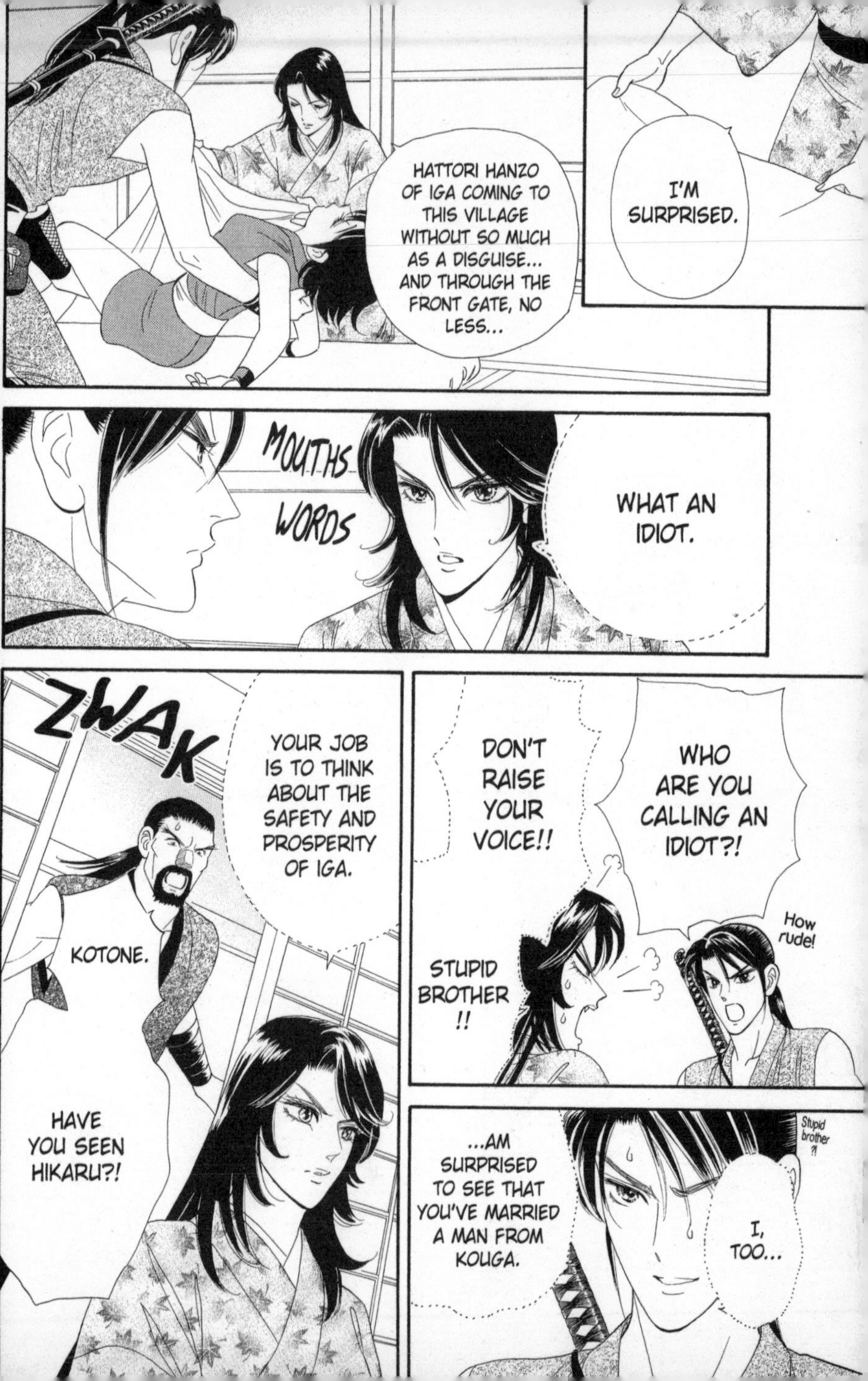
I'M SURPRISED.
HATTORI HANZO OF IGA COMING TO THIS VILLAGE WITHOUT SO MUCH AS A DISGUISE... AND THROUGH THE FRONT GATE, NO LESS...
WHAT AN IDIOT.
MOUTHS WORDS
WHO ARE YOU CALLING AN IDIOT?!
How rude!
DON'T RAISE YOUR VOICE!!
STUPID BROTHER!!
Stupid brother?!
I, TOO...
...AM SURPRISED TO SEE THAT YOU'VE MARRIED A MAN FROM KOUGA.
ZWAK
YOUR JOB IS TO THINK ABOUT THE SAFETY AND PROSPERITY OF IGA.
KOTONE.
HAVE YOU SEEN HIKARU?!

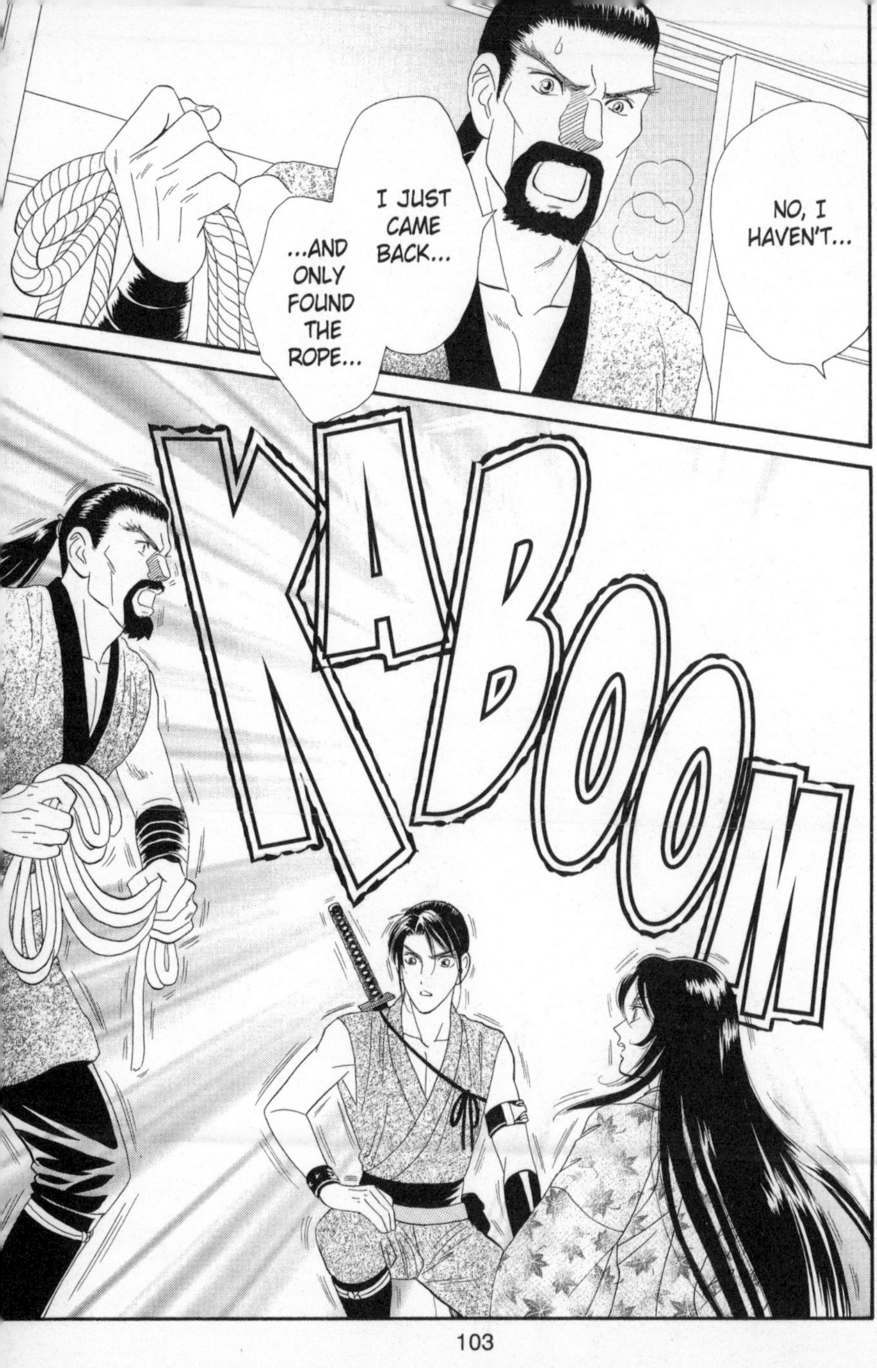
NO, I HAVEN'T...
I JUST CAME BACK...
...AND ONLY FOUND THE ROPE...
KABOOM

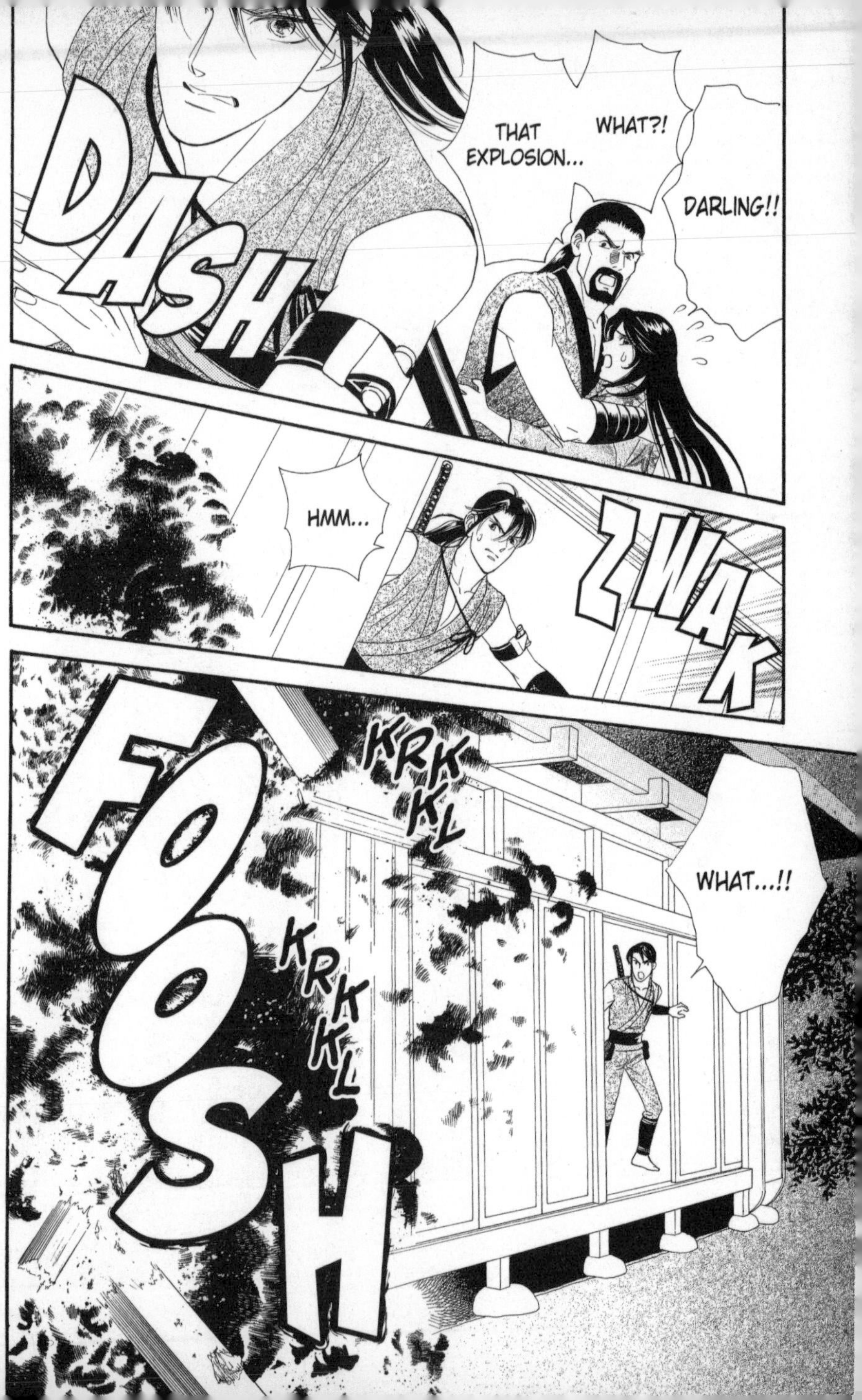
WHAT?!
THAT EXPLOSION...
DARLING!!
DASH
ZWAK
HMM...
WHAT...!!
KRK KL
KRKKL
FOOSH

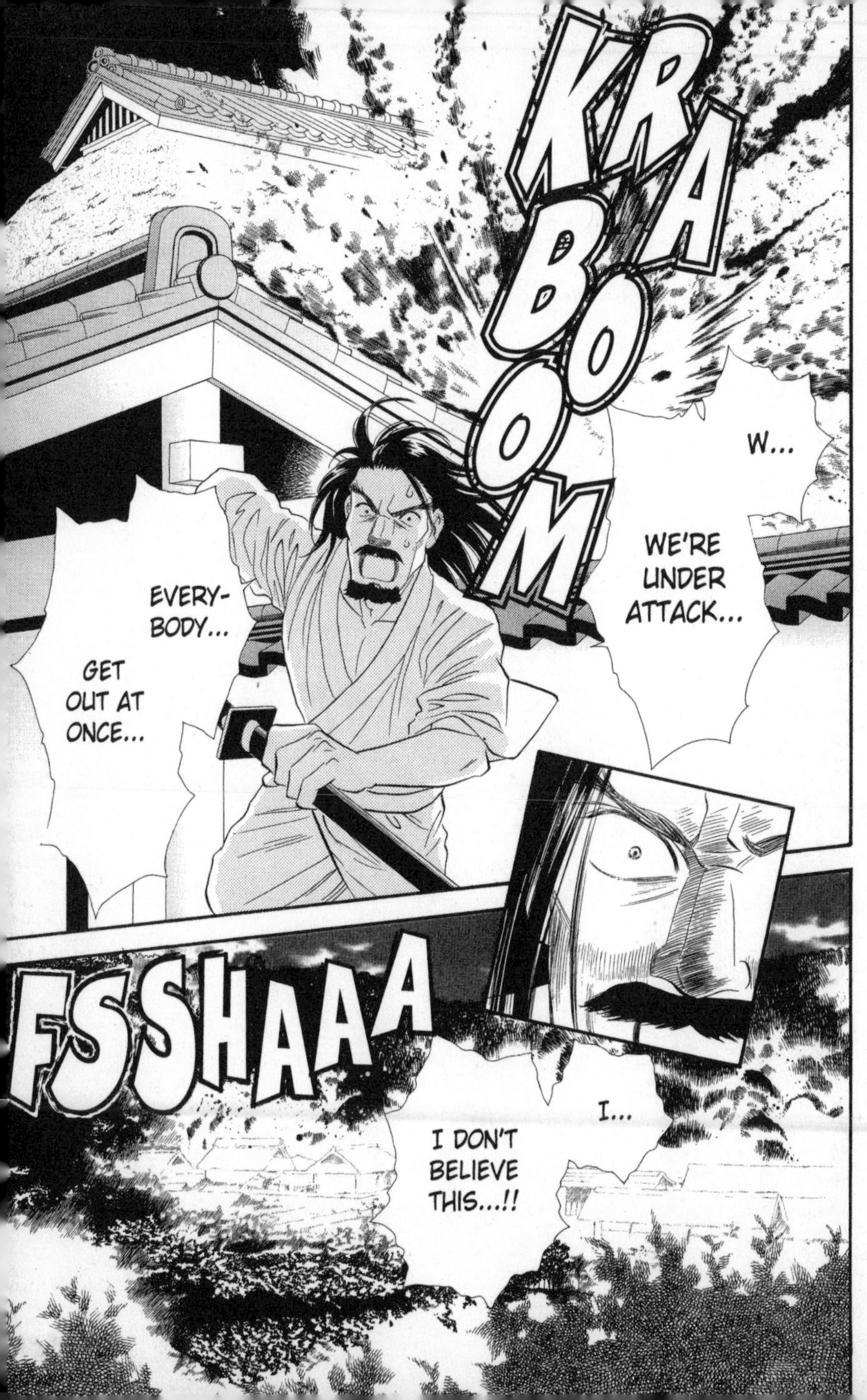
KRABOOOM
W...
WE'RE UNDER ATTACK...
EVERY-BODY...
GET OUT AT ONCE...
FSSHAAA
I...
I DON'T BELIEVE THIS...!!

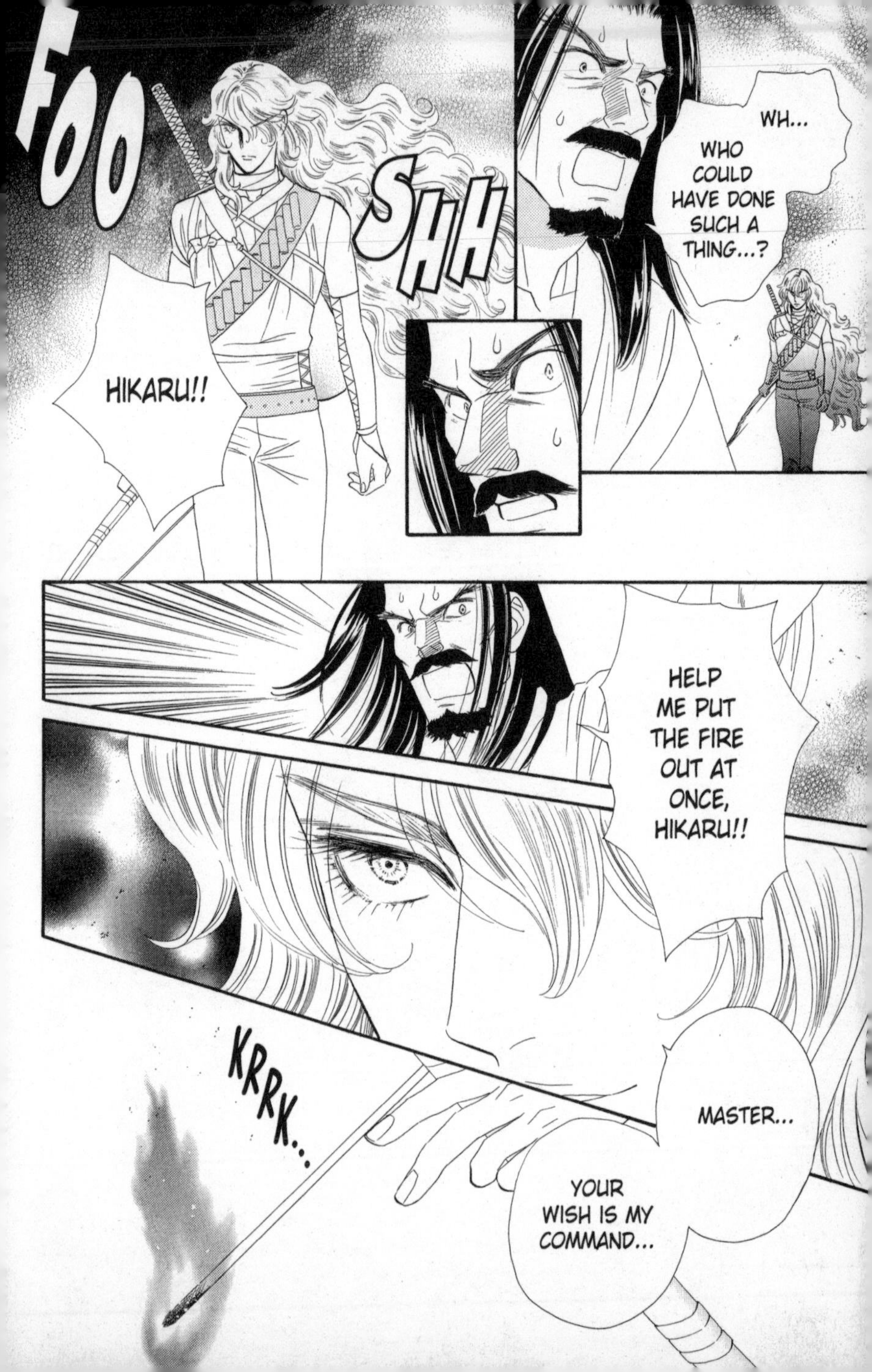
WH... WHO COULD HAVE DONE SUCH A THING...?
FOO
SHH
HIKARU!!
HELP ME PUT THE FIRE OUT AT ONCE, HIKARU!!
MASTER...
YOUR WISH IS MY COMMAND...
KRRK...

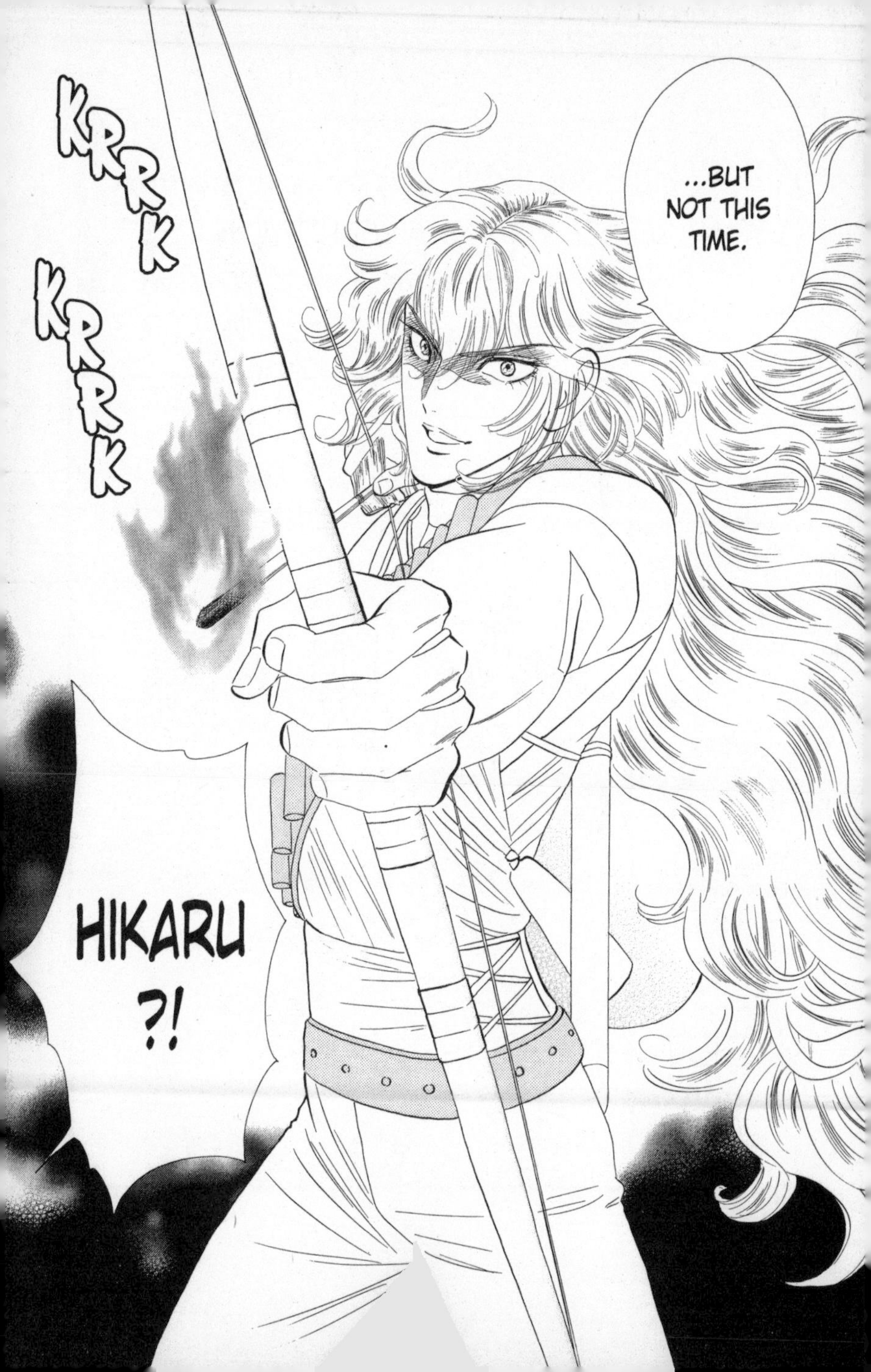
...BUT NOT THIS TIME.
KRRRK KRRRK
HIKARU ?!

TAIL OF THE MOON EXTRA: TODAY'S MISSION

"I WANT TO SEE YURI AS A BEAUTIFUL NURSE."

-GOEMON, SHIMANE PREFECTURE

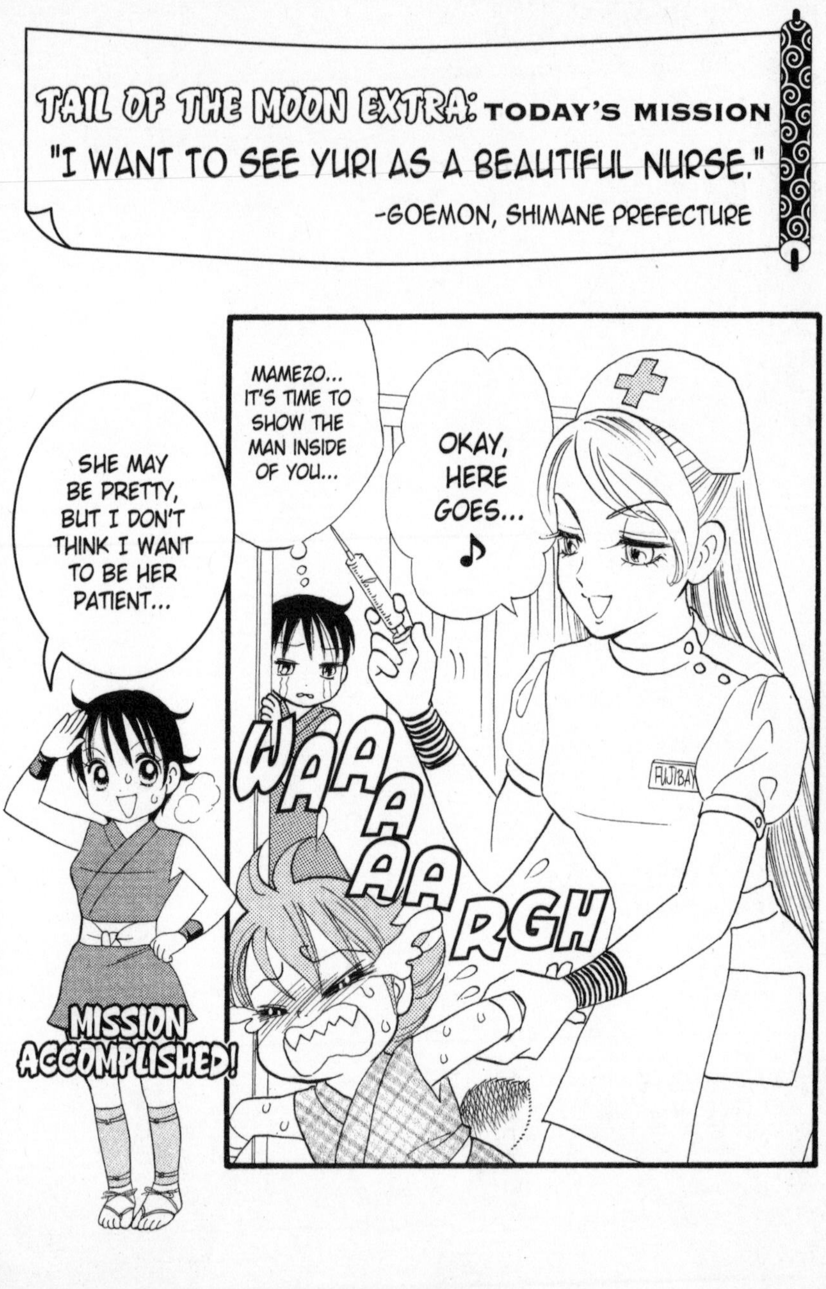
OKAY, HERE GOES... ♪
MAMEZO... IT'S TIME TO SHOW THE MAN INSIDE OF YOU...
FUJIBAY
WAAAAARGH
SHE MAY BE PRETTY, BUT I DON'T THINK I WANT TO BE HER PATIENT...
MISSION ACCOMPLISHED!

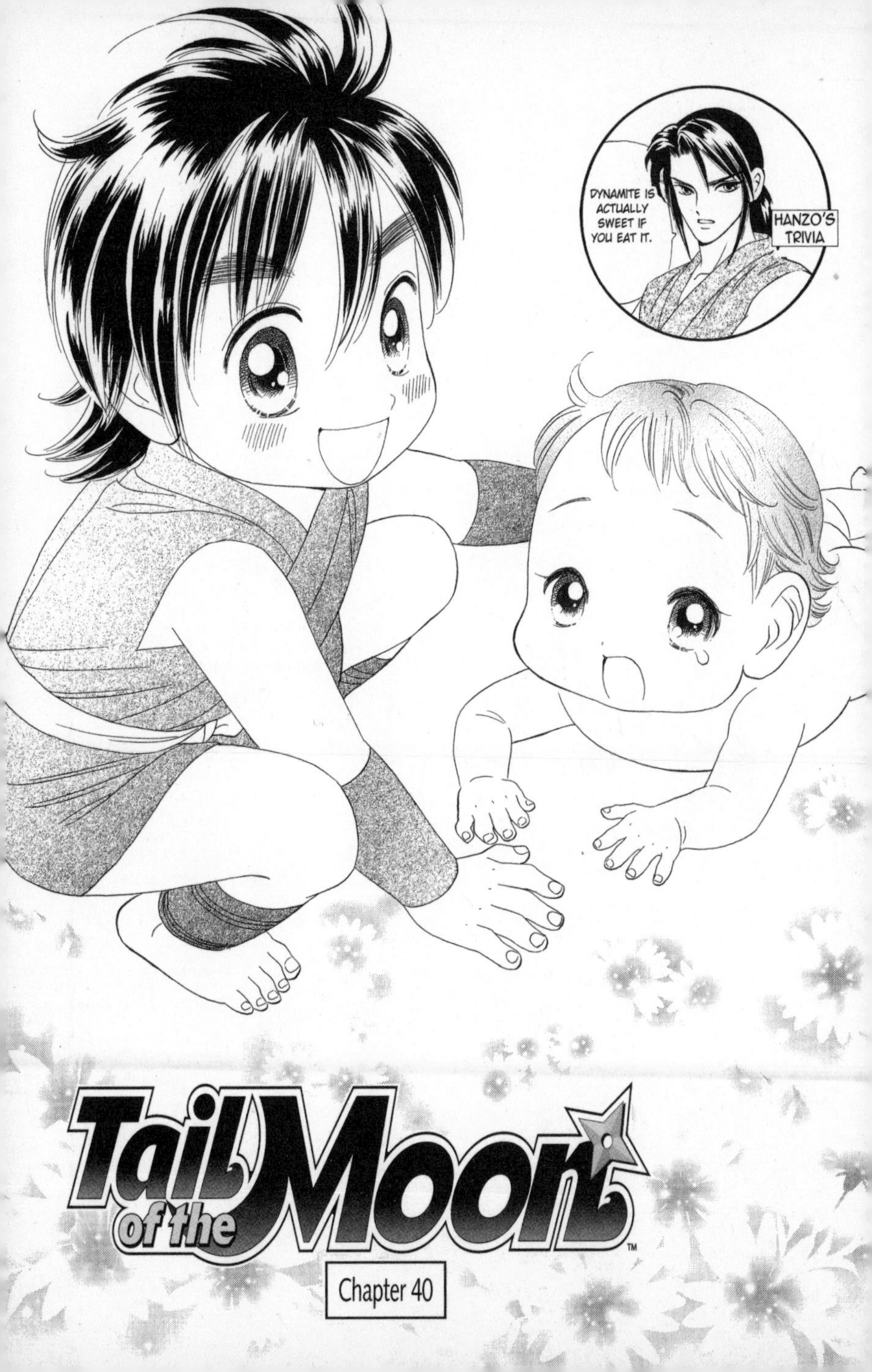

HANZO'S TRIVIA
DYNAMITE IS ACTUALLY SWEET IF YOU EAT IT.
Tail of the Moon™
Chapter 40

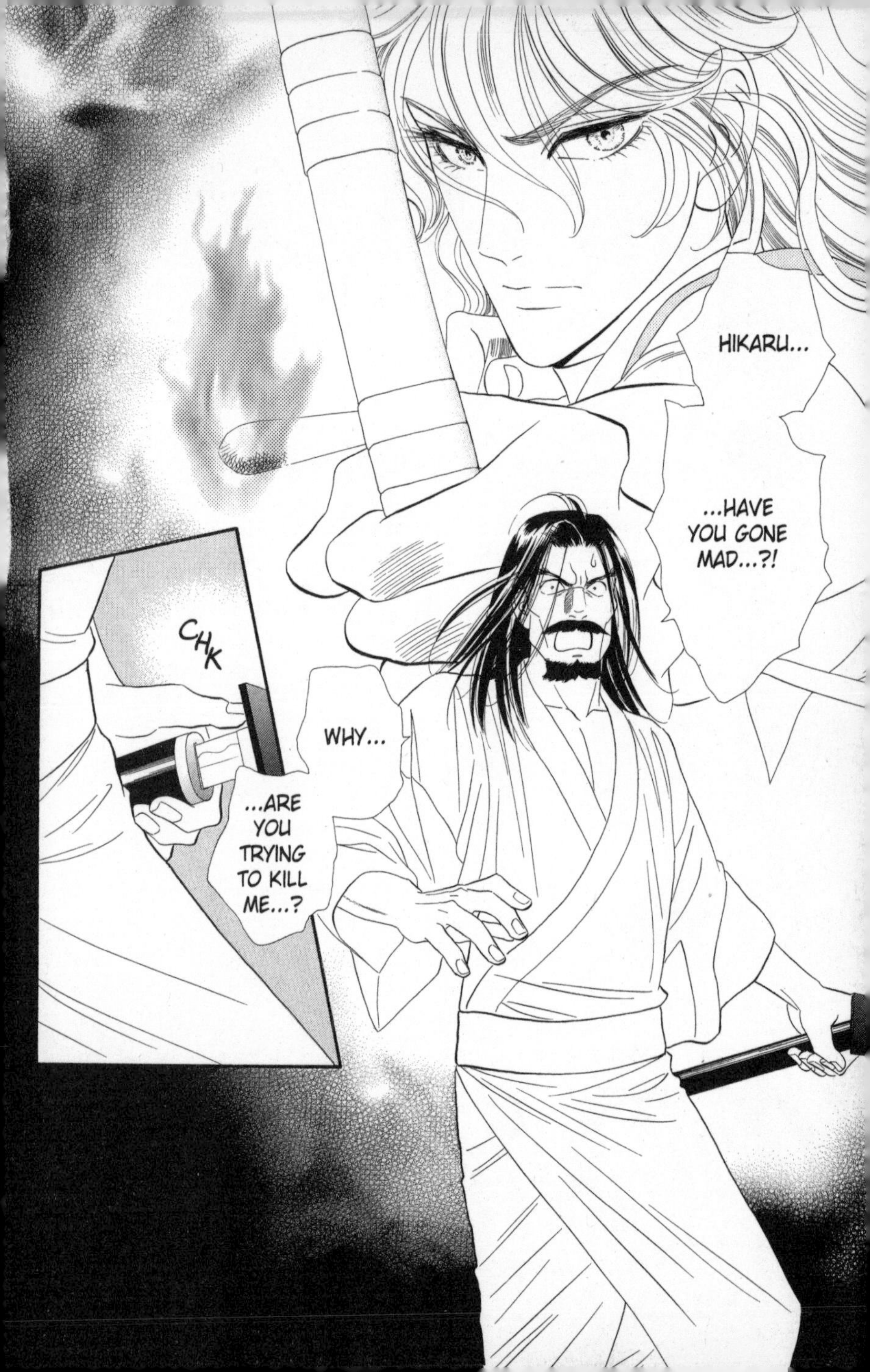
HIKARU...
...HAVE YOU GONE MAD...?!
WHY...
...ARE YOU TRYING TO KILL ME...?
CHK

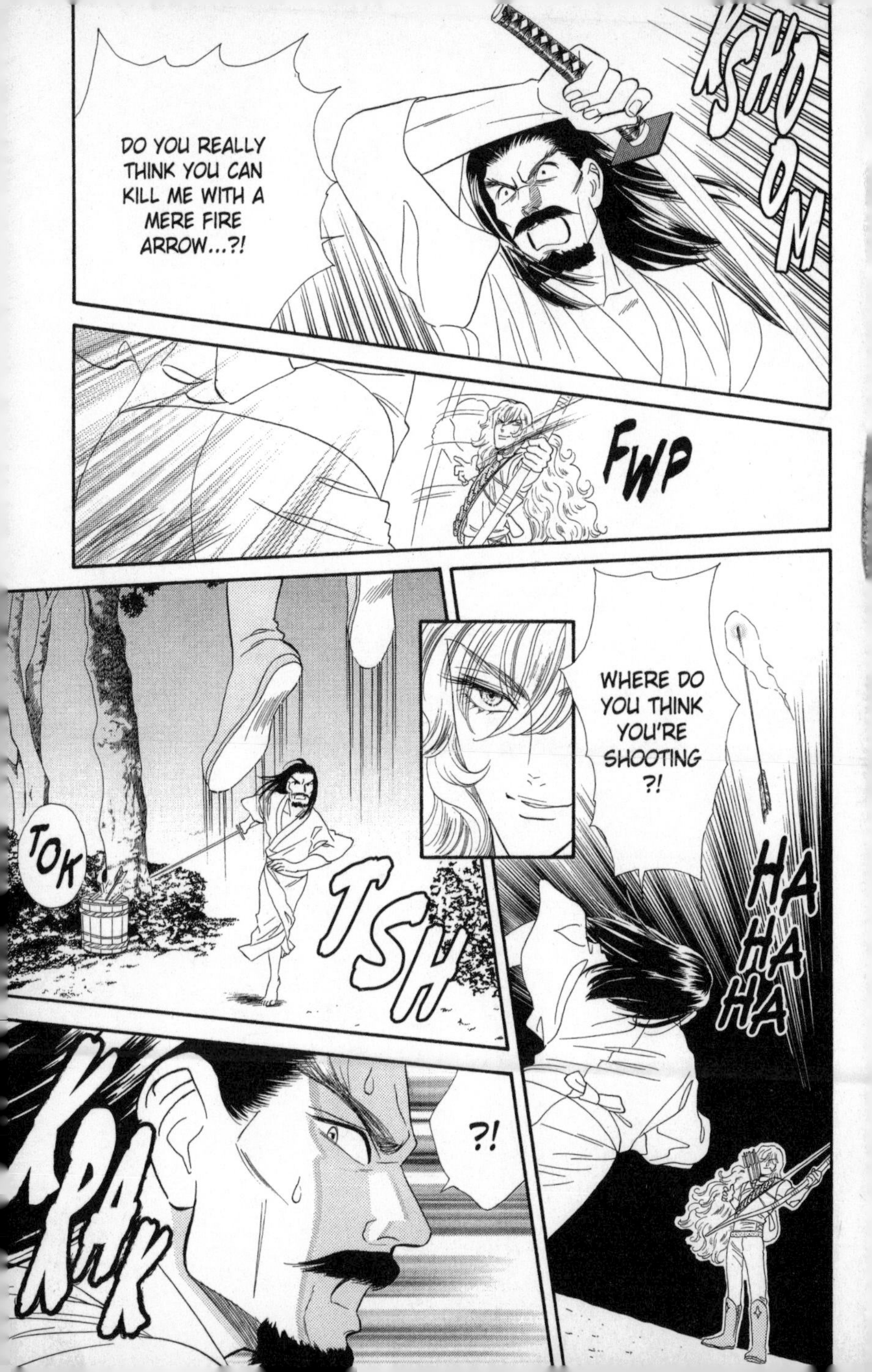
KSHOOM
DO YOU REALLY THINK YOU CAN KILL ME WITH A MERE FIRE ARROW...?!
FWP
WHERE DO YOU THINK YOU'RE SHOOTING ?!
HA HA HA HA
TSH
TOK
?!
KPAK

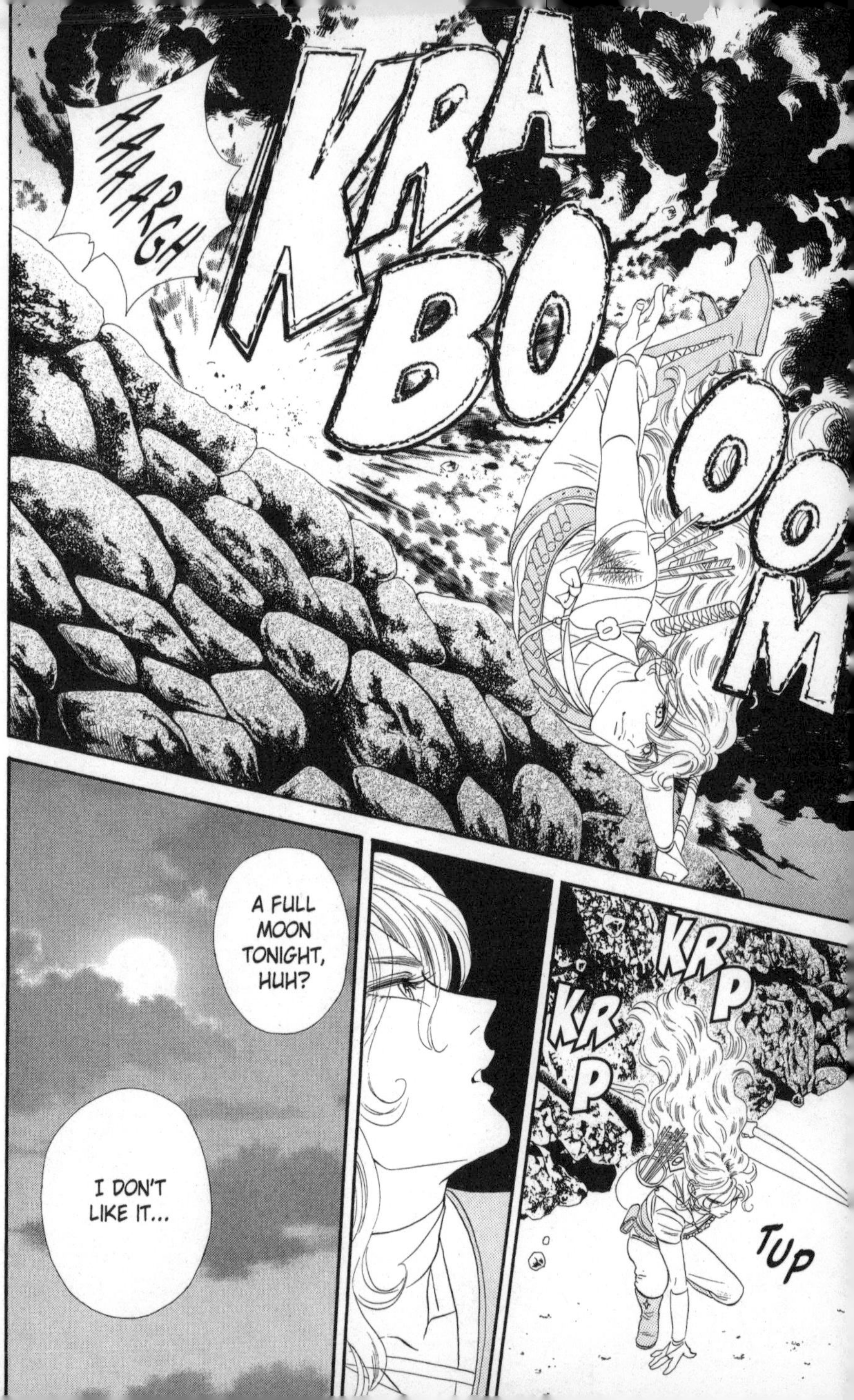
KRABOOOM
AAAARGH
KRP
KRP
TUP
A FULL MOON TONIGHT, HUH?
I DON'T LIKE IT...

UE-RIN'S WAY OF THE MANGA ④

Then came the painting tools... Since I lived in the countryside of Nara, I had no idea where I could buy paper and dip pens. I asked my art teacher about it and spent what little I had to buy the minimum necessities to draw manga.

(Kent paper, pen holder, pen nib)

For those who want to draw manga but don't know where to buy materials, you should ask your art teacher.

As I wondered whether to apply to *Ribon* or *Margaret* (both of which I was buying back then), I noticed that *Ribon* came out once a month whereas *Margaret* came out four times a month. This meant that there was a higher chance for me on *Margaret*, and that is why I chose it. I wasn't smart, but I sure was a very calculating 8th grader.

H... how embarrassing...

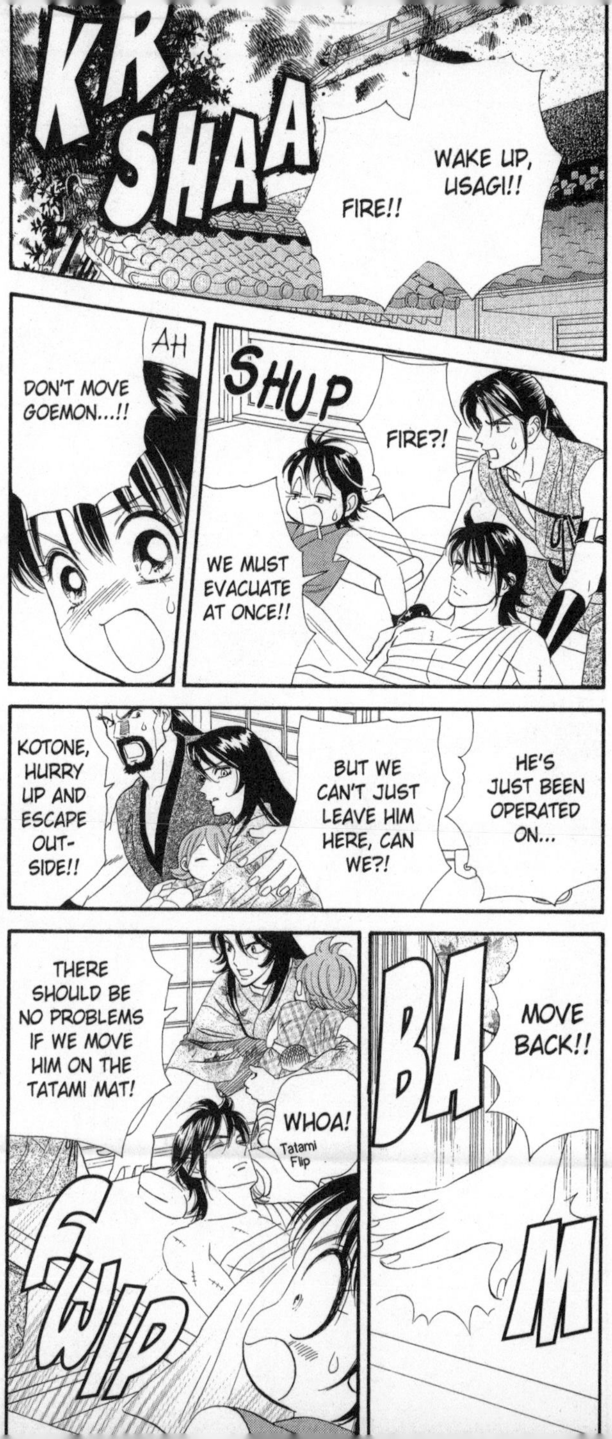
KRSHAA
WAKE UP, USAGI!!
FIRE!!
SHUP
FIRE?!
WE MUST EVACUATE AT ONCE!!
AH
DON'T MOVE GOEMON...!!
HE'S JUST BEEN OPERATED ON...
BUT WE CAN'T JUST LEAVE HIM HERE, CAN WE?!
KOTONE, HURRY UP AND ESCAPE OUTSIDE!!
BAM
MOVE BACK!!
THERE SHOULD BE NO PROBLEMS IF WE MOVE HIM ON THE TATAMI MAT!
WHOA!
Tatami Flip
FWIP

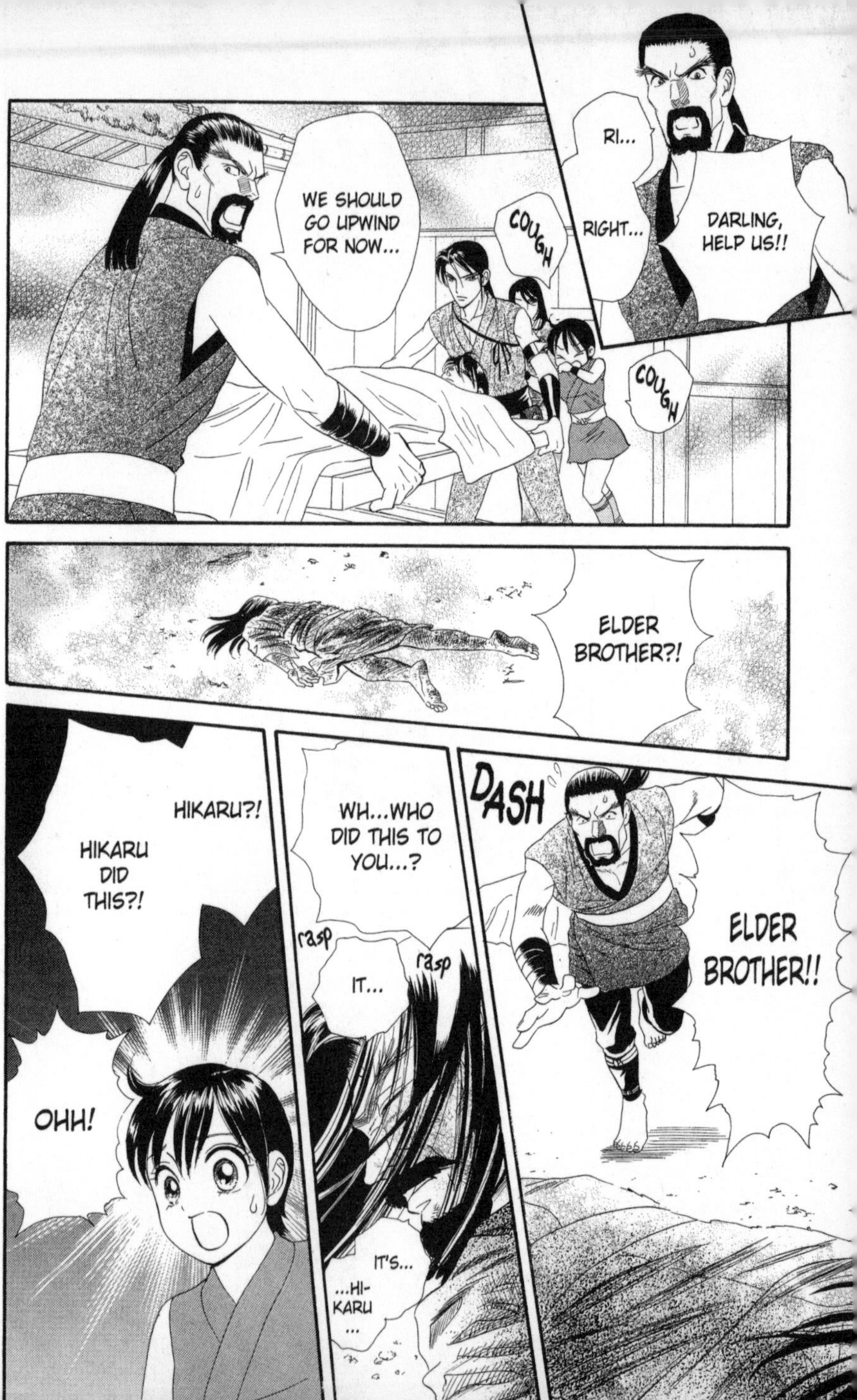
DARLING, HELP US!!
RI...
RIGHT...
WE SHOULD GO UPWIND FOR NOW...
COUGH
COUGH
ELDER BROTHER?!
DASH
ELDER BROTHER!!
WH...WHO DID THIS TO YOU...?
rasp
rasp
IT...
IT'S...
...HI-KARU...
HIKARU?!
HIKARU DID THIS?!
OHH!

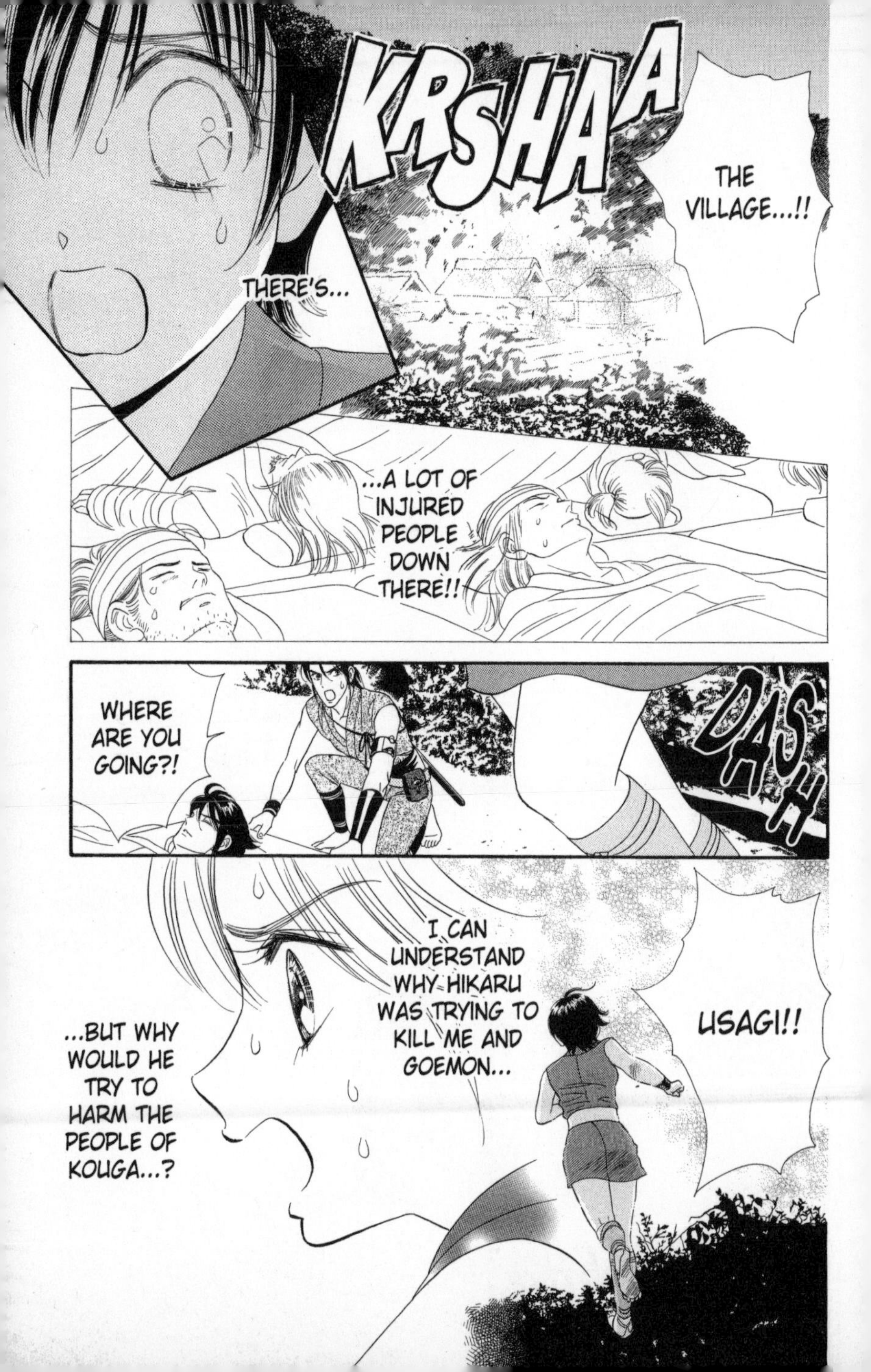
THE VILLAGE...!!
KRSHAA
THERE'S...
...A LOT OF INJURED PEOPLE DOWN THERE!!
DASH
WHERE ARE YOU GOING?!
USAGI!!
I CAN UNDERSTAND WHY HIKARU WAS TRYING TO KILL ME AND GOEMON...
...BUT WHY WOULD HE TRY TO HARM THE PEOPLE OF KOUGA...?

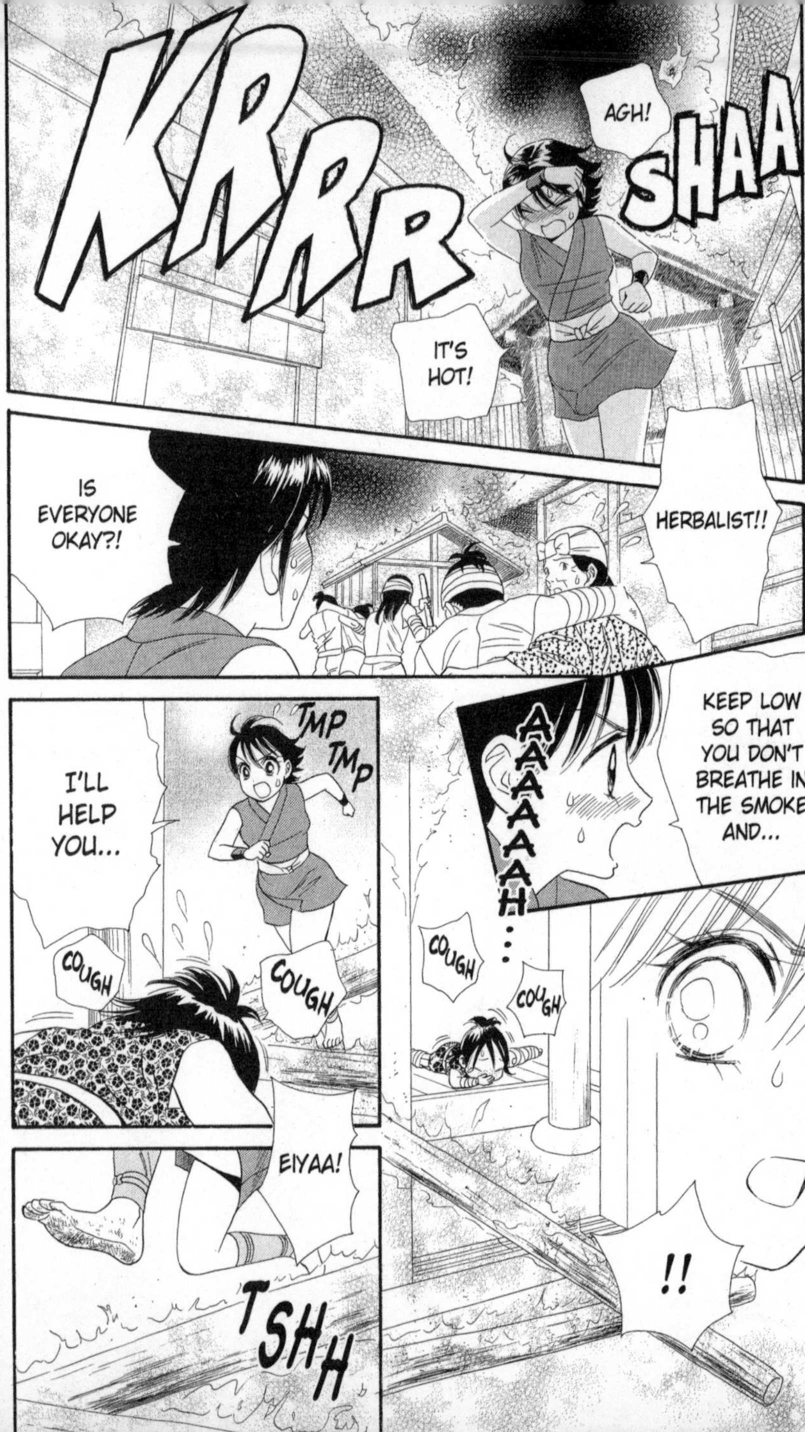
AGH!
SHAA
KRRR
IT'S HOT!
HERBALIST!!
IS EVERYONE OKAY?!
KEEP LOW SO THAT YOU DON'T BREATHE IN THE SMOKE AND...
AAAAAAAH...
COUGH
COUGH
TMP TMP
I'LL HELP YOU...
COUGH
COUGH
!!
EIYAA!
TSHH

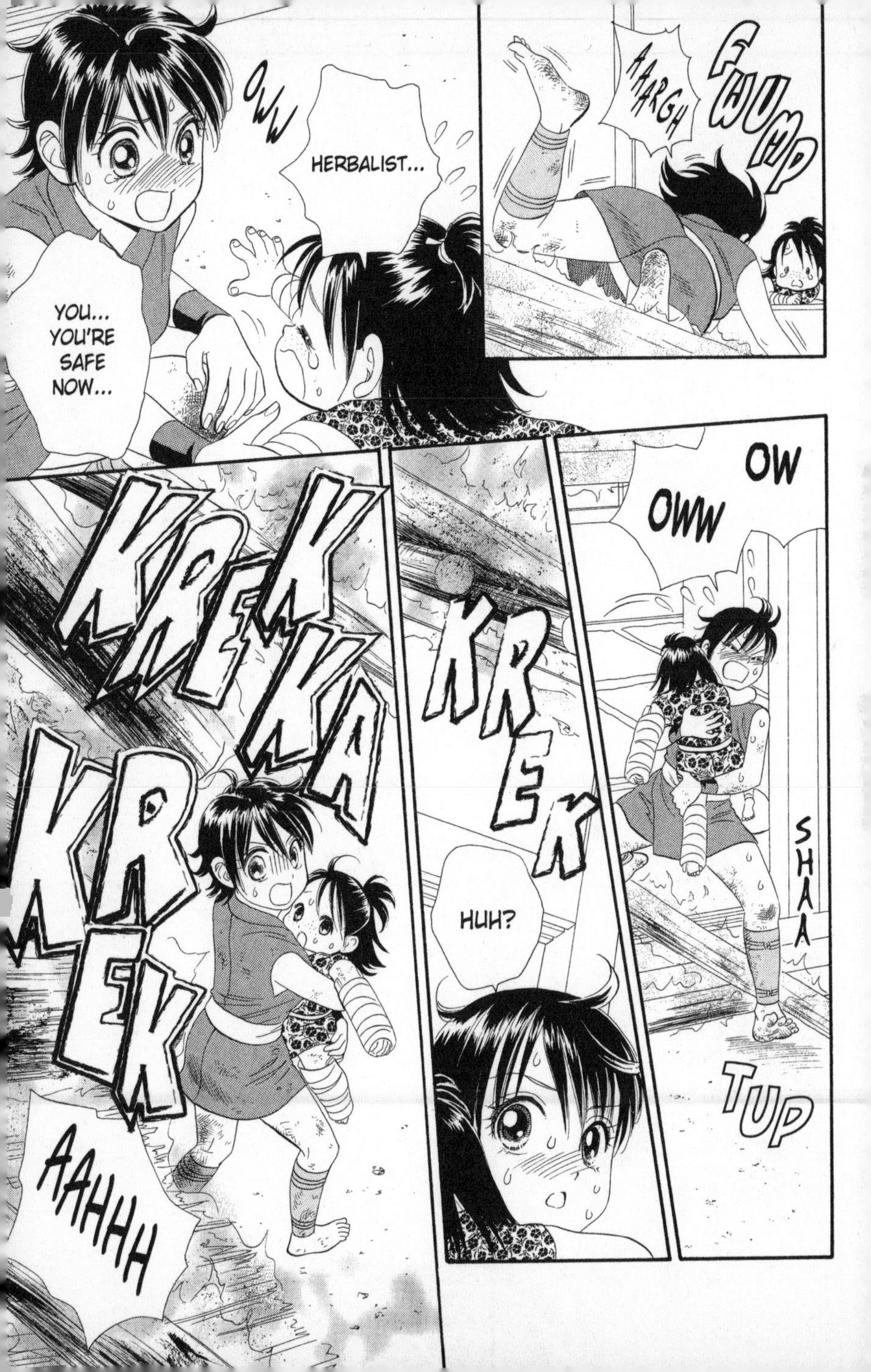
FWUMP
AAARGH
OWW
HERBALIST...
YOU... YOU'RE SAFE NOW...
OW
OWW
SHAA
TUP
KREK
HUH?
KREKA
KREK
AAHHH

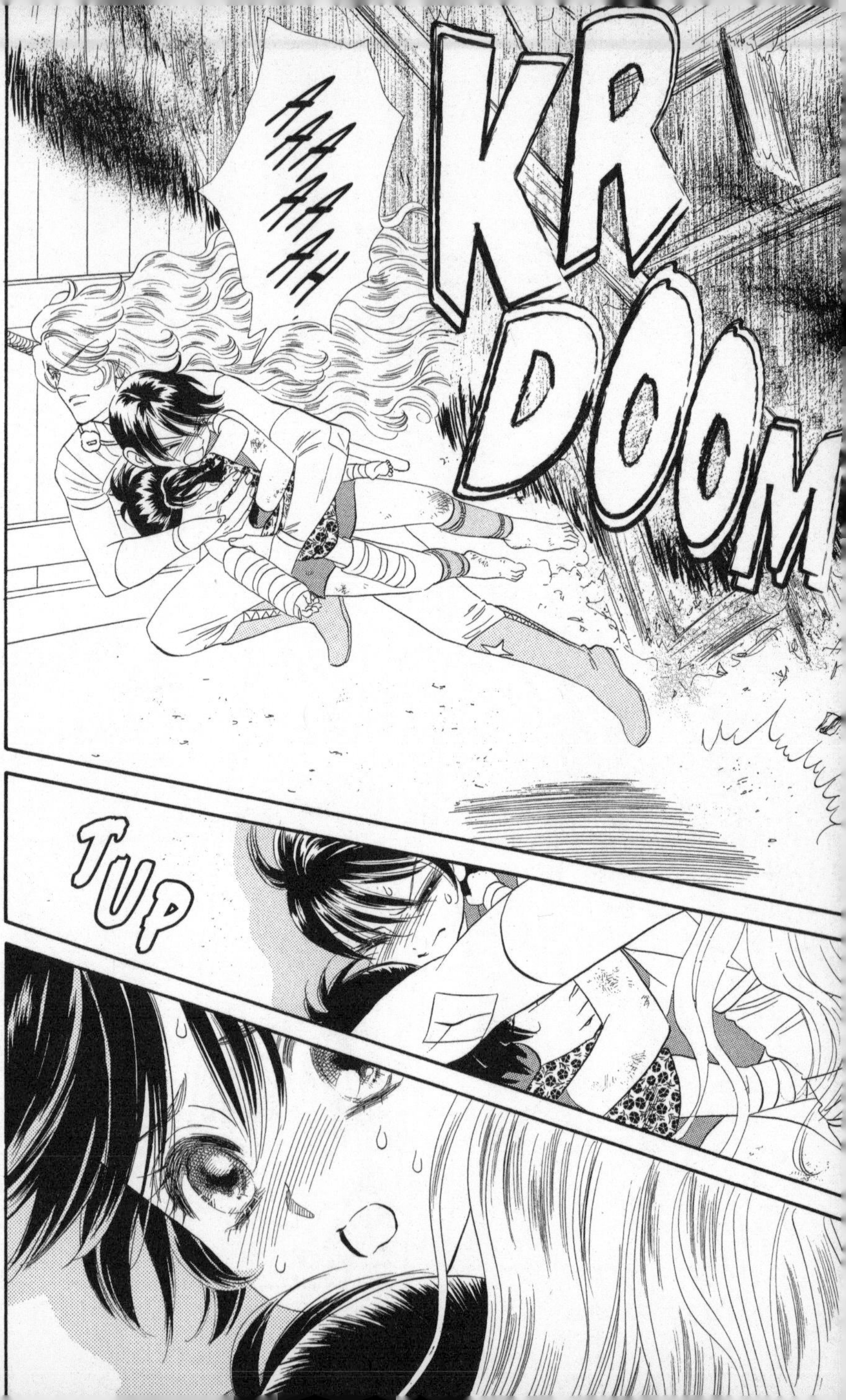
KR DOOM
AAAAAAAAH
TUP

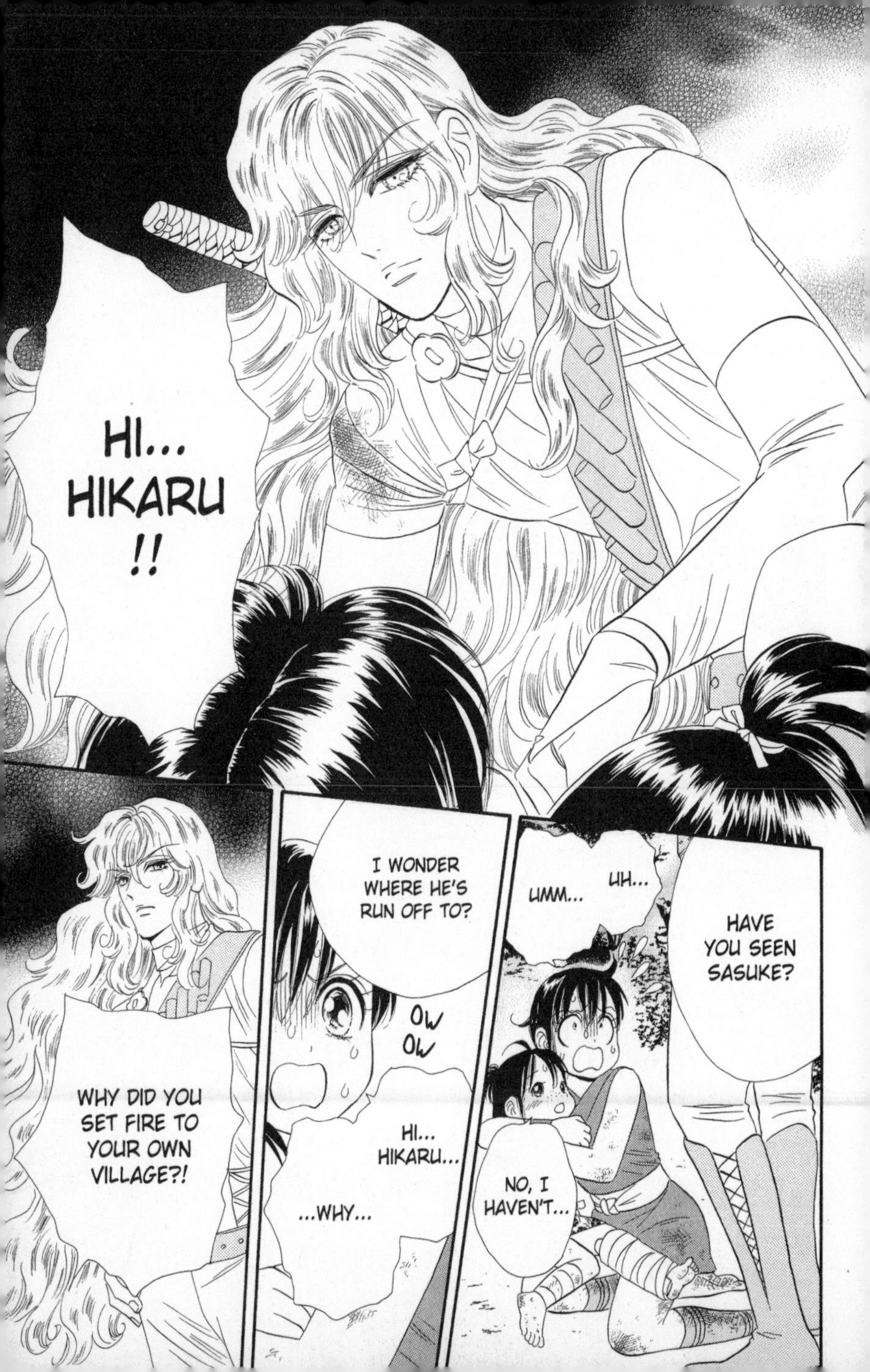

HI... HIKARU !!
HAVE YOU SEEN SASUKE?
UH...
UMM...
NO, I HAVEN'T...
I WONDER WHERE HE'S RUN OFF TO?
OW OW
HI... HIKARU...
...WHY...
WHY DID YOU SET FIRE TO YOUR OWN VILLAGE?!

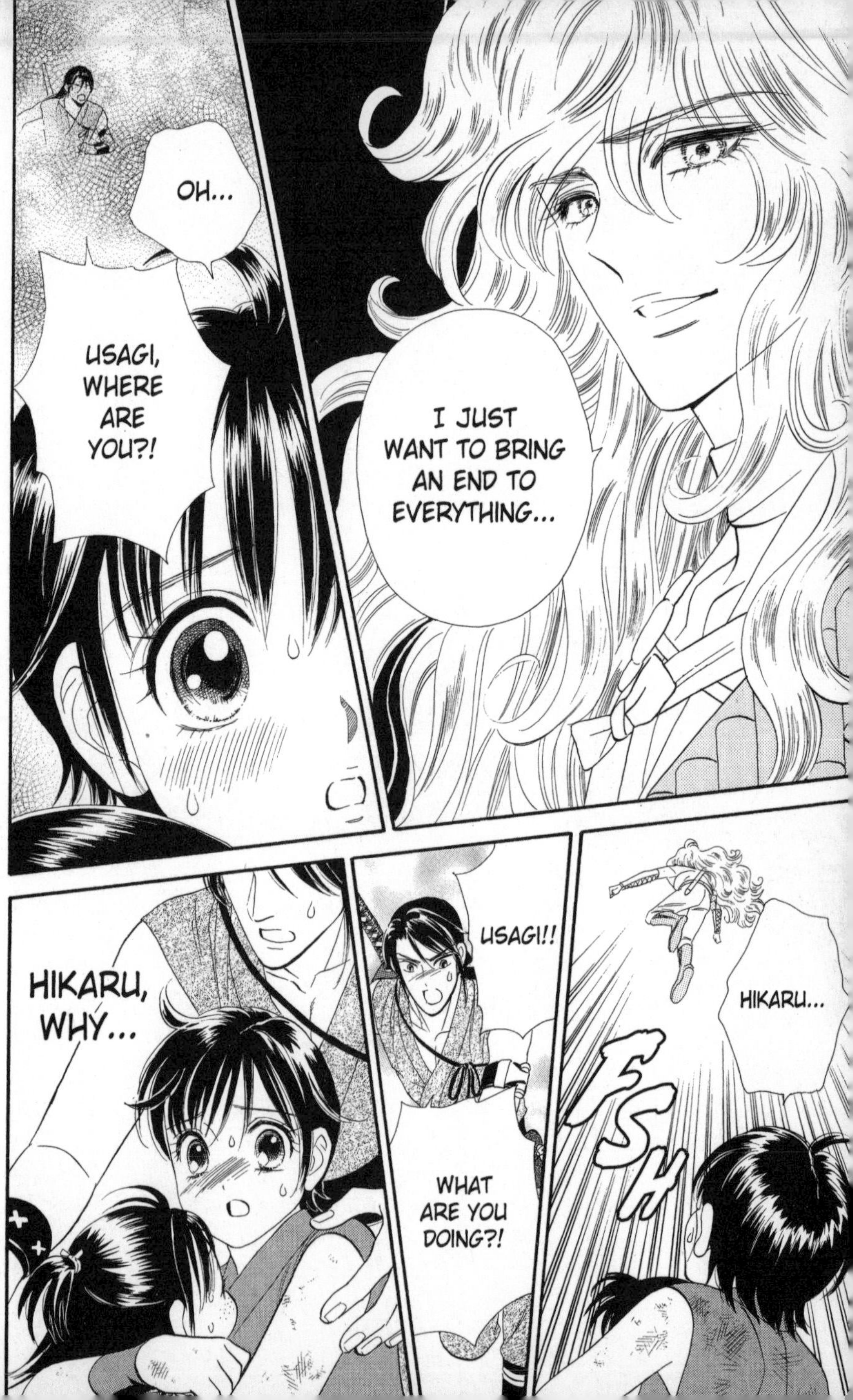
I JUST WANT TO BRING AN END TO EVERYTHING...
OH...
USAGI, WHERE ARE YOU?!
HIKARU...
FSH
USAGI!!
WHAT ARE YOU DOING?!
HIKARU, WHY...

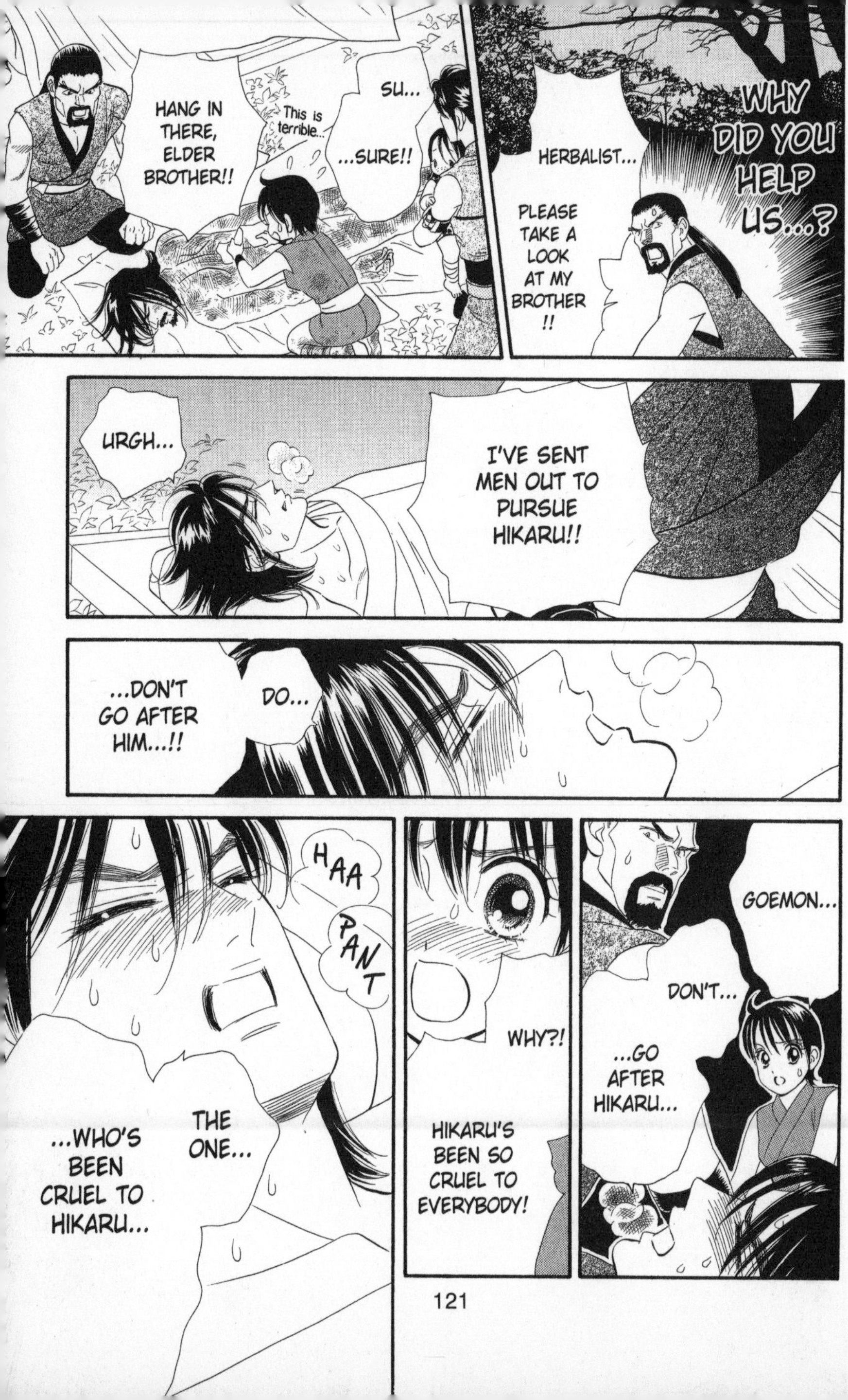
WHY DID YOU HELP US...?
HERBALIST...
PLEASE TAKE A LOOK AT MY BROTHER !!
SU...
...SURE!!
This is terrible...
HANG IN THERE, ELDER BROTHER!!
I'VE SENT MEN OUT TO PURSUE HIKARU!!
URGH...
DO...
...DON'T GO AFTER HIM...!!
GOEMON...
DON'T...
...GO AFTER HIKARU...
WHY?!
HIKARU'S BEEN SO CRUEL TO EVERYBODY!
HAA
PANT
THE ONE...
...WHO'S BEEN CRUEL TO HIKARU...

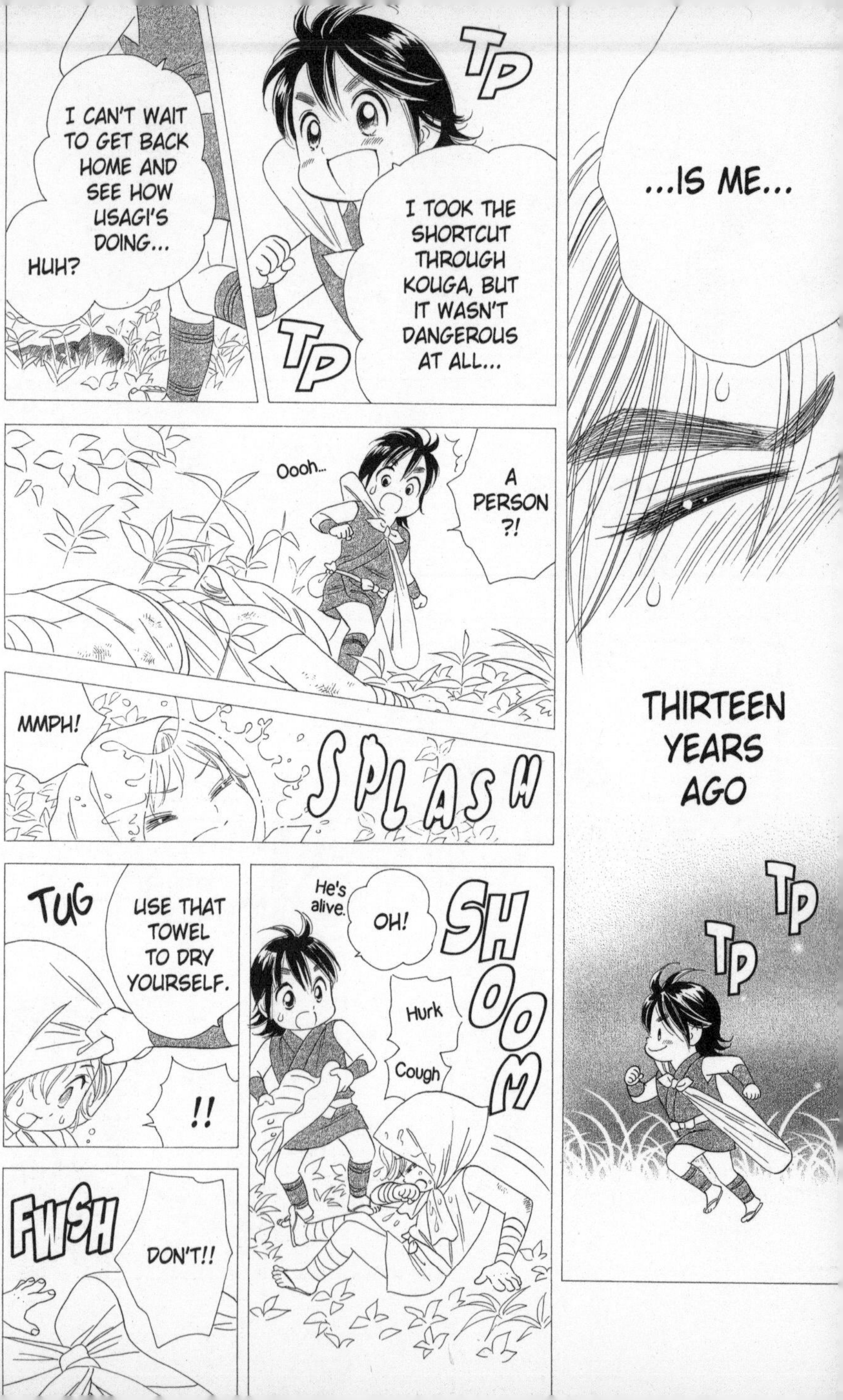
...IS ME...
THIRTEEN YEARS AGO
TP
TP
TP
I TOOK THE SHORTCUT THROUGH KOUGA, BUT IT WASN'T DANGEROUS AT ALL...
TP
I CAN'T WAIT TO GET BACK HOME AND SEE HOW USAGI'S DOING...
HUH?
A PERSON ?!
Oooh...
SPLASH
MMPH!
SHOOOM
OH!
He's alive.
Hurk
Cough
TUG
USE THAT TOWEL TO DRY YOURSELF.
!!
DON'T!!
FWSH

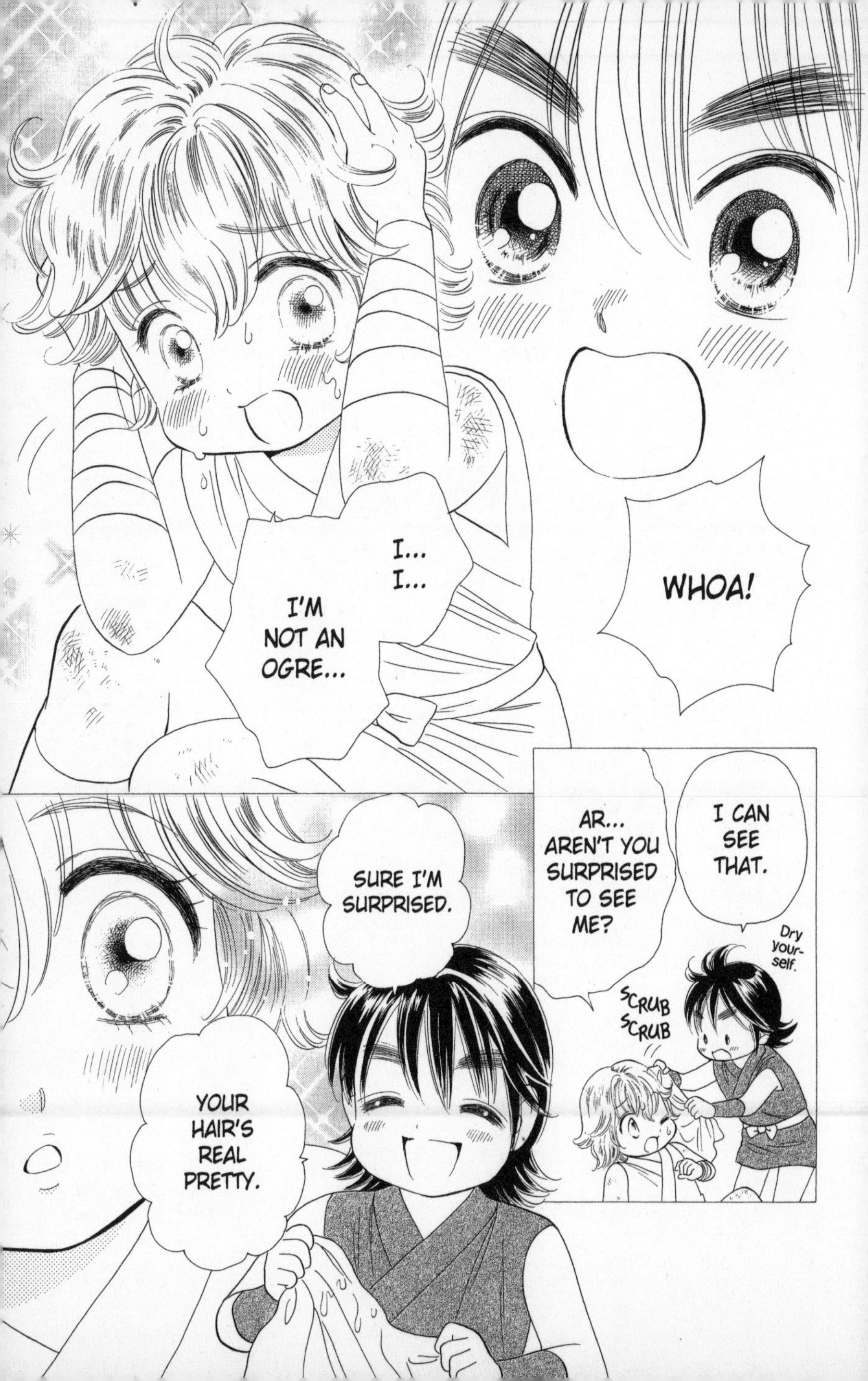
WHOA!
I... I...
I'M NOT AN OGRE...
I CAN SEE THAT.
AR... AREN'T YOU SURPRISED TO SEE ME?
Dry your-self.
SCRUB SCRUB
SURE I'M SURPRISED.
YOUR HAIR'S REAL PRETTY.

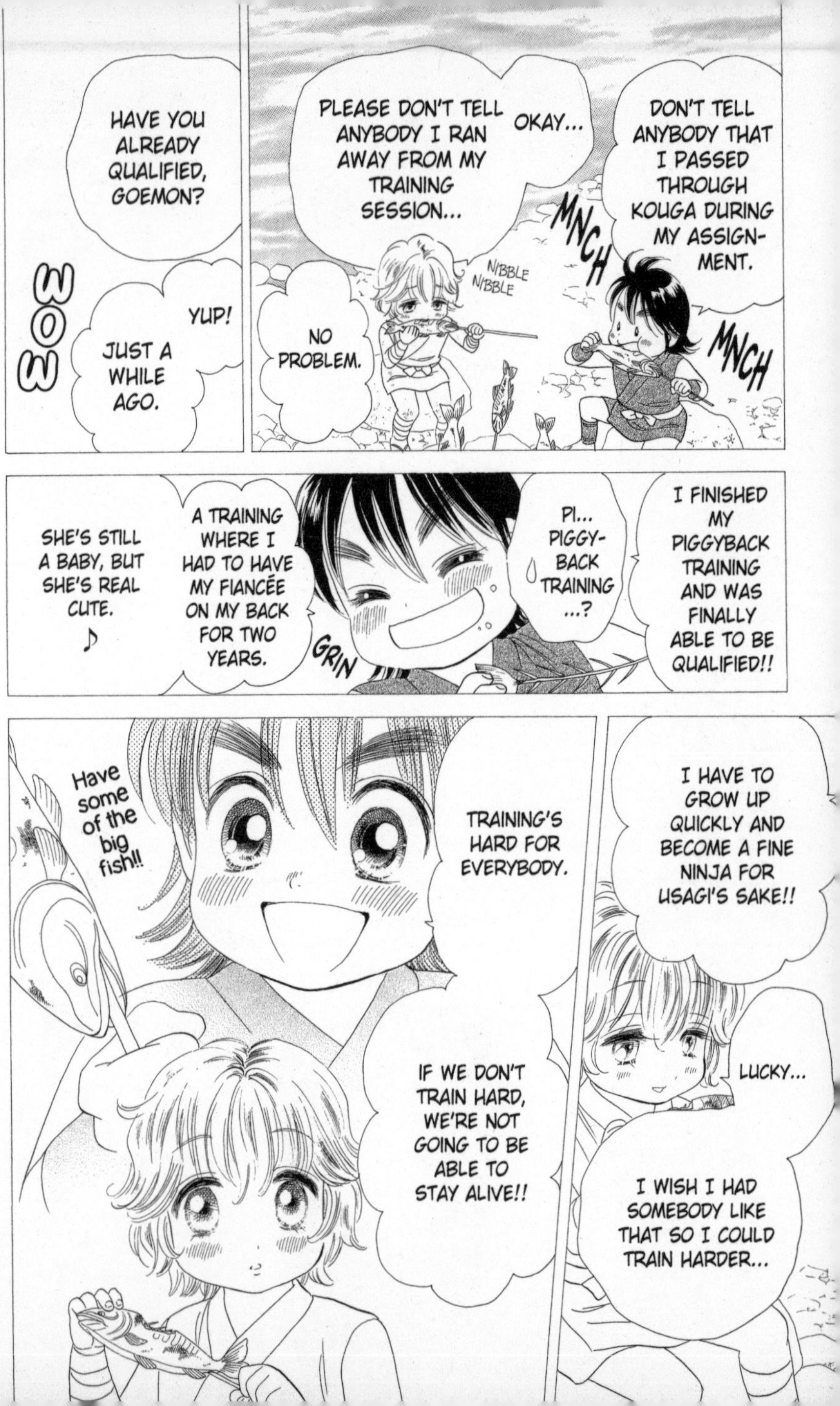
DON'T TELL ANYBODY THAT I PASSED THROUGH KOUGA DURING MY ASSIGN-MENT.
MNCH
MNCH
OKAY...
PLEASE DON'T TELL ANYBODY I RAN AWAY FROM MY TRAINING SESSION...
NIBBLE NIBBLE
NO PROBLEM.
HAVE YOU ALREADY QUALIFIED, GOEMON?
YUP!
JUST A WHILE AGO.
WOW
I FINISHED MY PIGGYBACK TRAINING AND WAS FINALLY ABLE TO BE QUALIFIED!!
PI... PIGGY-BACK TRAINING ...?
A TRAINING WHERE I HAD TO HAVE MY FIANCÉE ON MY BACK FOR TWO YEARS.
GRIN
SHE'S STILL A BABY, BUT SHE'S REAL CUTE. ♪
I HAVE TO GROW UP QUICKLY AND BECOME A FINE NINJA FOR USAGI'S SAKE!!
LUCKY...
I WISH I HAD SOMEBODY LIKE THAT SO I COULD TRAIN HARDER...
TRAINING'S HARD FOR EVERYBODY.
Have some of the big fish!!
IF WE DON'T TRAIN HARD, WE'RE NOT GOING TO BE ABLE TO STAY ALIVE!!

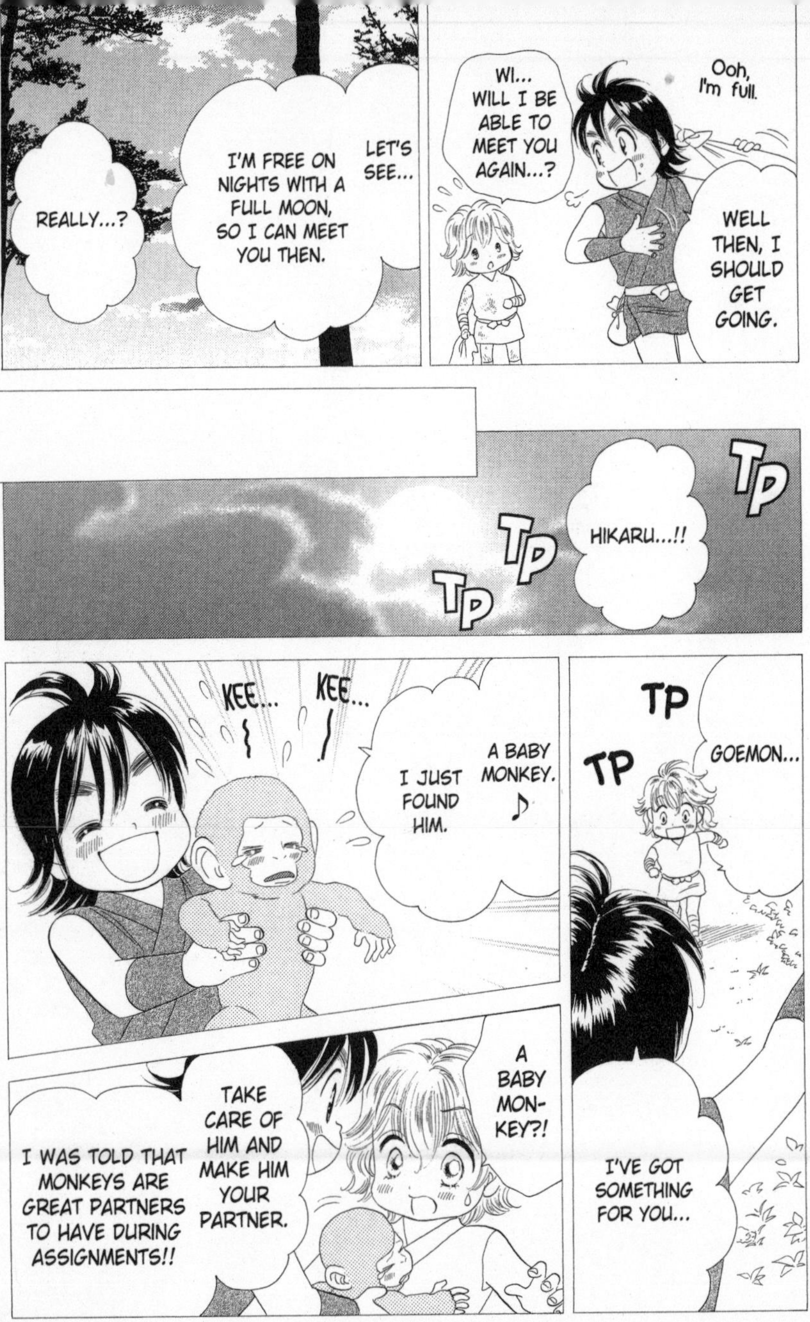
Ooh, I'm full.
WELL THEN, I SHOULD GET GOING.
WI... WILL I BE ABLE TO MEET YOU AGAIN...?
LET'S SEE...
I'M FREE ON NIGHTS WITH A FULL MOON, SO I CAN MEET YOU THEN.
REALLY...?
TP
HIKARU...!!
TP
TP
TP
TP
GOEMON...
TP
I'VE GOT SOMETHING FOR YOU...
KEE...
KEE...
A BABY MONKEY. ♪
I JUST FOUND HIM.
A BABY MON-KEY?!
TAKE CARE OF HIM AND MAKE HIM YOUR PARTNER.
I WAS TOLD THAT MONKEYS ARE GREAT PARTNERS TO HAVE DURING ASSIGNMENTS!!

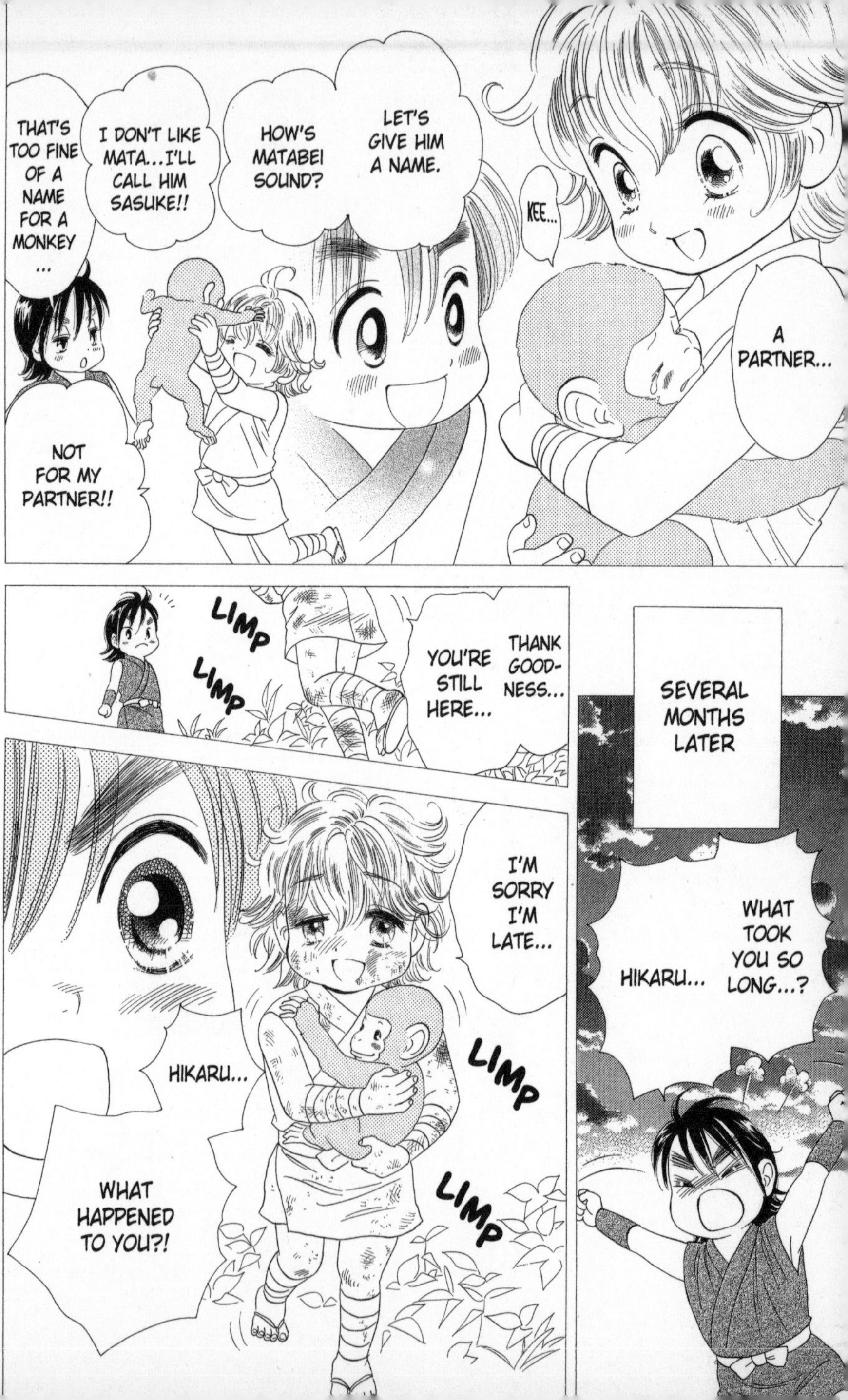
A PARTNER...
KEE...
LET'S GIVE HIM A NAME.
HOW'S MATABEI SOUND?
I DON'T LIKE MATA...I'LL CALL HIM SASUKE!!
THAT'S TOO FINE OF A NAME FOR A MONKEY ...
NOT FOR MY PARTNER!!
SEVERAL MONTHS LATER
WHAT TOOK YOU SO LONG...?
HIKARU...
THANK GOODNESS...
YOU'RE STILL HERE...
LIMP
LIMP
I'M SORRY I'M LATE...
LIMP
LIMP
HIKARU...
WHAT HAPPENED TO YOU?!

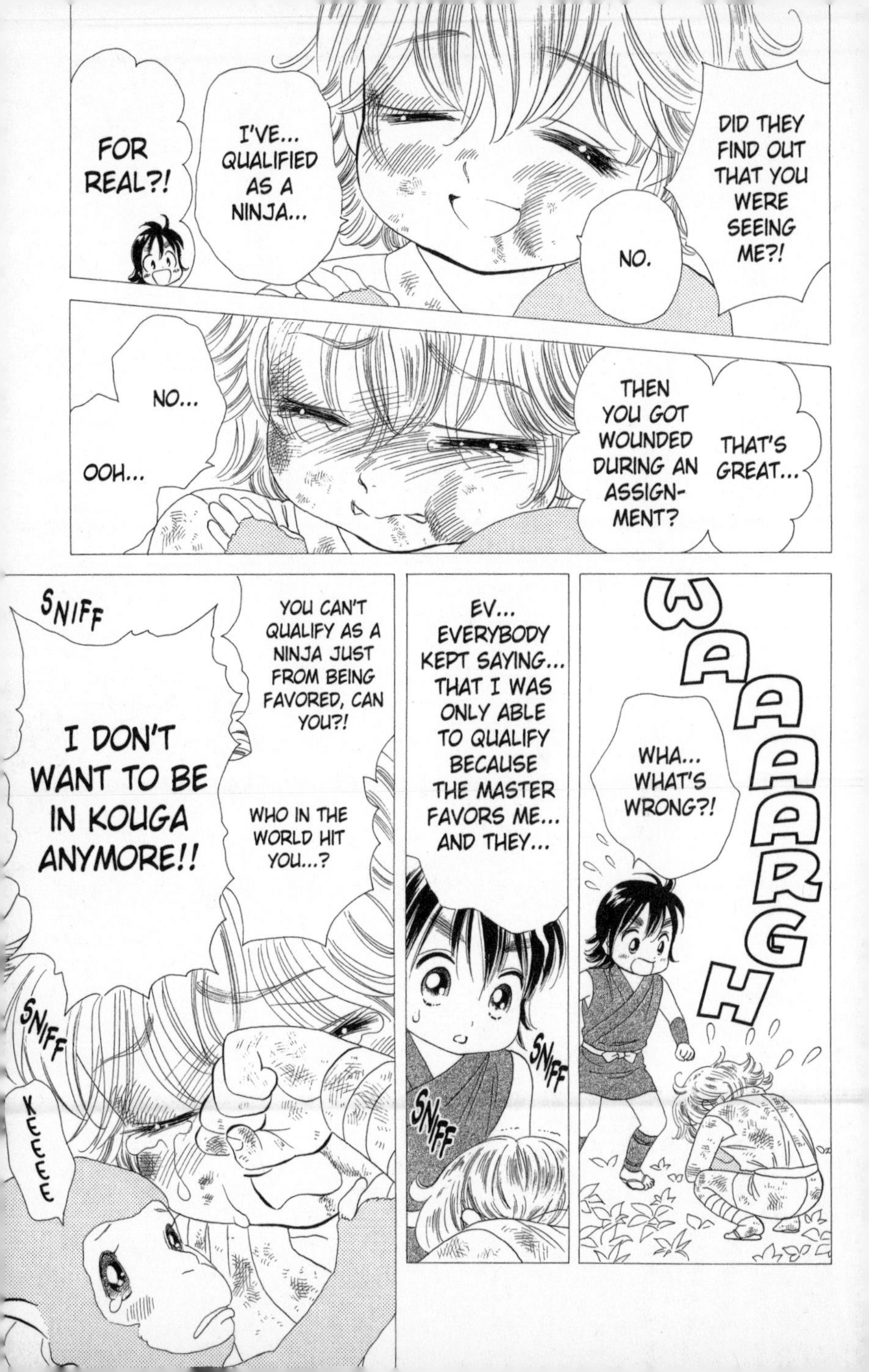
DID THEY FIND OUT THAT YOU WERE SEEING ME?!
NO.
I'VE... QUALIFIED AS A NINJA...
FOR REAL?!
THAT'S GREAT...
THEN YOU GOT WOUNDED DURING AN ASSIGNMENT?
NO...
OOH...
WAAAAARGH
WHA... WHAT'S WRONG?!
EV... EVERYBODY KEPT SAYING... THAT I WAS ONLY ABLE TO QUALIFY BECAUSE THE MASTER FAVORS ME... AND THEY...
SNIFF
SNIFF
YOU CAN'T QUALIFY AS A NINJA JUST FROM BEING FAVORED, CAN YOU?!
WHO IN THE WORLD HIT YOU...?
SNIFF
I DON'T WANT TO BE IN KOUGA ANYMORE!!
SNIFF
KEEEEE

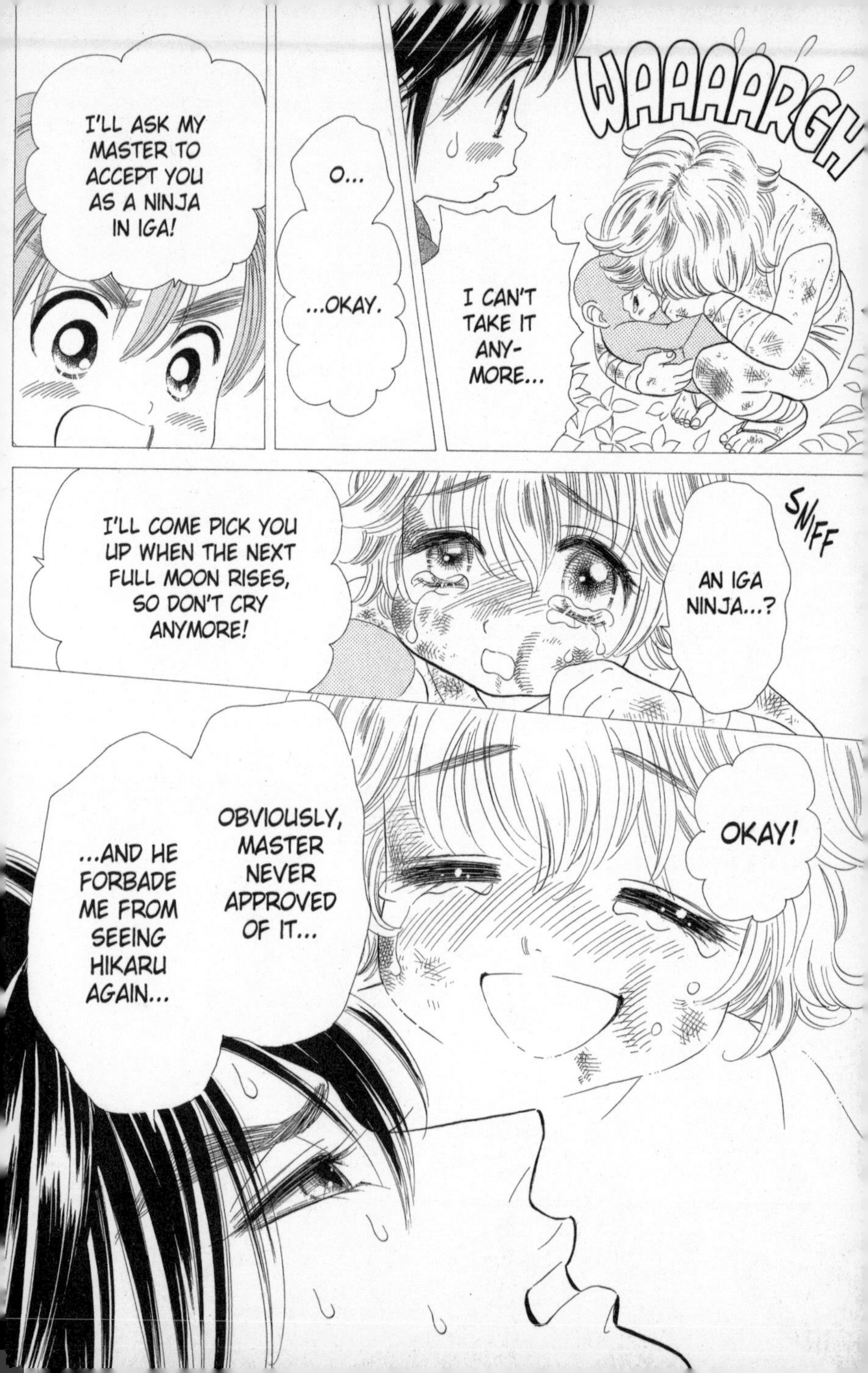
WAAAARGH
I CAN'T TAKE IT ANYMORE...
O...
...OKAY.
I'LL ASK MY MASTER TO ACCEPT YOU AS A NINJA IN IGA!
SNIFF
AN IGA NINJA...?
I'LL COME PICK YOU UP WHEN THE NEXT FULL MOON RISES, SO DON'T CRY ANYMORE!
OKAY!
OBVIOUSLY, MASTER NEVER APPROVED OF IT...
...AND HE FORBADE ME FROM SEEING HIKARU AGAIN...

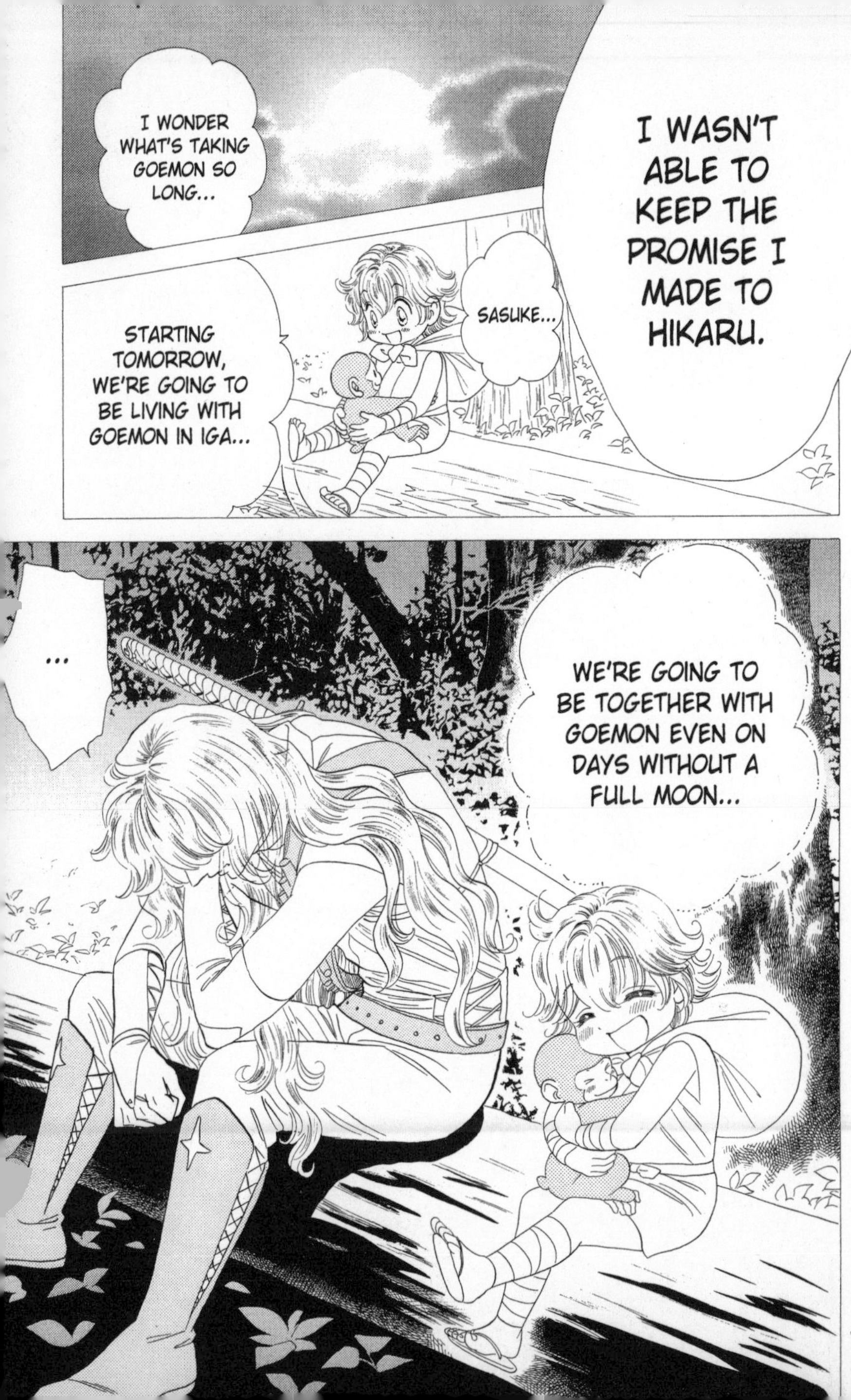

I WASN'T ABLE TO KEEP THE PROMISE I MADE TO HIKARU.
I WONDER WHAT'S TAKING GOEMON SO LONG...
SASUKE...
STARTING TOMORROW, WE'RE GOING TO BE LIVING WITH GOEMON IN IGA...
WE'RE GOING TO BE TOGETHER WITH GOEMON EVEN ON DAYS WITHOUT A FULL MOON...
...

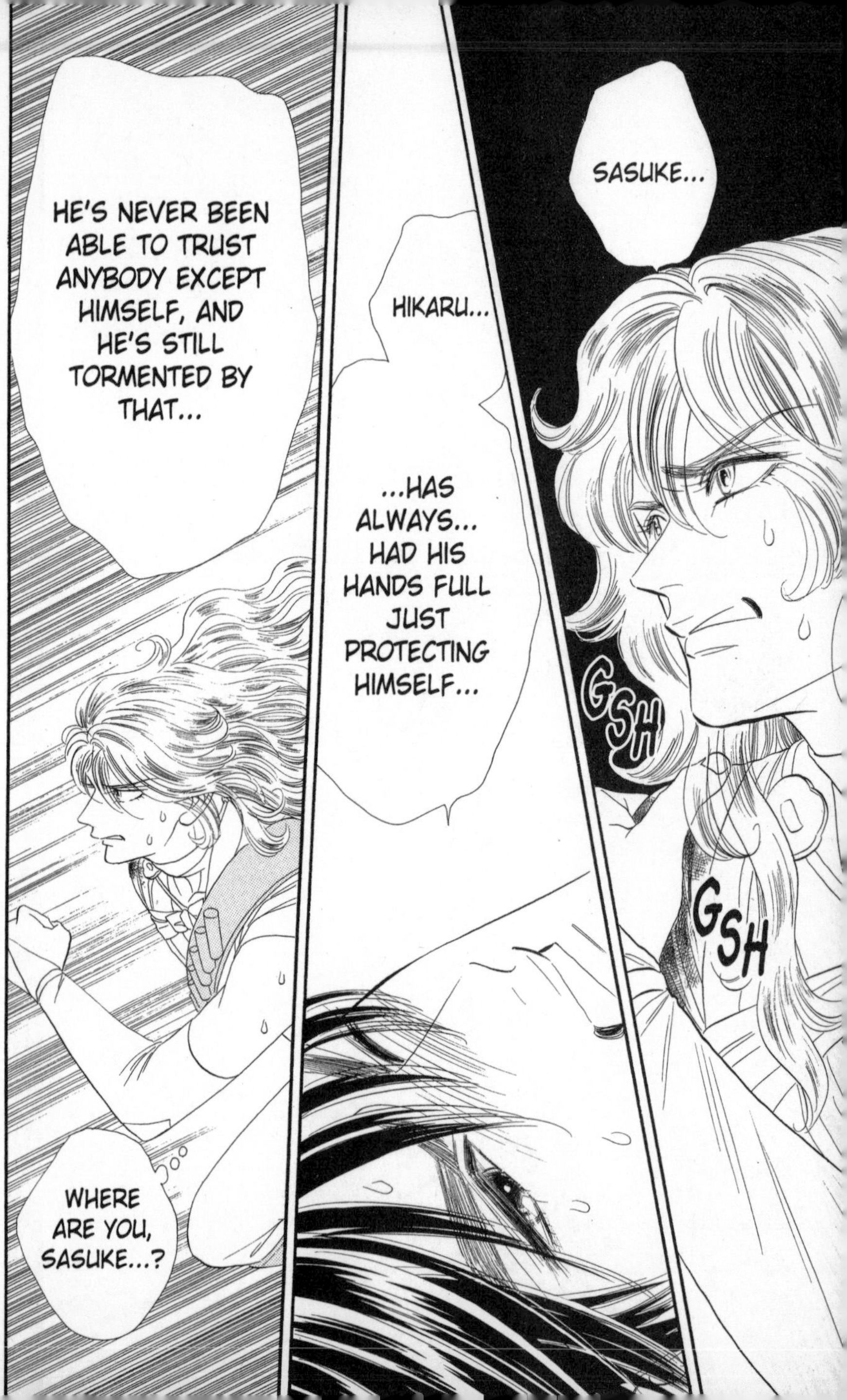
SASUKE...
GSH
GSH
HIKARU...
...HAS ALWAYS... HAD HIS HANDS FULL JUST PROTECTING HIMSELF...
HE'S NEVER BEEN ABLE TO TRUST ANYBODY EXCEPT HIMSELF, AND HE'S STILL TORMENTED BY THAT...
WHERE ARE YOU, SASUKE...?

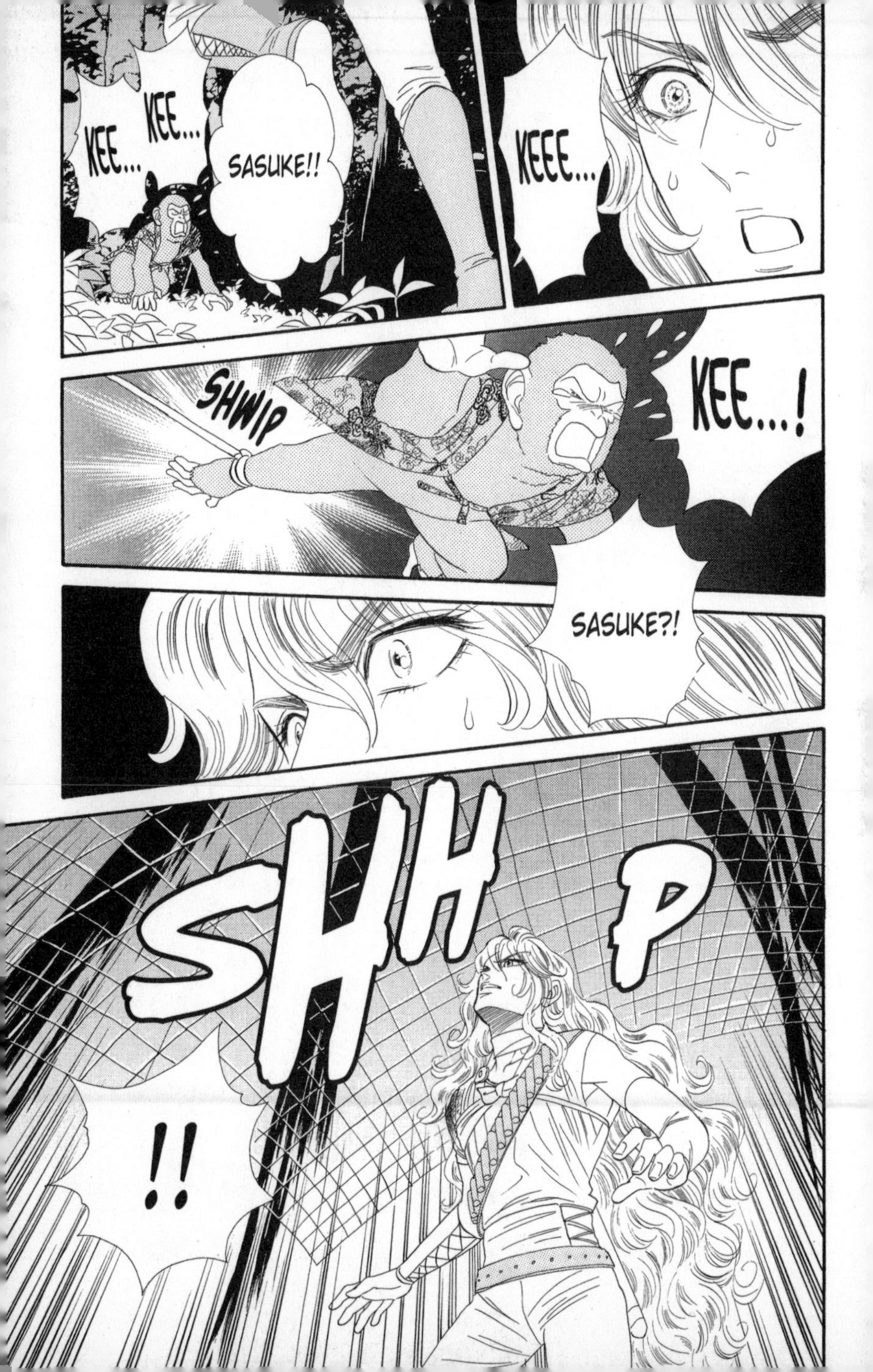
KEEE...
SASUKE!!
KEE...
KEE...
KEE...!
SHWIP
SASUKE?!
SHHP
!!

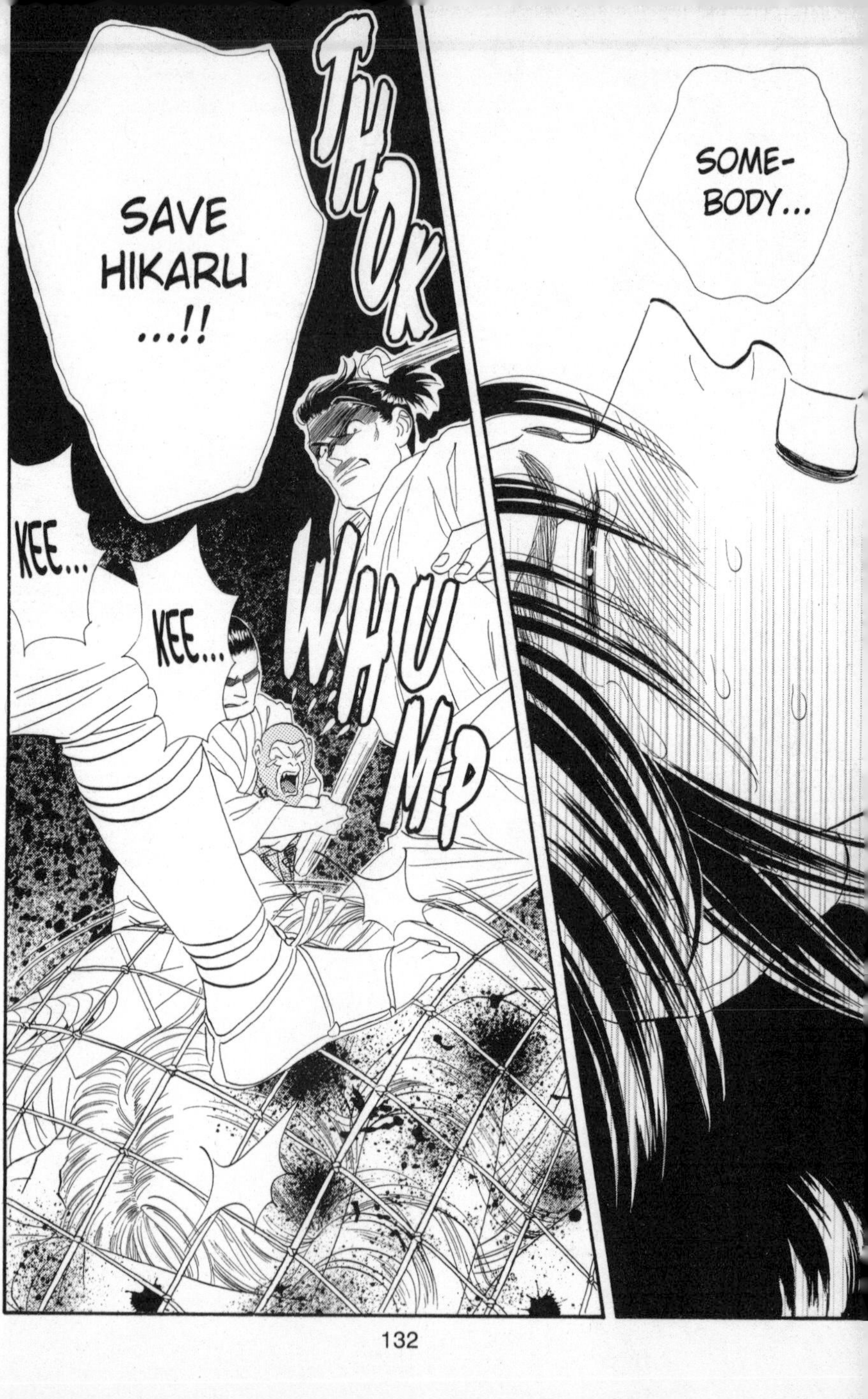
SOME-BODY...
SAVE HIKARU ...!!
THOK
WHUMP
KEE...
KEE...

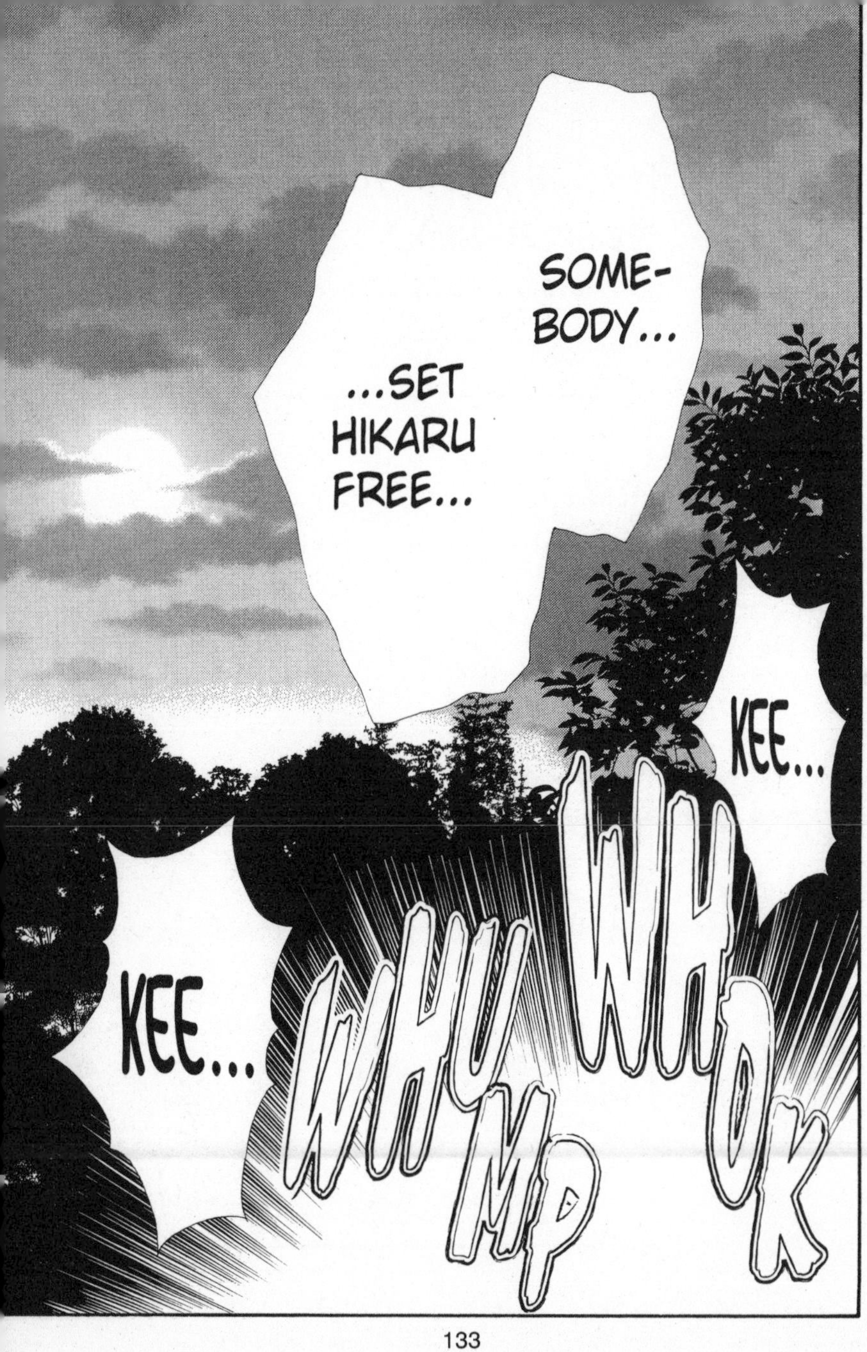
SOME-BODY...
...SET HIKARU FREE...
KEE...
WHAK
WHUMP
KEE...

TAIL OF THE MOON EXTRA: TODAY'S MISSION

"I WANT TO SEE GREAT-GRANDPA AS A MAGICIAN."

-GREAT-GRANDPA FAN, NARA PREFECTURE

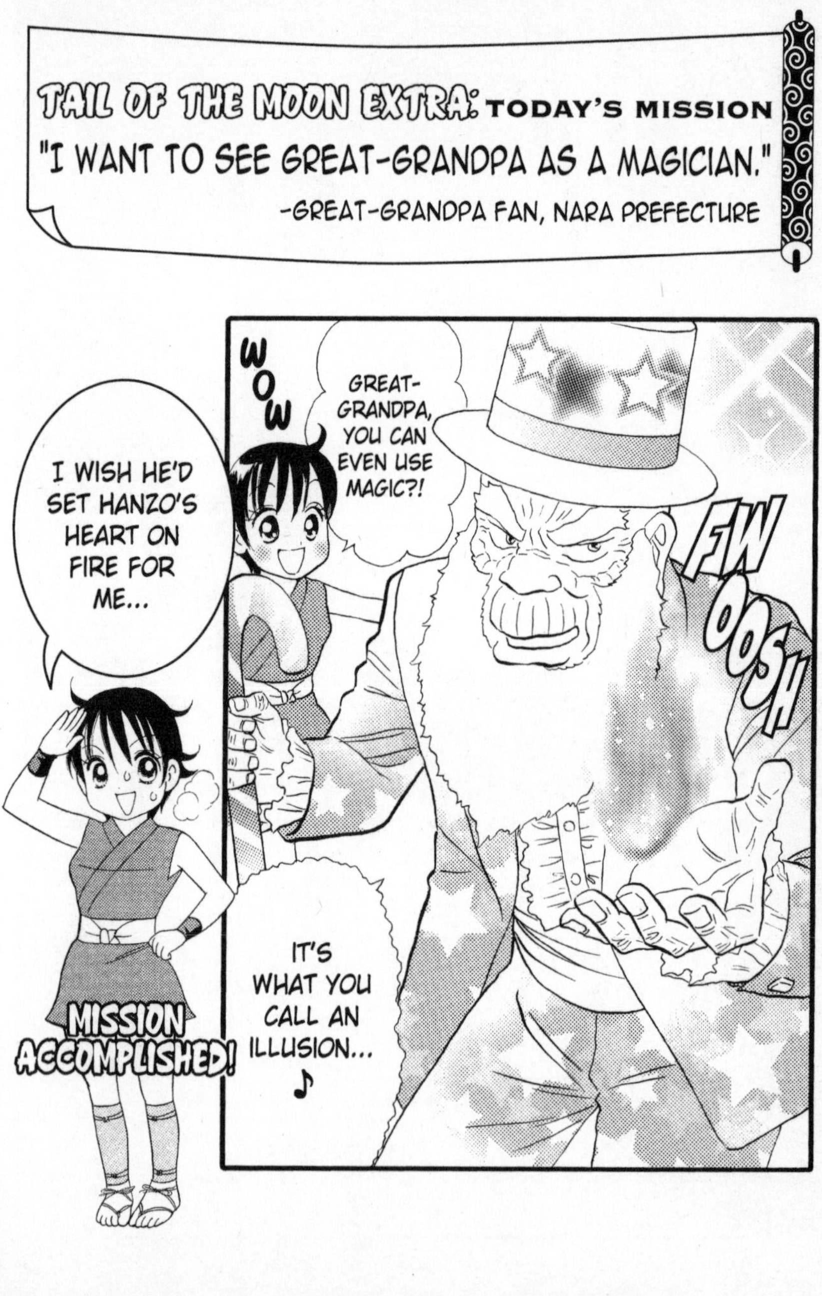
FWOOSH
WOW
GREAT-GRANDPA, YOU CAN EVEN USE MAGIC?!
IT'S WHAT YOU CALL AN ILLUSION... ♪
I WISH HE'D SET HANZO'S HEART ON FIRE FOR ME...
MISSION ACCOMPLISHED!

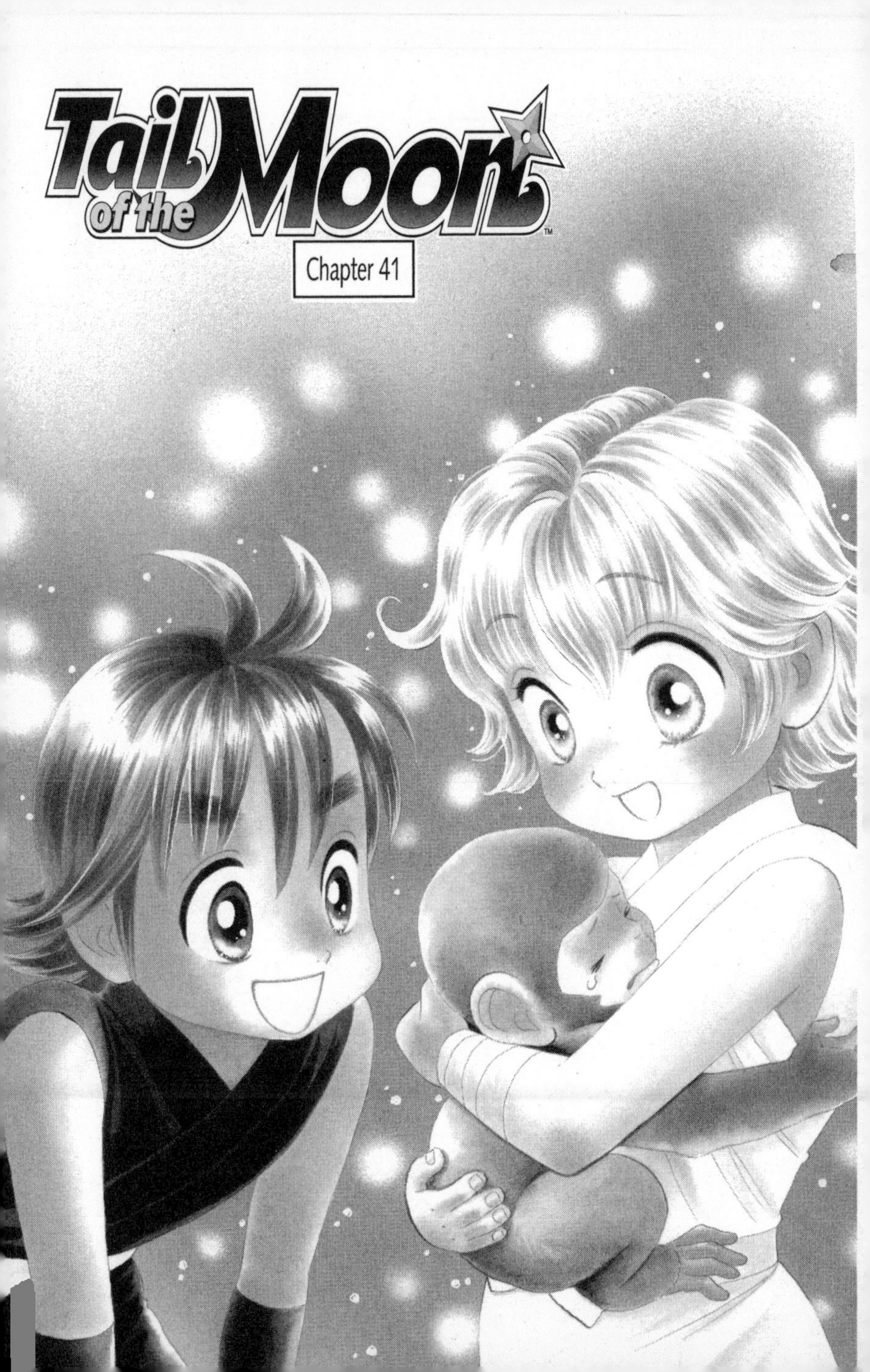
Tail of the Moon™
Chapter 41

TAIL OF THE MOON EXTRA: TODAY'S MISSION

"I WANT TO SEE USAGI IN GOTHIC LOLITA FASHION."

-KAATA, OKINAWA PREFECTURE

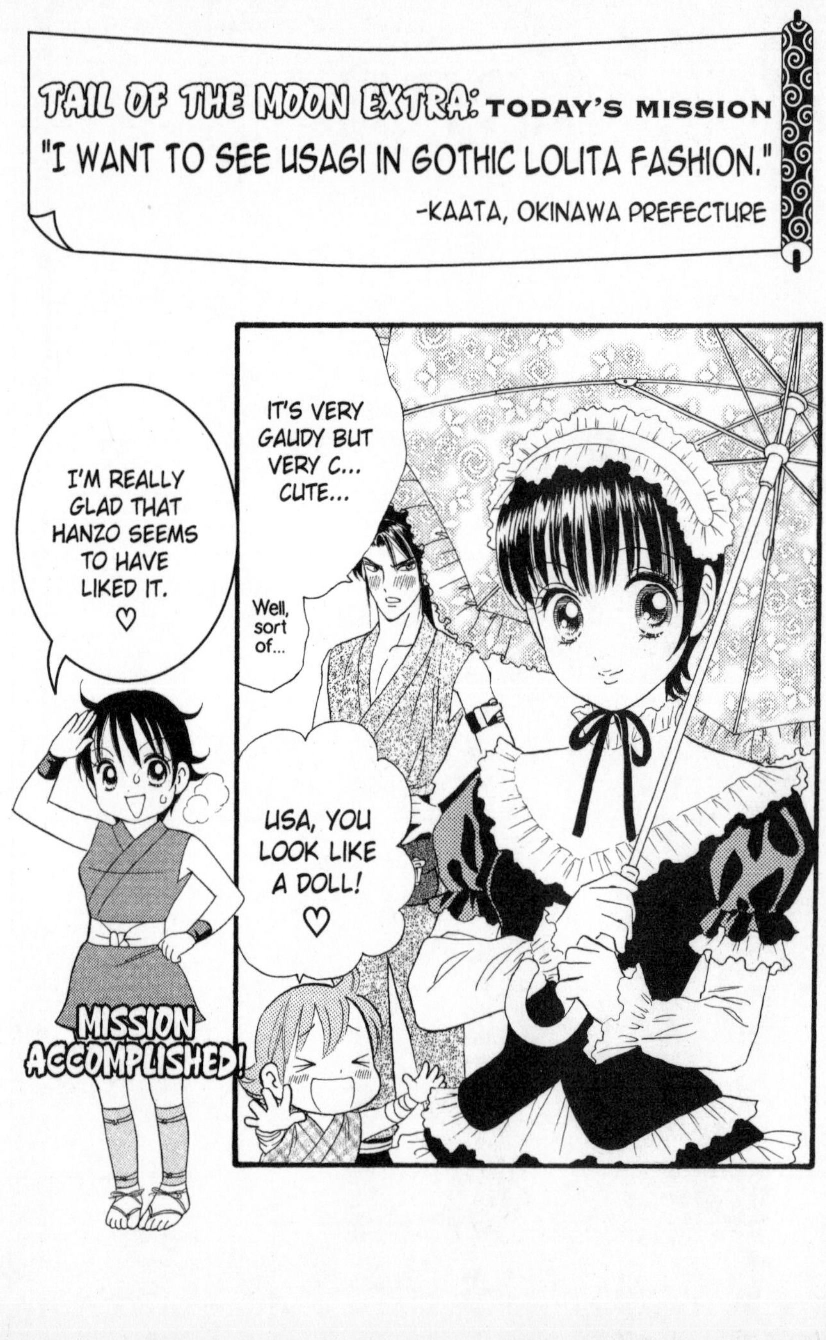
IT'S VERY GAUDY BUT VERY C... CUTE...
Well, sort of...
USA, YOU LOOK LIKE A DOLL! ♡
I'M REALLY GLAD THAT HANZO SEEMS TO HAVE LIKED IT. ♡
MISSION ACCOMPLISHED!

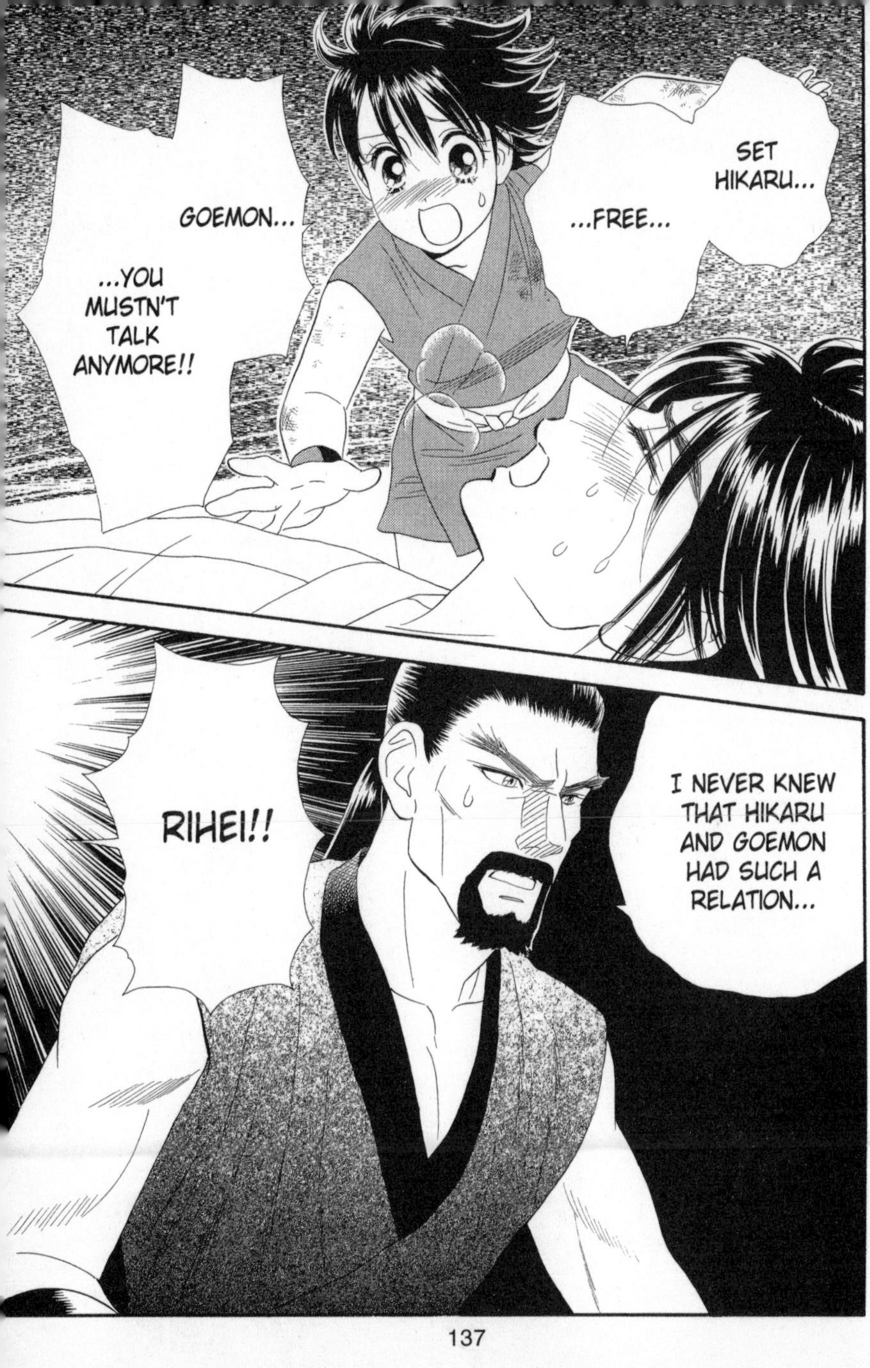
SET HIKARU...
...FREE...
GOEMON...
...YOU MUSTN'T TALK ANYMORE!!
I NEVER KNEW THAT HIKARU AND GOEMON HAD SUCH A RELATION...
RIHEI!!

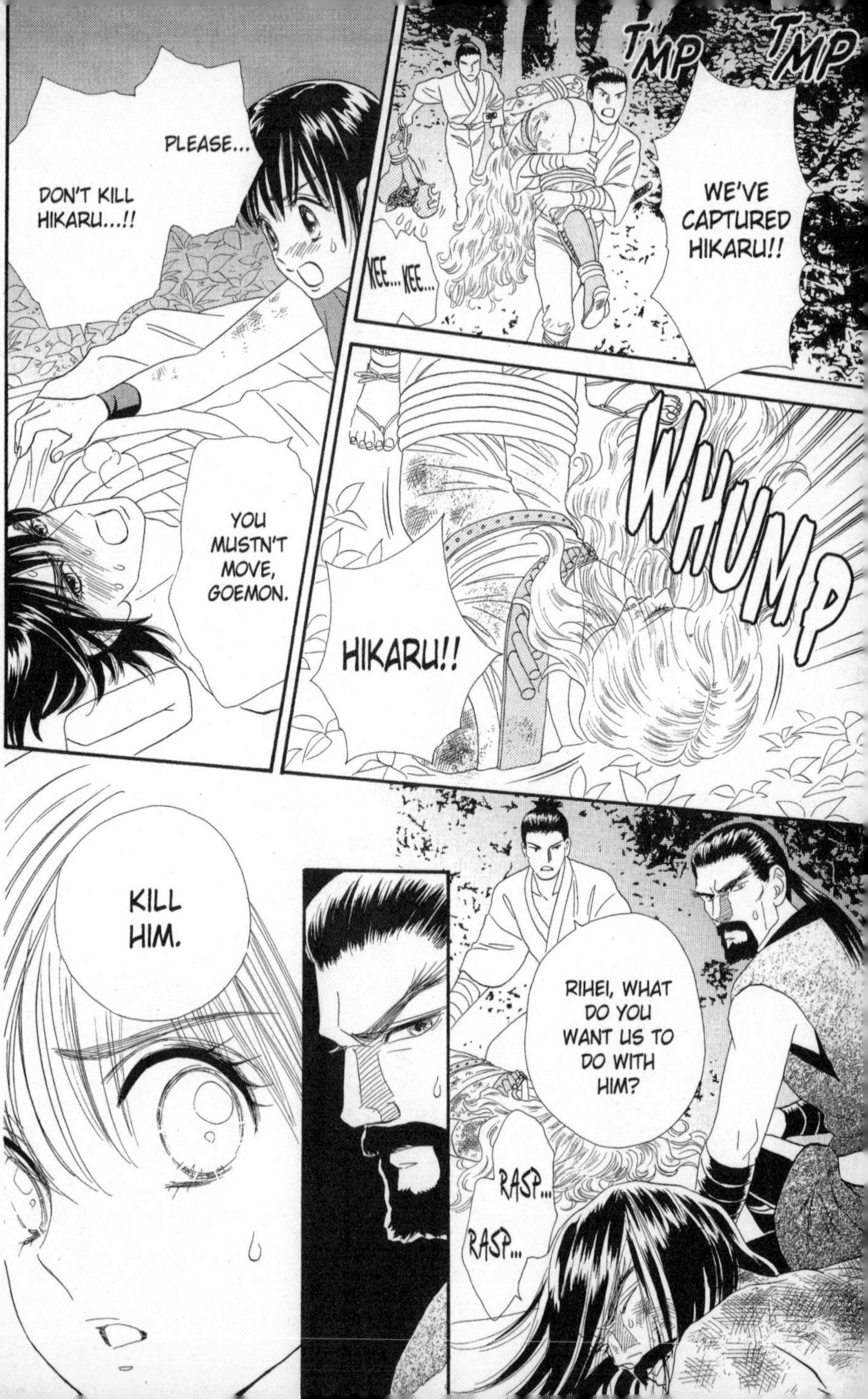
TMP
TMP
WE'VE CAPTURED HIKARU!!
KEE... KEE...
WHUMP
HIKARU!!
PLEASE...
DON'T KILL HIKARU...!!
YOU MUSTN'T MOVE, GOEMON.
RIHEI, WHAT DO YOU WANT US TO DO WITH HIM?
RASP...
RASP...
KILL HIM.

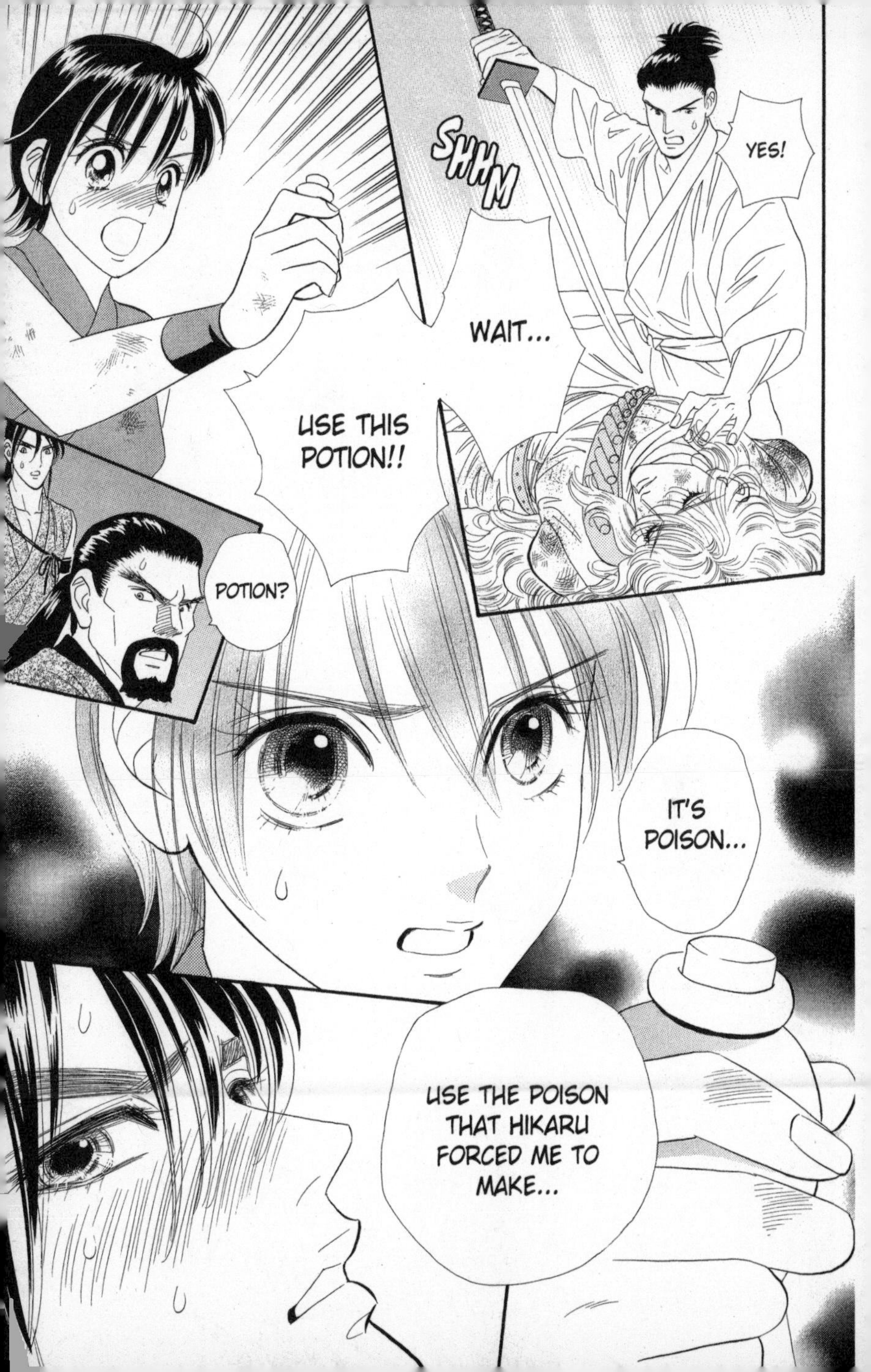
YES!
SHHM
WAIT...
USE THIS POTION!!
POTION?
IT'S POISON...
USE THE POISON THAT HIKARU FORCED ME TO MAKE...

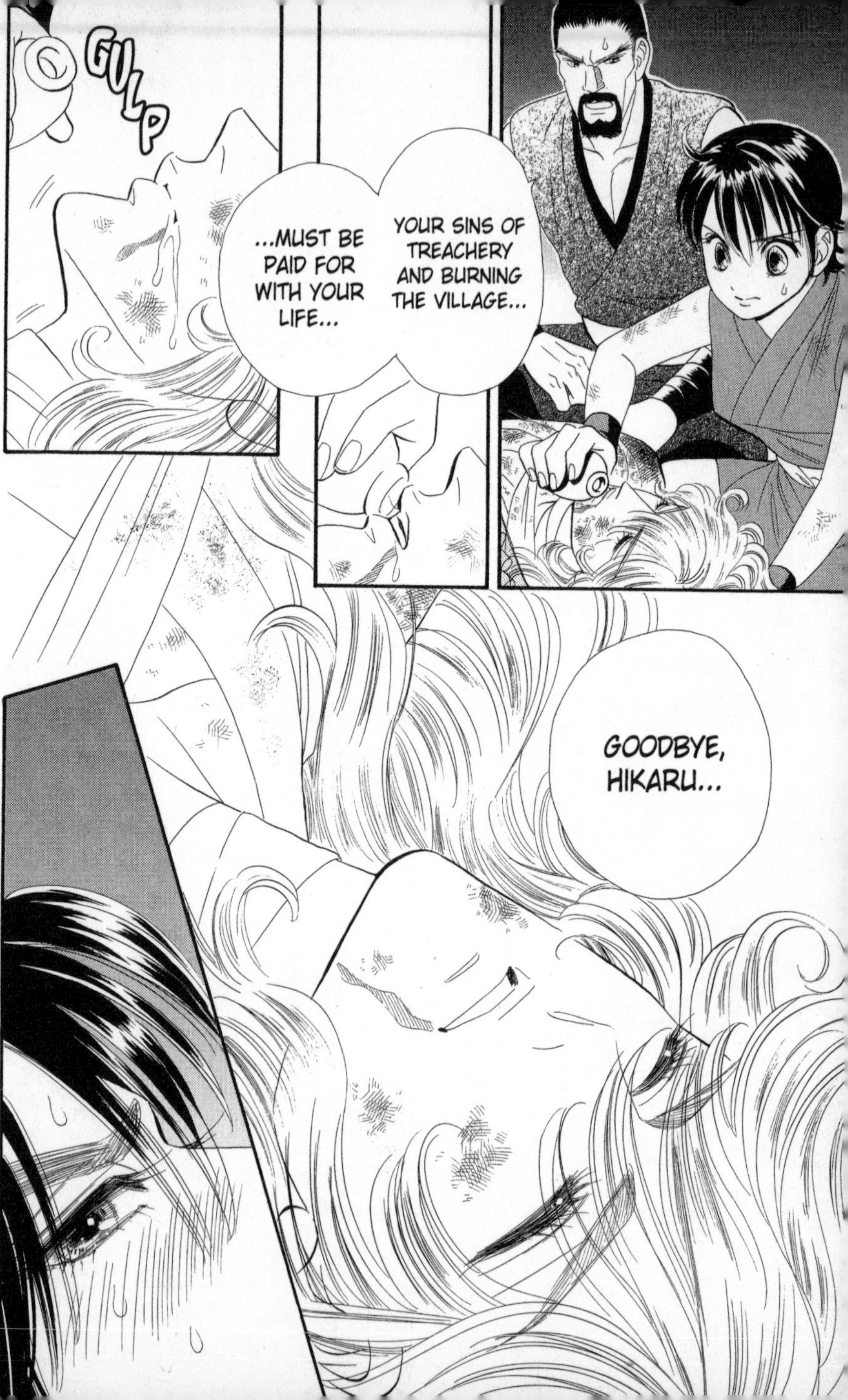
YOUR SINS OF TREACHERY AND BURNING THE VILLAGE...
...MUST BE PAID FOR WITH YOUR LIFE...
GULP
GOODBYE, HIKARU...

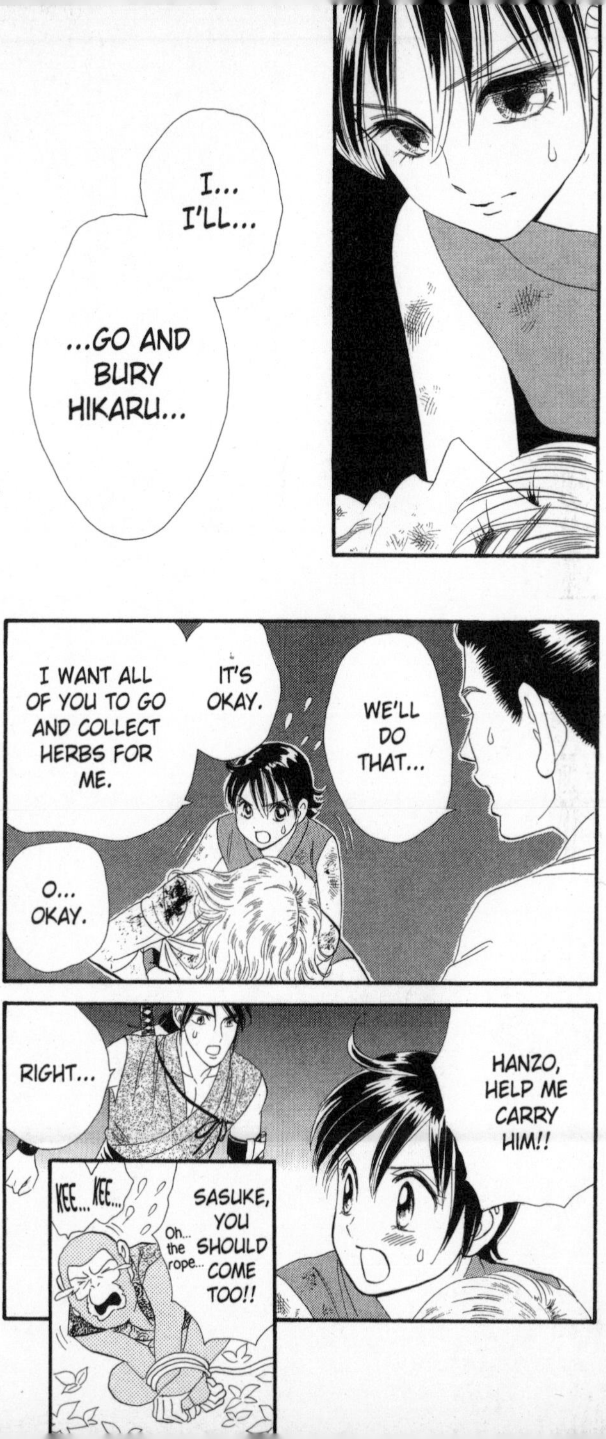
I... I'LL...
...GO AND BURY HIKARU...
WE'LL DO THAT...
IT'S OKAY.
I WANT ALL OF YOU TO GO AND COLLECT HERBS FOR ME.
O... OKAY.
HANZO, HELP ME CARRY HIM!!
RIGHT...
SASUKE, YOU SHOULD COME TOO!!
Oh... the rope...
KEE... KEE...

UE-RIN'S WAY OF THE MANGA ⑤

Back then, I didn't know the basics of drawing manga, including creating the storyboard first. I went straight to drawing manga onto drawing paper and had to squeeze my story within the number of pages I had to turn in.

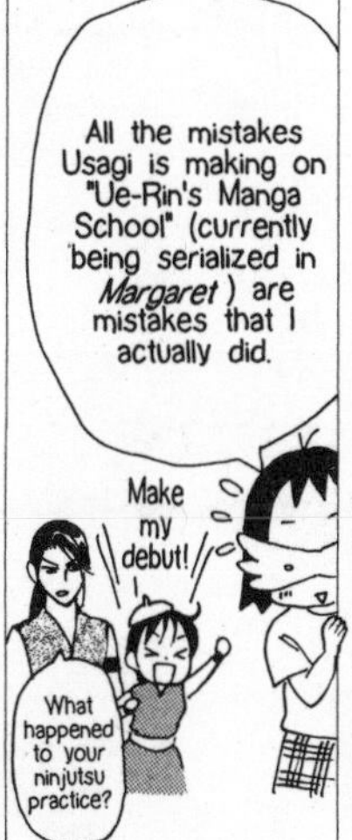
All the mistakes Usagi is making on "Ue-Rin's Manga School" (currently being serialized in *Margaret*) are mistakes that I actually did.
Make my debut!
What happened to your ninjutsu practice?

As for the result of the first manga I drew at night while attending middle school...

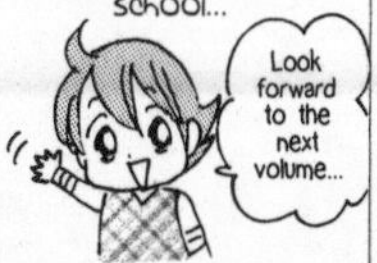
Look forward to the next volume...

See you in volume 7♪

Rinko Ueda

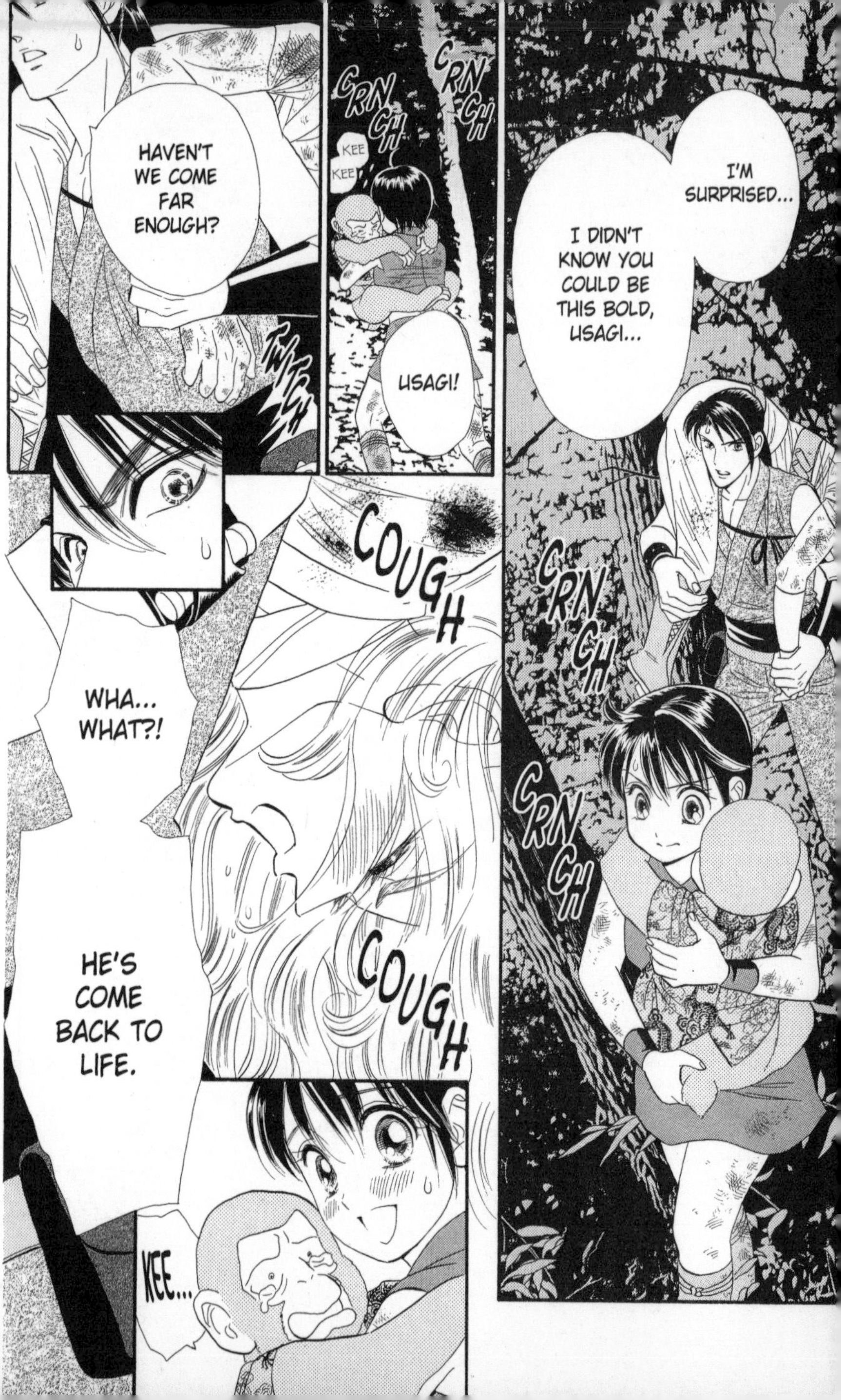
I'M SURPRISED...
I DIDN'T KNOW YOU COULD BE THIS BOLD, USAGI...
CRNCH
CRNCH
CRNCH
CRNCH
KEE
KEE
USAGI!
HAVEN'T WE COME FAR ENOUGH?
TWITCH
COUGH
COUGH
WHA... WHAT?!
HE'S COME BACK TO LIFE.
KEE...

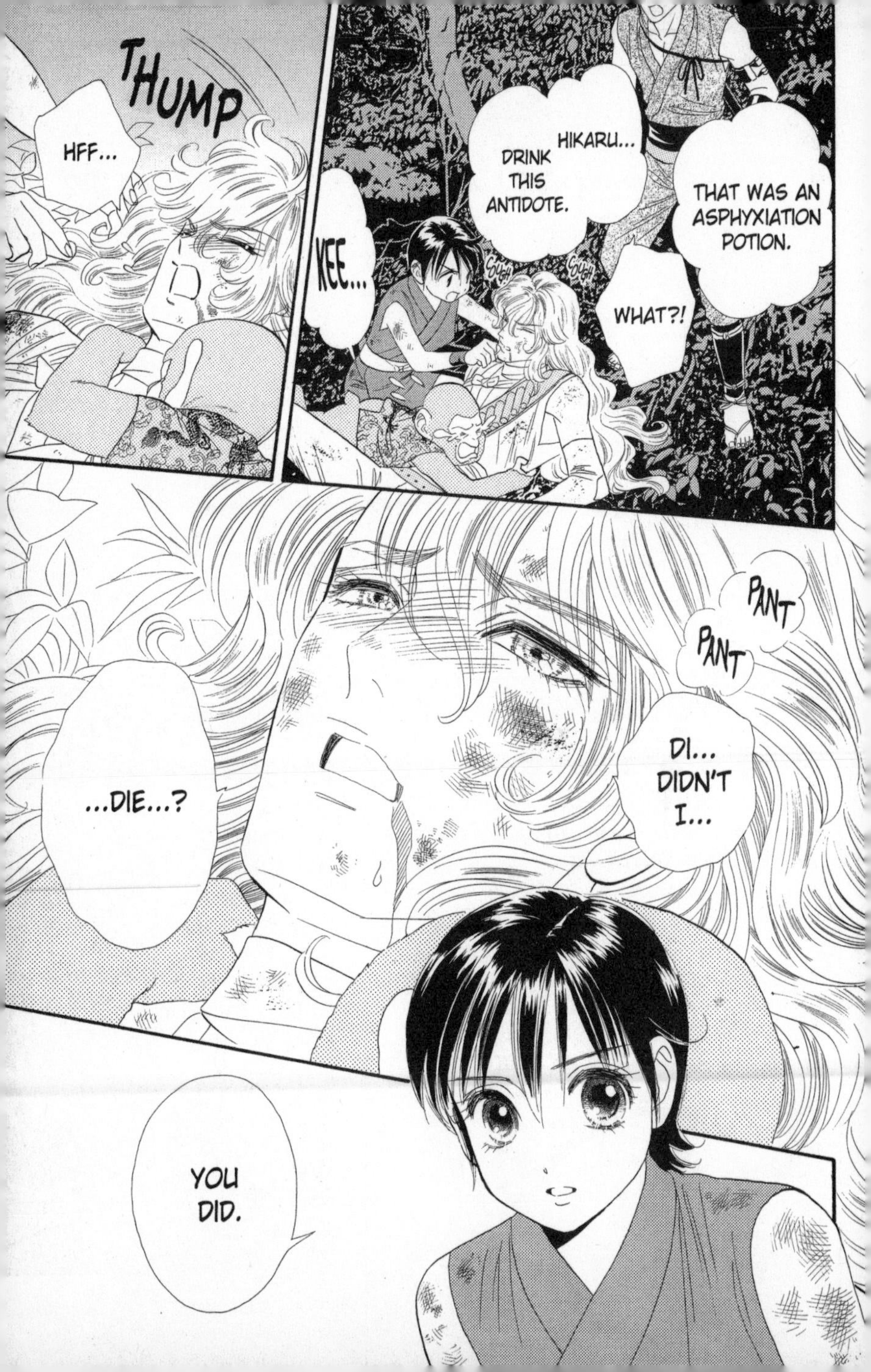
HIKARU... DRINK THIS ANTIDOTE.
WHAT?!
THAT WAS AN ASPHYXIATION POTION.
COUGH
COUGH
KEE...
THUMP
HFF...
PANT PANT
DI... DIDN'T I...
...DIE...?
YOU DID.

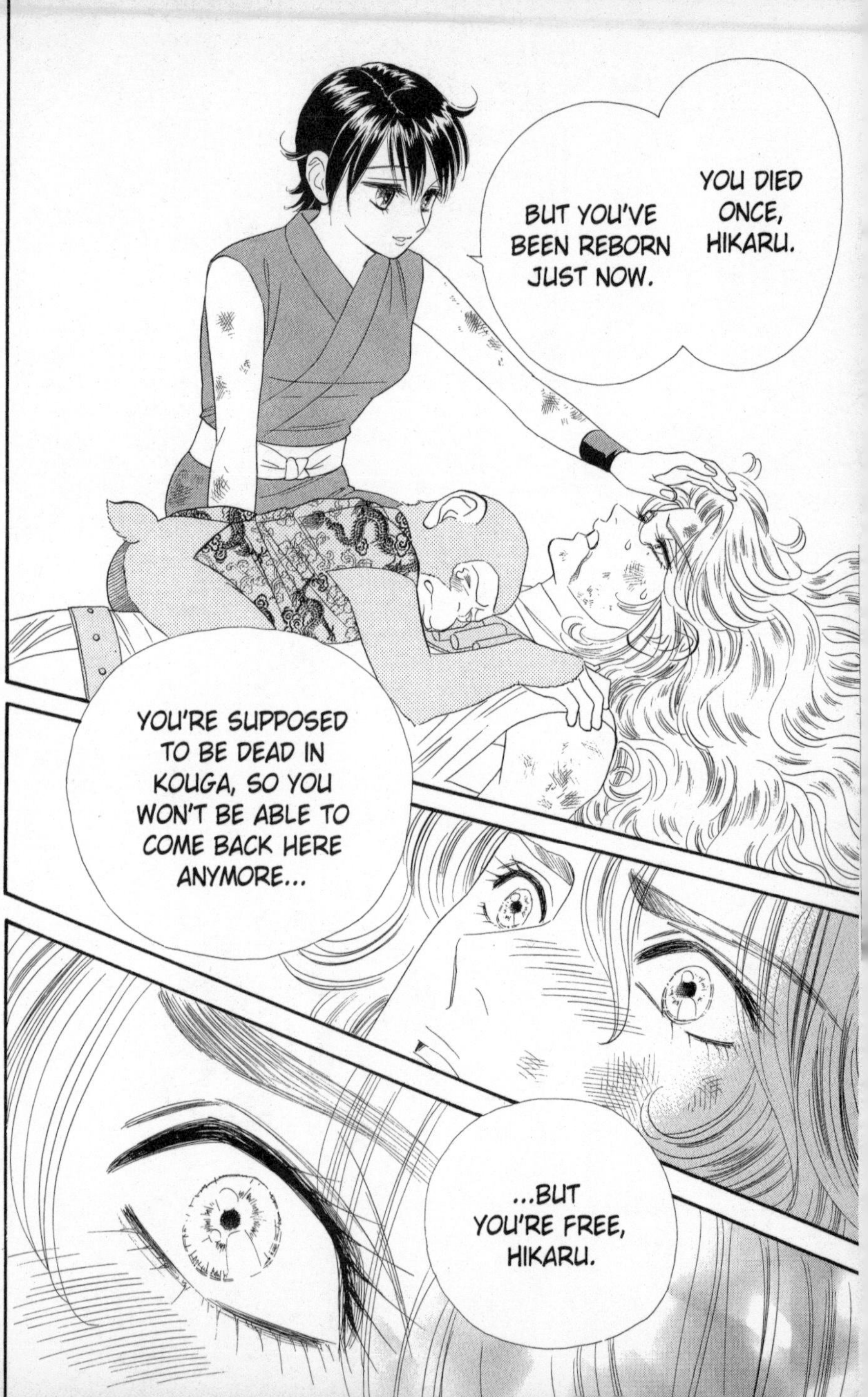
YOU DIED ONCE, HIKARU.
BUT YOU'VE BEEN REBORN JUST NOW.
YOU'RE SUPPOSED TO BE DEAD IN KOUGA, SO YOU WON'T BE ABLE TO COME BACK HERE ANYMORE...
...BUT YOU'RE FREE, HIKARU.

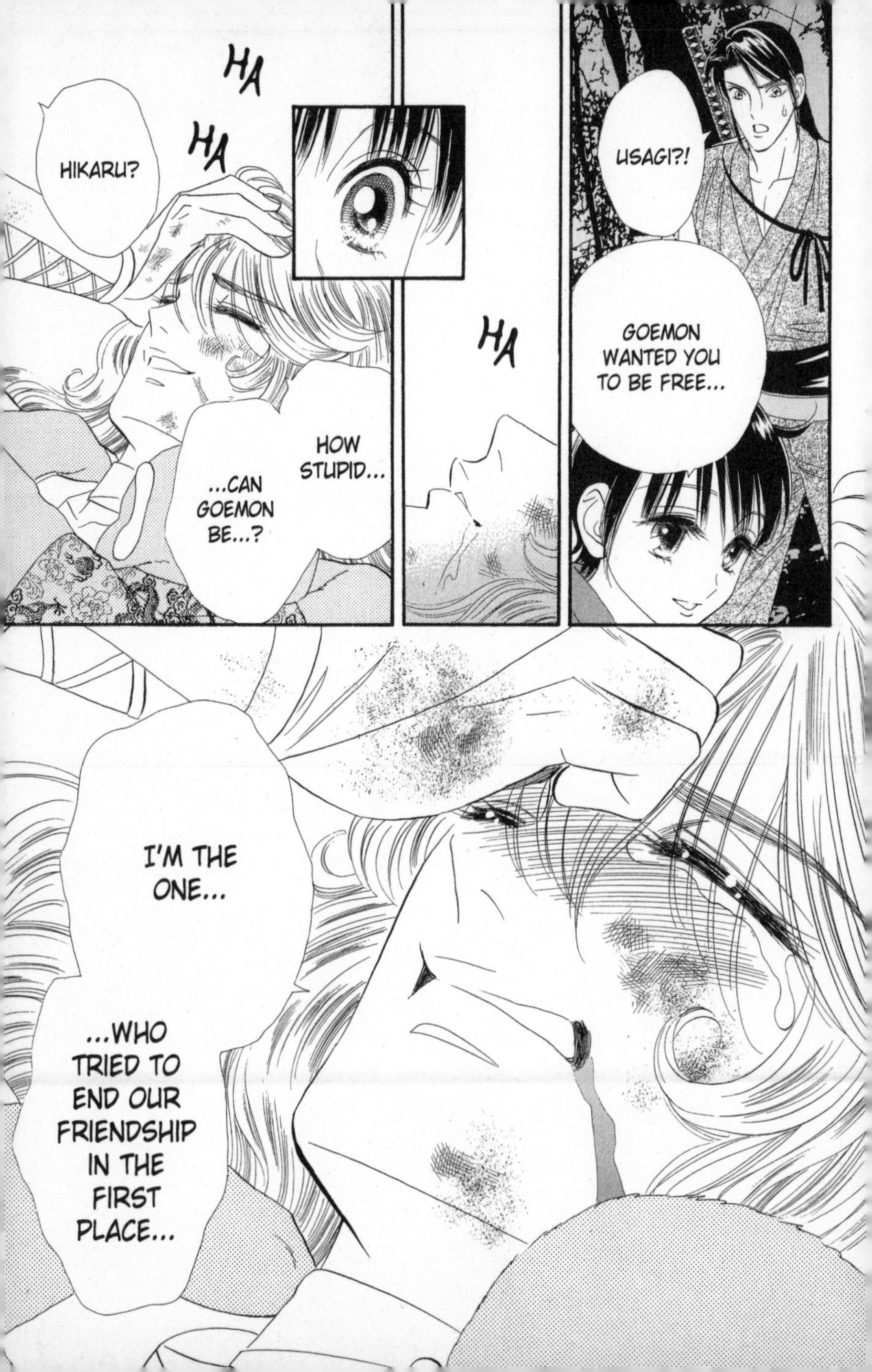
USAGI?!
GOEMON WANTED YOU TO BE FREE...
HA
HA
HA
HIKARU?
HOW STUPID...
...CAN GOEMON BE...?
I'M THE ONE...
...WHO TRIED TO END OUR FRIENDSHIP IN THE FIRST PLACE...

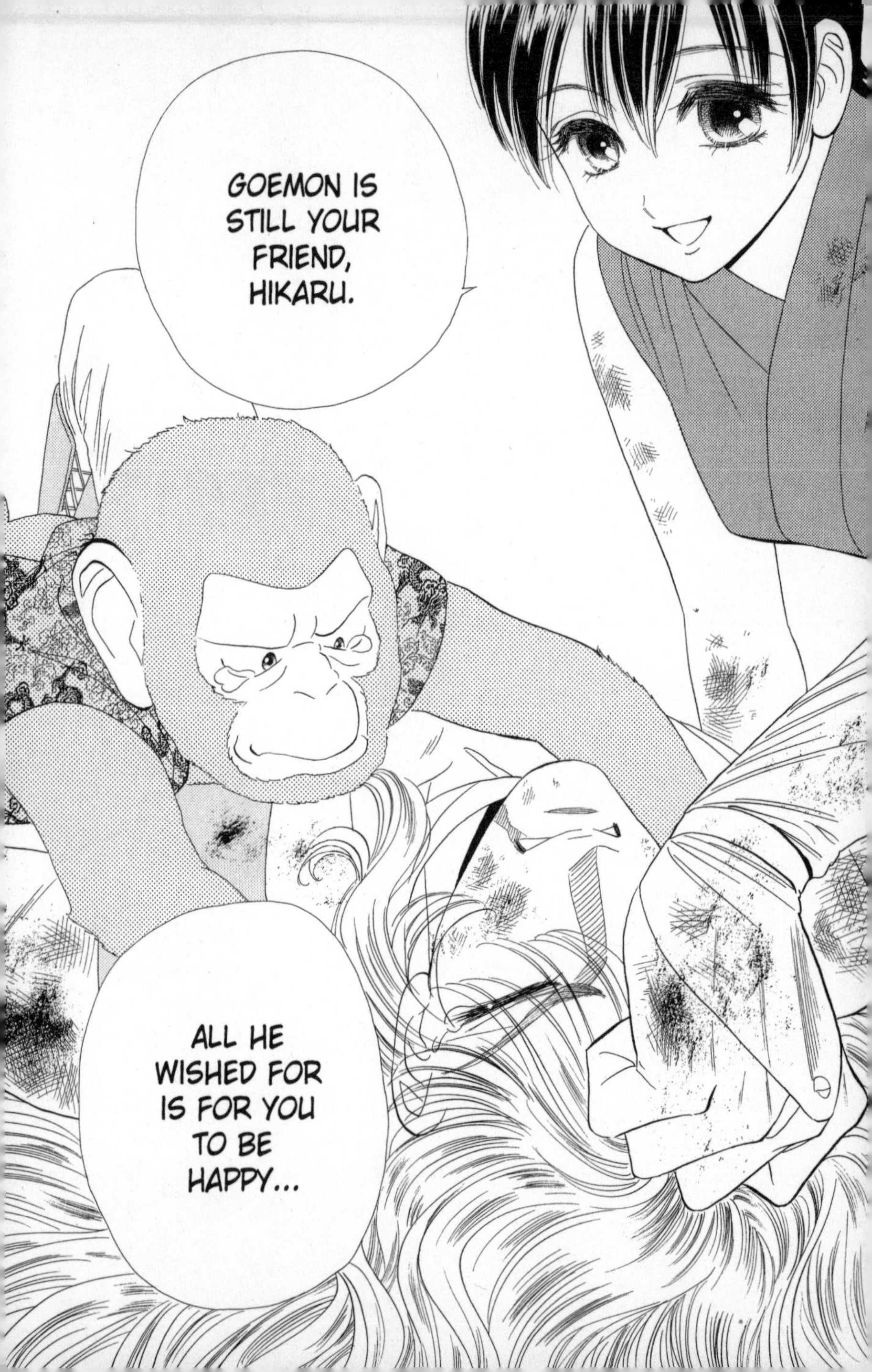
GOEMON IS STILL YOUR FRIEND, HIKARU.
ALL HE WISHED FOR IS FOR YOU TO BE HAPPY...

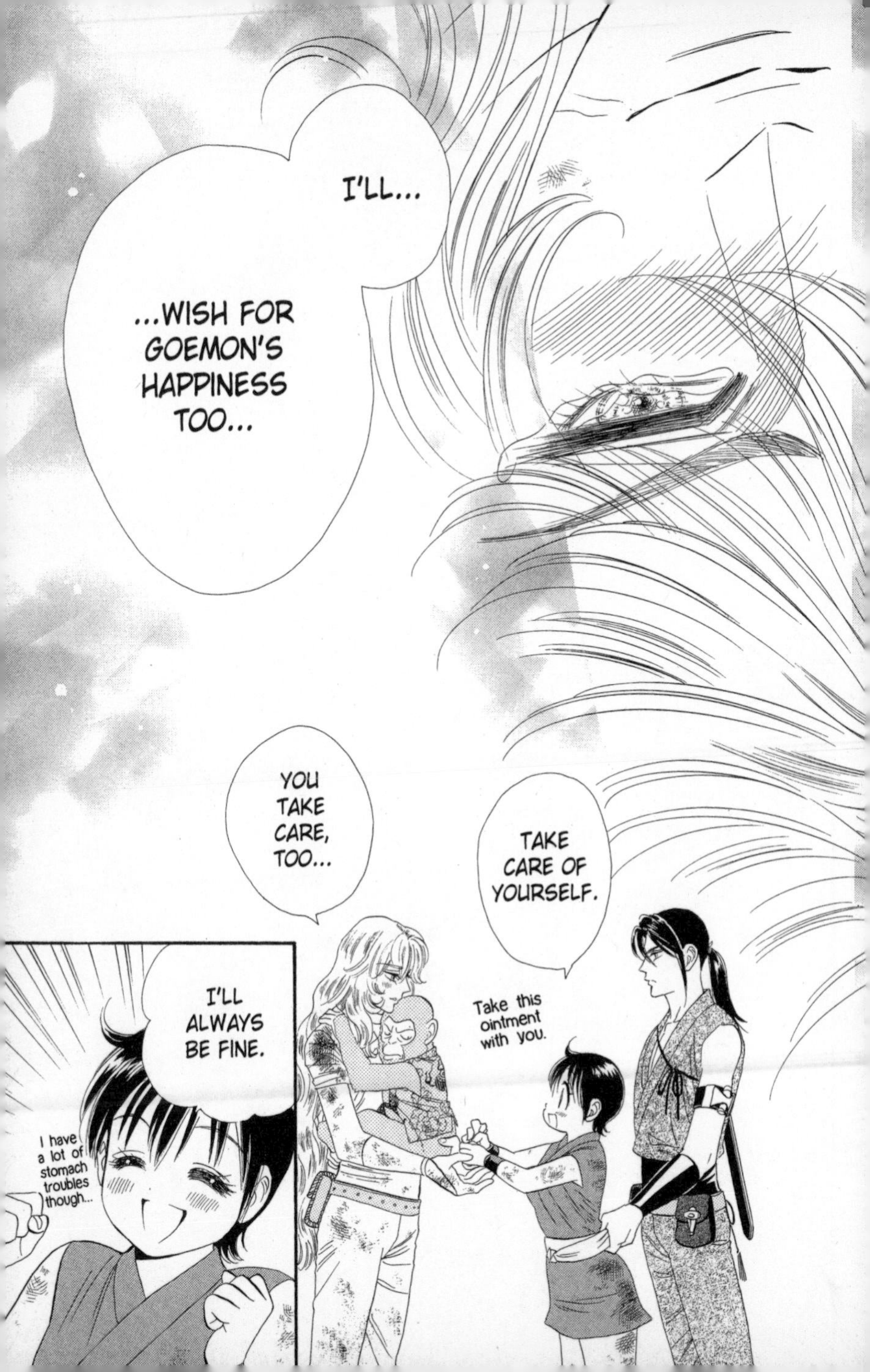
I'LL...
...WISH FOR GOEMON'S HAPPINESS TOO...
TAKE CARE OF YOURSELF.
YOU TAKE CARE, TOO...
Take this ointment with you.
I'LL ALWAYS BE FINE.
I have a lot of stomach troubles though...

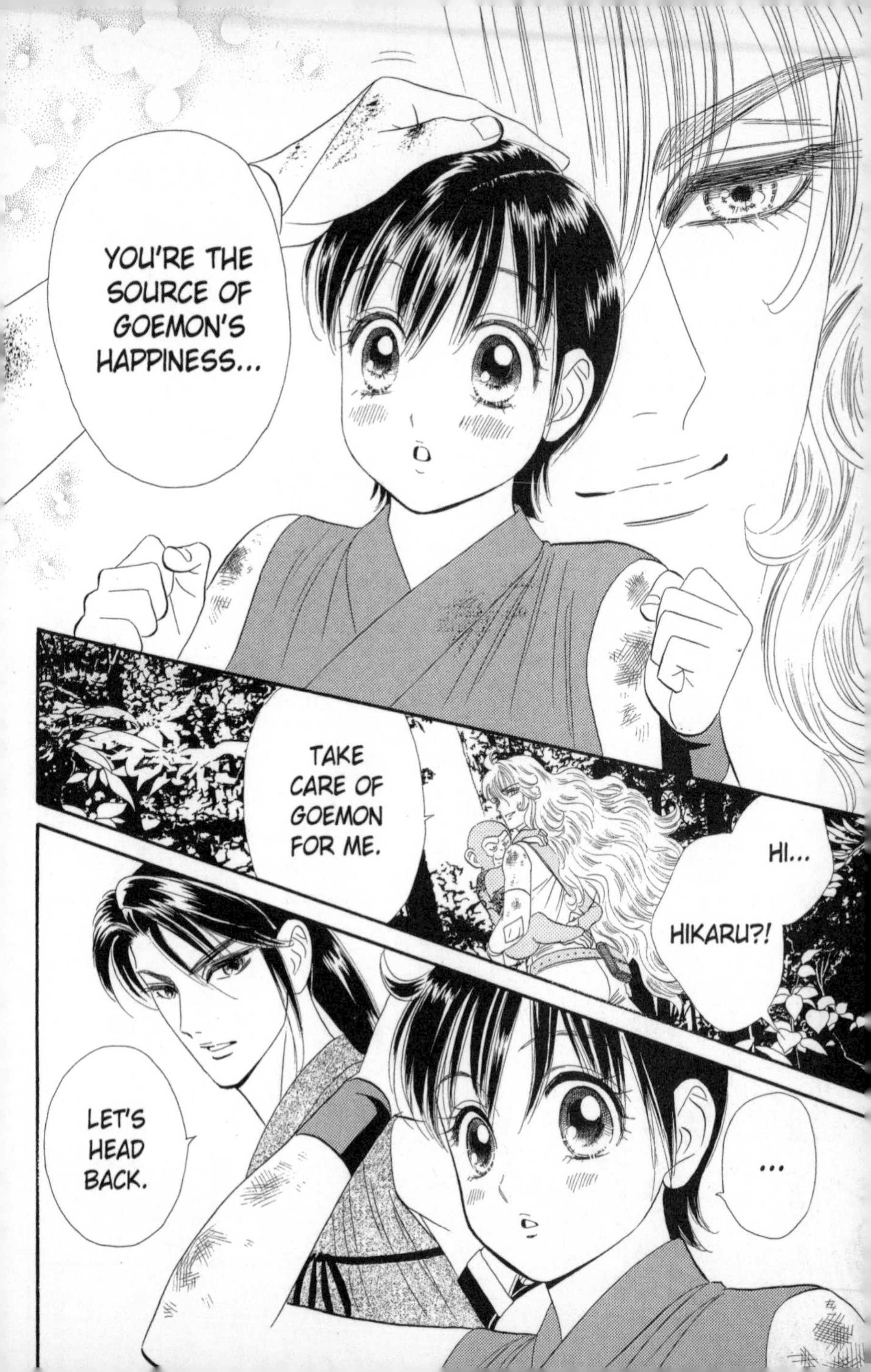
YOU'RE THE SOURCE OF GOEMON'S HAPPINESS...
TAKE CARE OF GOEMON FOR ME.
HI...
HIKARU?!
...
LET'S HEAD BACK.

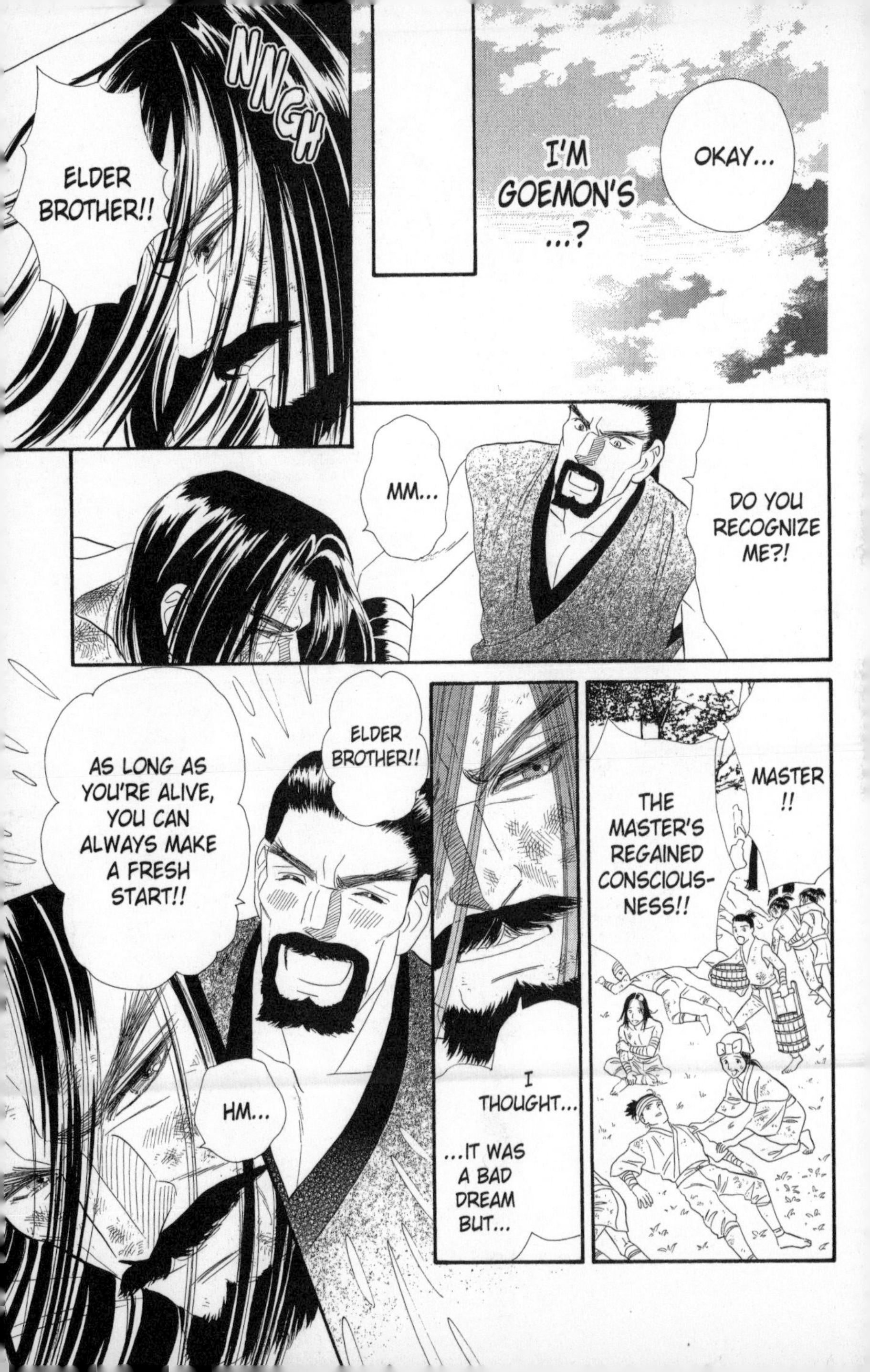
OKAY...
I'M GOEMON'S ...?
NNGH
ELDER BROTHER!!
DO YOU RECOGNIZE ME?!
MM...
MASTER !!
THE MASTER'S REGAINED CONSCIOUS-NESS!!
I THOUGHT...
...IT WAS A BAD DREAM BUT...
ELDER BROTHER!!
AS LONG AS YOU'RE ALIVE, YOU CAN ALWAYS MAKE A FRESH START!!
HM...

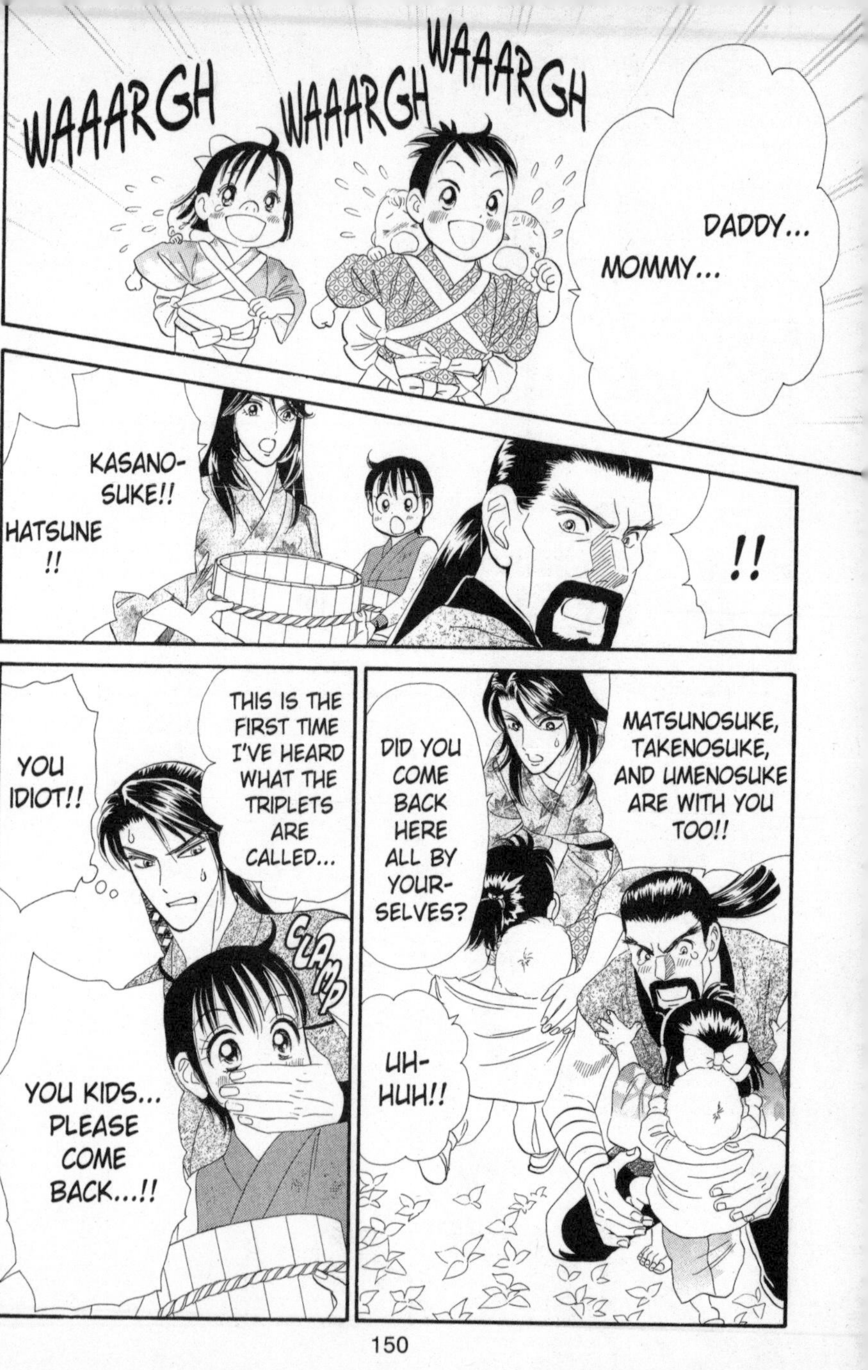
WAAARGH
WAAARGH
WAAARGH
DADDY... MOMMY...
!!
KASANO-SUKE!!
HATSUNE !!
MATSUNOSUKE, TAKENOSUKE, AND UMENOSUKE ARE WITH YOU TOO!!
DID YOU COME BACK HERE ALL BY YOUR-SELVES?
UH-HUH!!
THIS IS THE FIRST TIME I'VE HEARD WHAT THE TRIPLETS ARE CALLED...
YOU IDIOT!!
CLAMP
YOU KIDS... PLEASE COME BACK...!!

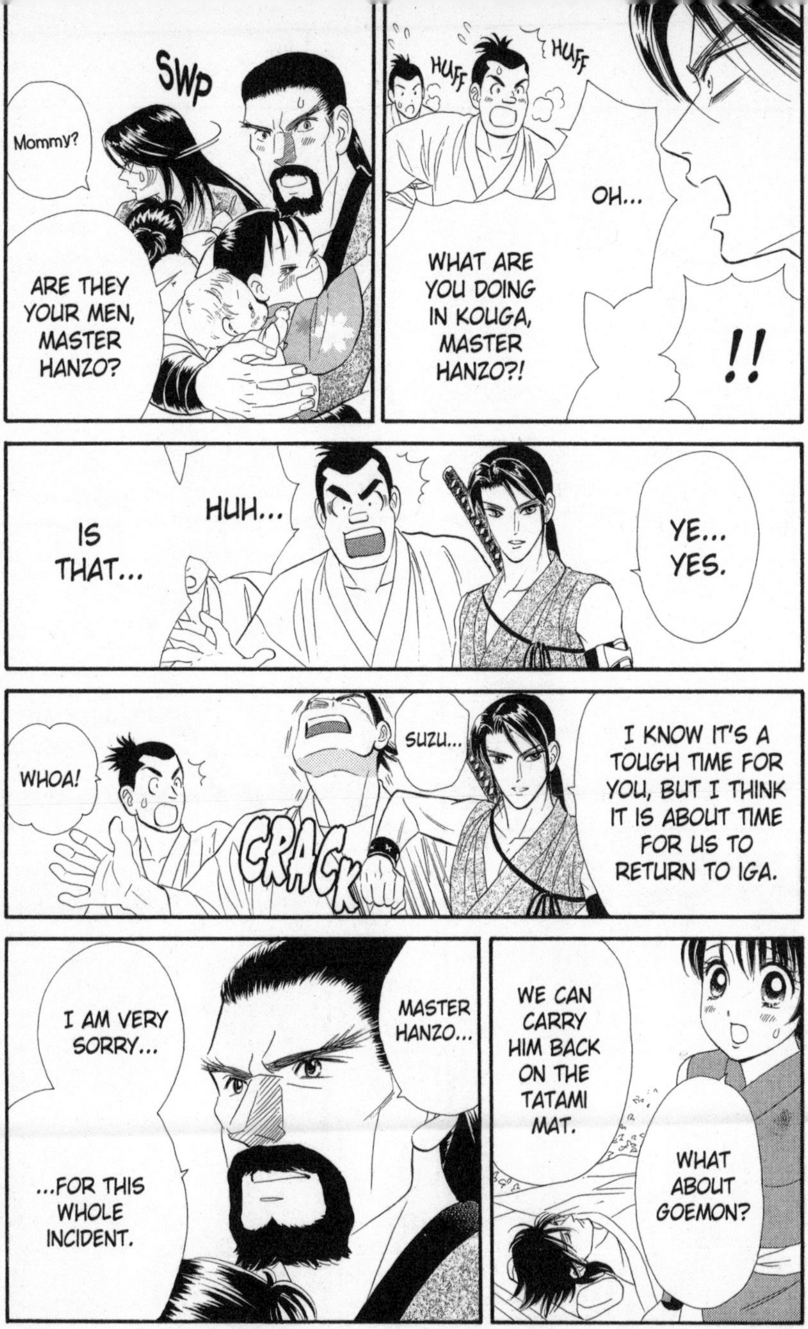
HUFF
HUFF
OH...
!!
WHAT ARE YOU DOING IN KOUGA, MASTER HANZO?!
SWP
Mommy?
ARE THEY YOUR MEN, MASTER HANZO?
YE... YES.
HUH...
IS THAT...
I KNOW IT'S A TOUGH TIME FOR YOU, BUT I THINK IT IS ABOUT TIME FOR US TO RETURN TO IGA.
SUZU...
CRACK
WHOA!
WE CAN CARRY HIM BACK ON THE TATAMI MAT.
WHAT ABOUT GOEMON?
MASTER HANZO...
I AM VERY SORRY...
...FOR THIS WHOLE INCIDENT.

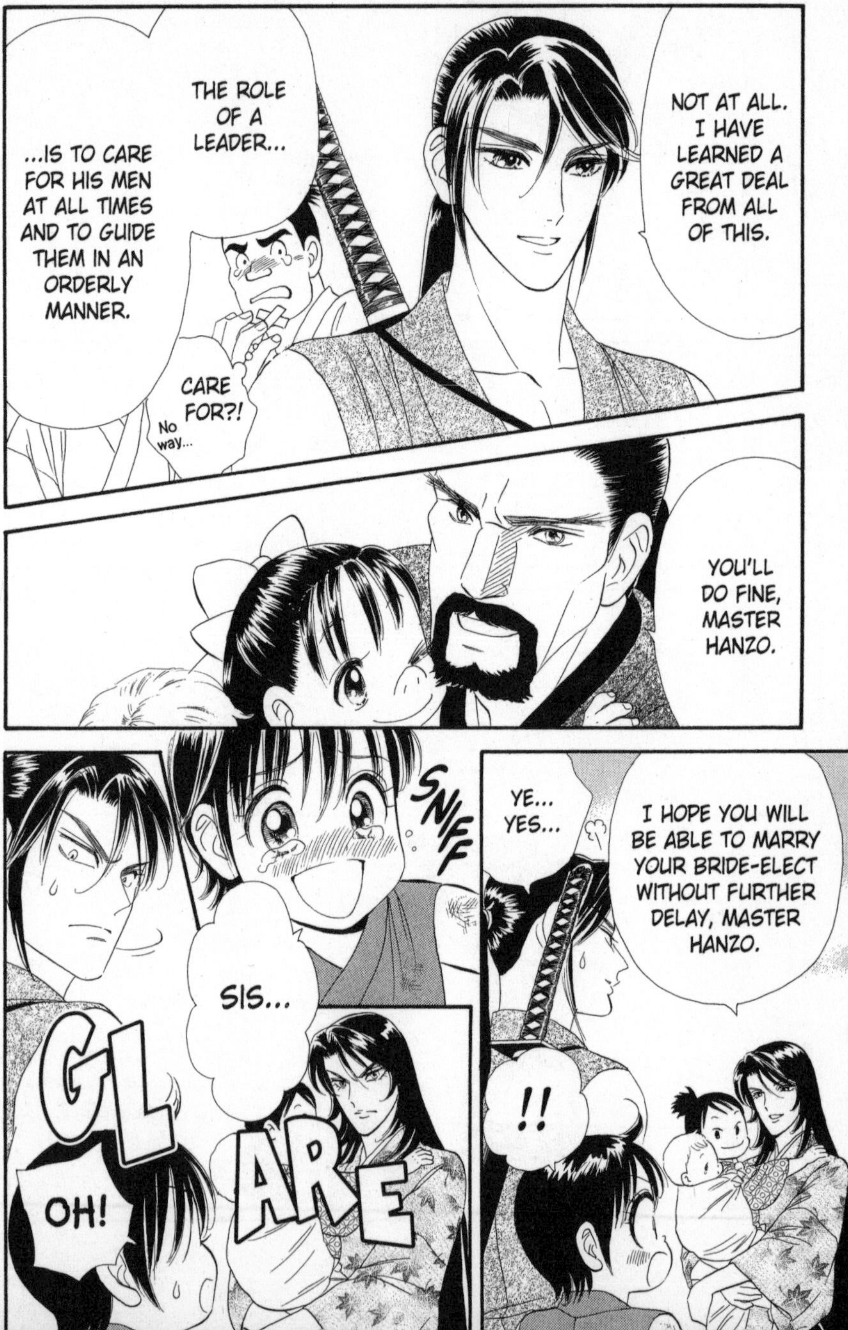
NOT AT ALL. I HAVE LEARNED A GREAT DEAL FROM ALL OF THIS.
THE ROLE OF A LEADER...
...IS TO CARE FOR HIS MEN AT ALL TIMES AND TO GUIDE THEM IN AN ORDERLY MANNER.
CARE FOR?!
No way...
YOU'LL DO FINE, MASTER HANZO.
I HOPE YOU WILL BE ABLE TO MARRY YOUR BRIDE-ELECT WITHOUT FURTHER DELAY, MASTER HANZO.
YE... YES...
!!
SNIFF
SIS...
GLARE
OH!

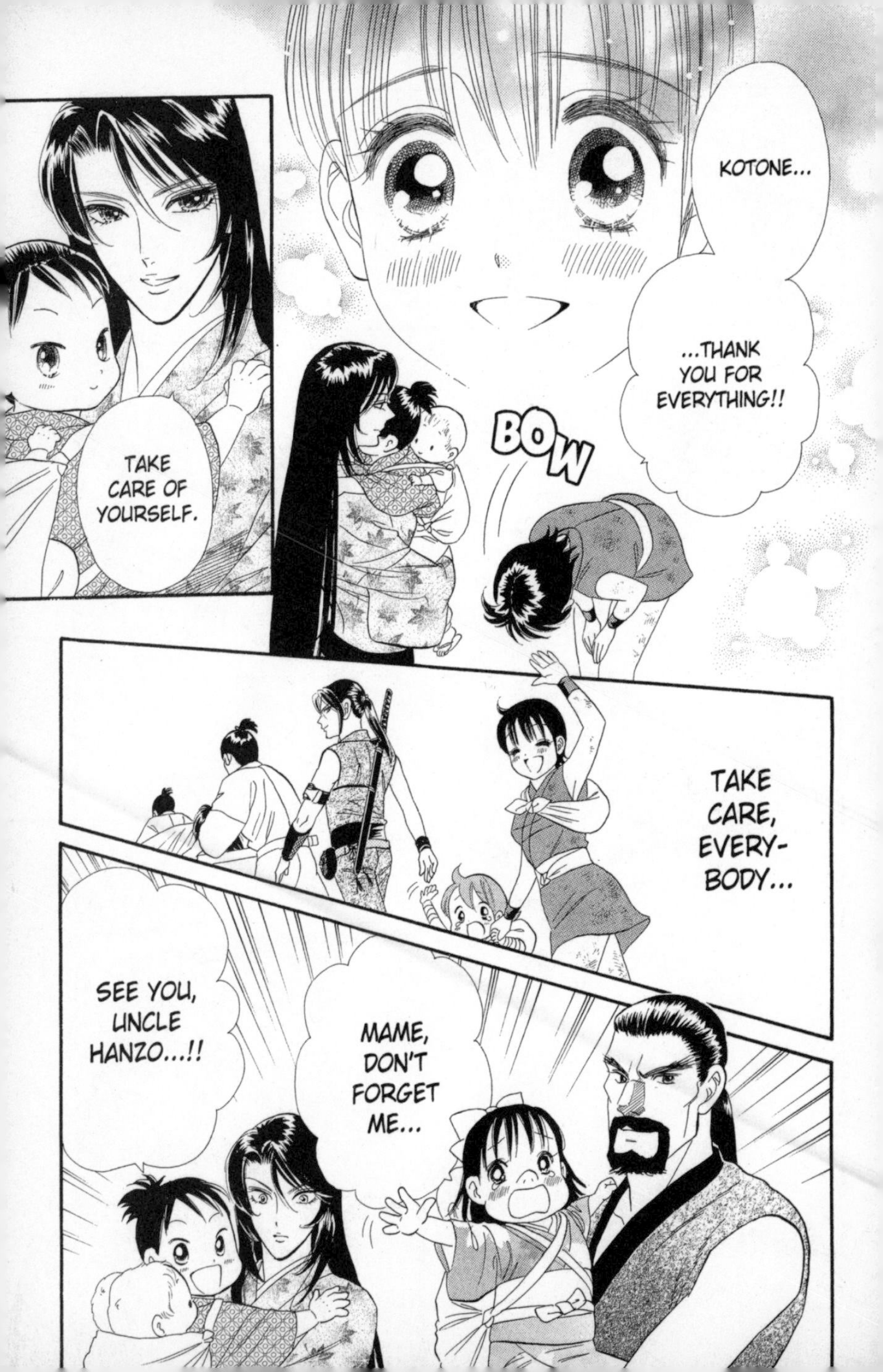
KOTONE...
...THANK YOU FOR EVERYTHING!!
BOW
TAKE CARE OF YOURSELF.
TAKE CARE, EVERY-BODY...
MAME, DON'T FORGET ME...
SEE YOU, UNCLE HANZO...!!

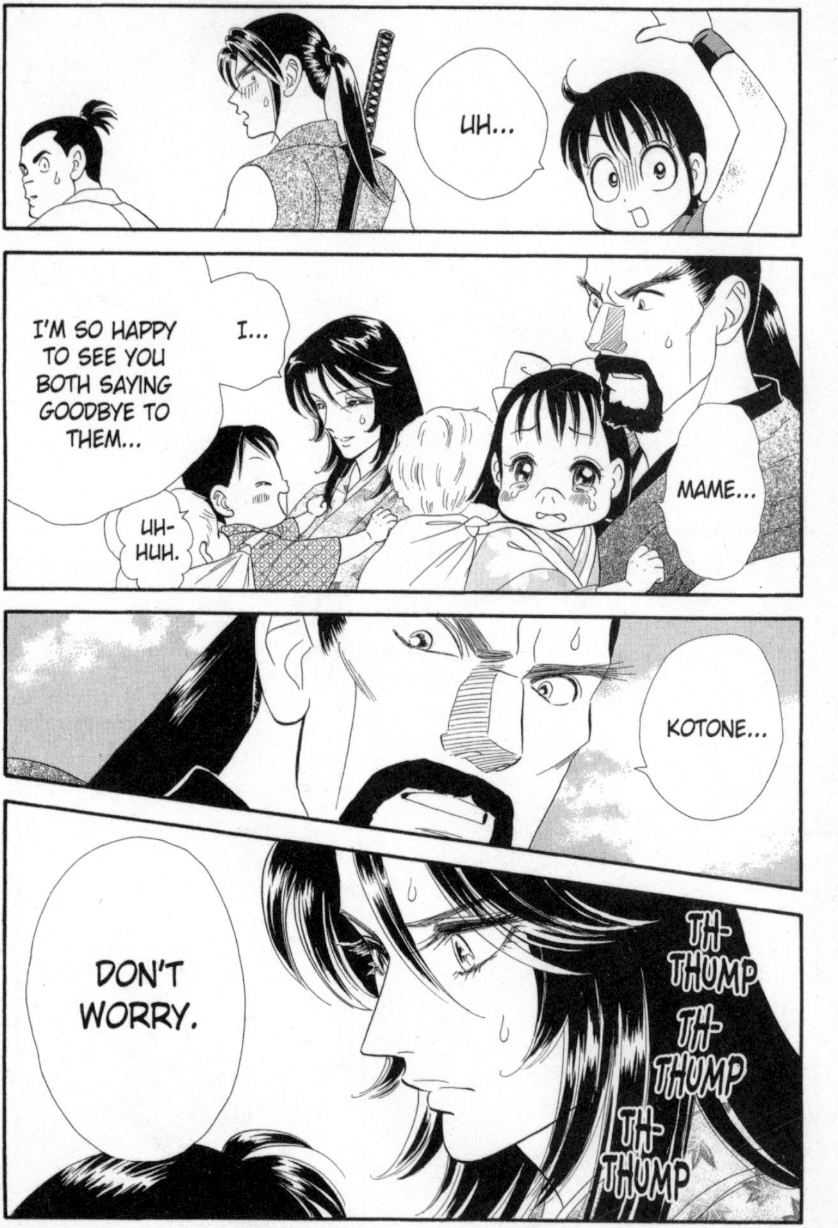
UH...
MAME...
I...
I'M SO HAPPY TO SEE YOU BOTH SAYING GOODBYE TO THEM...
UH-HUH.
KOTONE...
DON'T WORRY.
TH-THUMP
TH-THUMP
TH-THUMP

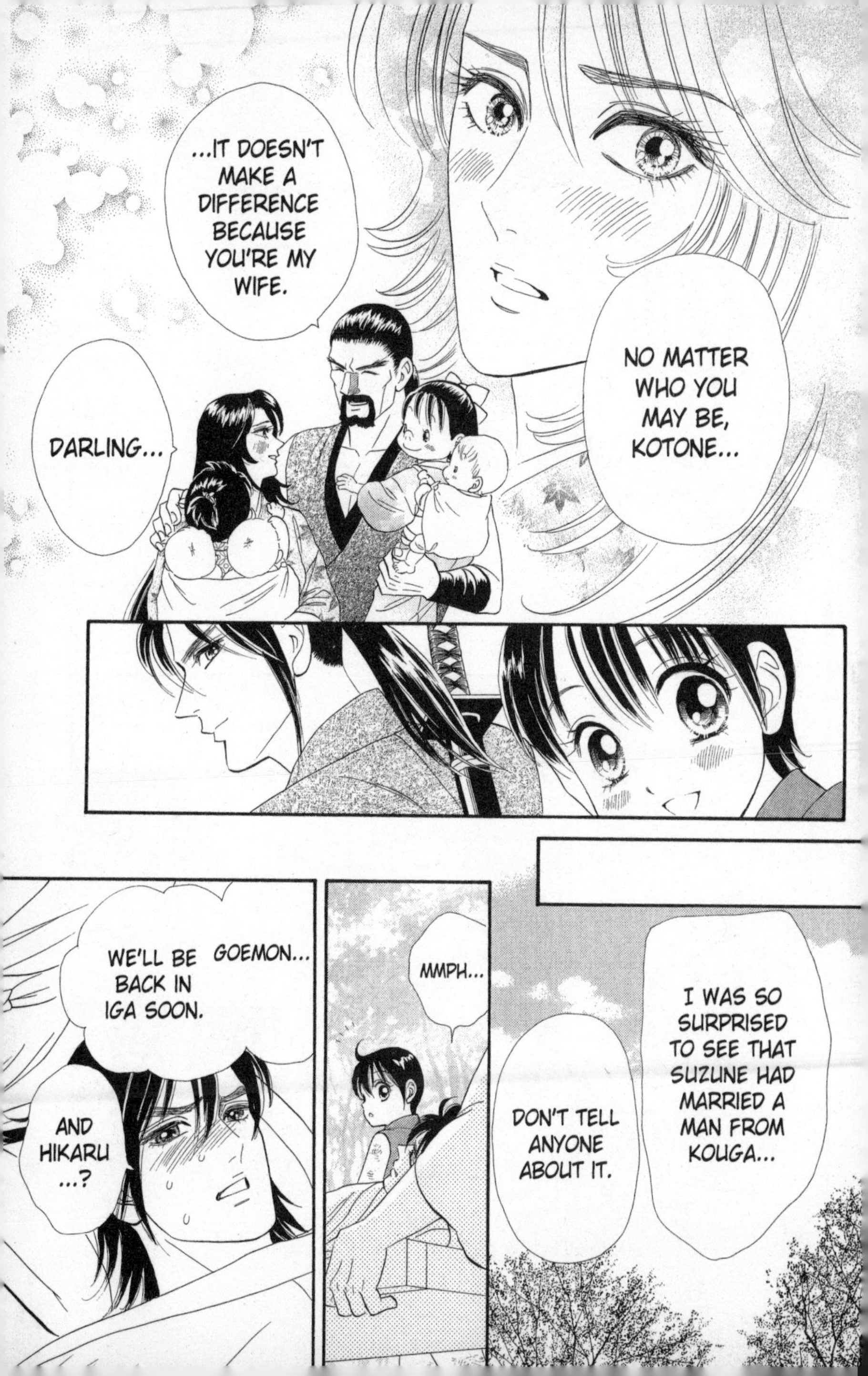
NO MATTER WHO YOU MAY BE, KOTONE...
...IT DOESN'T MAKE A DIFFERENCE BECAUSE YOU'RE MY WIFE.
DARLING...
I WAS SO SURPRISED TO SEE THAT SUZUNE HAD MARRIED A MAN FROM KOUGA...
DON'T TELL ANYONE ABOUT IT.
MMPH...
GOEMON...
WE'LL BE BACK IN IGA SOON.
AND HIKARU ...?

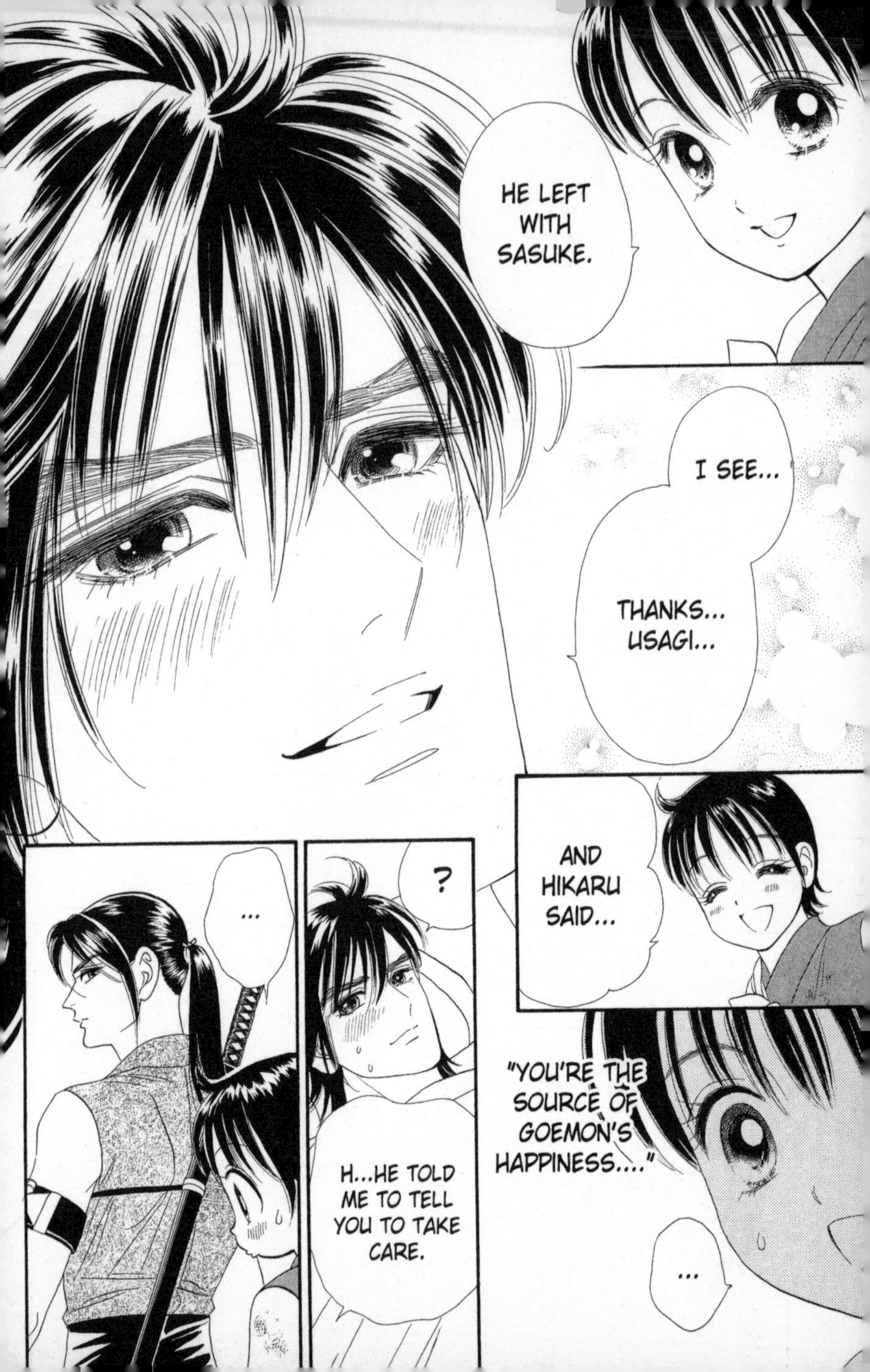
HE LEFT WITH SASUKE.
I SEE...
THANKS... USAGI...
AND HIKARU SAID...
"YOU'RE THE SOURCE OF GOEMON'S HAPPINESS...."
...
?
H...HE TOLD ME TO TELL YOU TO TAKE CARE.
...

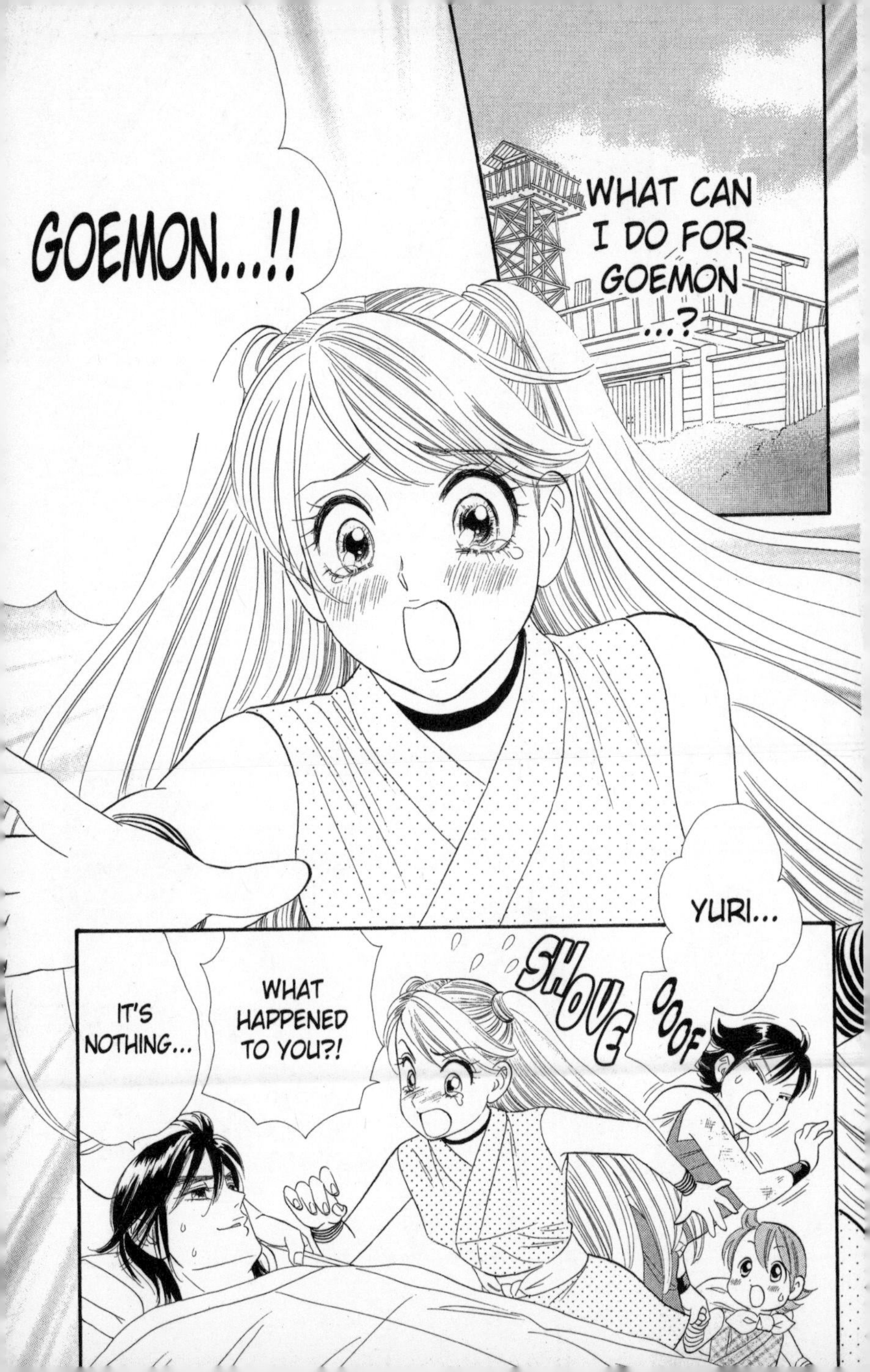

WHAT CAN I DO FOR GOEMON ...?
GOEMON...!!
YURI...
OOOF
SHOVE
WHAT HAPPENED TO YOU?!
IT'S NOTHING...

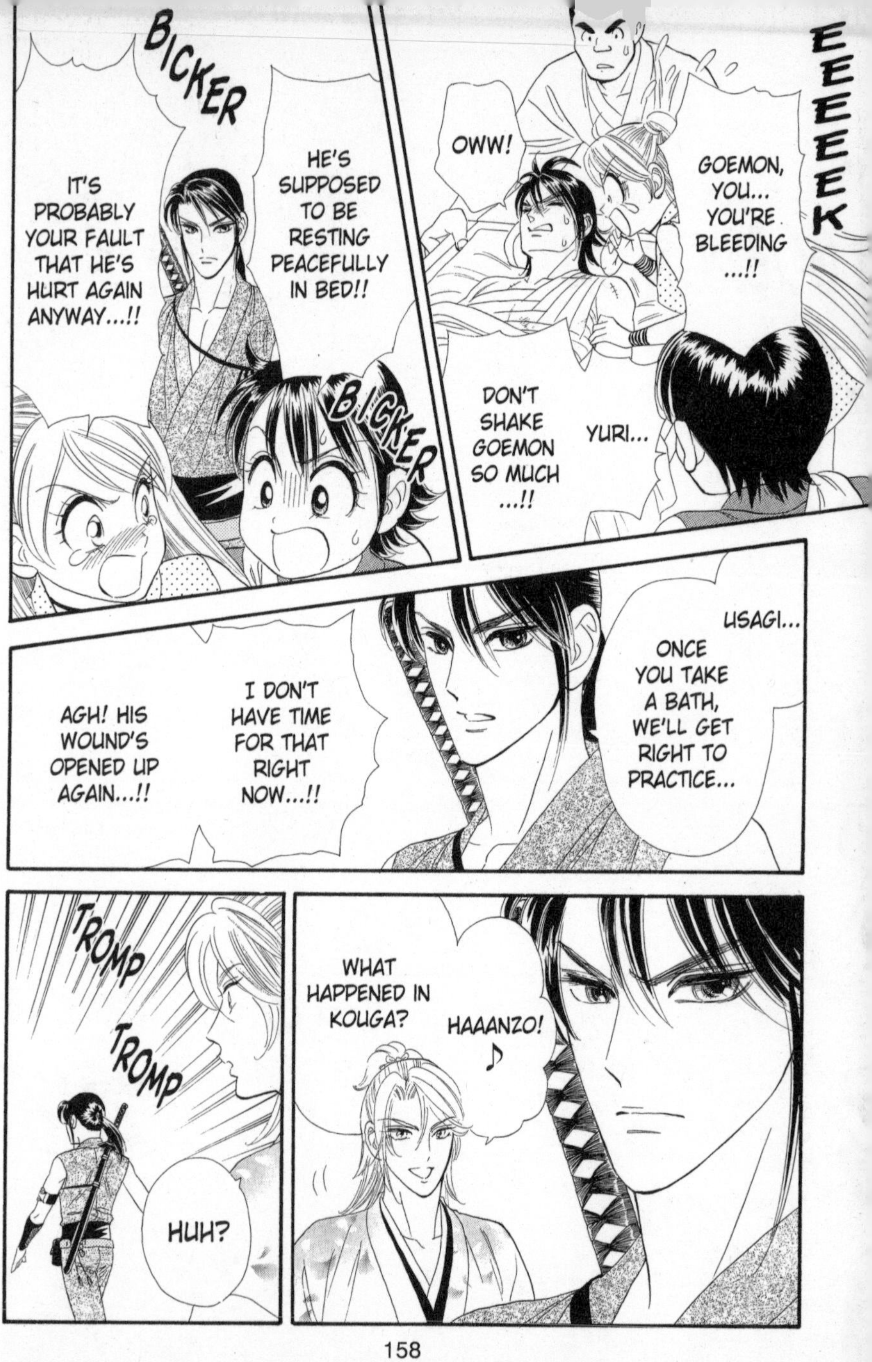
EEEEEEK
GOEMON, YOU... YOU'RE BLEEDING ...!!
OWW!
YURI...
DON'T SHAKE GOEMON SO MUCH ...!!
BICKER
HE'S SUPPOSED TO BE RESTING PEACEFULLY IN BED!!
IT'S PROBABLY YOUR FAULT THAT HE'S HURT AGAIN ANYWAY...!!
BICKER
USAGI...
ONCE YOU TAKE A BATH, WE'LL GET RIGHT TO PRACTICE...
I DON'T HAVE TIME FOR THAT RIGHT NOW...!!
AGH! HIS WOUND'S OPENED UP AGAIN...!!
HAAANZO! ♪
WHAT HAPPENED IN KOUGA?
TROMP
TROMP
HUH?

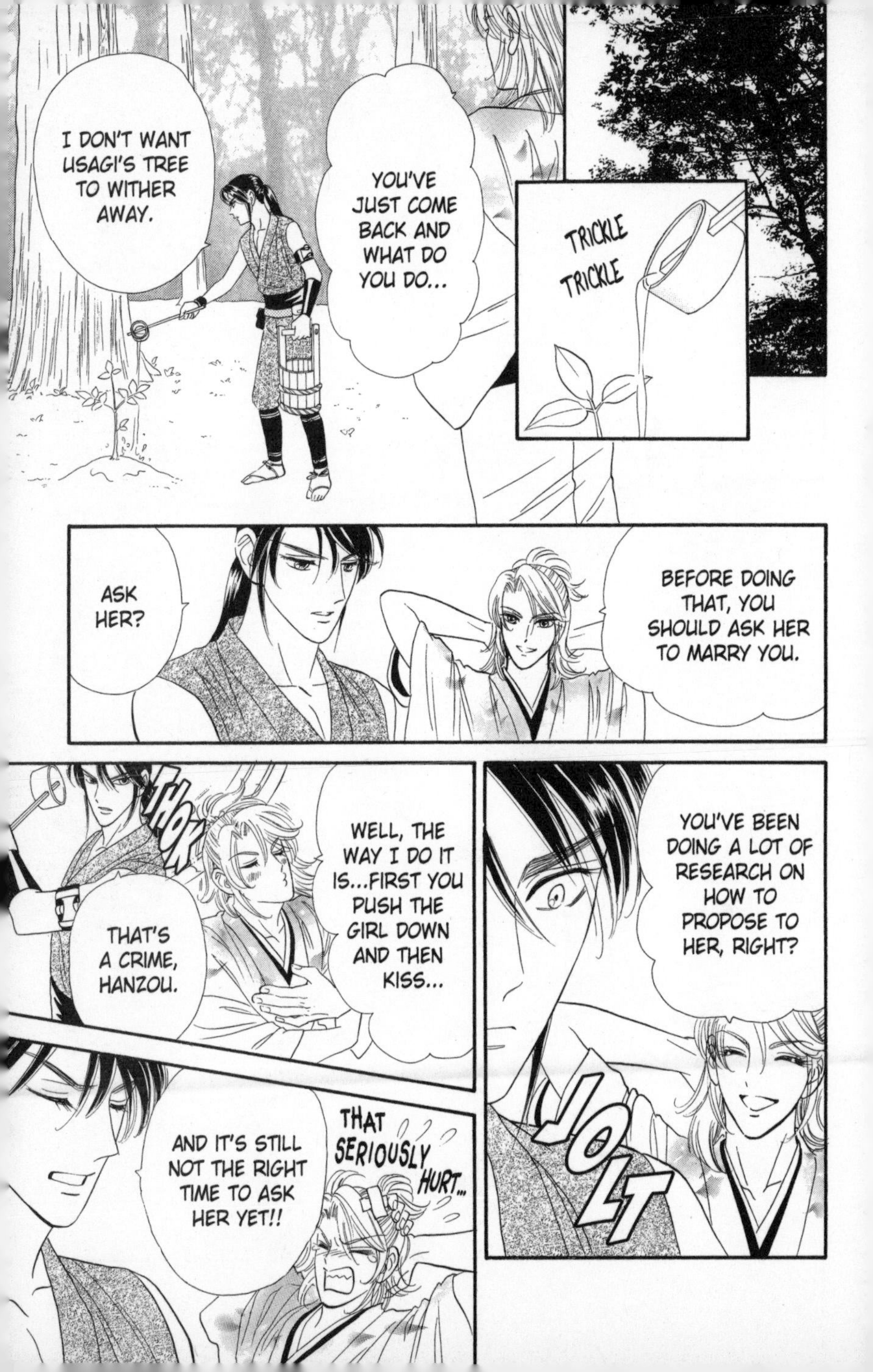
TRICKLE
TRICKLE
YOU'VE JUST COME BACK AND WHAT DO YOU DO...
I DON'T WANT USAGI'S TREE TO WITHER AWAY.
BEFORE DOING THAT, YOU SHOULD ASK HER TO MARRY YOU.
ASK HER?
YOU'VE BEEN DOING A LOT OF RESEARCH ON HOW TO PROPOSE TO HER, RIGHT?
JOLT
WELL, THE WAY I DO IT IS...FIRST YOU PUSH THE GIRL DOWN AND THEN KISS...
THAT'S A CRIME, HANZOU.
THAT SERIOUSLY HURT...
AND IT'S STILL NOT THE RIGHT TIME TO ASK HER YET!!

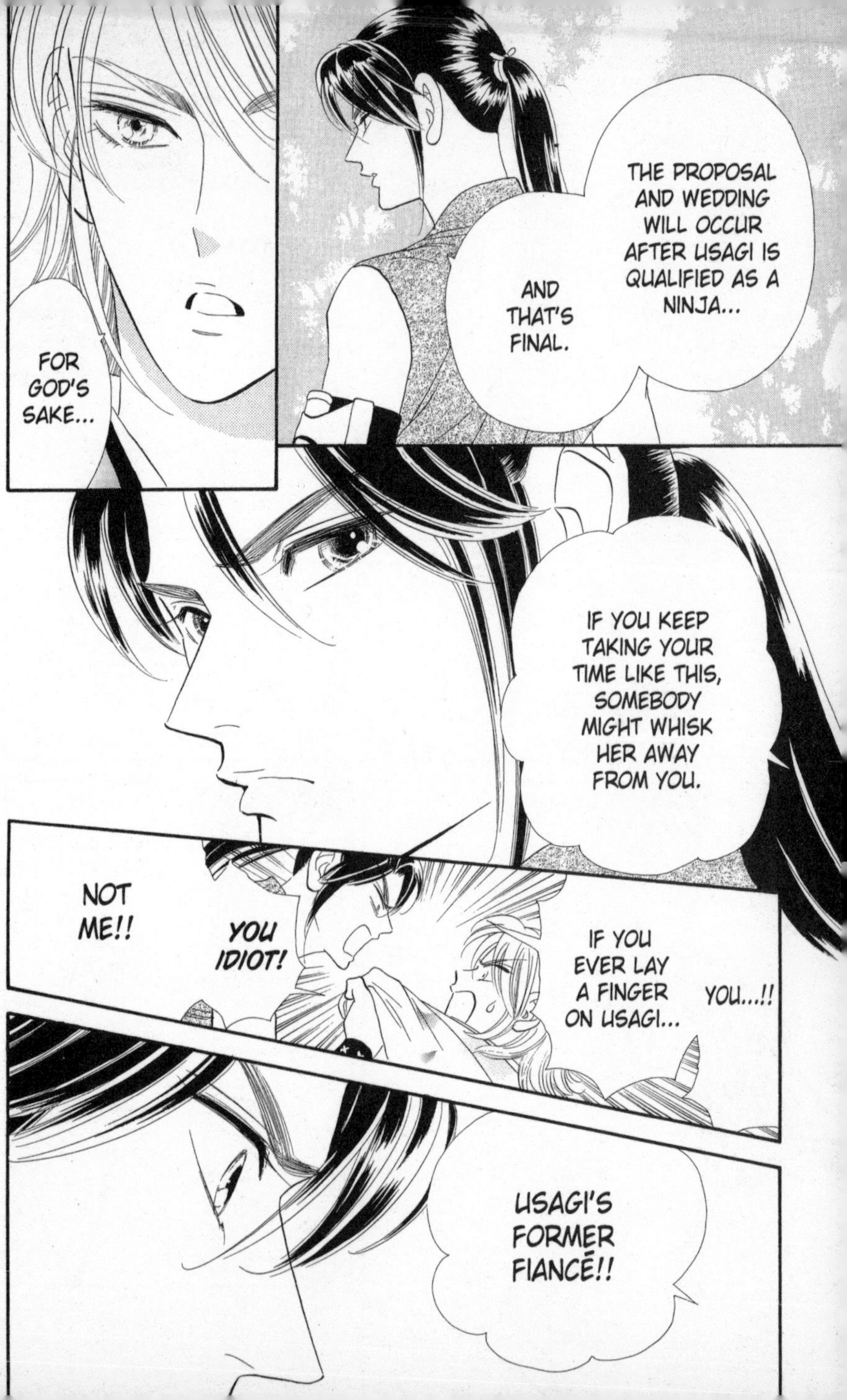
THE PROPOSAL AND WEDDING WILL OCCUR AFTER USAGI IS QUALIFIED AS A NINJA...
AND THAT'S FINAL.
FOR GOD'S SAKE...
IF YOU KEEP TAKING YOUR TIME LIKE THIS, SOMEBODY MIGHT WHISK HER AWAY FROM YOU.
YOU...!!
IF YOU EVER LAY A FINGER ON USAGI...
YOU IDIOT!
NOT ME!!
USAGI'S FORMER FIANCÉ!!

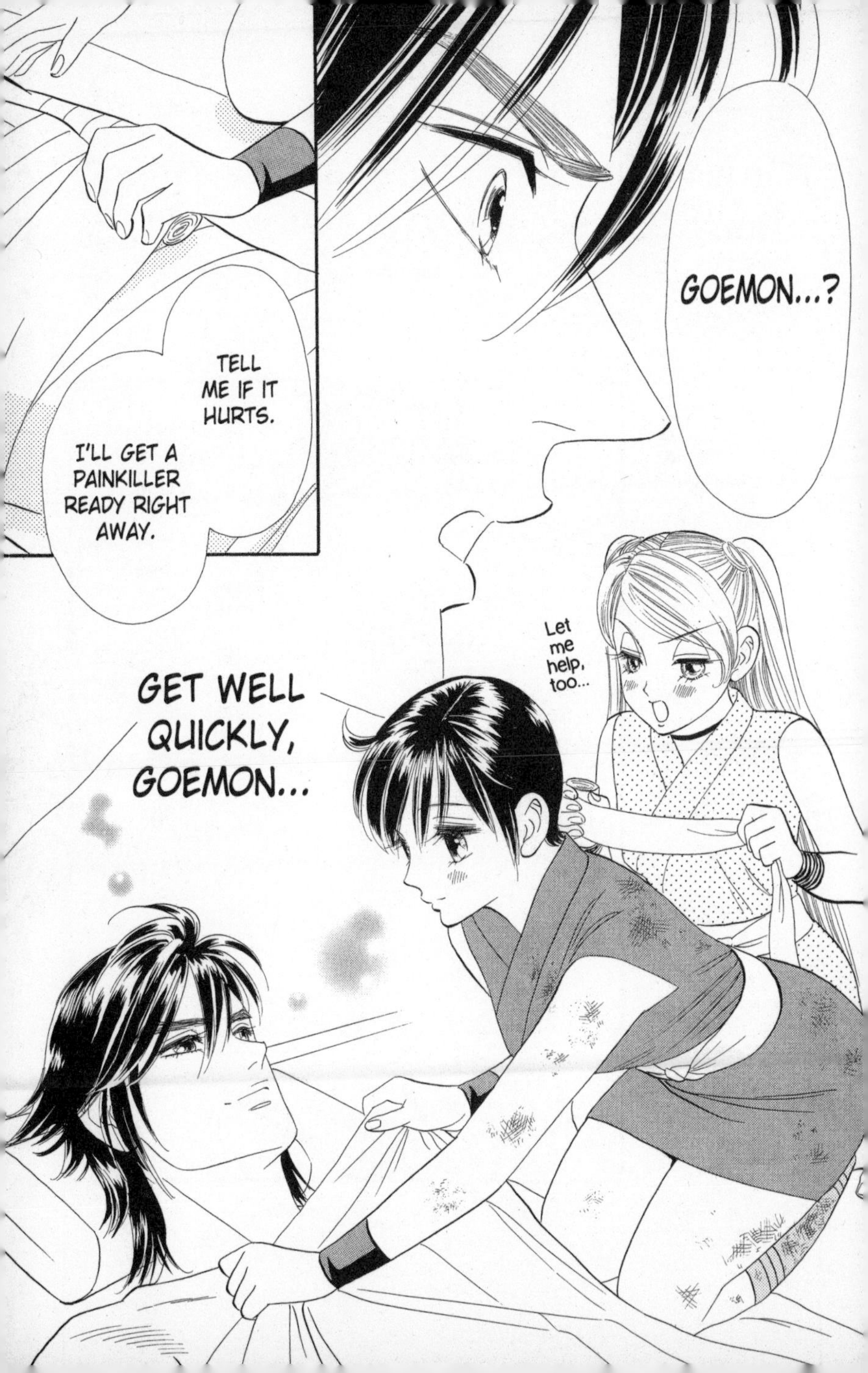
GOEMON...?
TELL ME IF IT HURTS.
I'LL GET A PAINKILLER READY RIGHT AWAY.
Let me help, too...
GET WELL QUICKLY, GOEMON...

TAIL OF THE MOON EXTRA: TODAY'S MISSION
"I WANT TO SEE HANZO IN A SWIMSUIT!"
-NAOPU, AKITA PREFECTURE

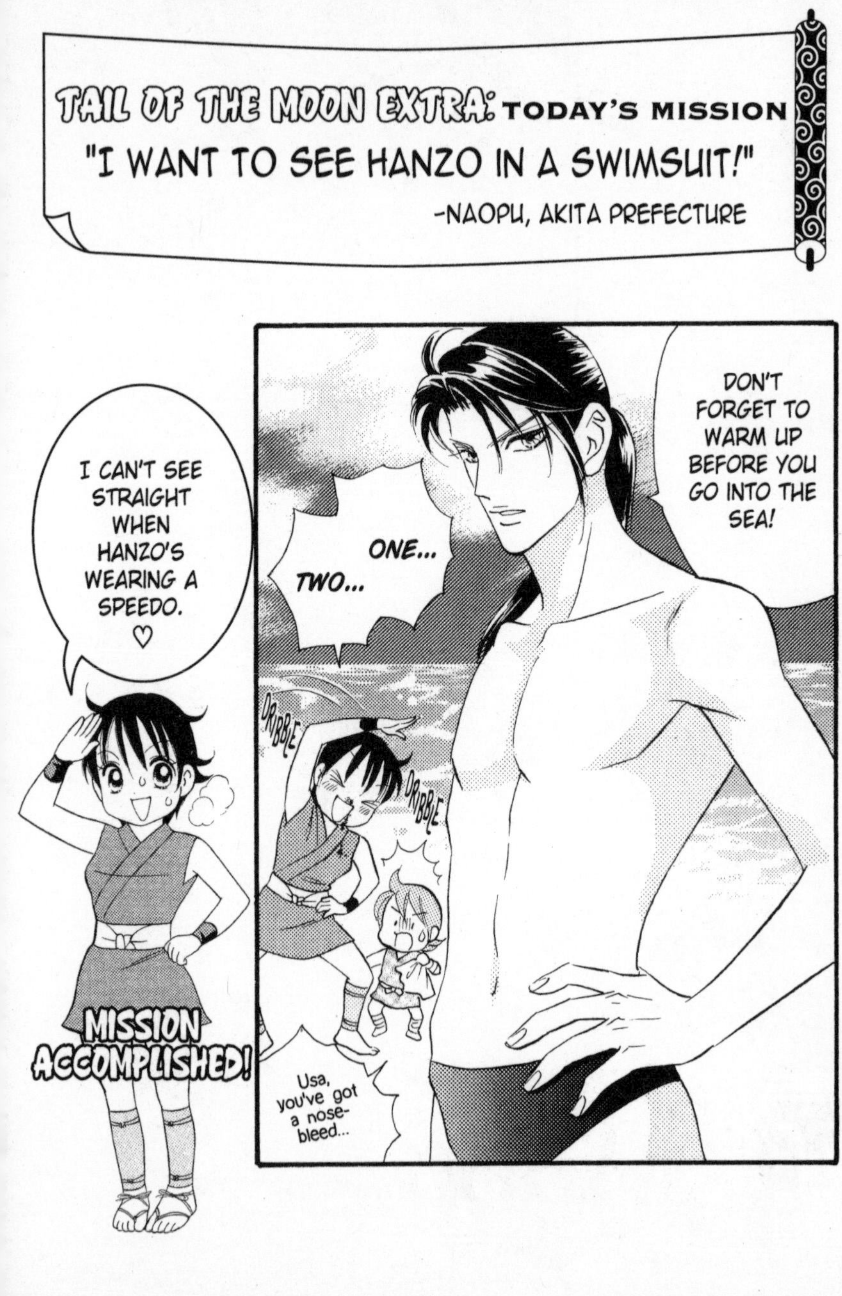
DON'T FORGET TO WARM UP BEFORE YOU GO INTO THE SEA!
ONE... TWO...
DRIBBLE
DRIBBLE
Usa, you've got a nose-bleed...
I CAN'T SEE STRAIGHT WHEN HANZO'S WEARING A SPEEDO. ♡
MISSION ACCOMPLISHED!

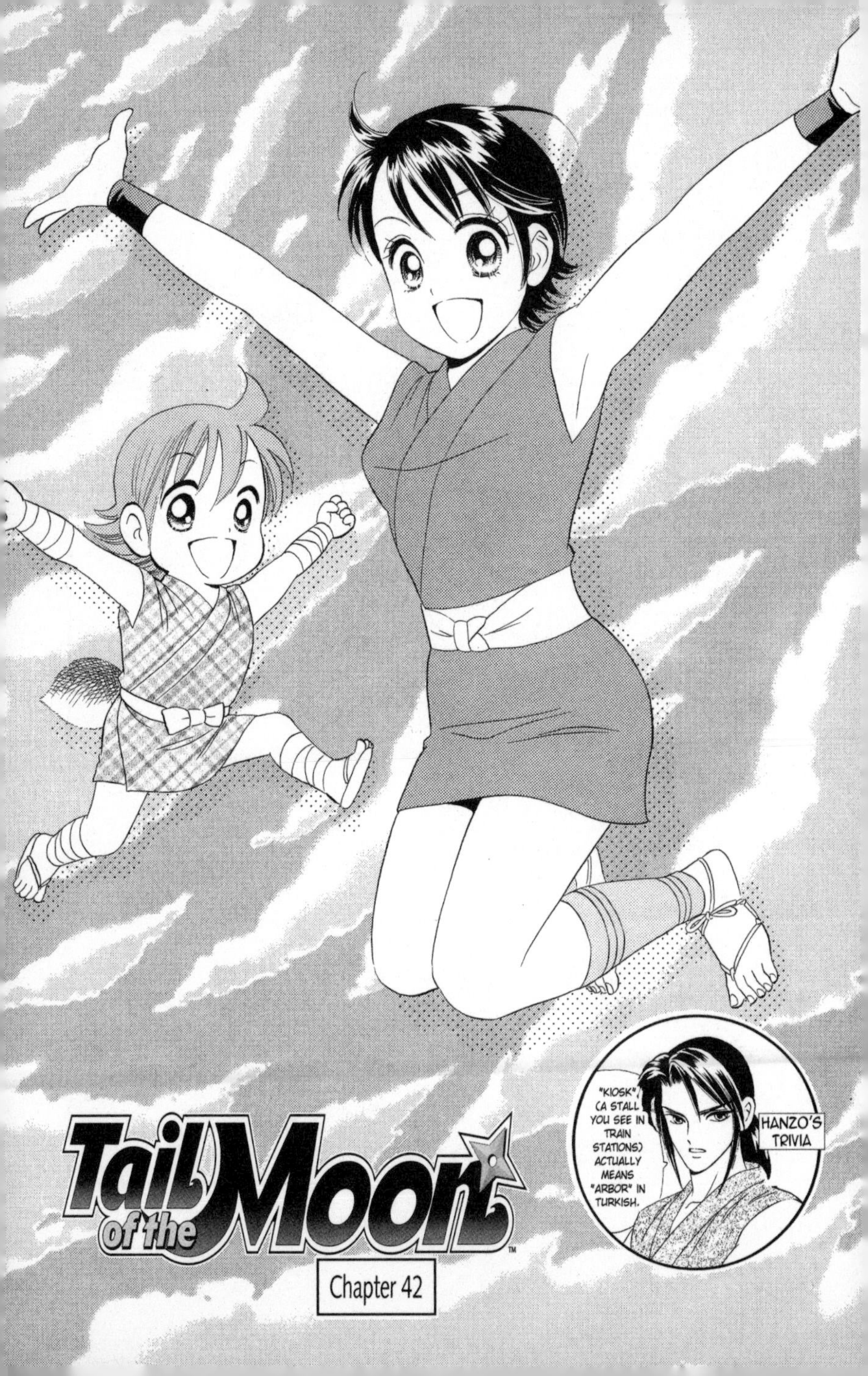
HANZO'S TRIVIA
"KIOSK" (A STALL YOU SEE IN TRAIN STATIONS) ACTUALLY MEANS "ARBOR" IN TURKISH.
Tail of the Moon™
Chapter 42

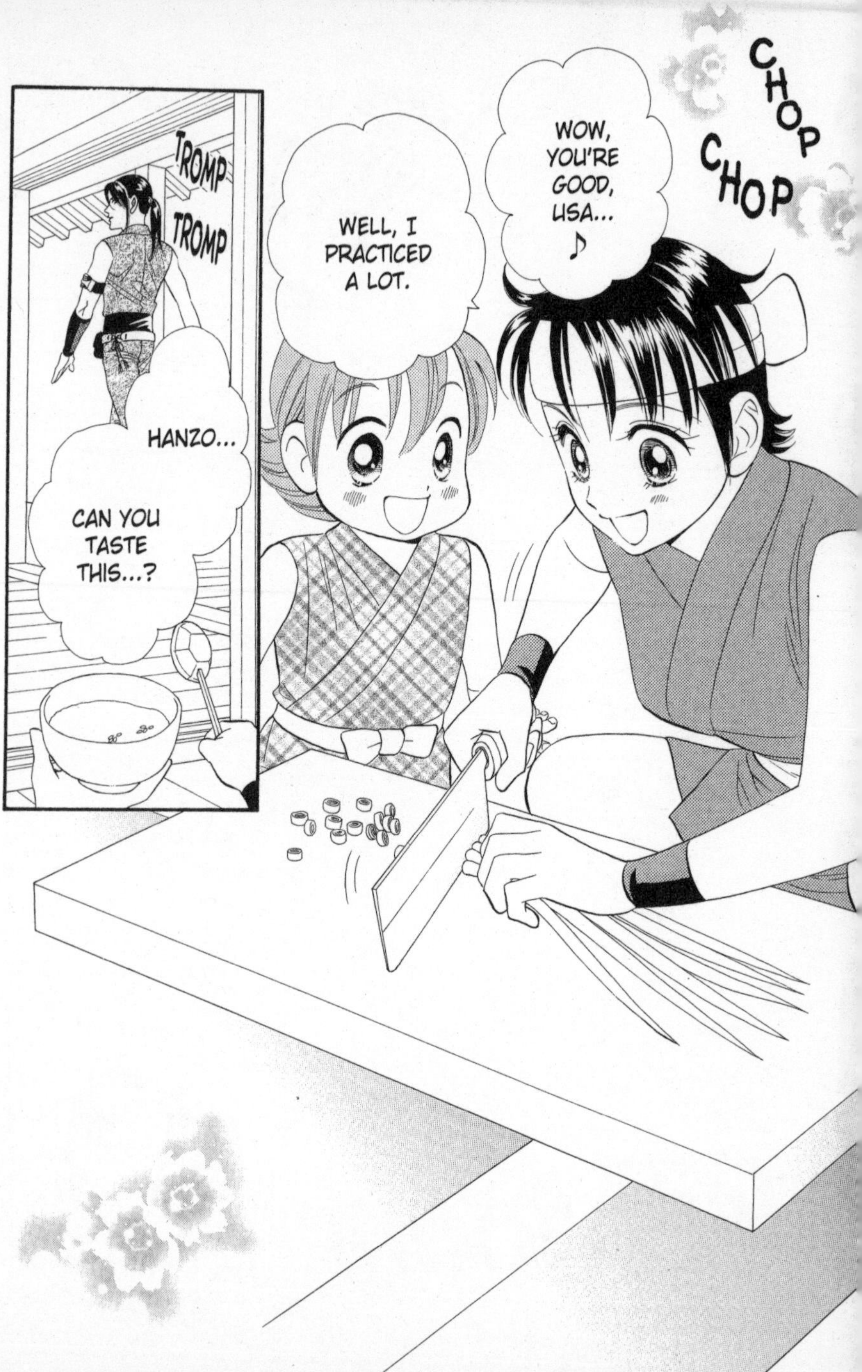
CHOP CHOP
WOW, YOU'RE GOOD, USA... ♪
WELL, I PRACTICED A LOT.
TROMP TROMP
HANZO...
CAN YOU TASTE THIS...?

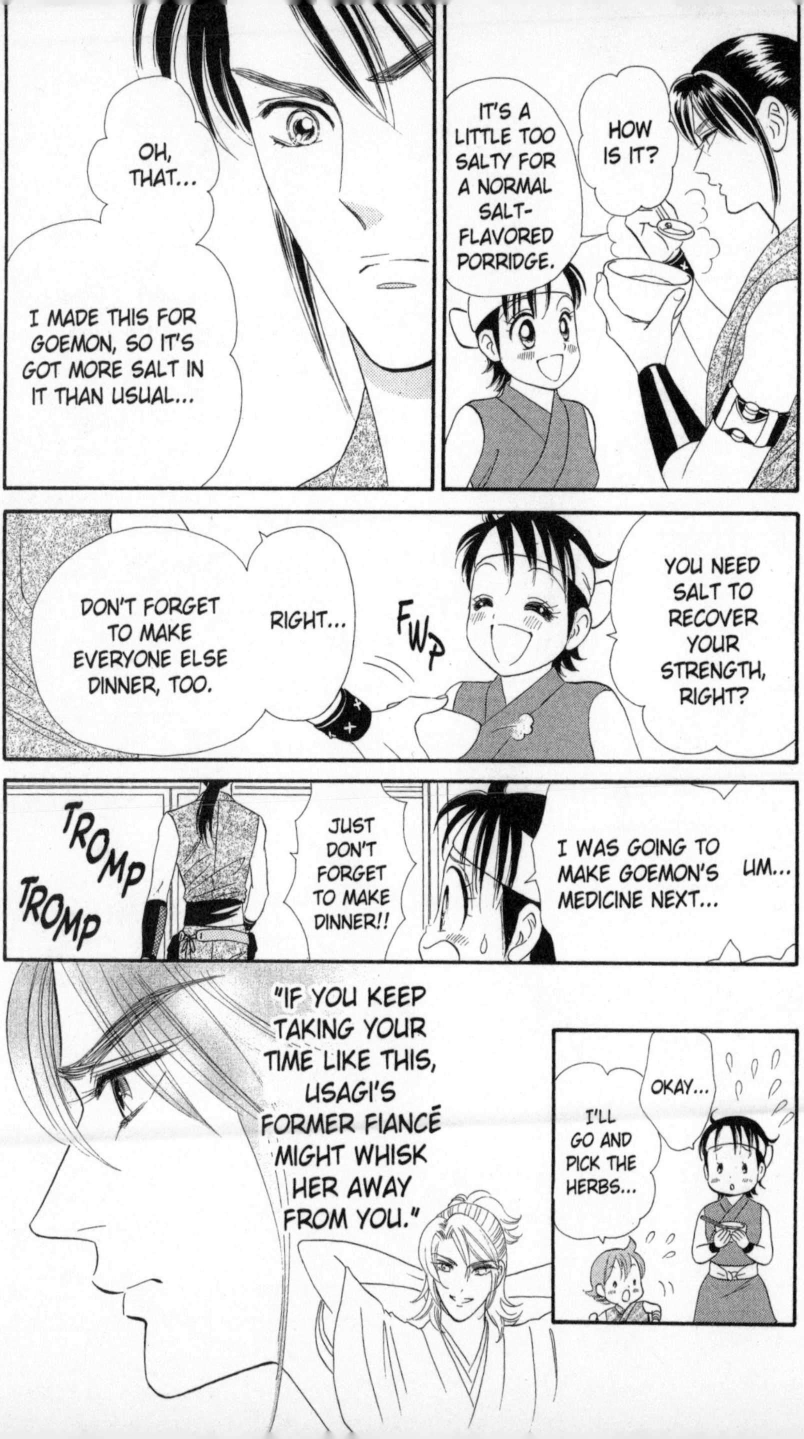

HOW IS IT?
IT'S A LITTLE TOO SALTY FOR A NORMAL SALT-FLAVORED PORRIDGE.
OH, THAT...
I MADE THIS FOR GOEMON, SO IT'S GOT MORE SALT IN IT THAN USUAL...
YOU NEED SALT TO RECOVER YOUR STRENGTH, RIGHT?
FWP
RIGHT...
DON'T FORGET TO MAKE EVERYONE ELSE DINNER, TOO.
UM...
I WAS GOING TO MAKE GOEMON'S MEDICINE NEXT...
JUST DON'T FORGET TO MAKE DINNER!!
TROMP
TROMP
OKAY...
I'LL GO AND PICK THE HERBS...
"IF YOU KEEP TAKING YOUR TIME LIKE THIS, USAGI'S FORMER FIANCÉ MIGHT WHISK HER AWAY FROM YOU."

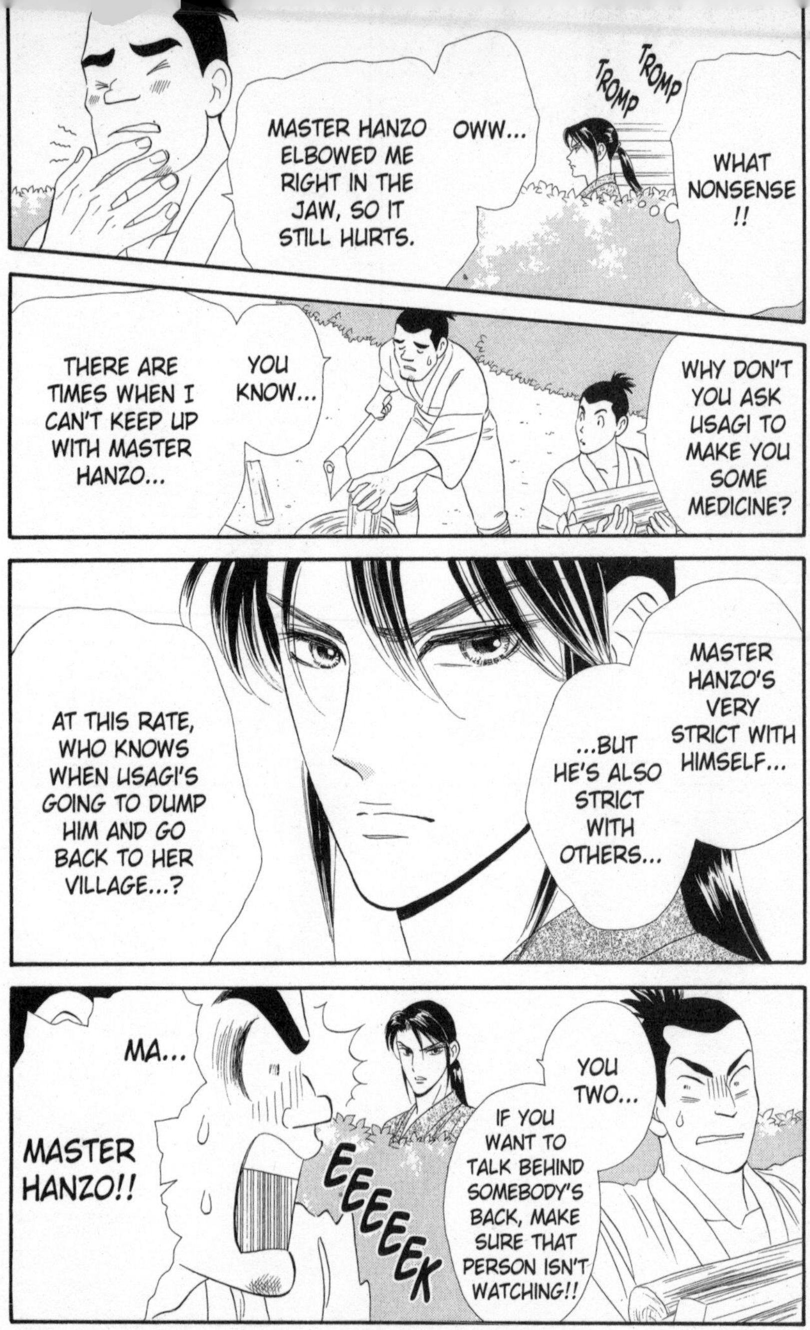
TROMP
TROMP
WHAT NONSENSE!!
OWW...
MASTER HANZO ELBOWED ME RIGHT IN THE JAW, SO IT STILL HURTS.
WHY DON'T YOU ASK USAGI TO MAKE YOU SOME MEDICINE?
YOU KNOW...
THERE ARE TIMES WHEN I CAN'T KEEP UP WITH MASTER HANZO...
MASTER HANZO'S VERY STRICT WITH HIMSELF...
...BUT HE'S ALSO STRICT WITH OTHERS...
AT THIS RATE, WHO KNOWS WHEN USAGI'S GOING TO DUMP HIM AND GO BACK TO HER VILLAGE...?
YOU TWO...
IF YOU WANT TO TALK BEHIND SOMEBODY'S BACK, MAKE SURE THAT PERSON ISN'T WATCHING!!
EEEEEEK
MA...
MASTER HANZO!!

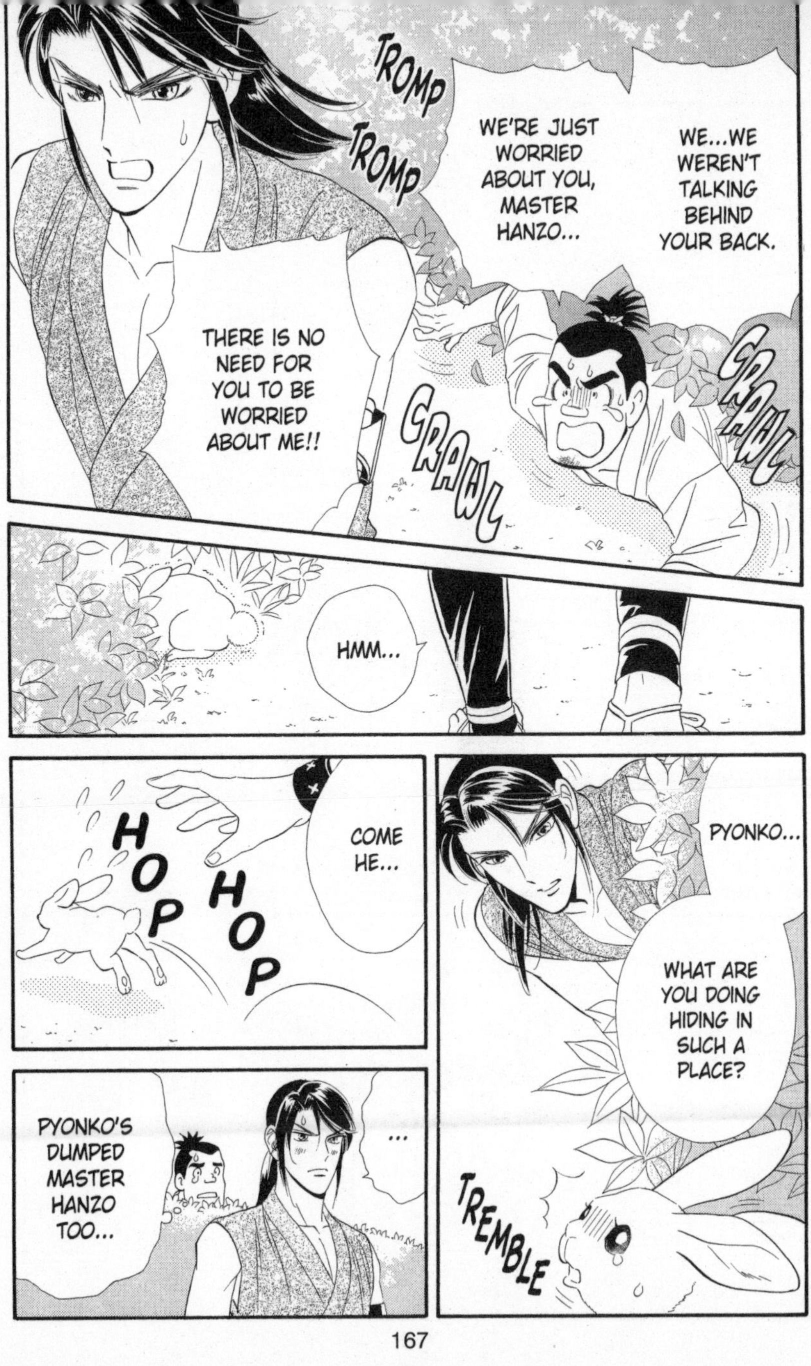

WE...WE WEREN'T TALKING BEHIND YOUR BACK.
WE'RE JUST WORRIED ABOUT YOU, MASTER HANZO...
TROMP TROMP
CRAWL
THERE IS NO NEED FOR YOU TO BE WORRIED ABOUT ME!!
CRAWL
HMM...
PYONKO...
WHAT ARE YOU DOING HIDING IN SUCH A PLACE?
TREMBLE
COME HE...
HOP HOP
...
PYONKO'S DUMPED MASTER HANZO TOO...

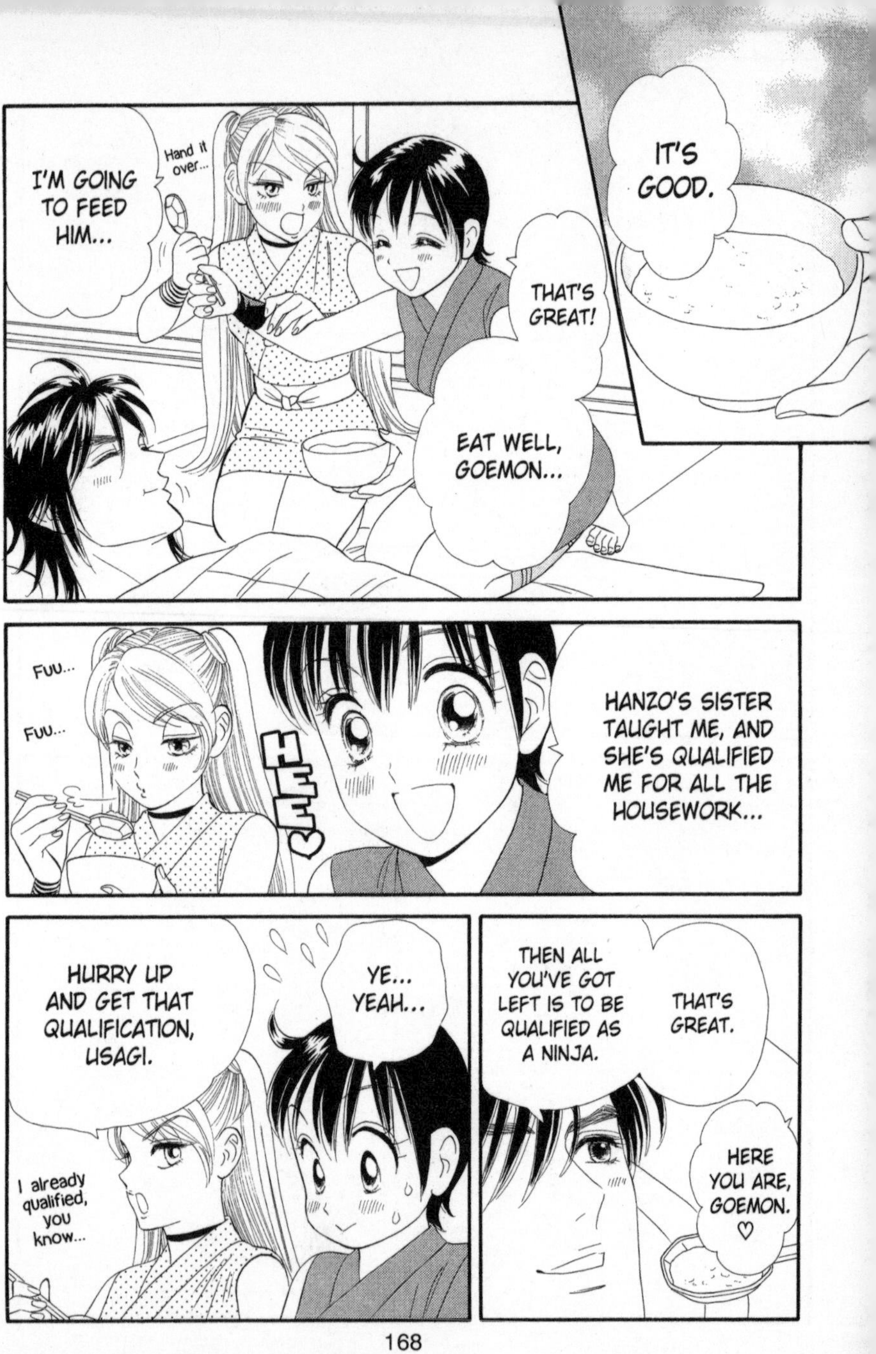
IT'S GOOD.
THAT'S GREAT!
EAT WELL, GOEMON...
Hand it over...
I'M GOING TO FEED HIM...
HANZO'S SISTER TAUGHT ME, AND SHE'S QUALIFIED ME FOR ALL THE HOUSEWORK...
HEE♡
Fuu...
Fuu...
THAT'S GREAT.
THEN ALL YOU'VE GOT LEFT IS TO BE QUALIFIED AS A NINJA.
HERE YOU ARE, GOEMON. ♡
YE... YEAH...
HURRY UP AND GET THAT QUALIFICATION, USAGI.
I already qualified, you know...

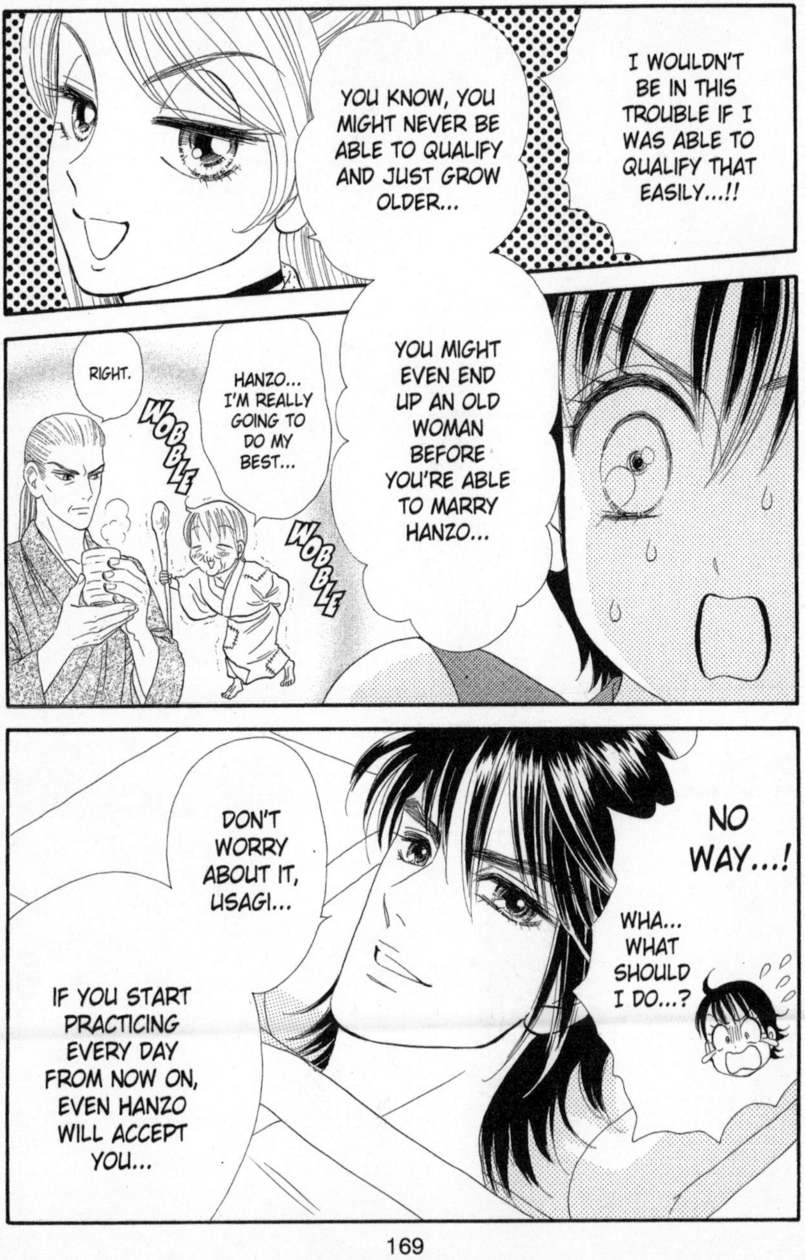
YOU KNOW, YOU MIGHT NEVER BE ABLE TO QUALIFY AND JUST GROW OLDER...
I WOULDN'T BE IN THIS TROUBLE IF I WAS ABLE TO QUALIFY THAT EASILY...!!
YOU MIGHT EVEN END UP AN OLD WOMAN BEFORE YOU'RE ABLE TO MARRY HANZO...
HANZO... I'M REALLY GOING TO DO MY BEST...
WOBBLE
WOBBLE
RIGHT.
NO WAY...!
DON'T WORRY ABOUT IT, USAGI...
WHA... WHAT SHOULD I DO...?
IF YOU START PRACTICING EVERY DAY FROM NOW ON, EVEN HANZO WILL ACCEPT YOU...

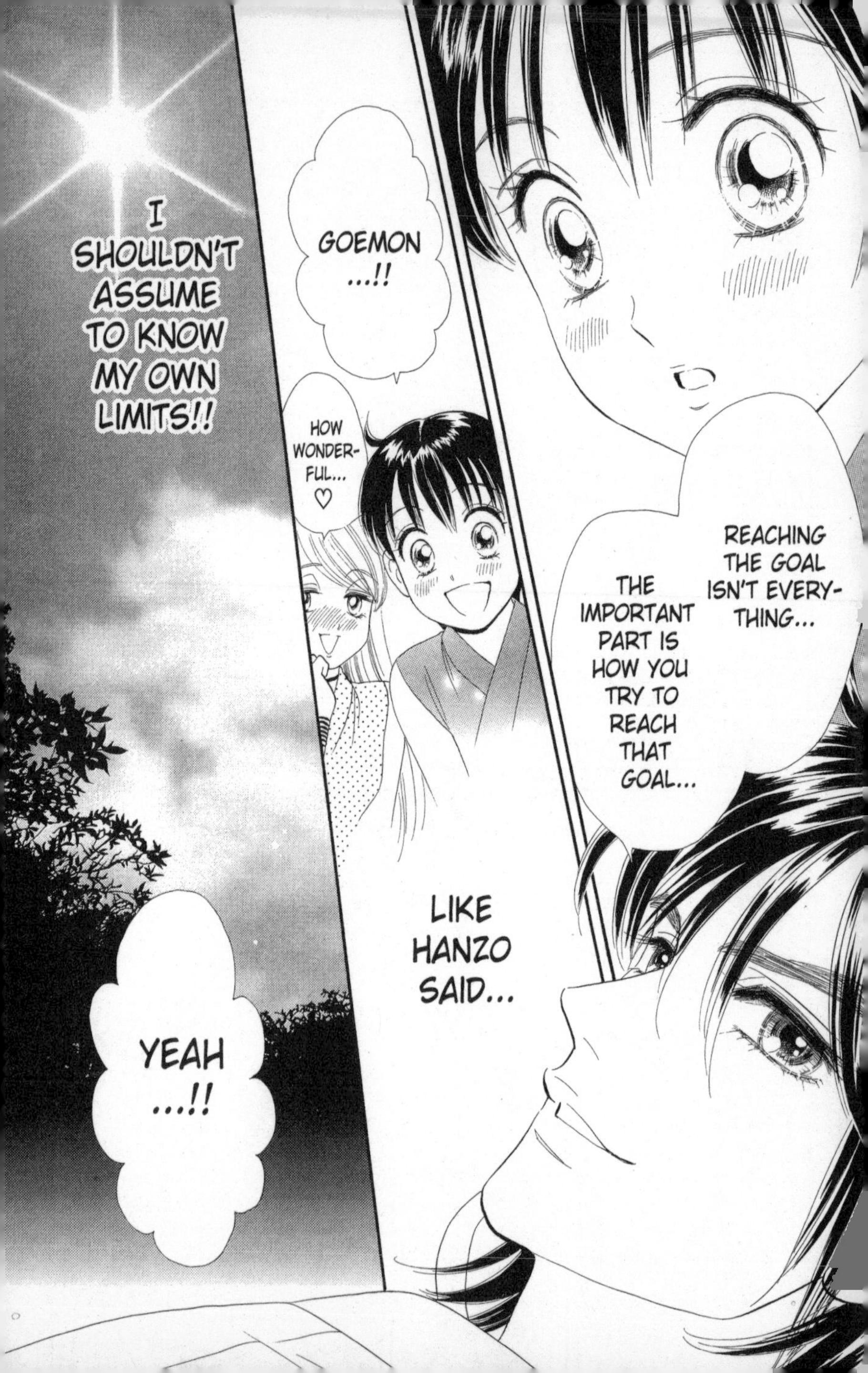
REACHING THE GOAL ISN'T EVERYTHING...
THE IMPORTANT PART IS HOW YOU TRY TO REACH THAT GOAL...
LIKE HANZO SAID...
GOEMON ...!!
HOW WONDERFUL... ♡
I SHOULDN'T ASSUME TO KNOW MY OWN LIMITS!!
YEAH ...!!

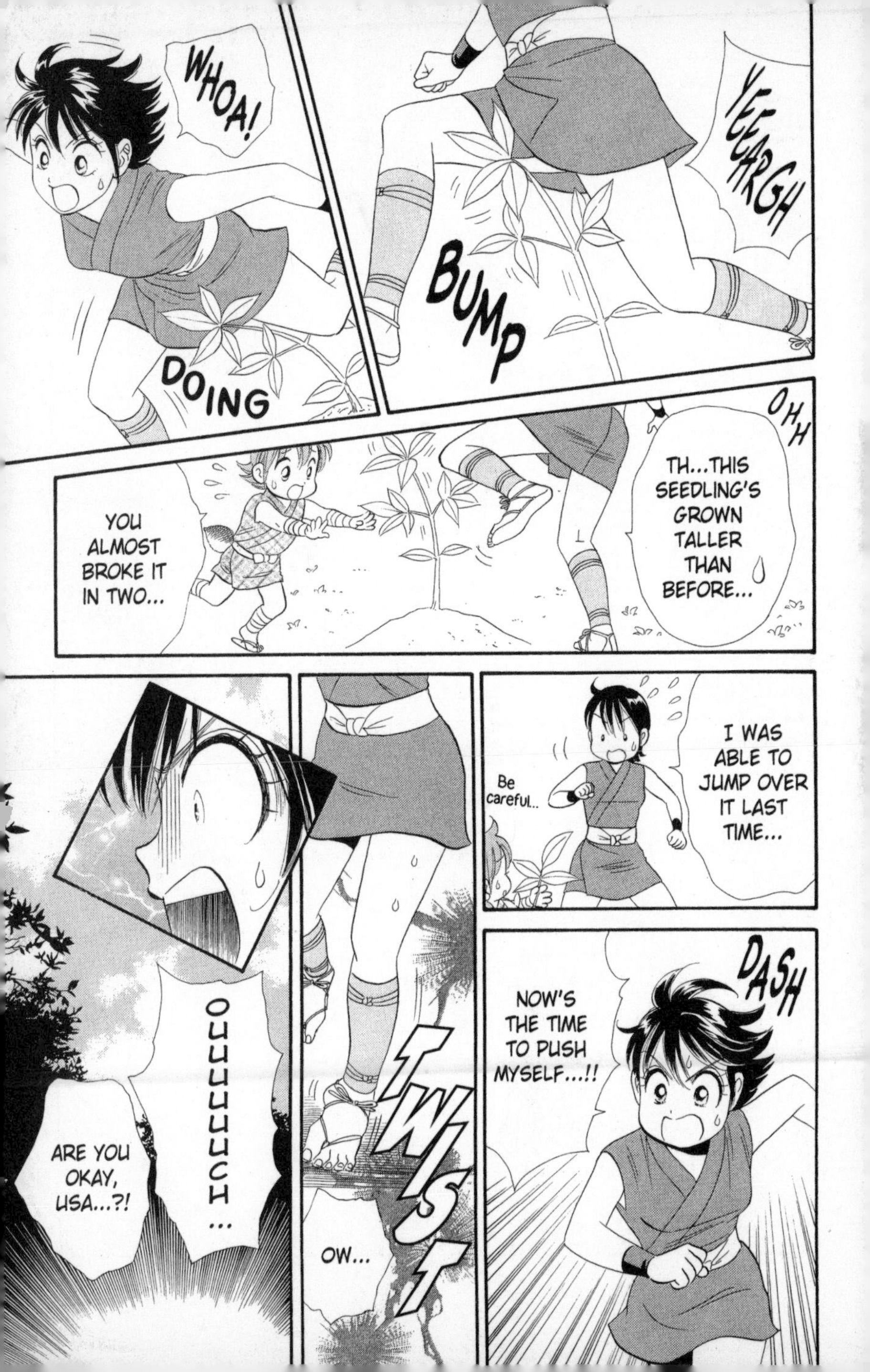
YEEARGH
BUMP
WHOA!
DOING
OHH
TH...THIS SEEDLING'S GROWN TALLER THAN BEFORE...
YOU ALMOST BROKE IT IN TWO...
I WAS ABLE TO JUMP OVER IT LAST TIME...
Be careful...
DASH
NOW'S THE TIME TO PUSH MYSELF....!!
TWIST
OW...
OUUUUUCH...
ARE YOU OKAY, USA...?!

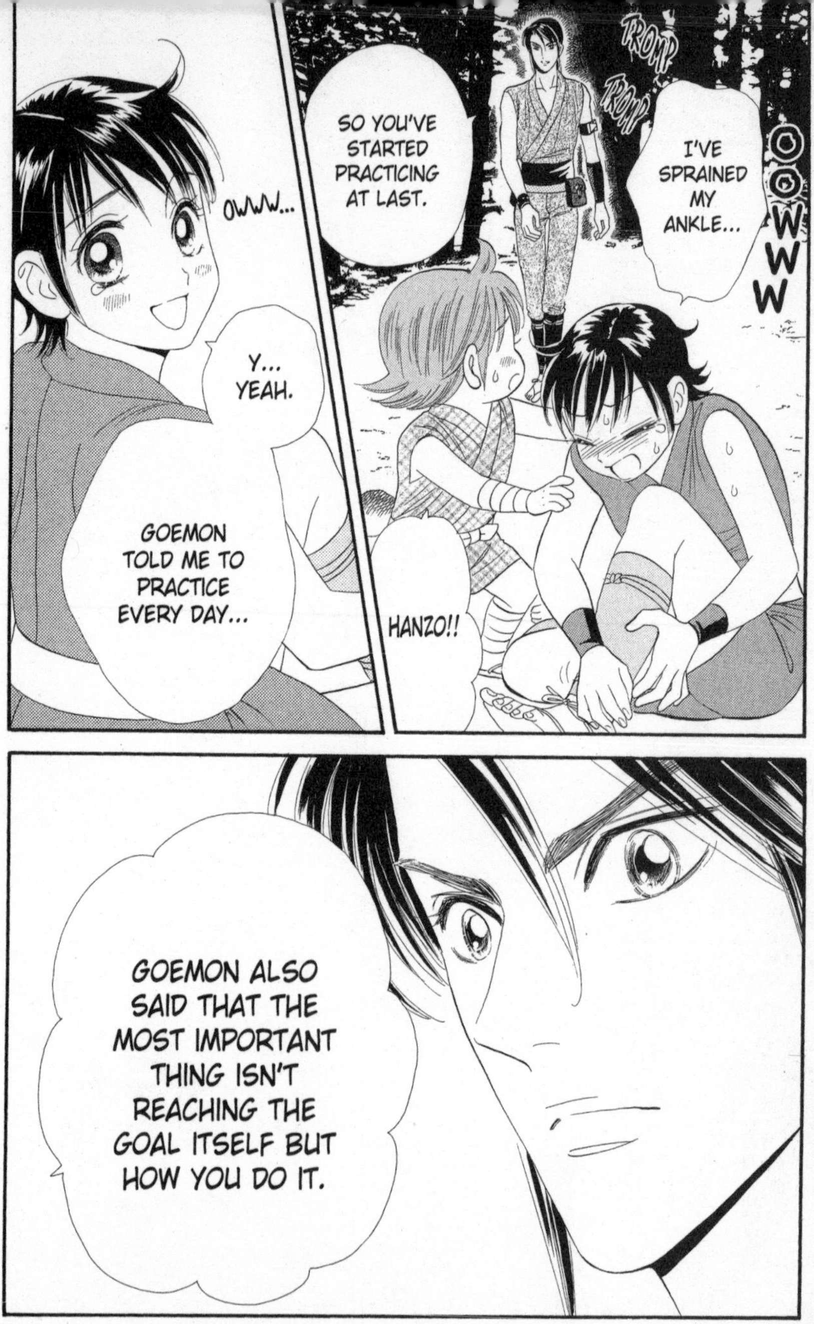
TROMP
TROMP
OOOWWW
I'VE SPRAINED MY ANKLE...
SO YOU'VE STARTED PRACTICING AT LAST.
HANZO!!
OWWW...
Y... YEAH.
GOEMON TOLD ME TO PRACTICE EVERY DAY...
GOEMON ALSO SAID THAT THE MOST IMPORTANT THING ISN'T REACHING THE GOAL ITSELF BUT HOW YOU DO IT.

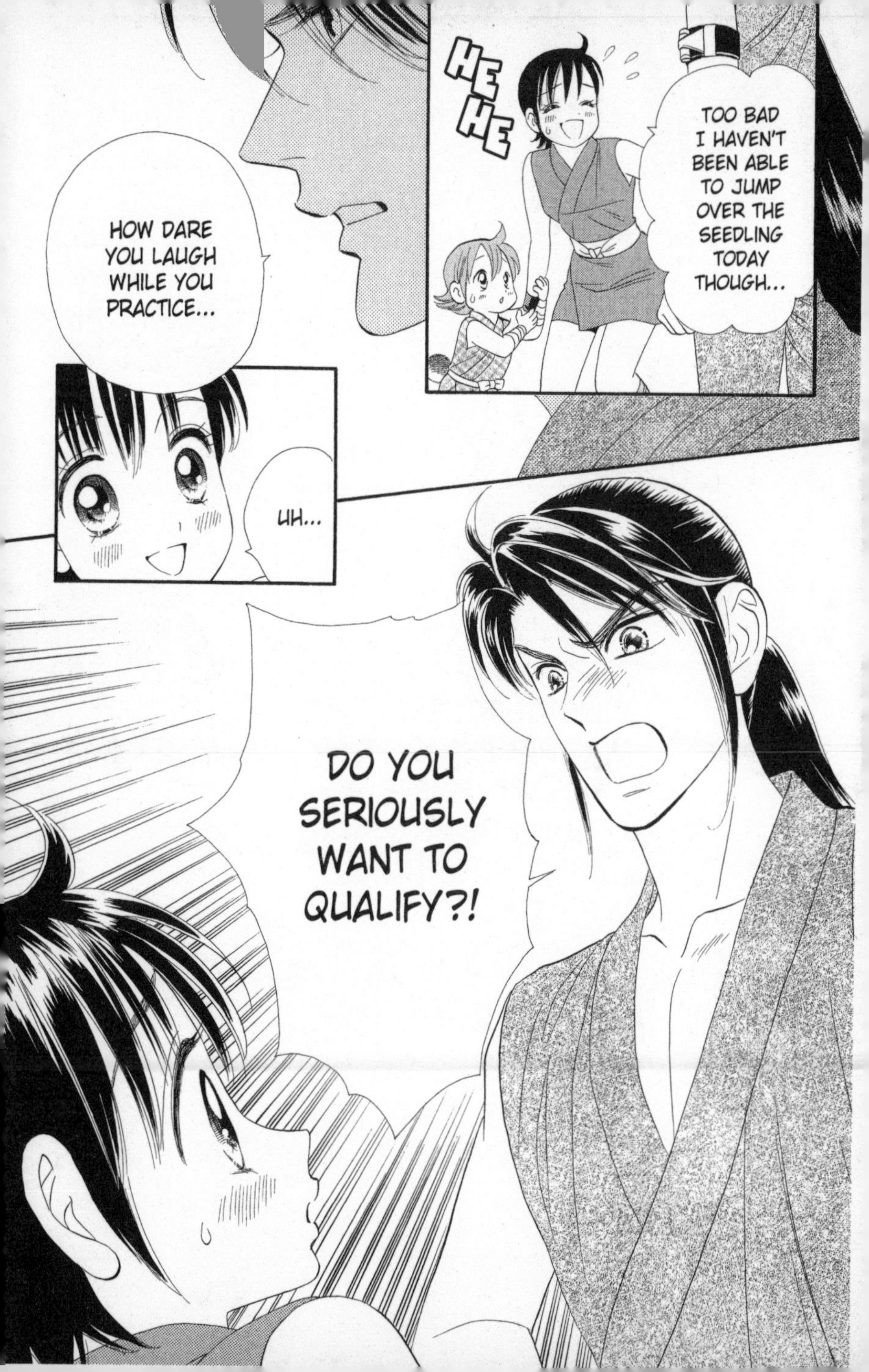
HE HE
TOO BAD I HAVEN'T BEEN ABLE TO JUMP OVER THE SEEDLING TODAY THOUGH...
HOW DARE YOU LAUGH WHILE YOU PRACTICE...
UH...
DO YOU SERIOUSLY WANT TO QUALIFY?!

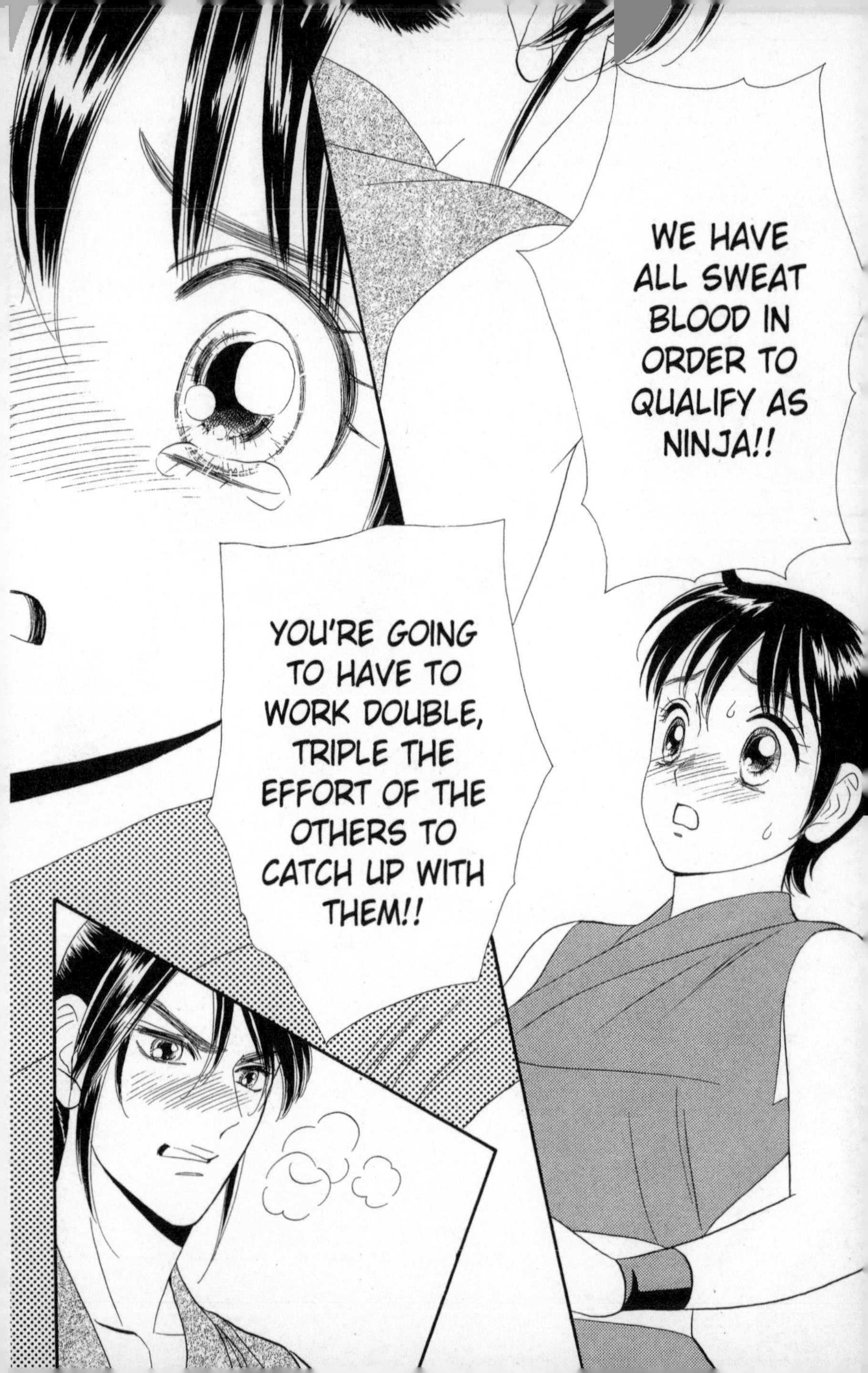
WE HAVE ALL SWEAT BLOOD IN ORDER TO QUALIFY AS NINJA!!
YOU'RE GOING TO HAVE TO WORK DOUBLE, TRIPLE THE EFFORT OF THE OTHERS TO CATCH UP WITH THEM!!

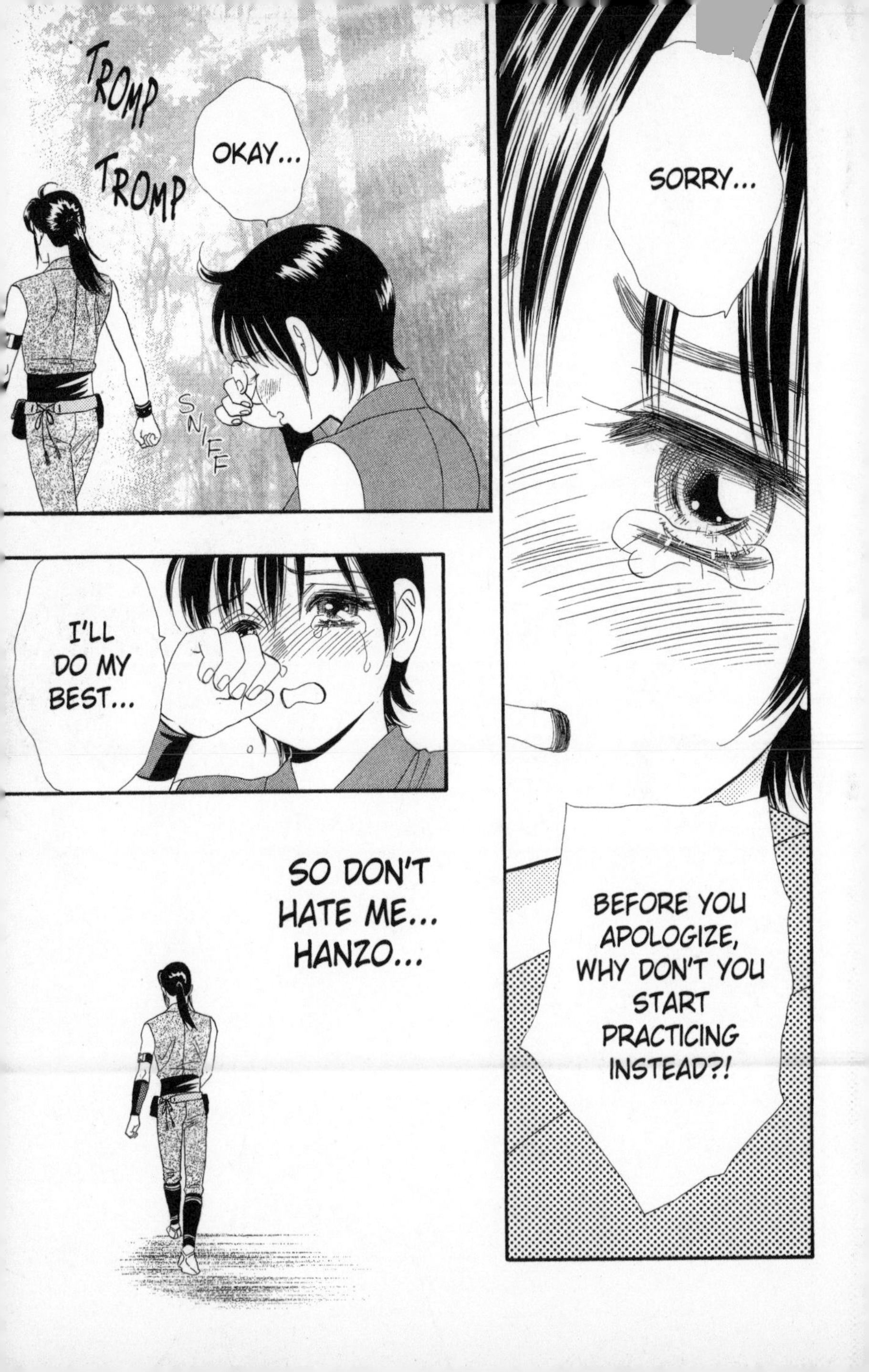
SORRY...
BEFORE YOU APOLOGIZE, WHY DON'T YOU START PRACTICING INSTEAD?!
OKAY...
TROMP TROMP
SNIFF
I'LL DO MY BEST...
SO DON'T HATE ME... HANZO...

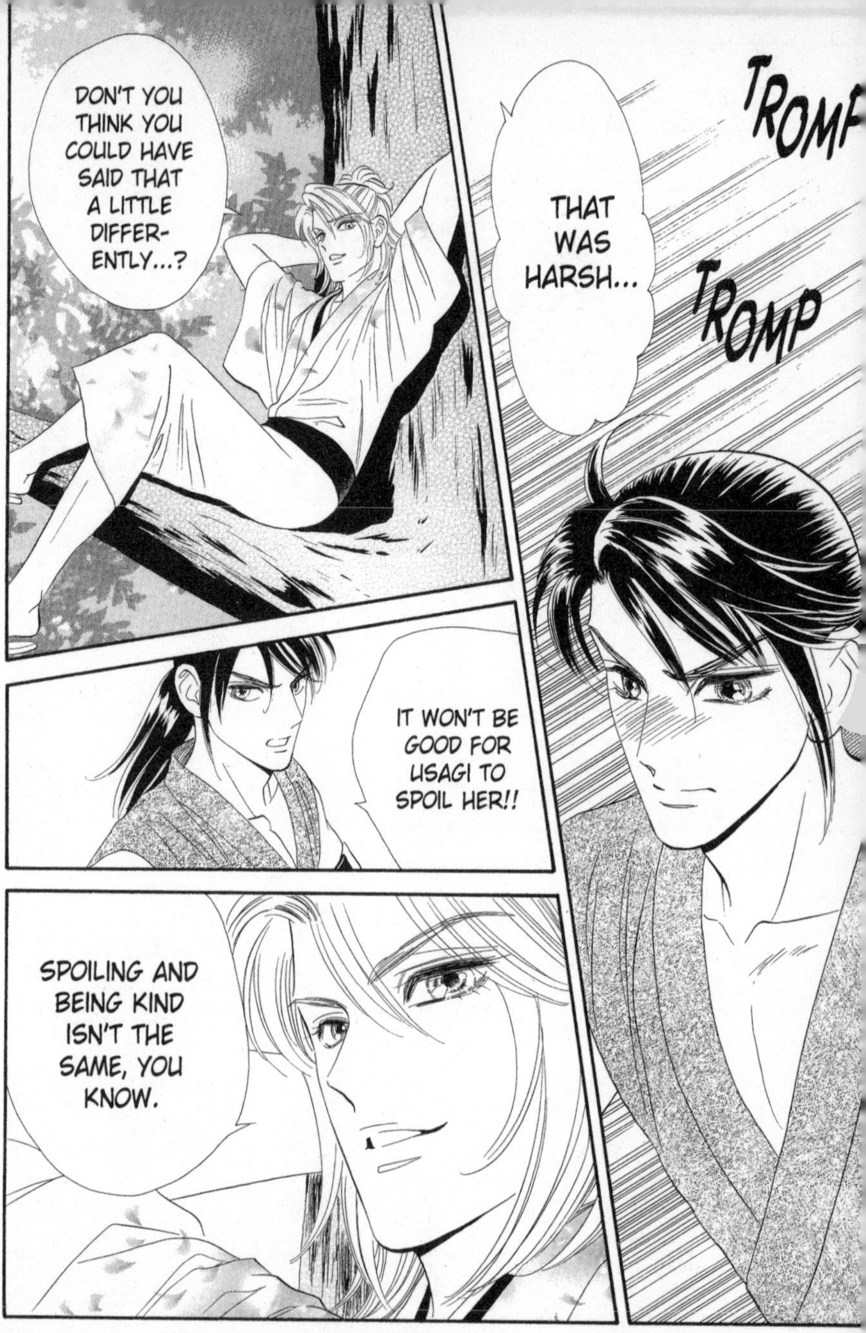
TROMP
TROMP
THAT WAS HARSH...
DON'T YOU THINK YOU COULD HAVE SAID THAT A LITTLE DIFFER-ENTLY...?
IT WON'T BE GOOD FOR USAGI TO SPOIL HER!!
SPOILING AND BEING KIND ISN'T THE SAME, YOU KNOW.

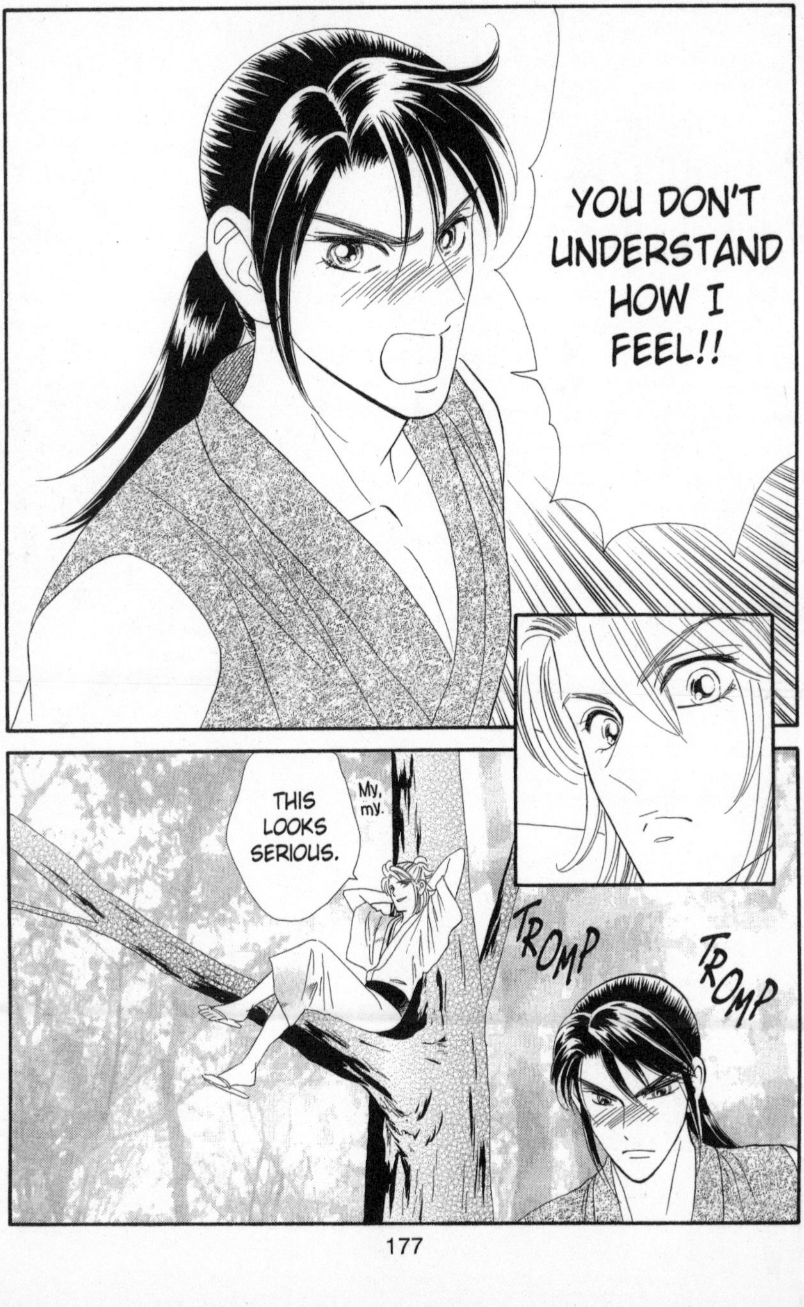
YOU DON'T UNDERSTAND HOW I FEEL!!
My, my.
THIS LOOKS SERIOUS.
TROMP
TROMP

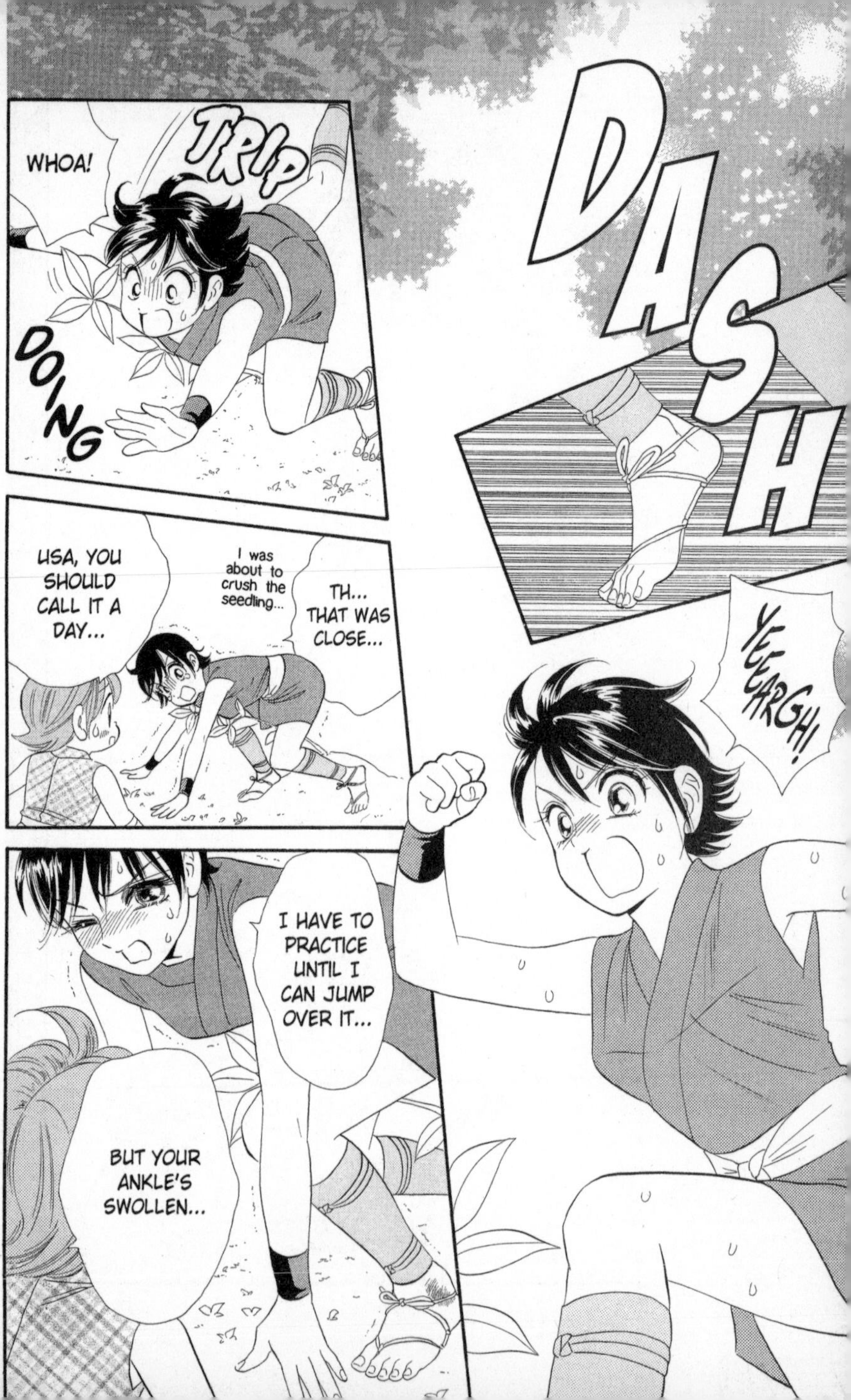
DASH
YEEARGH!
TRIP
WHOA!
DOING
TH... THAT WAS CLOSE...
I was about to crush the seedling...
USA, YOU SHOULD CALL IT A DAY...
I HAVE TO PRACTICE UNTIL I CAN JUMP OVER IT...
BUT YOUR ANKLE'S SWOLLEN...

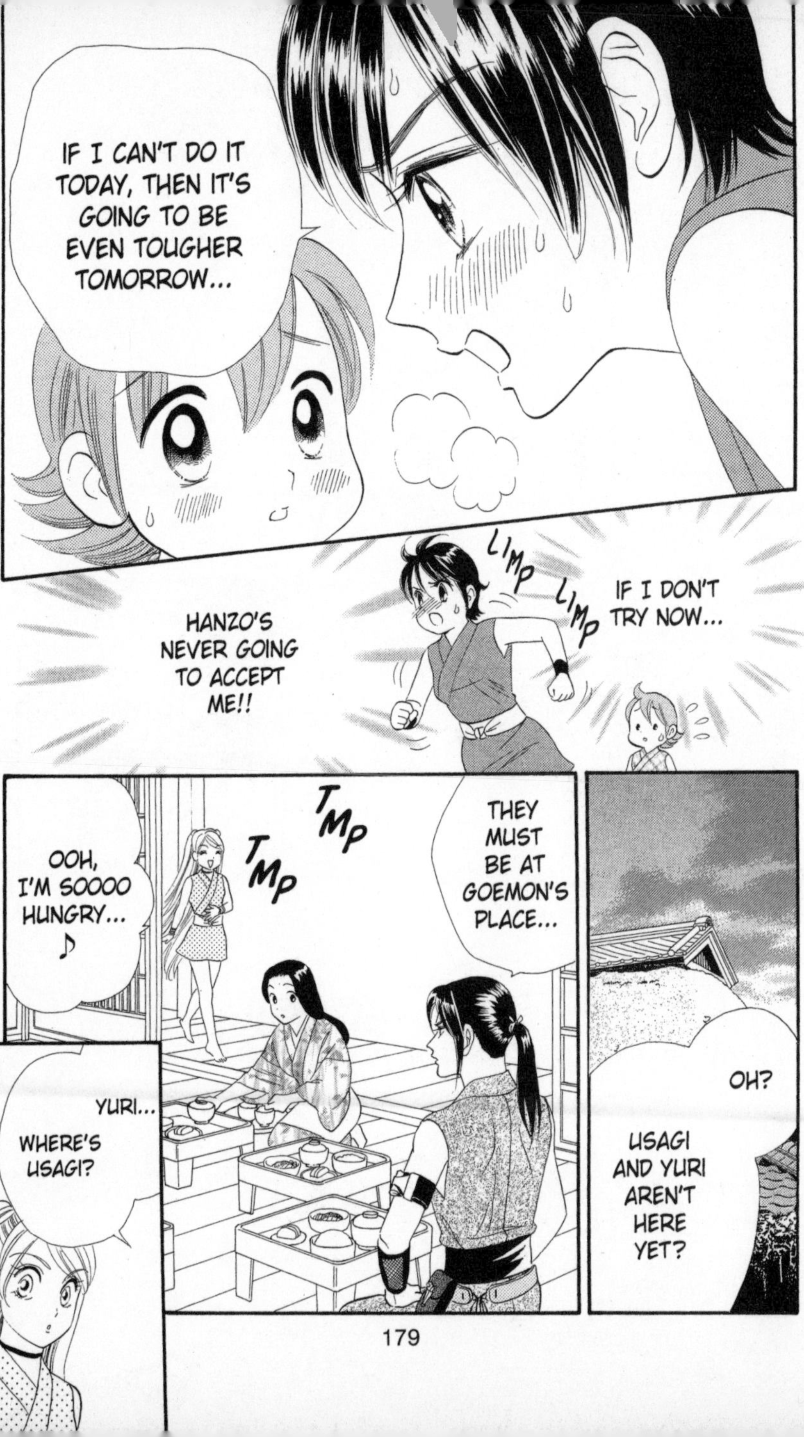
IF I CAN'T DO IT TODAY, THEN IT'S GOING TO BE EVEN TOUGHER TOMORROW...
IF I DON'T TRY NOW...
LIMP LIMP
HANZO'S NEVER GOING TO ACCEPT ME!!
OH?
USAGI AND YURI AREN'T HERE YET?
THEY MUST BE AT GOEMON'S PLACE...
TMP TMP
OOH, I'M SOOOO HUNGRY... ♪
YURI...
WHERE'S USAGI?

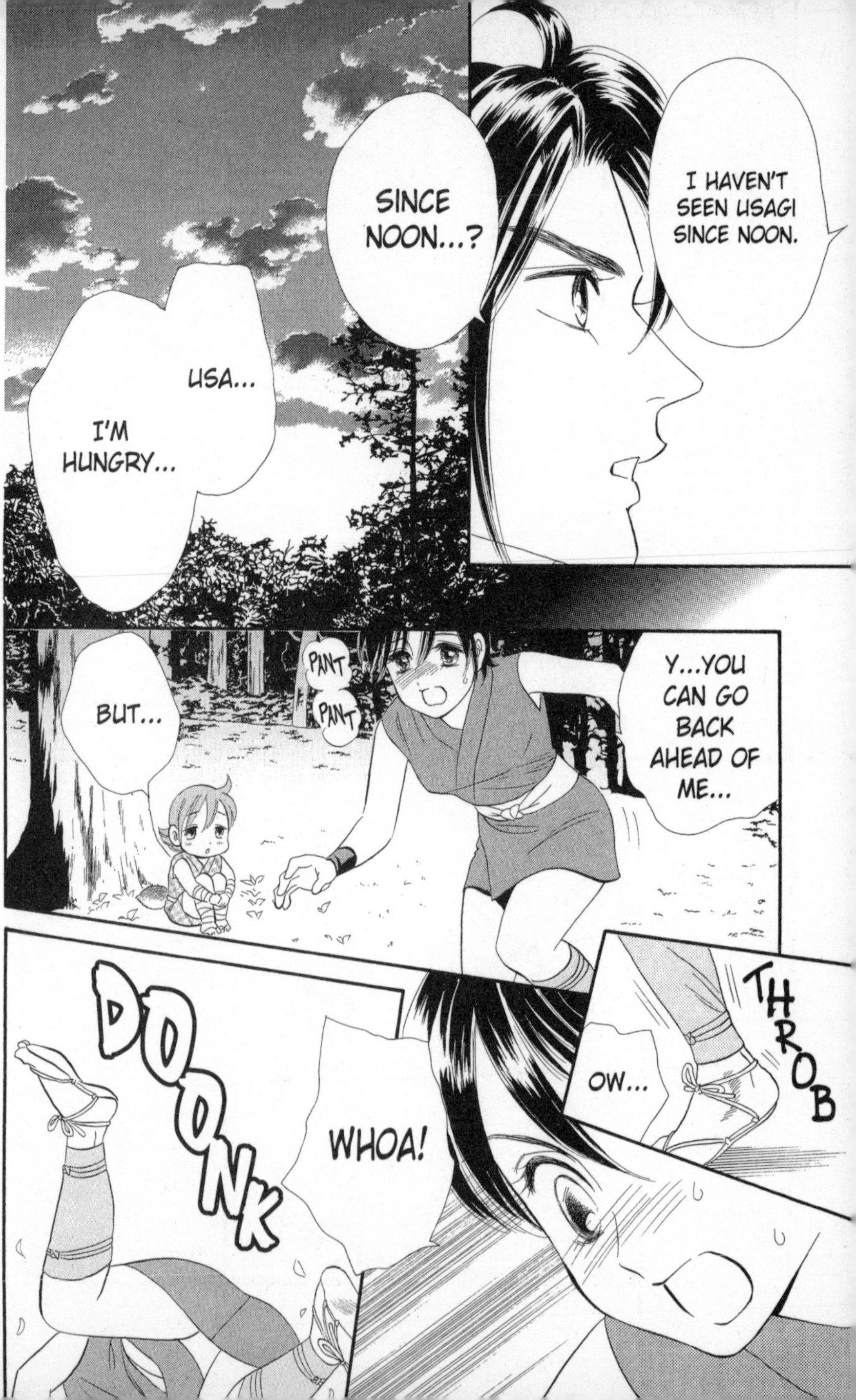
I HAVEN'T SEEN USAGI SINCE NOON.
SINCE NOON...?
USA...
I'M HUNGRY...
Y...YOU CAN GO BACK AHEAD OF ME...
PANT PANT
BUT...
THROB
OW...
WHOA!
DOONK

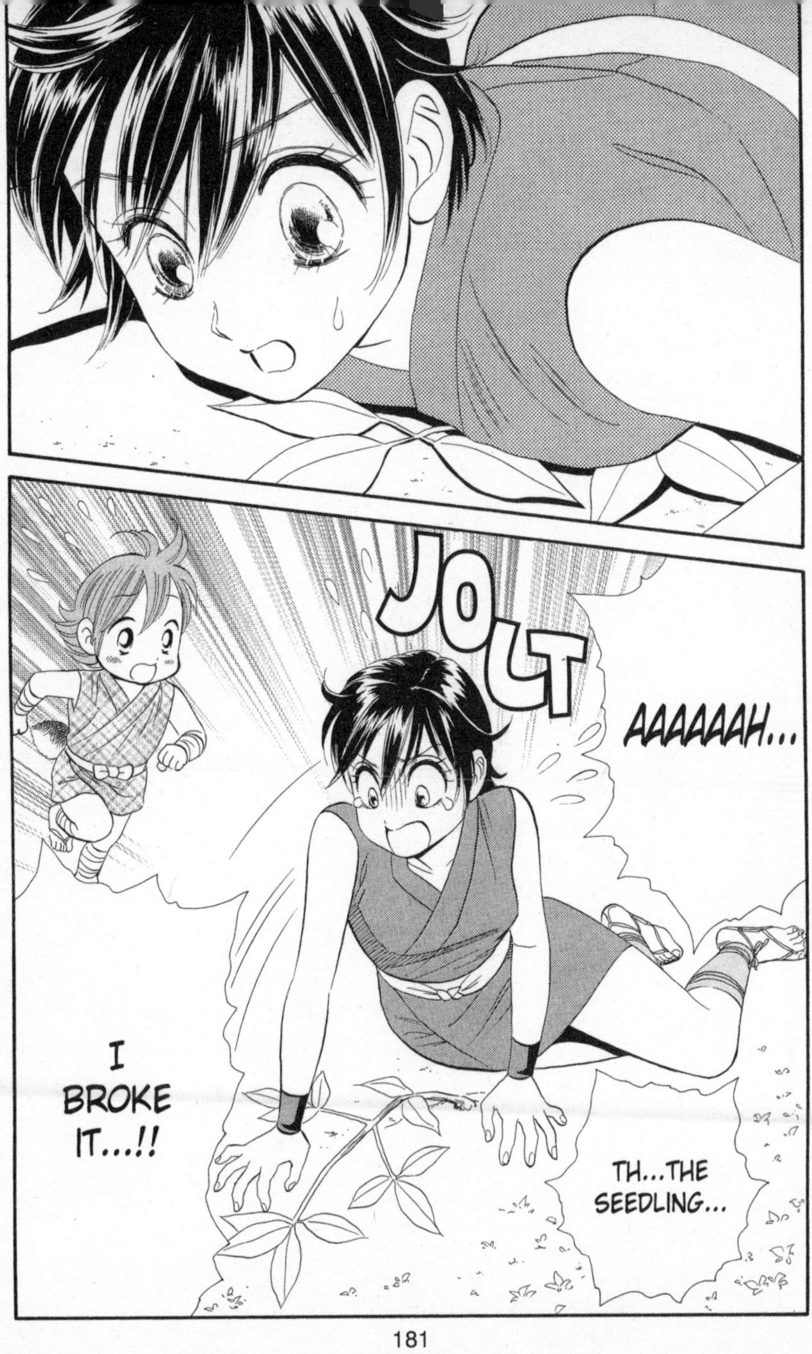
JOLT
AAAAAAH...
TH...THE SEEDLING...
I BROKE IT...!!

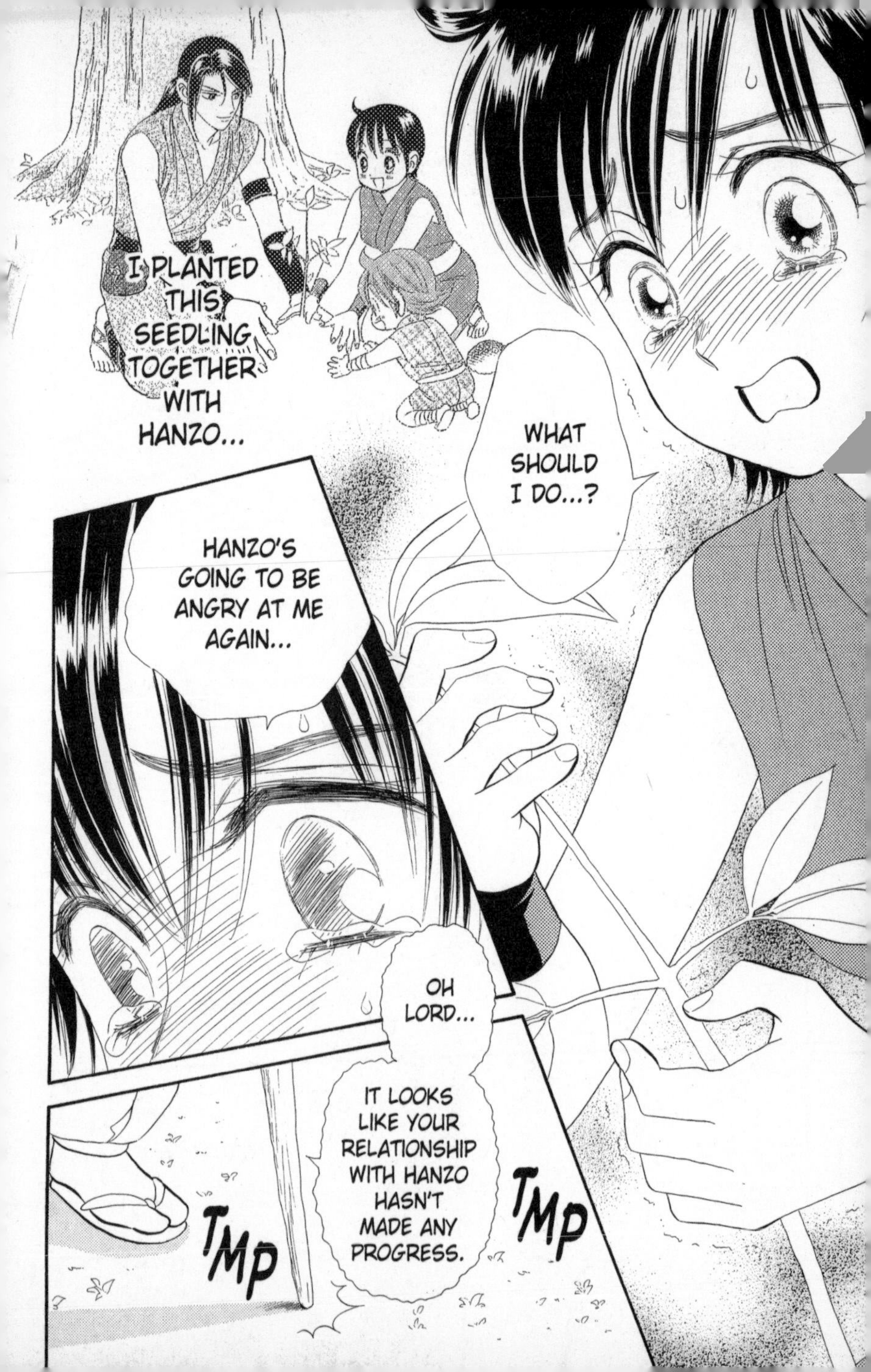
I PLANTED THIS SEEDLING TOGETHER WITH HANZO...
WHAT SHOULD I DO...?
HANZO'S GOING TO BE ANGRY AT ME AGAIN...
OH LORD...
IT LOOKS LIKE YOUR RELATIONSHIP WITH HANZO HASN'T MADE ANY PROGRESS.
TMP
TMP

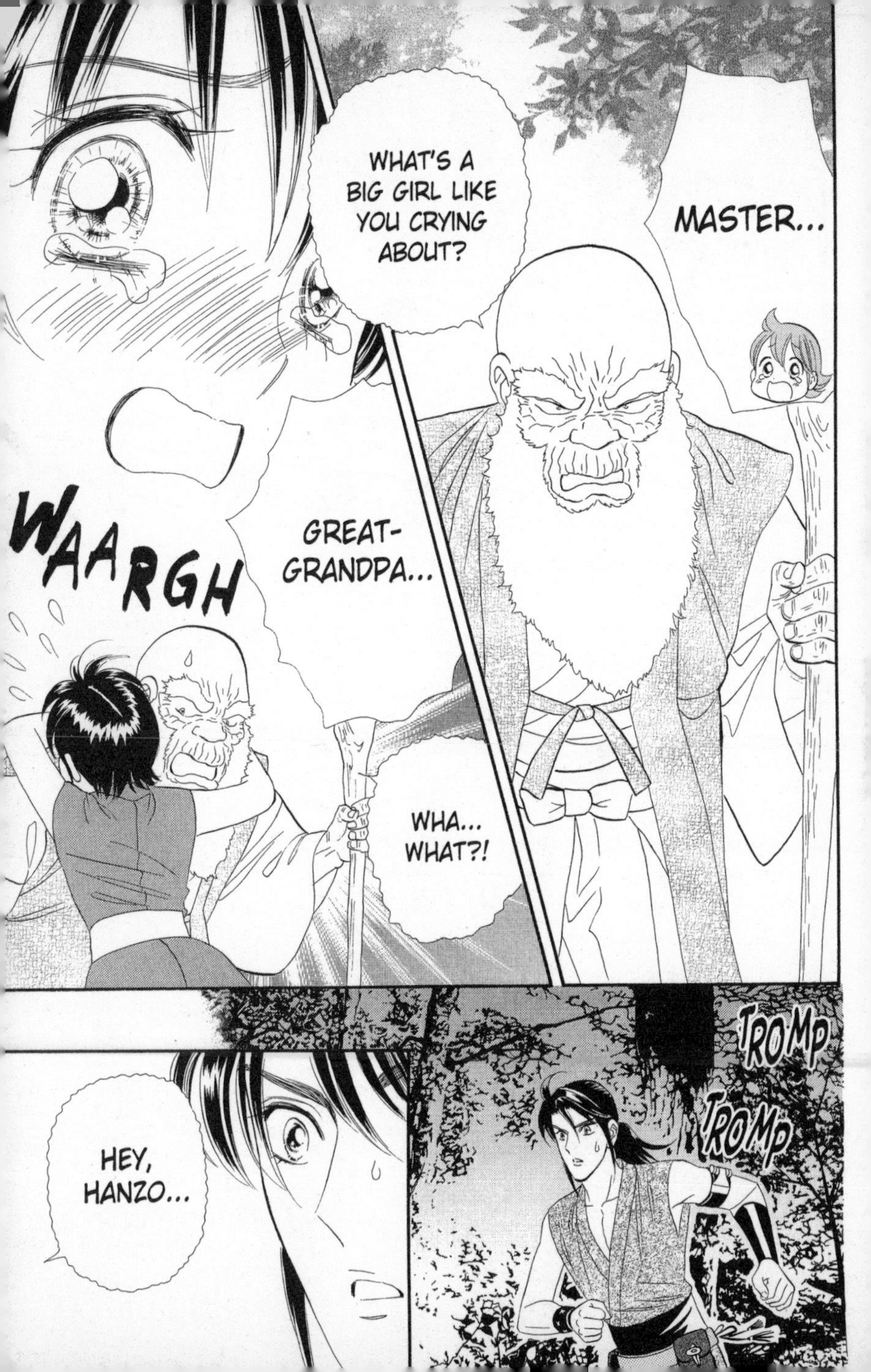
MASTER...
WHAT'S A BIG GIRL LIKE YOU CRYING ABOUT?
GREAT-GRANDPA...
WAARGH
WHA... WHAT?!
TROMP
TROMP
HEY, HANZO...

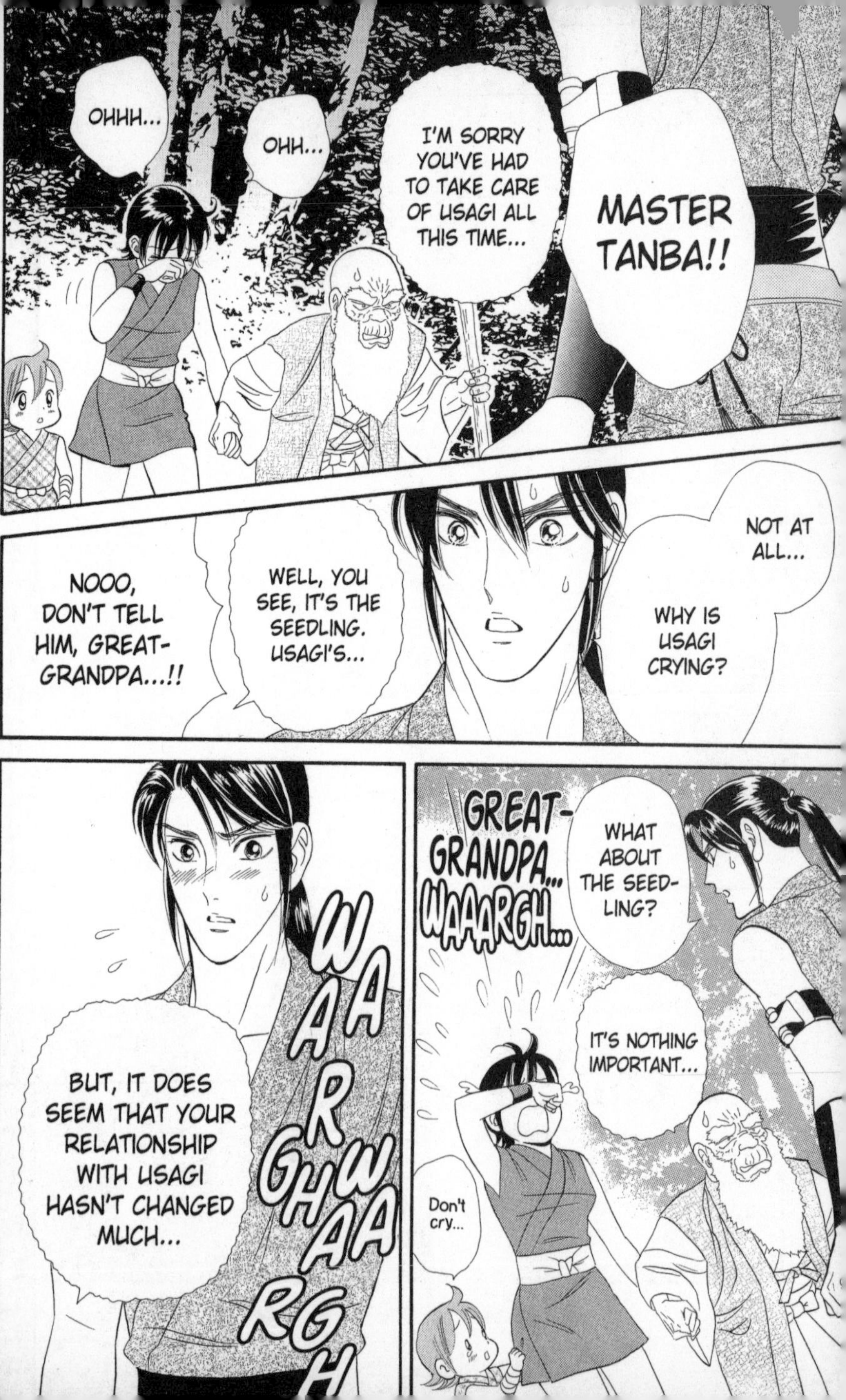
MASTER TANBA!!
I'M SORRY YOU'VE HAD TO TAKE CARE OF USAGI ALL THIS TIME...
OHH...
OHHH...
NOT AT ALL...
WHY IS USAGI CRYING?
WELL, YOU SEE, IT'S THE SEEDLING. USAGI'S...
NOOO, DON'T TELL HIM, GREAT-GRANDPA...!!
WHAT ABOUT THE SEED-LING?
GREAT-GRANDPA... WAAARGH...
IT'S NOTHING IMPORTANT...
Don't cry...
WAARGH WAARGH
BUT, IT DOES SEEM THAT YOUR RELATIONSHIP WITH USAGI HASN'T CHANGED MUCH...

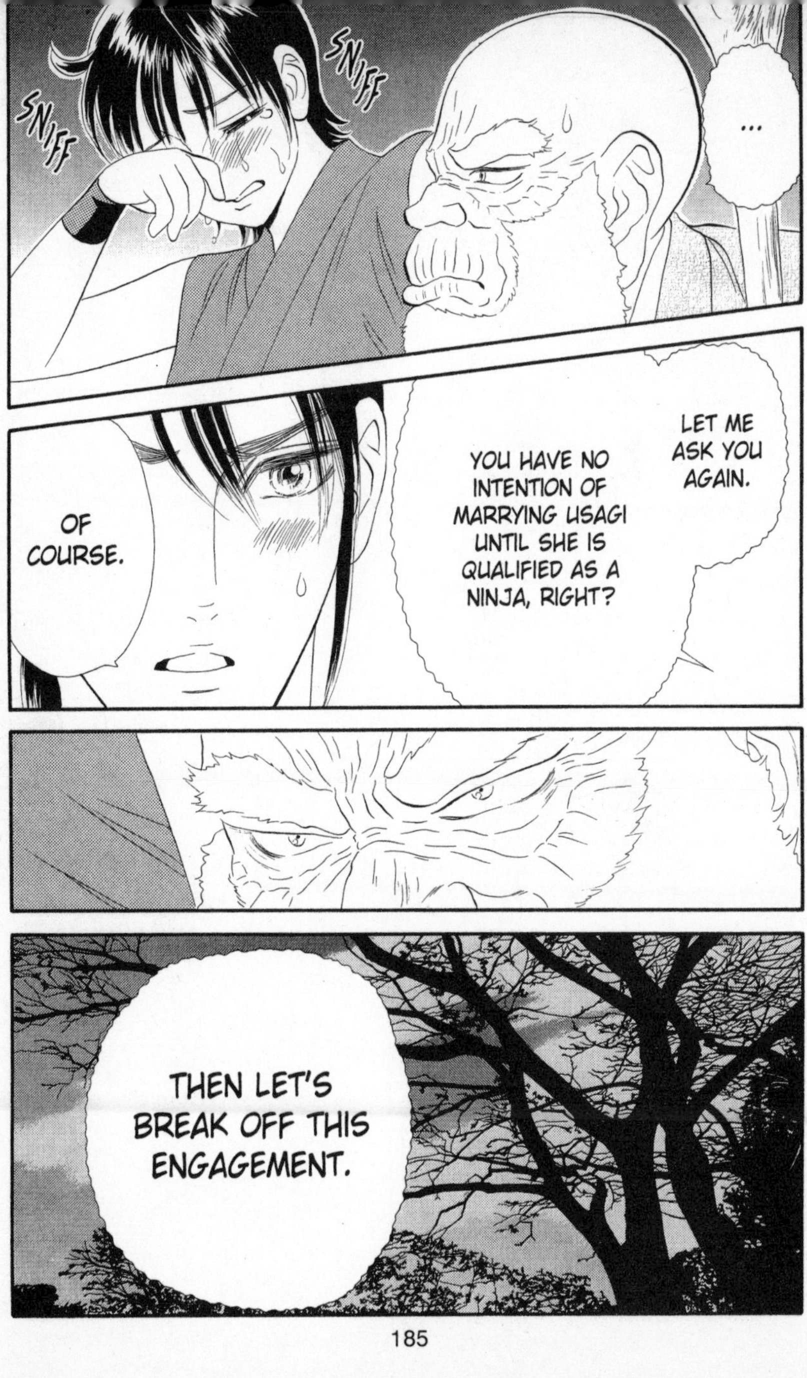
...
SNIFF
SNIFF
LET ME ASK YOU AGAIN.
YOU HAVE NO INTENTION OF MARRYING USAGI UNTIL SHE IS QUALIFIED AS A NINJA, RIGHT?
OF COURSE.
THEN LET'S BREAK OFF THIS ENGAGEMENT.

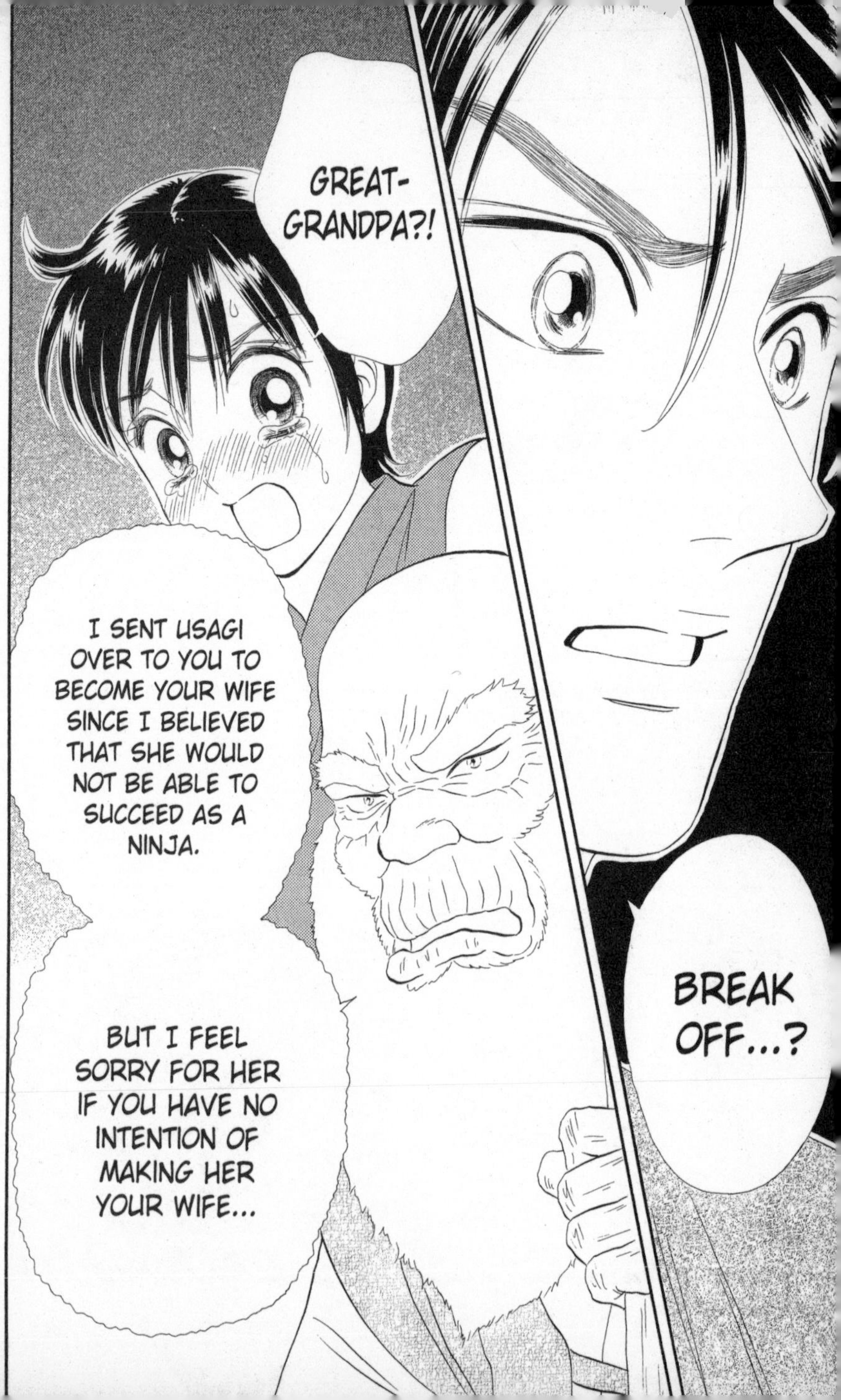

BREAK OFF...?
GREAT-GRANDPA?!
I SENT USAGI OVER TO YOU TO BECOME YOUR WIFE SINCE I BELIEVED THAT SHE WOULD NOT BE ABLE TO SUCCEED AS A NINJA.
BUT I FEEL SORRY FOR HER IF YOU HAVE NO INTENTION OF MAKING HER YOUR WIFE...

CONSIDER THIS ENGAGEMENT CANCELLED.
GREAT-GRANDPA!!
TO BE CONTINUED...

> *The ways of the ninja are mysterious indeed, so here is a glossary of terms to help you navigate the intricacies of their world.*

Page 19: Papillon
Papillon means "butterfly" in French. Japanese people often call the type of glasses Ue-Rin wears "Papillon(-style) glasses" because of how they look like a butterfly.

Page 42, panel 3: Ao Tsuzura Fuji
Ao Tsuzura Fuji is a type of vine traditionally used as a medicinal herb. It is found mainly in Asia, and its scientific name is *Cocculus trilobus*.

Page 42, panel 3: Otogiriso
Otogiriso is also a plant found mainly in Asia, but it has a slightly infamous name. In Japanese, the kanji characters break down into "young brother," "cut," and "plant." This name derives from a Heian legend where an elder brother killed his younger brother for disclosing the secret of how to make medicine using this plant. Its scientific name is *Hypericum erectum*.

Page 54: War of the Roses
Between 1455-1485, an intermittent civil war occurred in England between the House of Lancaster and the House of York, both branches of the royal house. The war was not called the "War of the Roses" back then, but the name derives from the badges of the two houses: the Red Rose of Lancaster and the White Rose of York.

Page 62, panel 2: Ninjutsu
Ninjutsu means the skill or ability of a ninja.

Page 2: Shimo no Hanzo
Shimo no means "the Lower," and in this case refers to Hanzo's geographic location rather than social status.

Page 9, panel 2: Kimikageso
Also known as "lily of the valley," Kimikageso is a poisonous plant that was originally found throughout Japan. The "lily of the valley" that is often seen in Japan now is from Germany, whereas the original Japanese type is said to be rare these days. Its scientific name is *Convallaria majalis*.

Page 11, panel 5: Iga
Iga is a region on the island of Honshu and also the name of the famous ninja clan that originated there. Another area famous for its ninja is Kouga, in the Shiga prefecture on Honshu. Many books claim that these two ninja clans were mortal enemies, but in reality inter-ninja relations were not as bad as stories might suggest.

Page 18, panel 5: Tokugawa Ieyasu
Tokugawa Ieyasu (1543-1616) was the first Shogun of the Tokugawa Shogunate. He made a small fishing village named Edo the center of his activities. Edo thrived and became a huge town, and was later renamed Tokyo, the present capital.

Page 87: **Manga School**
"Manga School" is a section in Japanese manga magazines for people who want to become manga artists. Participants who receive high scores for their sample manga submissions get an award along with a chance to make their debut in the magazine.

Page 87: **Ribon**
Ribon is a monthly Japanese shojo (girls) manga magazine published by Shueisha.

Page 87: **Hikaru Yuzuki**
Hikaru Yuzuki, a former *Ribon* manga artist, is still active in creating manga. He currently has a series in *Business Jump*, which is a Japanese Shonen (boys) manga magazine.

Page 113: **Margaret**
Margaret is a biweekly Japanese shojo (girls) manga magazine published by Shueisha.

Things are finally starting to turn out like a ninja manga series. The story is a lot more serious than before, and I had a lot of fun drawing mini-Goemon and mini-Hikaru. It seems as if the Kouga ninja are the bad guys, but please understand that they aren't bad in any way. Both Iga and Kouga have their reasons for doing things, and the clashes between those reasons are what cause the "disputes," so I believe that they are both neither good nor evil.

–Rinko Ueda

Rinko Ueda is from Nara prefecture. She enjoys listening to the radio, drama CDs, and Rakugo comedy performances. Her works include *Ryo*, a series based on the legend of Gojo Bridge, *Home*, a story about love crossing national boundaries, and *Tail of the Moon (Tsuki no Shippo)*, a romantic ninja comedy.

TAIL OF THE MOON

Vol. 6

The Shojo Beat Manga Edition

STORY & ART BY
RINKO UEDA

Translation & Adaptation/Tetsuichiro Miyaki
Touch-up Art & Lettering/Mark McMurray
Design/Izumi Hirayama
Editor/Amy Yu

Editor in Chief, Books/Alvin Lu
Editor in Chief, Magazines/Marc Weidenbaum
Sr. Director of Acquisitions/Rika Inouye
VP of Sales/Gonzalo Ferreyra
Sr. VP of Marketing/Liza Coppola
Publisher/Hyoe Narita

Printed in Canada

Published by VIZ Media, LLC
P.O. Box 77064
San Francisco, CA 94107

Shojo Beat Manga Edition
10 9 8 7 6 5 4 3 2 1
First printing, August 2007

www.viz.com
store.viz.com

PARENTAL ADVISORY
TAIL OF THE MOON is rated T+ for Older Teen and is recommended for ages 16 and up. This volume contains brief nudity and ninja violence.

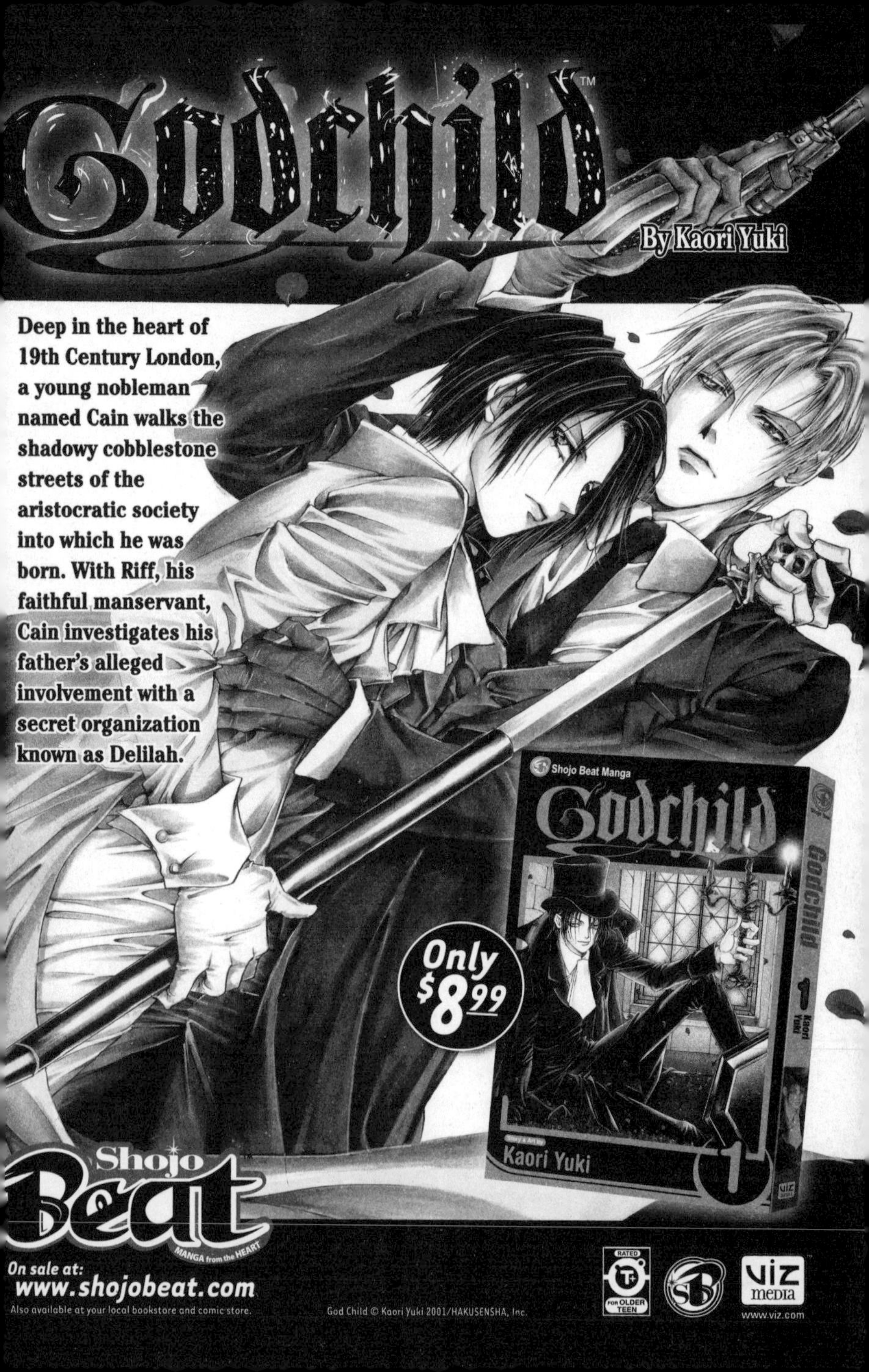
Godchild™
By Kaori Yuki
Deep in the heart of 19th Century London, a young nobleman named Cain walks the shadowy cobblestone streets of the aristocratic society into which he was born. With Riff, his faithful manservant, Cain investigates his father's alleged involvement with a secret organization known as Delilah.
Shojo Beat Manga
Godchild
Kaori Yuki
Only $8.99
Shojo Beat
MANGA from the HEART
On sale at:
www.shojobeat.com
Also available at your local bookstore and comic store.
God Child © Kaori Yuki 2001/HAKUSENSHA, Inc.
RATED T+ FOR OLDER TEEN
VIZ media
www.viz.com